Show and Tell

SHOW AND TELL

The New Book of Broadway Anecdotes

Ken Bloom

OXFORD
UNIVERSITY PRESS

OXFORD
UNIVERSITY PRESS

Oxford University Press is a department of the University of Oxford. It furthers
the University's objective of excellence in research, scholarship, and education
by publishing worldwide. Oxford is a registered trade mark of Oxford University
Press in the UK and certain other countries.

Published in the United States of America by Oxford University Press
198 Madison Avenue, New York, NY 10016, United States of America.

Library of Congress Cataloging-in-Publication Data
Names: Bloom, Ken, 1949– author.
Title: Show and tell : the new book of Broadway anecdotes / Ken Bloom.
Description: New York, NY : Oxford University Press, [2016]
Identifiers: LCCN 2016000396| ISBN 9780190221010 (pbk. : alk. paper) |
ISBN 9780190221034 (epub)
Subjects: LCSH: Musicals—New York (State)—New York—Anecdotes.
Classification: LCC ML1711.8.N3 B58 2016 | DDC 792.609747/1—dc23
LC record available at http://lccn.loc.gov/2016000396

9 8 7 6 5 4 3 2 1

Printed by R.R. Donnelley, United States of America

Members of the original company of *South Pacific* had a reunion on the stage of the Majestic Theatre fifty years after *South Pacific*'s opening. Sue Hight, of the original company, thanked the cast of *The Phantom of the Opera* for being there. One of the actors replied, "Don't you understand, you're the reason we're here today. We're the ones that came after you."

This book is dedicated to all the people who came before us.

CONTENTS

ACKNOWLEDGMENTS

First and foremost, I'd like to thank the friends and acquaintances who told me so many of these anecdotes. Barry Kleinbort, Ken Kantor, and Peter Filichia kindly went through the manuscript catching errors, fleshing out some stories, and adding stories of their own. Thanks to Howard Mandelbaum, a great friend and the guy who came up with the title of this book! A number of friends helped with both the book and my sanity, so thanks are due to the aforementioned Kleinbort, Kantor, and Filichia, as well as David Schmittou, Caesar Rodriguez, Pat Plowman, Harry Bagdasian, Bill Rudman, Helene Blue, Jay and Dixie Morse, John Winson, Laura Lee Johnson, Bari Biern, Scott Sedar, Penny Fuller, and Anita Gillette. Thanks also to two friends at Oxford University Press, Richard Carlin and my excellent editor Norm Hirschy. And, finally, thanks to my copy editor, Bonnie Kelsey, whose astute eye for grammar and clarity helped me tell these stories.

And special thanks to those who graciously agreed to be interviewed either for this book or my NPR pieces, as well as those who are also good friends: Lee Adams, Ben Bagley, Lucinda Ballard, Elaine Cancilla, Martin Charnin, Chris Denny, Howard Dietz, Kevin Duda, Josh Ellis, Peter Filichia, Penny Fuller, Rita Gardner, Anita Gillette, E.Y. Harburg, Joseph Hardy, Sheldon Harnick, Susan Hight, Craig Jacobs, Edward Jablonski, John Kander, Kenneth Kantor, Barry Kleinbort, Burton Lane, Lynn Lane, Michele Lee, Ronnie Lee, Jerry Orbach, Don Pippin, Michael Price, Chita Rivera, Harold Rome, Robert Schear, David Schmittou, Thomas Z. Shepard, Charles Strouse, Jule Styne, and Sara Zahn.

Show and Tell

Introduction

The stories in this book have been passed down orally, in books, and through interviews. I can definitively state that all these anecdotes are true, inadvertent lies, or apocryphal. When compiling this list, I found several of these tales retold in different fashions or ascribed to different shows or people. In a few cases, I noted these differences. Not all anecdotes are humorous in nature. Some are sad, some are tragic, and some are clearly told as cautionary tales. Taken as a whole, they reflect the rich history of the theatre and its myriad of practitioners, each with their own unique personality.

Many of the names herein may not be known to you, but each of them devoted themselves to the theatre and every one of them has a larger story to tell. A glance through Wikipedia or other internet sites can greatly expand one's knowledge and appreciation of these stalwarts. A bibliography follows at the end of the book and some of these biographies, auto and otherwise, can give hours of pleasure if you're truly into the history of the people and places of the theatre. But if your curiosity ends with the last page of this book, that's all right too. The names themselves are not the point of the anecdotes.

It's amazing how some stories get reinvented as they get passed on from storyteller to storyteller, much like the game of telephone. Sometimes these stories are completely different from what actually happened. I've tried to refer to the originals, but even different biographies, auto and otherwise, give variations on the same stories. Likewise, many autobiographies are written by ghostwriters, who didn't know the real facts and didn't know enough to correct their subjects.

This book is roughly organized to follow the paths of most shows from the idea, to the writing, producing, casting, etc., with occasional pauses for diversions. The shows covered include those on Broadway and off, national tours, regional theatres, and presentation houses. There's even a bit of London peppered throughout when the stories were too delicious not to include.

CHAPTER 1

Personalities

Here are some stories that aren't necessarily linked to a specific show but illustrate who their subjects were better than any biographies.

GEORGE ABBOTT

The man with the longest and perhaps most successful career in musical theatre was George Abbott. All through his long career, he was known to cast and crew as Mr. Abbott—never George—although when he was directing *A Funny Thing Happened on the Way to the Forum*, Larry Gelbart asked if he could call him just plain "George." Mr. Abbott replied, "Of course." Gelbart then inquired why everyone else always called him "Mr. Abbott," and his response was "Damned if I know."

While working on *Where's Charley?* Abbott would fly first class between Hollywood where Loesser was writing the show and New York where the show was in production. First-class airfare was expensive and producers Feuer and Martin were conscious of how much it was costing the production. Feuer told his partner Ernie Martin, "From now on, I'm calling him George!"

Abbott was a no-nonsense kind of guy. After one tryout performance of a musical, Abbott said to the songwriters, "This song is out, that song is out." The songwriters got their hackles up and threatened to send for their lawyer. Abbott replied, "Don't send for your lawyer unless he can write songs."

In 1936, Jose Ferrer was in the Abbott show *Brother Rat* at the Biltmore Theatre. Being an ambitious young actor, Ferrer built on the performance Mr. Abbott had crafted for him and made a lot of "improvements." Strangely enough, a lot of the laughs began disappearing one by one as Ferrer's performance "improved." Six weeks into the run, Mr. Abbott called a rehearsal and instructed Ferrer to take all the "improvements" out. Ferrer was furious and said to himself, "I'll take it all out and teach him a lesson and see who's right and who's wrong." He took out all the "improvements" and the laughs returned. He then began improving his performance again and six weeks later, Mr. Abbott told him to take it all out. This happened again for a third time. It was then that Ferrer learned the lesson of keeping a performance exactly the way a director sets it.

When Abbott was unhappy with one of Sheldon Harnick's lyrics in *Fiorello!* Abbott walked over to Harnick, put his arm around him, and simply asked, "Sheldon, would Larry Hart have been satisfied with that lyric?"

With George Abbott, no matter how a show was going, bad or good, evenings were spent dancing. Sometimes he'd even take out the leading lady as a kind of audition. During *New Girl in Town*, Abbott took Gwen Verdon out to dance and she had the temerity to tell him he wasn't on the beat! Abbott told Jule Styne when they took a pair of girls out dancing during the tryout of *High Button Shoes*, "If the girl has a good time with you, it's OK to ask her to pay for her portion of the bill." George Abbott could be parsimonious.

One day, when *The Fig Leaves Are Falling* was rehearsing on Broadway, Abbott and composer Albert Hague went to the Howard Johnson's restaurant on 46th Street and Broadway. Abbott ordered a bowl of soup. Albert Hague ordered a bowl of soup and a hot dog. When the waiter brought Mr. Hague his hot dog, Abbott told Hague, "You live well."

Abbott would take notes on yellow lined legal pads and then tear the notes off, crumple them into a ball, and throw them in a corner. Just writing down the note put it in his mind and he didn't need to refer to them anymore. During rehearsals of *The Fig Leaves Are Falling*, Dorothy Loudon would wait until rehearsal was over and pick up the crumpled notes. Then she'd go home and iron them to read what he wrote.

Under Abbott's tutelage, Harold Prince rose up the ranks to assistant stage manager and then to casting director of *Call Me Madam* (which he got because both Abbott's and Leland Hayward's casting directors were working elsewhere). One day, Prince got his draft notice to serve in Korea. He told Abbott the news and Abbott assured Prince that there'd be a job waiting for him when he returned.

After two years including extensions, Prince got out and landed in Hoboken. He called his parents and told them he was back. He bought *The New York Times* and opened it to the theatre section. There he learned that the play *In Any Language* was opening that night at the Cort Theatre, starring Uta Hagen and Walter Matthau and directed by George Abbott.

Prince called his parents again and told them he'd be late and then made his way to the Cort Theatre and talked the stage doorman into letting him in about a half hour before curtain. Sitting on the stage were Abbott and his stage manager Robert Griffith. Prince, still in uniform, walked over to them and Abbott, without missing a beat, said, "Are you back already?"

Around 1970, George Abbott was at a party and ran into Maureen Stapleton. "You must allow me to take you home," he said to her. So they got into a cab and he started making moves on Stapleton. "George, what are you doing," she asked in amazement. Mr. Abbott replied in a matter-of-fact manner, "I'm trying to go to bed with you." Now, Abbott was eighty-one and Stapleton was forty-three. Naturally, Stapleton's reply was, "Oh, all right. Why didn't you say so?" So they did and had a wonderful time together. In fact, they had a wonderful time for a decade. It only ended when Abbott, at age ninety-one, started dating his future wife Joy.

HAROLD ARLEN

Cy Coleman was at a party playing "Stormy Weather" on the piano. Harold Arlen was sitting on a bench next to Burton Lane's wife Lynn. Arlen leaned over to Lynn and whispered, "You know, I never liked that song."

BEN BAGLEY

Ben Bagley is today perhaps best known for his series of "Revisited" albums on his Painted Smiles label. But before those, he was a wonderful producer and director of off-Broadway musical revues including *The Littlest Revue* and *The Shoestring Revue*. These shows and Julius Monk's Upstairs at the Downstairs nightclub revues introduced audiences to the talents of Kaye

Ballard, Charlotte Rae, Strouse and Adams, Jones and Schmidt, and other future greats.

He named his *Shoestring Revue* for a good reason. Bagley never had any money. In fact, when Charlotte Rae was auditioning for the show, he asked her if he could borrow a quarter so he could get home to New Jersey.

TALLULAH BANKHEAD

Tallulah loved to shock people. There are a million stories, but we'll try to stick to the ones about her on Broadway.

Howard Dietz once said of her, "A day without Tallulah is like a month in the country."Mrs. Patrick Campbell, of whom similar stories were told, said, "She's always skating on thin ice. And the British public wants to be there in case the ice breaks."

Dorothy Parker said, "She would give you the shirt off her back even if you didn't want it."

When Bankhead was in New Haven trying out *Crazy October*, the fire marshal at the Shubert Theatre instructed the stage manager to tell Tallulah that she wasn't allowed to smoke in her dressing room. The stage manager looked the marshal in the eye and said, "You tell her!"

She opened on Broadway in a revival of *Rain* by Somerset Maugham though she had wanted to premiere the play in London but wasn't cast because she had insulted Maugham. So Broadway it was. In the show, her character Sadie Thompson seduces the Reverend Davidson and leaves him alone onstage in horror of what he's done. When he'd make his exit, Tallulah was waiting in the wings, her dress hiked up around her neck, her legs apart, and her maid holding a silver tray upon which was a single condom. The show was not a success.

She stopped a rehearsal of the play *Something Gay* saying she was just not in the mood. When the director Thomas Mitchell (the actor known for *Gone with the Wind*) asked her, "Well, what would you like to do?" she replied, "I'd like two bottles of champagne, a big double bed and Hugh Sinclair (her handsome leading man in the show)." By the way, the show was already doomed for failure having gone through three other directors before Mitchell came on the scene.

The show opened on March 1, 1933, otherwise known as Bank Day, the day on which every bank in the country was closed down by the government. So the box office could only accept checks. The play was not a success though it ran for three and a half months, a run that was only made possible by Bankhead pouring $40,000 into its coffers.

Even though her previous outing with a Somerset Maugham play was not a success, in 1938, she opened in *The Circle*. Let's allow Miss Bankhead to tell the story herself: "It was opening night in New York, and there was a line in Maugham's dialogue about Mary Anderson, who had been a great beauty in England many years before, but because this was a revival, and in America, at that, we decided to make it Maxine Elliott, who had been a very, very great American beauty indeed, and in the scene in which a man was turning over the pages of a photograph album with me, he was supposed to say, 'Ah, Maxine Elliott, her beauty took your breath away,' and instead on opening night the poor actor said, 'Ah, Maxine Elliott, her breath took her beauty away,' and there was an instant of the most terrible silence, and then Grace George nearly fell off the sofa laughing, and at that moment I was supposed to say, with a perfectly straight face, of course, 'Oh, Lady Kitty,' but I couldn't bring out a thing, and the audience started laughing, and they laughed and laughed, stopping for a while to try to get hold of themselves, as *we* were trying to get hold of *ourselves*, and then starting up again, and it's a wonder we're all not still there laughing!"

(Years later, *The Circle* was revived on Broadway with Rex Harrison in the lead. The cast changed so much during the run, the producer decided that, instead of taking new photos of each new company, he'd stick with the original cast photo and just change the heads as a new actor replaced the old.)

Back to Tallulah: Her next play was *I Am Different* in which she starred with Glenn Anders. The two of them were talking backstage, just before his cue to go back onstage. At the sound of a gun firing, he was supposed to run onto the stage exclaiming "I heard a shot!," look at the body on the stage floor, and say, "It's only a flesh wound." Anders's cue came but he was still thinking about Tallulah. He ran onstage and yelled, "I hear a flesh wound." He then examined the body and proclaimed, "It's only a shot." Tallulah, in the wings, broke up and, of course, the entire audience heard her laughing.

She hit the jackpot with *The Little Foxes* and soon thereafter *The Skin of Our Teeth*. In these shows, she proved that she wasn't just a narcissist who would do anything for attention. She was actually a fine actress, though it took a firm hand to keep her from excesses. When she was sent the script for *The Little Foxes*, she read only her lines and not the rest of the play.

Appearing in the short-lived play *The Eagle Has Two Heads*, Bankhead performed two great feats. Her opening monologue ran for seventeen minutes. It takes a great actress to hold an audience in thrall for that long. Out of town in Boston, it was twenty-two minutes long. While in the fair city, five minutes were trimmed from the monologue and Marlon Brando was trimmed from the cast.

The other great feat that Bankhead undertook was remarkable. Her character is standing at the top of a long staircase. She is shot and then falls head-first down the stairs to the floor below. John Lardner's review described what happened: "Miss Bankhead spared herself nothing on opening night at the Plymouth. In a plunge that I would hesitate to make with football pads on, she toppled headfirst, majestically and in a pure line, down several stairs. She was fresh as a daisy, however, for her curtain calls, which were up to the standards of the Bankhead public."

When Bankhead opened the play *The Dancers* in London under the auspices of Gerald du Maurier, she said, "My first night in London in the play, *The Dancers*. The final curtain. Then wild shrieks that shook the rafters. I had heard much of London audiences and their booing but I didn't know they could be so unanimous. I fainted. It took me days to realize they were not booing but doing just the opposite."

Tallulah had a marvelous time in London once she figured out that the audiences adored her. "I was making ready to leave when Noel Coward called to say he wanted me to take the lead in *Fallen Angels*. It was to open in four days. There were 150 pages to learn in that time. I did it, and the play proved the gateway to the hearts of the London audiences. . . . It was during my run in *Camille* that Ethel Barrymore came backstage one night and showed me a damp spot on the top of her head. She told me it was caused by the tears of a young girl in the balcony."

MARSHALL BARER

Barer was one of the most talented of Broadway lyricists, but he had, shall we say, his own peccadilloes. Barer had a vintage Mercedes convertible that was entirely covered in denim, everything but the windows, that is. And coming out of a zipper was the Mercedes hood ornament.

Barer was crashing at a friend's apartment in New York when the friend came home from work, and there was Barer leaning out the window, spray-painting his boots red to match his outfit.

When Barer gave up his Los Angeles apartment and moved to New Mexico, whenever he'd come back to Los Angeles, he'd stay in his storage unit.

The Disney Studio wanted to make a television version of *Once Upon a Mattress* and summoned the show's writers, Barer, Mary Rodgers, and Jay Thompson, out to the studio. Barer was against the project while Rodgers and Thompson wanted it to go ahead. During the meeting, the Disney executive told the writers that Disney only wanted to film the book and not include the songs. Barer became apoplectic. "Well then, you don't need our permission. It's a fairy tale!" He was so angry that he stormed out of the room. When he got to his car (the Mercedes with the jeans covering), he needed to pee, but he had made such a scene that he didn't want to go back into the office. So he relieved himself in the parking lot. When he got back to his house, he got a call from a junior executive who enthusiastically told him, "You showed 'em, pissing on the studio!" Disney went ahead and made the movie with a new score.

ETHEL BARRYMORE

The first family of Broadway was the Barrymores, and the grand dame of the family was Ethel Barrymore. Seeing her was a revelation. She was so correct with her perfect posture and regal attitude. In *Scarlet Sister Mary*, she played a young girl who was torn between being good and leading a life of sin. To practice being a young strumpet, Barrymore went to the Billy Pearce Dance Studio. Now, Billy Pearce was known as "Snake Hips" because of how he moved his hips. So Ethel Barrymore took lessons from Snake Hips. And, by the way, she played the role in blackface.

While acting in the now-forgotten play *Embezzled Heaven*, along with Ethel Barrymore, Madeline Gilford was slicing lemons during a scene. She accidentally cut herself. She then brought the plate of sliced lemons to Ethel Barrymore who noticed the blood on the edge of the plate. Barrymore was staring at the plate when she said her next line about getting some parsley. Instead, she said, "Zdenka, go in the garden and get me a plate of blood."

Barrymore was mad at George S. Kaufman about the way her family was depicted in the play *The Royal Family*. Kaufman asked Barrymore to appear at a benefit. She responded to the playwright, "I intend to have laryngitis on that night."

MAURICE BARRYMORE

The scion of the great Barrymore family of actors, Maurice Barrymore, was as excellent a performer as his children Lionel, John, and Ethel. Like his offspring, he was an exceptional person. Barrymore was a successful playwright in addition to his talents as an actor. Among his plays was *Najezda*, and it was an international success with performances in both the United States and in London in 1886.

With success behind the play, he sent it to the great Sarah Bernhardt hoping she would star in a Parisian production. But he heard nothing for over two years. Then the play *La Tosca* opened in Paris, and it was an obvious case of plagiarism. Bernhardt's response to the accusations against her was, "If a great man gets the germ of an idea from some—some obscure American, what does it matter? These things often happen." Barrymore's reply went as follows: "A man is no less a thief who steals from his own hat rack my walking stick, where I have confidently placed it, and builds an umbrella on it."

Later the play by Sardou was made into the opera by Puccini, and Barrymore never made a cent from it.

BLANCHE BATES

Blanche Bates started acting out West when the West was still the West. Admission to the theatre was in the form of gold nuggets. She eventually came to New York and was a star in such hits as *A Doll's House*, a bunch of Belasco productions including *Madame Butterfly* and *The Girl of the Golden West*, and other plays nobody today has ever heard of. In her time, the beginning of the last century, there was decorum on the stage. And an unwritten set of rules. She was a great star and acted and dressed the part both onstage and off.

Late in her career, a young Ruth Gordon acted with her in *Mrs. Partridge Presents*. In the first scene of act one, Bates sat at a table serving chowder out of a big tureen. Gordon made her exit to vociferous applause from the audience. This was unheard of, a supporting player getting applause when the star was still onstage. So, as soon as Gordon exited, Bates put down the ladle and left the stage too. When the applause abated, Bates returned to the table, picked up the ladle and continued the play.

At one performance of the play, she exited to no applause at all. "What!" she cried out in disbelief. So she started the applause from backstage and the audience picked it up. "That's more like it!" she harrumphed and regally retook the stage.

DAVID BELASCO

As one of the greatest producers/directors/playwrights in American theatre history, David Belasco was certainly a unique individual. Though Jewish, he dressed in black with a priest's collar and thus was dubbed "The Bishop of Broadway."

Belasco believed in realism in the theatre. If there was a kitchen in a play, you could bet that a real breakfast would be cooked in it. One time, when he instructed an actor to squirt soda water into a highball glass, the actor asked if the sound of the soda would kill his laugh. Belasco drew himself up and proclaimed, "This play is about bachelors. I'd rather have the sound of that soda than a dozen laughs."

He wrote the plays *Madame Butterfly* and *The Girl of the Golden West*. Puccini was paying attention. *Madame Butterfly* almost went unseen and unknown. Belasco tore apart the script to *Madame Butterfly* into tiny pieces. His secretary Miss Ginty was shocked! Belasco knew he had a second copy in his office, but Miss Ginty fainted on the floor.

What he didn't know was that Miss Ginty had knocked over an inkwell onto the copy and it was ruined. Miss Ginty spent the next days pasting the tiny scraps of paper together. Some said that Miss Ginty actually was Belasco's collaborator on the script, but whether it was true or not, without her, there would be no *Madame Butterfly*.

Belasco would work his actors hard in the days before Actors' Equity. He'd serve lunch in the basement of his namesake theatre so the actors wouldn't wander off and have their minds on other things. And if rehearsals ran into overtime, he'd have dinner served. Much of the time in rehearsals was taken up by Belasco thinking, standing and thinking while the actors waited.

If an actor made Belasco angry, he'd deal with him harshly. He'd scream at the performer, his anger rising until he was practically apoplectic. He was so angry that he'd pull out his pocket watch and throw it to the floor. That got the actor's attention. Little did they know that he had boxes of cheap watches in his office just to achieve this effect.

In one show, he became so incensed that he took a fire axe and attacked the scenery. He was crazed. How dare an actor be so stupid! The axe flew through the air and took another chunk out of the set. The actors were frozen. The axe continued to swing until the set was a pile of kindling. He definitely got their attention. What they didn't know was that Belasco had never liked the set and had already ordered a new one that was in the process of being built.

Belasco loved his leading ladies. Ina Claire, Jeanne Eagels, Lenore Ulric, and Frances Starr were his favorites. On opening nights, he loved when they'd beckon him onstage to take a bow. And he loved when they'd visit his private apartment in the theatre.

IRVING BERLIN

Berlin lived on Beekman Place overlooking the East River. His pals Harold Arlen and E. Y. Harburg would look out the window and point out the barges sailing up the river. They'd tease Berlin, telling him, "There's another barge of money going up to Richard Rodgers' house."

Irving Berlin wrote some quite risqué songs, including one named "Trader Horny." They are not in the *Complete Lyrics of Irving Berlin* book. In fact, late in his life, Berlin and his caretaker/nurse would attend x-rated movies together.

Likewise, Harold Arlen and Ted Koehler wrote risqué lyrics for the Cotton Club shows. But Arlen's estate wouldn't release them after his death.

Arlen and Berlin spoke on the phone almost everyday. And when there was a ball game, be it baseball or football, they'd make little bets with each other. Whoever lost would send a check for five dollars or so to the other one.

Speaking of Arlen and Berlin, Martin Charnin was collaborating with Harold Arlen on the musical *Softly*. They'd start work at ten in the morning and promptly at noon, work would stop. Irving Berlin would call from Arlen's lobby and the two of them would take a daily perambulation. After a while, Charnin said to Arlen, "You meet Irving Berlin every day when we're working and he never comes up. I'd like to meet him." The next day,

Berlin came upstairs to Arlen's door and Charnin shook the great composer's hand. Charnin told Berlin, "I'm delighted to meet you." When Arlen returned from the walk, he told Charnin that Berlin felt insulted. Charnin couldn't understand what he could have done to insult Berlin. After all, they only saw each other for maybe a minute. Arlen explained, "Irving felt you should have said, 'I'm *honored* to meet you.'"

Irving Berlin had a secretary, Hilda Schneider, who was what was then called a tough broad. When people called his office, they had to get past Schneider. That's why she was nicknamed "The Berlin Wall."

When Anita Gillette was on *The Tonight Show*, she got a call the next morning from Irving Berlin's office. "Hello, Anita, it's Hilda, Hilda Schneider," as though Anita wouldn't know which Hilda it was. "We saw you last night on the Carson show and Mr. B. wants to talk to you." Berlin got on the phone: "Hello, Anita, it's Irving, I saw you last night with Johnny Carson. Anita, you sang Jule Styne. Anita, I got a lotta songs!"

HUMPHREY BOGART

The Cradle Snatchers was Humphrey Bogart's fifth Broadway play though the role of the gigolo wasn't a large one. Apparently, the general consensus was that his acting was terrible. When the company would retire to a speakeasy after the performance, the teasing got so bad, Bogart would get plastered and go to the kitchen where he would spend an hour or two standing on his head. The cast dubbed him "Bogey" and the name stuck.

CORAL BROWNE

Browne once said of a writer of a play she was doing, "He couldn't write fuck in the dust of a Venetian blind."

BILLIE BURKE

Burke was one of the great beauties on the American stage at the turn of the last century. She's best known today as Glinda in the film version of *The Wizard of Oz*. She toured relentlessly across the country under the auspices of producer Charles Frohman. One day, a newspaper reporter asked her what was in the vast amount of luggage she carried from town to town. Burke demurely stated, "Why, that's Billie Burke."

DAVID BURNS

David Burns was a great performer, but he had an extremely crude sense of humor. Someone once wrote that if you ever had your hand behind your back, Burns would put his cock in it.

Once he came into a rehearsal of *The Music Man* late and apologized to the company in a very upper-class accent. "I beg your pardon everyone. Please forgive me. I was in the lavatory having my cock sucked by the most charming cleaning lady." Pert Kelton couldn't believe it. Or rather, she could believe it but didn't want to. "Oh, Davey, you are disgusting." Burns drew himself up and looked down his nose at Kelton and said, "Some cleaning woman I never met is sucking my cock and you call *me* disgusting?"

Burns was the third choice to play Horace Vandergelder in *Hello, Dolly!* David Merrick originally wanted Burl Ives, and then Art Carney was offered the part and turned it down. So Merrick got in touch with Burns who insisted on a salary of $2,000 a week. When Merrick offered $1,250, Burns told him, "I mean this from the bottom of my heart, go fuck yourself."

Merrick again made the offer with the same response from Burns. Merrick then asked Burns to come to his office. Merrick's secretary told Burns that Mr. Merrick would see him and to go right in. Burns went to the door of Merrick's private office and took off all his clothes except his socks and shoes. Burns knocked and Merrick said, "Come in." Burns knocked again and Merrick said, "Come in." Finally Burns knocked again and Merrick went to the door and opened it. Burns said to Merrick, "Any casting today?" He got the $2,000.

Gower Champion was lambasting the cast of *Hello, Dolly!* Things were not going well with the show and Champion was not having it. During the tirade, David Burns whispered in Carol Channing's ear, "Carol, let me tell you about my vasectomy."

EARL CARROLL

The third in the revue-producing triumvirate that also included George White and Florenz Ziegfeld, Earl Carroll's shows were built upon showing as much of a woman's assets as could legally be allowed on the stage. That didn't get him in hot water with the law, but another stunt did. At an after-theatre party, Carroll had a bathtub brought to center stage and filled it with champagne. Note that this was in the midst of prohibition. The impresario then had seventeen-year-old beauty Joyce Hawley take off her clothes and get into the tub for a good, long soak.

The guests were invited to take in the waters (champagne) or take in the view (Hawley). The girl soon became hysterical and her tears mixed with the champagne. The event was written up in the press and came to the attention of the Federal Prohibition Bureau, which brought Carroll to trial. He professed that the bathtub was only filled with ginger ale, but he wasn't believed and was fined $2,000 and sent to jail for a year and a day. Carroll was paroled after four months, his image greatly improved.

Carroll got into trouble with the law again when, during the *Vanities of 1930*, he hired Faith Bacon, a fan dancer by trade. The only thing separating her flesh from the eyes of the audience was the artful manipulation of two fans. The morals squad of the city objected to the display and also a skit with comic Jimmy Savo where he played a window dresser, changing the fashions of a bevy of chorus girls pretending to be mannequins.

GOWER CHAMPION

He was called "The Presbyterian Hitler."

CAROL CHANNING AND CHARLES LOWE

Channing and her husband Charles Lowe created three-by-five-inch cards on which were written the name of the interviewer, the publication, date of the interview, and some personal information. Years later, when the same interviewer would meet Channing, she would refer to her cards and ask about the interviewer's wife or child or an event in their lives.

Channing would also keep cards on people she worked with but never update them. Buster Davis, a musical genius who first worked with Channing on *Gentlemen Prefer Blondes*, recalled that seven years after his mother had died, Channing was still asking him how she was doing.

PADDY CHAYEFSKY

Sidney Chayefsky turned into Paddy Chayefsky, and this is how it happened. He was in the Army and managed to get leave for the Jewish holiday of Passover. When it was Good Friday, Chayefsky asked to be given leave for that also. His captain asked him why he was taking off both religious holidays. Chayefsky replied that his father was Jewish and his mother was Catholic. The Captain, speaking in an Irish brogue and tweaking Chayefsky's nose with his fingers, replied, "And I suppose now your first name would be Paddy." From then on and until the end of his life, it was "Paddy."

NOEL COWARD

Noel Coward was on the phone with Western Union dictating a telegram to Gertrude Lawrence. When he was finished, he asked the operator to sign the telegram "Fiorello LaGuardia." "Are you Mayor LaGuardia?" asked the operator. "No," answered Coward, "I am not." "In that case, you can't sign his name." "Oh. Well, sign it Noel Coward." "Are you Mr. Coward?" "Yes I am." "Oh," replied the operator, "in that case, you can sign any name you want to."

That telegram might have been meant for Lawrence when she opened in *Skylark*, the first time she appeared in a straight play on Broadway. The telegram read: "Legitimate at last. Won't Mummy Be Pleased."

HOWARD DIETZ

"Composers should not be allowed to think. It gets in the way of their plagiarism. When composers are illiterate they look up to the lyric writers. Lyric writers should be looked up to by somebody."

Dietz was a remarkable talent. He wrote some of the greatest popular songs, he was head of publicity at MGM, he invented the MGM lion, he brought the game charades from Paris to the U.S., and he directed the first truly sophisticated musical revue, *The Band Wagon*, for which he also wrote sketches and the lyrics.

"Arthur Schwartz is the most intelligent composer I know. He once took an assignment, which required him to write a large number of songs a week. I asked if that would take a lot out of him. 'Yes,' he replied, 'but it will also take a lot out of Bach, Beethoven, and Brahms.'"

When Dietz and his wife Lucinda Ballard would hold a party at their townhouse on West 11th Street in Greenwich Village, a moving van would pull up to the house and the entire contents would be loaded onto the truck.

Then tables and chairs would be brought in for the party. Afterward, the entire process was reversed and the house put back in order.

Years later, the townhouse would become notorious when a radical group was making a bomb in the basement that went off, destroying part of the building.

And later still, the house was a local landmark because a teddy bear was put into the bay window and was dressed appropriately for the weather and holidays.

HOWARD DIETZ AND THE SHUBERT BROTHERS

When the show *Between the Devil* was in negotiations for the film rights, Lee Shubert wanted an extraordinary amount of money. When Dietz objected to the amount being asked, Shubert in reply handed Dietz a piece of paper. On it were written the names of other great producers: Charles Dillingham, Charles Frohman, Florenz Ziegfeld, and others. What did they have in common Shubert asked Dietz. Well, they were all dead. But that's not the answer Shubert was looking for. He said to Dietz, "They all died broke." The movie was never made.

When the Shuberts produced *At Home Abroad*, Dietz bought thirty-eight house seats for the opening night. When he was sent his first royalty check, a deduction was made for one hundred seats. The Shuberts had charged critics' tickets against Dietz as one of their expenses.

Five years later, the Shuberts wanted Dietz to work on additional numbers for the show *Keep Off the Grass*. He refused to do so until he was repaid for the critics' tickets. They told him not to worry about it, and he replied that he was going to worry about it. He did the numbers and they did pay him, eventually.

VERNON DUKE

Duke once told producer/director Ben Bagley that the greatest sound in the world was the sound of a fat woman's thighs slapping together.

When Duke was collaborating with Martin Charnin on the ill-fated musical *Zenda*, Charnin was thrilled to announce that he was going to have a baby. Duke asked what the name would be and Charnin told him, "Alexandra." Duke was apoplectic. "I will never call her Alexandra. That is the name of the Tsarina who was married to the worse Tsar, Nicholas II." "Well, what would you call her then? asked Charnin. "Sascha," replied Duke and that's what she was named.

LARRY FAY

Larry Fay wasn't a performer or a director or much of anything in the theatre. Actually, he had only one credit. He produced a flop revival of *Under the Gaslight* in 1929. But he nevertheless had an influence on the theatre.

Fay was a gentleman gangster. He dressed impeccably, didn't carry a gun, and was a rumrunner out of Canada. He had an interest in a couple of clubs and was known up and down Broadway.

One day, David Burns and Benny Baker were at Dinty Moore's, a favorite hangout. They ran into Fay, who asked what they were doing. They said that they were making $125 a week with Gus Edwards. Fay told them, "Tell Gus I said to give you more." They thought it was a joke, but they went to Edwards and, indeed, he raised their salary to $175.

CHARLES FROHMAN

Frohman was one of the greatest producers of the American theatre. Among his shows was one that forever captured the imagination of audiences and provided one of the most remarkable evenings at the theatre. The play was just one of twenty-five produced by Frohman in 1905. James M. Barrie's *Peter Pan* opened on November 6th. On that evening and every other evening, Maude Adams as Peter asked the audience if they believed in fairies. To a man they stood up and shouted, "Yes!" That innocence, that sense of fun and romance is largely gone from the theatre.

Even in modern times when Jean Arthur or Mary Martin or Sandy Duncan or Cathy Rigby asks the audience if they believe in fairies, they still clap even if it's without the same conviction and innocence of the original audiences. We may be more jaded or even take the word "fairies" ironically, but somewhere down deep we secretly in our hearts still believe in fairies.

Frohman's career was tragically cut short when the boat upon which he was sailing was sunk by a German ship. That boat was the Lusitania, and its sinking heralded World War I and the loss of innocence. It also robbed the American and London theatre of one of its greatest showmen.

FAYE EMERSON

Faye Emerson was an actress and a popular television personality. She was on a crowded midtown bus, and a guy was saying, "Stop shoving. Stop shoving." He turned and saw Faye Emerson and said, "You're Faye Emerson, aren't you?" And she said, "Why, yes I am." He replied, "Well, watch who you're shoving, Faye!"

ABRAHAM ERLANGER

Abe Erlanger and Marcus Klaw were the heads of the Theatrical Syndicate, the theatre monopoly founded in the late 1800s that controlled theatres throughout the country and built several Broadway houses, including the New Amsterdam Theatre, home of *The Ziegfeld Follies*, and the theatre that is now named the St. James. They presented many of the greatest plays in the early 1900s including *Dracula, Ben-Hur,* and *The Jazz Singer,* as well as *The Ziegfeld Follies.* It was only when the Shubert Brothers came on the scene that the Theatrical Syndicate had any real competition.

As an example of exactly how much money could be made even in those early days when tickets cost only a few dollars or less is the story of when Florenz Ziegfeld approached Erlanger for a bigger cut from the *Follies.* After all, Ziegfeld put the shows together, cast them, picked out the scenery and costumes, and oversaw the productions.

"My percentage is all out of proportion to the earnings of the show," stated Ziegfeld to Erlanger. "You're a rich man and you can afford to make my bit larger. Why, you're worth $40,000,000 if you're worth a nickel." Erlanger stopped Ziegfeld short: "Stop right there—I am worth $60,000,000 and a flock of nickels besides."

CY FEUER AND ERNEST MARTIN

Feuer and Martin were highly successful producers and certainly had an eye for a hit, though they had their fair share of failures. But people often didn't like them, even more than they didn't like David Merrick. Some wags dubbed them "The Nazi and the Liar." George S. Kaufman called them, alternately, "Jed Harris rolled into one" and "Mr. Hyde and Mr. Hyde." Jed Harris was a genius at producing hits, but he was one of the most reviled figures in the theatre of his time.

PETER GENNARO

Choreographer Peter Gennaro lost his hearing late in his career. Since he couldn't hear the music well, a new plan had to be devised. So, in the rehearsal room, the pianist opened the lid of the upright piano and Gennaro would put his hand on the soundboard to feel the rhythms.

GEORGE AND IRA GERSHWIN

George Gershwin wanted to study with Maurice Ravel in Paris. Ravel was worried that the young artist wouldn't have enough money for an extended stay. Ravel asked Gershwin, "How much do you make from your Broadway shows?" Gershwin replied, "About a thousand dollars a week." Ravel was surprised and said, "Oh, Mr. Gershwin, may I study with you?" In the end, Ravel refused to mentor Gershwin, thinking that further classical education might impair his natural abilities as a composer.

George Gershwin was no shrinking violet. In fact, he loved nothing more than to commandeer a piano during a party and become the center of attention. Not that the host or hostess minded. But sometimes, it was annoying to others.

Kaufman claimed to be working on an invention with the comic Joe Cook. "I'm going to patent an invention which will keep composers away from pianos at parties. It might be expensive, though; eight strong men would probably be needed to make it work. Maybe I'd better come up with something which'll keep pianos away from composers." Once, a friend stopped George S. Kaufman on the street. He informed the playwright/director that the songs for Kaufman's new show were terrific. "What music?" inquired Kaufman. "The title song particularly, 'Of Thee I Sing,' I mean. I also liked the other new one for the show, 'Who Cares?' " responded the friend. "Gershwin played them at a party when I was in California last week."

At another occasion, Kaufman chided Gershwin, "If you play that score one more time before we open, people are going to think we're doing a revival."

Oscar Levant said to Gershwin, "Tell me, George, if you had to do it all over, would you fall in love with yourself again?"

George and Ira Gershwin had a 70/30 split on royalties of their songs. Later it was amended to a 60/40 split.

Noel Coward invited Hal David and Ira Gershwin to come out to Las Vegas to see his act. David went to Gershwin's house and got in his car. As they went down the driveway, David exclaimed, "Isn't this a marvelous trip!" As they turned onto the street, Ira replied, "So far."

David once went to Ira's house when a package arrived. In the envelope was a record with a note from Ira's publisher. The note explained that the record was the 300th recording of "I Got Rhythm." David was impressed. "Imagine, Ira, 300 artists have recorded your song!" Ira responded, "Some people seem to like it."

JOHN GIELGUD

John Gielgud was dining at the Ivy Restaurant with this very attractive young man and Gladys Cooper was at the next table. Gielgud was doing his best trying to pretend that he doesn't see Cooper, but he finally realized that he couldn't ignore her any longer, so he turned to her and said, "Gladys how lovely to see you. I'd like you to meet my nephew." And Gladys Cooper turned to the boy and said, "I'm glad to meet you, I've known your aunt for many years."

John Gielgud was at a dinner party when he said, "Margalo is a cunt!" To his surprise, he noticed Margalo Gilmore seated right next to him. Thinking fast, he averred, "I wasn't talking about you Margalo, I'm talking about another Margalo, darling."

ANITA GILLETTE

Anita Gillette was playing the ingénue in the musical *All American*. Even though she played a nymphomaniac in the show, people treated her as an innocent young girl. In fact, she was married and pregnant. During the opening night party, Mel Brooks, the librettist, came up to Gillette and squeezed her cheek like a Jewish mama, "Oooh, she's so cute. I could eat her up! How'd a little girl like you get pregnant?" Gillette was so annoyed, she answered in a loud voice, "I got fucked!"

Gillette went home to Baltimore and found an old *Life Magazine* in the attic. Inside was a story about the big, new Broadway stars, Barbara Harris, Barbra Streisand, and Anita Gillette. Paging through the magazine, she cried, feeling that her career didn't measure up to those of the other women. Of course, she was wrong. She still has a successful career fifty years later.

JOHN GOLDEN

Golden was a terrific producer, actor, and playwright. And he was also a sometime lyricist, with the song "Poor Butterfly," written with Raymond Hubbell, being his biggest hit. When he opened his play *Three Wise Fools*, the critics were not kind. So he simply paid people to wait in line at the box office. Soon, they were joined by others who, seeing the long queue, figured the play must be a success.

Paul Muni, starring in Golden's 1927 production of *Four Walls*, was the proud recipient of the Italo-American Award. The many newspapers then in New York covered the award with photographers snapping away at Muni. A prominent member of the Italian-American community made the presentation. Afterward, in his office, Golden greeted the man who bestowed the award on Muni. The man was Tony, Golden's barber, and the scroll was made up by Golden the morning of the award.

Golden really believed in the theatre. Garson Kanin, author and director of *Born Yesterday*, decided, after a long, successful run, to finally close the show because it had only broken even in the previous two weeks. Golden marched down to Kanin's office and burst in, attacking Kanin for putting up the closing notice. "Don't close till there *is* a loss. Take five thousand dollars just for the hell of it, let's see how far *that* goes!" *Born Yesterday* played for seven more months.

ADOLPH GREEN

Barry Kleinbort asked lyricist/librettist Adolph Green when he knew he was a professional. Green told Barry that one would think it was when his first show, *On the Town*, had a triumphant opening on Broadway. But the truth was quite the opposite. Green said it was the show *Bonanza Bound* that proved to him he was a professional.

The show was a disaster out of town. After it closed for good there, Green and the company returned to New York "with our tails between our legs." The next day, he decided to go to Sardi's. He held his head up high as he entered the restaurant. Everybody swarmed around him asking him what went wrong with the show. Green thought about the question. "I was all ready to blame the cast and composer and director." But instead he stated, "We had an idea for the show and it wasn't very good." When he himself took part of the blame for the show's failure, he knew he was a real professional.

Green told everyone he wrote the screenplay to *Singin' in the Rain* which he did along with his writing partner, Betty Comden. He couldn't help but brag about it. When he ordered Chinese food over the phone, he informed the owner that he wanted a large order of General Tso's chicken, mu shu pork, and that he wrote *Singin' in the Rain*.

When he was quite elderly, Green fell down and his wife Phyllis Newman had him taken to the hospital. When she asked the doctor how he was doing, the doctor replied, "It's only a hairline break and shouldn't be a problem." But he implied that Green might have some mental problems: "He kept claiming that he wrote the film *Singin' in the Rain*."

MARTYN GREEN

Producer Jamie de Roy was working as an apprentice at the Bucks County Playhouse. The great Gilbert and Sullivan Savoyard Martyn Green was working on a show. During one of his changes, he told de Roy, "I need to put on black socks." She questioned him, "What do you want me to do?" He replied, "Just put them on me." She knelt down and he said to her, "No, here," and took off his wooden leg and handed it to her, which freaked her out since she didn't know he had one.

Radie Harris, the columnist, also had a wooden leg. She was holding court and all these people were milling around her. Harris's bitter enemy, the actress Coral Browne, said to her, "Oh, Radie, it must be so wonderful to have the whole world at your *foot*."

OSCAR HAMMERSTEIN I

Oscar Hammerstein I, uncle of Oscar the second, bet $100 that he could write a complete opera in one day. He succeeded, but the result, *The Kohinoor Diamond*, did not. Hammerstein produced his opera himself and lost much more than the $100 he won.

OSCAR HAMMERSTEIN II

Before *Oklahoma!* opened on Broadway, Oscar Hammerstein's career was in decline. To show he had a sense of humor, Hammerstein took out the following ad in *Variety*:

SUNNY RIVER (6 weeks at the St. James)
VERY WARM FOR MAY (7 weeks at the Alvin)
THREE SISTERS (7 weeks at the Drury Lane)

FREE FOR ALL (3 weeks at the Manhattan)
"I've Done It Before And I Can Do It Again"

Here's an apparently true story that is one of the most oft-told of Broadway anecdotes. Mrs. Oscar Hammerstein and Mrs. Jerome Kern were at a party and the hostess introduced them to another guest by saying, "My husband wrote 'Ol' Man River.'" Dorothy Hammerstein corrected her: "Mrs. Kern's husband wrote dum, dum, dum, dum. My husband wrote 'Ol' Man River.'"

MARVIN HAMLISCH

By the time Marvin Hamlisch was writing *Sweet Smell of Success*, he had already won the Tony, Grammy, Emmy, and Pulitzer Prize. He told Barry Kleinbort, "I'm excited about this show. This one's gonna legitimize me." Then he refused to write a new ballad for the show when asked to by the producers.

Marvin Hamlisch never wrote anything down. He would play numbers on a cassette and send them to a transcriber who would notate them, so people started calling cassette tapes "Hamlisches."

E. Y. "YIP" HARBURG

Howard Dietz once said, "Yip Harburg, who argues if bluebirds can fly over the rainbow, why can't he?"

Harburg was quite the ladies' man. His song from *Finian's Rainbow*, "When I'm Not Near the Girl I Love," summed up his philosophy of life. But Harburg wasn't just looking to bed a woman; he was legitimately looking for love.

Harburg's first great success was "Brother Can You Spare a Dime," with music by Jay Gorney. Later, Harburg married the former Mrs. Gorney. In fact, she often stated, "I never marry anyone who didn't write "Brother Can You Spare a Dime."

Harburg at a party once introduced the girl on his arm with "This is Mrs. Harburg for tonight."

One summer, Burton Lane and his wife Lynn were visiting the Harburgs at a house in Martha's Vineyard. Lane and Harburg were looking out the window enjoying the beautiful view. The sand, the sea, the surf—it was right out of a picture book. Harburg turned to Lane and enthused, "One day I'm going to own a house like this." Lane, surprised, replied, "But Yip, this *is* your house!"

MOSS HART

Despite all his success, Moss Hart was terribly insecure. Since he had so many successes collaborating with other writers, chiefly George S. Kaufman, he was unsure whether he could successfully write a play by himself. At one point, he was paralyzed with fear that he would never be successful again. S. N. Behrman told Hart, "You're a professional writer. You must write. Go to your desk and write every day, even if it's only a diary." Hart wrote in his diary for over a year and then tore it up and began work on his autobiography, *Act One*.

Hart once said of people in general and himself specifically, "It's interesting that the great mystery of unhappiness is not about fate, about bad breaks, and you can understand it. But when you're completely successful and you're unhappy, it becomes a mystery. Most of the successful people I know are unhappy. Success is like anesthesia. You can increase the dosage and increase it and finally it doesn't work."

Hart had three shows on Broadway including *You Can't Take It with You*, for which he received the Pulitzer Prize along with Kaufman. And still he was in analysis for seven years. He finally concluded that "in the theatre you get more than you deserve and sometimes less than you deserve—and there is no use being bitter about it."

Though his last show *Camelot* was a horrible experience resulting in Hart suffering a heart attack and Alan Jay Lerner developing a very serious case of bleeding ulcers, Hart summed up the whole affair by saying, "Well, at least we aspired."

JUNE HAVOC

June Havoc was forever influenced by her mother Rose Hovick, the subject of the musical *Gypsy*. You might remember that Rose and Herbie are in a Chinese restaurant and at the end of the meal, Rose opens a big bag and puts in the leftovers and also all the silverware.

When June Havoc was an adult, she had a specially lined bag in which she'd stuff wheels of cheese and other foods when she went to benefits and dinners. Gypsy Rose Lee also scrimped and saved. People referred to her as a cheapskate Auntie Mame. She'd eat baked beans out of a can in her Sutton Place apartment. After Gypsy's death, it was said that her son Eric Preminger wasted all the money that Gypsy saved by eating out of cans.

HELEN HAYES

Helen Hayes told Miles Kreuger about what it was like to be an ingénue in the theatre of the 1920s. She told him that ingénues didn't walk, they hopped. They wouldn't sit down on a seat; they plunked down on it. They had nothing to do with reality; they just bounced around empty-headed.

JERRY HERMAN'S MOTHER

Jerry Herman was born in the Polyclinic Hospital on 50th Street between 8th and 9th Avenues. The building is still there across the street from the New World Stages. Jerry's mother told him that from her hospital bed, she could see the Winter Garden Theatre. And she told Jerry that he would one day have a big hit show at the Winter Garden. Well, you probably know that Jerry did have an immense success at the Winter Garden, *Mame*. But Jerry's mother never saw any of his success. She died of cancer in 1954.

Herman's mother Ruth was a wonderful person, and her influence on him was tremendous. One day, young Jerry came home and the house was festively decorated. Jerry asked his mother, "Mom, this isn't a holiday. It isn't a birthday. Why does the house look like this?" His mother answered, "It's today." That led to Herman writing the song "It's Today" for *Mame*.

SHIRLEY HERZ

Shirley Herz was the first press agent to win the Tony (the second was Adrian Bryan-Brown). Columnist extraordinaire Liz Smith, a longtime friend of Herz, told her, "I was stunned when you won the Tony." Herz replied, "Well, I never thought you'd amount to anything either."

Young Shirley Herz was hired by Sam Friedman, a press agent who now has a Broadway theatre named after him. "By the end of the first week when he handed me my paycheck, he said, 'I can't have you working here anymore. Having a woman in the office. It's fucking difficult, I can't swear and I can't say shit and all those words so you have to leave.' I told him, 'You just said them.'"

Herz also said: "I was working on *Oh, Calcutta!*, which had a lot of nudity. A beautiful girl was in it. We had to take her down to City Hall in her costume. A sheer costume. Her coat was open and the wind was blowing. We were arrested."

Shirley Herz was the person who dubbed Rosalind Russell's husband, producer Frederick Brisson, "The Lizard of Roz."

AL HIRSCHFELD

There were many great caricaturists in the history of Broadway, but the greatest of all was Al Hirschfeld. It was publicist Richard Maney who "discovered" Hirschfeld and brought his work to the *New York Herald-Tribune* where Hirschfeld drew his first theatre caricatures. Soon thereafter, he moved to *The New York Times*. Hirschfeld didn't have a contract with the *Times*. The deal was that he would dictate the size of the drawing when it would appear in the paper. That all changed on April 11, 1980, when his drawing of the revival of Paul Osborn's play *Mornings at Seven* appeared in the *Times*. The drawing appeared on the first page of the arts and leisure section in the space of only one column. Hirschfeld was incensed and, from then on, he had a contract with the *Times* that included his having the right to tell the editors what size to print his drawings.

Hirschfeld was known for the word "Nina" hidden in all his drawings. On Sunday mornings many readers turned immediately to the arts section for Hirschfeld's drawing and started counting the Ninas. Nina was the name of Hirschfeld's daughter and what began as a one-time tribute to her became his trademark.

Margo Feiden was Hirschfeld's representative, and she sold his drawings at her gallery. There was a student from NYU who kept returning to the gallery to look at a specific drawing that kept him hypnotized. He'd spend hours, days, and weeks looking at the drawing. Finally, Feiden asked him what it was about that drawing that was so mesmerizing. The man answered that he had found only eleven of the thirty-nine Ninas in the drawing. Feiden informed him that the number thirty-nine after Hirschfeld's name represented the year the drawing was completed. Nina was born six years later.

TWO CELESTE HOLM STORIES

Celeste Holm was at the top of the list of mean people. She would ask people to pay twenty-five cents to UNICEF for her autograph, or if you swore in her presence you had to drop a quarter in the box.

She'd also sit in the wings of her shows and take notes on the acting of her fellow cast members. When they exited the stage, she'd give them her notes.

GEORGE S. KAUFMAN'S MOTHER

George S. Kaufman could do nothing right in the theatre, at least according to his mother. She would call her son up and say, "Did you read what the critics said about Eugene O'Neill's new play? My, how they praised it!" She was intimating that if George was such a big deal, why didn't he direct O'Neill's play.

George would say to her, "But, Mama, other people have to write plays. Can I help it if they're good—and hits?"

"They're friends with the critics," stated Mrs. Kaufman said. "You should be more sociable."

One night, his eighty-year-old mother went to a rehearsal of one of her son's plays. Afterward, Kaufman asked her, "Mama, what do you think of this one? Like it, yes?" "Seems to me," she replied, "your producers might have spent a little more money on it. Seems pretty cheap."

"Cheap? Why, Mama, this is an expensive production. Didn't you notice—three sets?"

"Yes, yes," she admitted, "but all in the same house."

Kaufman's mother met George Gershwin's mother in Atlantic City. "How are you Mrs. Kaufman," inquired Mrs. Gershwin. "I am Mrs. Gershwin— my son wrote something in music with your son."

George's mother replied, "Maybe. My son writes with lots of people." And then she left.

JOHN KENLEY

When Paul Lynde came down with hepatitis the night before he was to open in John Kenley's production of *Don't Drink the Water* at E. J. Thomas Hall in Akron, Ohio, Barry Kleinbort had to go on for him.

Ten years later, Barry walked into Charley's Restaurant in New York and saw the producer sitting at a table. Kleinbort walked up to him and said, "I don't know if you'll remember me." Kenley, without missing a beat told everybody at his table, "This young man went on for Paul Lynde in *Don't Drink the Water*." Kleinbort was surprised. "Mr. Kenley, that's amazing, how did you remember that?" Kenley responded, "Darling, I remember everyone who ever saved me money."

Most readers will not know who John Kenley was, but he led a truly amazing life. Go to Wikipedia to find out about this remarkable talent.

JOE KIPNESS

Joe Kipness was a somewhat shady producer, though casts and crews loved him and nicknamed him "Kippy" and "Cryin' Joe." He once commented, "'Darling, the theater, despite everything, has given me more happiness than I ever received in my life from anything. I'm going to do other shows. I'll do it until I die."

He was extremely cagey about his business and sometimes had inventive solutions to problems. He once owed someone money after a failed show. The investor threw a big birthday party for his daughter at Kipness's faux Polynesian restaurant Hawaii Kai, next door to the Winter Garden Theatre. When the bill came, the investor told the waiter, "Tell Kipness to take it out of the money he owes me."

Kipness held auditions for *I Had a Ball* in Hawaii Kai.

One of Kipness's first producing ventures was *The Duke in Darkness* by Patrick Hamilton. The show was a bomb in New Haven. Kipness called together some theatricals to his hotel room and asked them what could be done to save the show. They started throwing around ideas left and right and Kipness's hopes grew.

Just then, Hamilton spoke up, "Let me remind you, Mr. Kipness, that we have a contract. The play you bought is the play that shall be done on Broadway. Not one word, not a comma, shall be changed." Kipness could not control his anger. He started sputtering, frustrated that he couldn't deck Hamilton. Finally, Kipness blurted out, "I'll be goddamned! This is the last time I ever do a play with an *author*!"

Another note about Kipness, who definitely deserves a Wikipedia article: His and Jule Styne's secretaries were sisters.

LISA KIRK

While riding down in an elevator in an office building, Lisa Kirk looked around at her fellow passengers, hoping that somebody would recognize her. They ignored her, so Kirk said in a loud voice, "Lisa Kirk, you naughty girl, you left your script upstairs."

BURTON LANE

When Burton Lane was a young man, he showed tremendous potential as a pianist. Burton's dad was one of the best fathers ever. He had heard that George Gershwin was staying at a hotel in Atlantic City. So he drove Burton down to the shore and they sat in the hotel's lobby until Gershwin came down in the elevator. Then Burton's father introduced himself and told Gershwin all about his son. Gershwin then became Burton's mentor.

Gershwin's mentoring and Lane's talents paid off when the Shubert brothers hired Lane to write his first musical theatre score. Still in his teens, he was the youngest Broadway composer. Sadly, the show never came to town. But a few years later, Maurie Rubens, the Shuberts' house composer, interpolated Lane's melodies into another Shubert show, but without giving credit to Lane. Burton's father saw to it that the songs were taken out of the score.

Lane and his wife Lynn were committed liberals. In fact, once Lynn called Lane to tell him that she was in jail in Washington, D.C., after she had been arrested during a protest march. At one point during the Nixon administration, there was a knock on their apartment door. When Lane answered it, a man informed him that he was "on the shit list" and he'd better watch out. Lane asked him if he would go on record and the man refused.

Lane was asked to collaborate with Dorothy Fields on the musical *A Tree Grows in Brooklyn*. One morning, Lane went to Fields's home to discuss the project and asked to go to the upstairs bathroom. On his way back downstairs, he noticed a large mirror in the living room. Fields was reflected in it taking a swig directly from a liquor decanter. Burton figured that if she was having a drink so early in the morning, he didn't want to work with her and he turned down the project.

Now we take a moment to tell a story that is not about the theatre, though it's close. Barbara Streisand and Burton Lane were in the recording studio listening to playbacks for "Hurry, It's Lovely Up Here." Streisand asked Lane what he thought of her performance.

Lane's wife could see his back stiffen. He knew he had two possible answers. He could lie and say he loved it, or he could tell her the truth and risk her walking off the picture. Burton said to Streisand, "I hate it!" Streisand asked what he didn't like and if he'd show her at the piano.

They went into the studio where Lane told Streisand that the sung should be sung like a lullaby, as if to a baby. Streisand replied that they should re-record the song. They went back into the studio and Lane called Howard Koch, the head of Paramount. Lane told Koch that they should re-record the song, that the performance was bad. Koch replied, "You mean in your opinion." Lane simply said, "There's someone else here who wants to talk to you." Streisand got on the phone and the number was recorded again.

Although Lane was extremely close to the Gershwin family, when he wrote the song "Says My Heart," George and Ira's mother Rose sued him for plagiarizing the tune from the Gershwin song "Tell Me More."

When Harry Warren's song "An Affair to Remember" became a hit, Lane noticed that it was extremely similar to "The Happiest Day of My Life" from *Royal Wedding*. But Lane refused to sue.

ALAN JAY LERNER AND FREDERICK LOEWE

Lerner wore white gloves while writing his lyrics. His excuse was that he didn't want to get ink on his hands. But the truth was that he bit his nails down to the cuticles and his fingers would bleed.

Lerner was a profligate spender. He'd walk down the street and spy two Queen Anne chairs in an antique store window, walk in, pay $50,000 for each of the chairs, and continue on his stroll.

When Lerner was dying, he called up Turnbull and Asser shirt makers and ordered new shirts. And on the night he died, he ordered champagne for the visitors and family.

He was also what Charles Strouse labeled "an automatic liar." There was often no cause for a lie, but Lerner simply found it more interesting to drop a lie into the conversation now and then.

Though his collaborators Burton Lane and Charles Strouse were frustrated by his slow working methods, both were extremely fond of Lerner, though their wives were not. Lerner would spend hours getting exactly the right word for a song. His collaborators knew there were so few good lyricists around and Lerner was one of the best.

It took Lerner six months to write the title song for *On a Clear Day You Can See Forever*. He wrote twenty-six different versions until he finally settled on the one used in the show.

When Lerner was told a pastor in California was using the lyric to "On a Clear Day" for his sermons, Lerner joked, "Tell him not to expect a second chorus."

Even after they had long stopped collaborating, Lerner called Frederick Loewe everyday.

Lerner wouldn't let theatres mount productions of *My Fair Lady* unless they guaranteed they'd have chandeliers in the ball scene. He didn't want cheap productions of the show, and he felt that scene was when the show really took off. Others thought that "On the Street Where You Live" was when the show really grabbed the audience.

When Kitty Carlisle was rehearsing her first Broadway role in 1933's *Champagne Sec*, the pit pianist was Frederick Loewe. At one rehearsal, he came up to Carlisle and proclaimed, "Some day I will write the best musical on Broadway." Carlisle thought, "There are a lot of pit pianists. You and who else?"

Thirty-three years later, Carlisle and her husband Moss Hart were standing in the back of the Mark Hellinger Theatre watching *My Fair Lady*. Loewe came up to Carlisle and said, "Well, I wrote the best musical on Broadway."

Lerner had rented a house so that he could work on *My Fair Lady*. The house was supposed to be haunted, but Lerner paid the ghost no mind. Loewe joined Lerner, but was nervous about a ghost being on the premises. The ghost appeared one night in Loewe's room. He felt a cold draft as the ghost went through the room and into the bathroom. Lerner told Loewe not to worry about it. One week later, the ghost appeared again. Loewe felt the chill, heard the footsteps across the floor, the sound of the toilet flushing, and the footsteps going back out into the hall. Lerner went downstairs the next morning and discovered Loewe was gone. Lerner found a note that read, "I don't mind the ghost coming into my bedroom or the bathroom, but the ghost taking a crap is too much."

Outside the Mark Hellinger Theatre, every night after the curtain came down on *My Fair Lady*, there was a queue around the block lined up for standing room for the following night's show. Loewe was so excited about the show's success, he spent hours talking to people on the line about the show and his life.

By the way, "I Could Have Danced All Night" was originally written as a waltz.

Loewe, Hart, and Carlisle had booked a cruise around the world. The night before they were to leave, Hart died in Palm Springs. The following morning, Loewe showed up at Carlisle's door. Surprised, Carlisle said, "I thought you were going around the world, Fritzie?" Loewe replied, "Could I ever leave you now?"

Frederick Loewe was a great ladies' man. He would often be found naked, playing the piano with a comely beauty less than half his age sitting on his lap. At one point, he was living in Las Vegas with an eighteen-year-old when he could have been her grandfather.

MARCIA LEWIS

Marcia Lewis was one of the most beloved performers on Broadway. She could be both touching and a hilarious clown. When Lewis was nominated for a Tony for a revival of *Grease*, the cast chipped in and bought her a beautiful dress to wear to the ceremony.

ROBERT LEWIS

A few years before his death, famed director Robert Lewis was at a birthday party for the brilliant actress and comedian Julie Kurnitz. The party was held in a second-floor loft that overlooked a crowded parking lot. It was evening, and Lewis, who couldn't see very well, looked out the window at the jam-packed parking lot and noted, "The traffic is terrible tonight."

GODDARD LIEBERSON

"Send in the Clowns" was supposed to be Len Cariou's big moment in *A Little Night Music*, but the song was given to Glynis Johns. Johns was skeptical: "You really think that's my moment?"

When it came to recording the original cast album, Thomas Shepard was hired to produce the album. But Goddard Lieberson showed up at the recording studio ready to take charge. Though Shepherd already had the job, he felt there was nothing to do but welcome Lieberson into the studio and give him control.

"Send in the Clowns" was the last number to be recorded so the cast was sent home. But Cariou stayed around to record the reprise at the end of the show. He offered to stand next to Johns when she was singing the song to give her confidence and she agreed. After the take was completed, Johns and Cariou heard nothing from the booth.

Finally, Lieberson came up to Johns and asked if he could talk to her for a second. She went with him into the booth and Lieberson said, "I want you to remember that it's a torch song. I want you to do it that way." And that second take was the one that was used. Though it isn't really a torch song, Lieberson knew what to say to Johns to get the precise feeling that was going to come across in a listening experience.

BEATRICE LILLIE

If at first you don't succeed, as they say. John Kander told the story of when he was accompanist to Beatrice Lillie. At one performance, she came out and did a surefire bit but got no laugh. She went into the wings, came out onstage, and did the bit again. She went off, came out, and did the bit again. The third time was lucky; the audience was in stitches.

FRANK LOESSER AND EDWIN H. MORRIS

Frank Loesser called Charles Strouse his "little colored boy," an allusion to the rumor that Irving Berlin had a little colored boy in Harlem who actually wrote his songs. Charles was around twenty years old at the time and was paid $75 a week for about three years for helping around the office. During that time, Strouse would sit up with Loesser until three or four in the morning, keeping the composer company, when he was so unhappy with his marriage to Lynn Loesser.

Lynn Loesser was dubbed "The Evil of Two Loessers." While the Loessers were living in Hollywood, Frank had a girlfriend living back in New York. Writer Harry Kurnitz dubbed the girlfriend "East Lynn." For those of you who don't get the joke, there was an extremely famous melodrama titled *East Lynne*.

Loesser always thought that his brother was the talented one.

Edwin H. Morris had a boutique publishing company. Morris was a great believer in up-and-coming talent. He'd put them on a small salary with the understanding that if they wrote something publishable, he'd have the rights to publish it. When Morris decided to retire, instead of selling his catalogue, he returned the copyrights to the songwriters, probably the only time in history that happened.

Loesser learned from Morris when he started his own publishing company. On salary for Loesser were Martin Charnin (*Annie*) and Robert Kessler, Alfred Uhry, and Robert Waldman (*The Robber Bridegroom*). Moose Charlap and Norman Gimbel (who started with Morris) were with Morris, but when they wrote *Whoop-Up*, Loesser published that score (and probably ghost-wrote the song "Flattery"). Meredith Willson (*The Music Man*) was also signed with Frank Music, but not as a contract writer (though Loesser probably wrote the song "My White Knight" for *The Music Man*). Richard Adler and Jerry Ross were on salary, though Loesser turned down writing *The Pajama Game* (but still probably wrote the songs "A New Town is a Blue Town" and "Her Is").

If they became a success, Loesser's deal with the songwriters was the same as with Morris. The publisher would have the publishing rights to the musical.

Morris was a very generous guy, as we noted. One day, he asked Charles Strouse, "What are you doing for Christmas?" Strouse told him that he had no plans and so Morris replied, "My boat is down in Fort Lauderdale with a captain and crew on board. Take it!" Strouse was overjoyed.

He and his wife Barbra Siman flew down to Florida and were shocked to find that "the boat" was an 80-foot yacht. They climbed aboard and the captain asked them where they'd like to go. Strouse requested that they just take a trip around the harbor and coastline. The captain fired up the engines and Siman said to Strouse, "I'm seasick." The motors were turned off and Strouse and spouse got off the boat. And that was the end of their Christmas holiday cruise.

We mentioned that Edwin Morris was so loyal to his composers that he returned their copyrights to them when he retired. Noel Coward did a similar act of generosity for producer Max Gordon. Gordon produced Coward's play *Design for Living* on Broadway. It was a success in every way, including in their relationship. Coward sent Gordon a signed portrait that read, "In memory of a long future association."

But Gordon didn't have the chance to produce another of Coward's plays. Coward had moved on to producing with John C. Wilson, but he wrote Gordon to say that he could have an interest in any of the shows that Wilson produced of Coward's in the U.S. So Gordon had a 25 percent interest in both *Tonight at 8:30* and *Blithe Spirit*.

ALFRED LUNT AND LYNN FONTANNE (AND NOEL COWARD)

When someone asked why the acting couple didn't bill themselves as Fontanne and Lunt, Alfred Lunt replied, "This is the theatre, dear boy, not a god-damned lifeboat."

When Joseph Hardy went backstage after winning his Tony Award at the 1970 awards, he was allowed to hang out. He saw Alfred Lunt, Lynn Fontanne, and Noel Coward behind a curtain waiting to make their entrance. They were standing there quietly waiting for the curtain to open so they could come downstage. They seemed to be the most elderly, tired, stooped-over people in the world. Then their names were called and as the curtain began to open, they straightened up and came out smiling and laughing as if they had just heard the most hilarious joke while waiting backstage. That's how it is done.

RICHARD MANEY

Probably the most successful press agent in Broadway history or at least the most visible, he was even profiled in *The New Yorker* by Wolcott Gibbs. Maney was nothing if not honest, or at least honest in his opinion. When Alexander Cohen was starting out, he hired Maney, but Maney returned the favor by telling Cohen, "You lack two things that make a good producer— talent and taste."

Others venerated Maney. Tallulah Bankhead insisted that he flog all her shows. She even had a clause in her contracts that guaranteed Maney the job. She showed him the clause in a contract she had with the Theatre Guild. "Now, whose your favorite actress?" she asked of Maney. He replied, "Helen Hayes."

AUDREY MEADOWS

Audrey Meadows goes into the bakery Ecce Panis on Third Avenue and orders some bread and asks the woman behind the counter how much she owes. The owner gushes, "Miss Meadows I have loved you so much over the years, I couldn't take any money from you" and hands Meadows the bread. Meadows says to the saleslady, "Gee, thanks, do you love me enough to throw in that cake too?" Then she turned to writer David Levy and said, "You don't know if you don't ask." The owner threw in the cake too.

ETHEL MERMAN

Even as early as *Something for the Boys*, Ethel Merman commanded the stage, really commanded it. By this I mean that, when she was singing, everyone else in the cast had to fade off the stage. She did the same thing when acting in *Hello, Dolly!* As Cy Feuer once said of Merman when she sang, "No one else could share the same atmosphere."

Merman, when asked if she was ever nervous onstage would reply, "If any of them out there could do what I'm doing, they'd be up here doing it."

DAVID MERRICK

When Merrick decided to move *Do Re Mi* from the St. James Theatre to the smaller 54th Street Theatre, Phil Silvers, the star of the show, heard about the move from his barber while getting his hair cut.

Bruce Laffey briefly worked as the receptionist in David Merrick's office before stage-managing Betty Grable's tour in *Hello, Dolly!* Merrick rarely came into the office, but one day, the door flew open and Merrick burst in with his entourage. Laffey had never met Merrick, and the great producer didn't introduce himself. Instead, he glared at Laffey, and said, "Aren't you guarding the door! I might have been an actor!"

One afternoon, David Merrick and his aide de camp Jack Schlissel grabbed their coats, told the office staff to watch the phones, and ran downstairs. That seemed strange, but the staff soon went back to their jobs. A few minutes later, a couple of firemen came up the stairs and into the office. "What are you two doing here," asked the firemen. "There's a bomb scare in the building and you've got to get out!"

Stories about Merrick the tyrant are legendary, but he was also the ultimate showman and a brilliant producing genius. As Penny Fuller says of him, "He loved to be mischievous." Sometimes it might be taken as meanness, but he did have a soft side as well.

Fuller, Elizabeth Ashley's understudy in *Barefoot in the Park*, went to the Tony Awards in Ashley's place since she was sick.

Every time *Hello, Dolly!* would win, Merrick would get up and get the award and the orchestra would play "Who's Afraid of the Big Bad Wolf." At the after party, Fuller went up to Merrick and said, "Mr. Merrick, I hope you weren't upset when they played 'Who's Afraid of the Big Bad Wolf.' When I was on tour in Philadelphia, you were sitting at a table all by yourself and I wanted to go over to you."

A few weeks later, Fuller was standing by herself at a Democratic fundraiser when Merrick came up the staircase with a business associate. They made a beeline for Fuller. Merrick was actually very shy, and he was glad to see someone from the theatre whom he could talk to.

Fuller said, "Mr. Merrick, I know you must be busy, but I'm opening in *Barefoot in the Park* on June 8th." And Merrick responded, "You may not open because we've just come from a Producers' League meeting and the actors might go on strike." Fuller's eyes filled with tears. Merrick patted her arm and said, "I'll fix it. We don't want anything to spoil your opening night."

The next Saturday night, the actors voted to go out on strike. Fuller went out to dinner and Robert Redford sent over a drink and said, "Good luck whenever you open." But, come Monday morning, the strike was over.

Fuller had two tickets left for the opening. She called Merrick's office and his secretary Helen Nickerson said, "He's too busy to talk to you." And Fuller said, "Just tell him that Penny Fuller said, 'Thank you.'" And then Fuller told Nickerson that she was worried about how she'd get rid of this pair of expensive tickets. They were $7.50 each.

Later that day, the phone rang and it was Nickerson. "Mr. Merrick would like to come tonight. Please put a pair of tickets in his name and guarantee them." That got Fuller off the hook.

That night, Fuller arrived at the theatre, her opening night on Broadway. There were a bunch of telegrams and the first one she read was from Merrick. He wrote, "I kept my promise, no one will ever know you settled the strike. Good luck, David Merrick."

When Jerry Herman was working on *Hello, Dolly!* he would intently watch the stage and take notes. Merrick put Herman in one of the boxes and told him to turn his chair around and watch the audience. "You'll learn more about your show than anything your producer or director can tell you."

Merrick was right, of course. Too many writers and directors don't listen to the audience during performances. And when an audience doesn't laugh or do what the artistic staff expects, they blame the audience instead of looking at why they are reacting that way.

For more about David Merrick, please see the Quotes section of this book.

ANN MILLER

Ann Miller was an extremely nice woman, as well as a terrific talent. Her first Broadway show was *George White's Scandals* in 1939. She had a brief run in *Mame* and then forty years after her Broadway debut, she joined Mickey Rooney in the exceptional revue *Sugar Babies*. While in the show, Miller was asked what she was going to do for Passover, and she replied that she didn't do game shows.

Miller would come to her dressing room three hours before a show. She'd spend a good part of the time putting cover-up makeup on the veins on her legs. Then she'd put on two pairs of panty hose. As she said, "The audience is coming for two reasons, to see my legs and to see Ann Miller onstage."

While in *42nd Street*, Carole Cook took Ann Miller for a drive and pointed out the oldest wooden house still standing in Brooklyn. When she heard the house was constructed around 1650, Miller exclaimed, "Really, Carole? I didn't know wood lived that long."

MARILYN MILLER

Marilyn Miller was the first person to be named "Marilyn," an amalgam of "Mary" and "Lynn."

JERRY ORBACH

Jerry Orbach gave more performances as a leading actor in Broadway musicals than any other actor in Broadway history. He also had the best track record of any actor with more hit shows during his career.

Jeff Berger, an agent, asked Orbach why he only had one flop on Broadway. The actor told him his secret: "And you can tell all your clients. Whenever I needed money, I said, 'Yes.'"

COLE PORTER

Porter suffered a horrific accident when horseback riding. The horse fell on him and rolled over Porter's legs crushing them. Porter spent the rest of his life undergoing a series of operations and in great pain. When Porter would be at the hospital, he'd have his valet there, his own furniture in the room, and his own food on his own china and crystal.

JOHN RAITT

Michael Hayden was appearing as Billy Bigelow in *Carousel* at Lincoln Center. He and John Raitt, who played Bigelow in the original production of *Carousel*, were both appearing as emcees at a Broadway Cares *Easter Bonnet* fundraiser. The producers asked Raitt if he'd sing the end of "Soliloquy" with Hayden. Raitt declined. The producer asked, "Why not? Can't you hit the high notes?" Raitt replied, "Oh, sure. No problem, it's just that I'll blow that guy off the stage." Raitt did sing the song, but not with Hayden.

CHARLES NELSON REILLY

When Charles Nelson Reilly was in *How to Succeed*, his teacher, Mrs. Tressky, who had predicted he'd be on Broadway one day, came to see him backstage. Mrs. Tressky was ninety-four and told Charles that the one person she'd like to meet was the great actress Molly Picon. Reilly went over to where Picon was playing in *Milk and Honey* and asked if she'd meet Mrs. Tressky. The next day, Mrs. Tressky and Charles went to Sardi's, and there was Molly Picon standing on a chair and holding a dozen long-stemmed roses enthusing, "Mrs. Tressky, I've always wanted to meet you!"

For those who think making it big is easy, Reilly was in twenty-two off-Broadway shows between 1950 and 1960. According to Reilly, Walter Kerr wrote in the *Herald-Tribune*, "If I see Mr. Reilly's energetic face in one more opening number, I'm going to be sick."

RICHARD RODGERS

Historian Miles Kreuger, who was working in Richard Rodgers's office, went past the composer's door and heard a recording of *The Boys from Syracuse*.

He mentioned to someone that it was nice that Mr. Rodgers could take time out of his busy day just to sit back and listen to his music.

Kreuger was told that wasn't the case, and that two young producers came up to the office wanting to mount an off-Broadway revival of the show. Rodgers didn't remember all of the score, so he was playing the Goddard Lieberson studio cast recording.

SIGMUND ROMBERG

It is said that he had an encyclopedic memory of other people's tunes that he often unconsciously appropriated. So people wagged, "On the opening night of his new shows, you could whistle his new songs going into the theatre, as well as going out."

BILLY ROSE

Billy Rose was dubbed "The Bantam Barnum." It was press agent extraordinaire Richard Maney who invented that soubriquet for Rose, as well as "The Mighty Midget," "The Mad Mahout," and "The Basement Belasco." Billy Rose was short as you might imagine.

Rose was also a king of the cut-in (i.e., when a song was written, if Rose took a liking to it and put it into one of his shows, his name was added to the songwriting credits and the ensuing royalties).

One such cut-in was a song titled "If You Believed in Me" by Harold Arlen and Yip Harburg that premiered in Rose's production of *The Great Magoo*. The show was a failure, but the song lives on, now known as "It's Only a Paper Moon." Harburg was amused at Rose's gall in cutting himself in: "The only thing Billy contributed was the use of the Selwyn Theatre for eleven performances."

At parties, Harburg would sing songs he ostensibly wrote with Billy Rose and say to the crowd, "I'll stop at the parts that Billy Rose wrote." He'd sing the song and stop at the words "the" and "a."

At a party thrown by Billy Rose and stripper/intellectual Gypsy Rose Lee, Burton Lane told the following story: "Rose sat right at the piano absorbing it as if it were part of his being. A couple of people asked me to play a hit song of mine and Yip Harburg's from the hit show *Hold on to Your Hats*, 'There's a Great Day Coming Manana.'" Burton kept ducking the request though he couldn't think exactly why. Later, it all came to him. The second verse has the lyric, "Income tax will grow small, Billy Rose will grow tall, and Gypsy Rose will take all . . . off manana."

Rose's ego knew no bounds, and he was such an unpleasant fellow it seemed impossible to find someone who actually liked him. He died in 1966, the largest individual stockholder in AT&T. Naturally, his family fought over his money and he wasn't even buried for months, since the family couldn't agree on anything at all except that they hated him and wanted his money. In death, he did one good deed: His money founded the New York Public Library's Theatre Collection, which is named after him.

JANE RUSSELL

Before Jane Russell found religion late in life, she was what was called a "live wire." Imagine the surprise of Tim Cahill, when he saw the great star walking toward him on the way to the *Night of 100 Stars* at Radio City Music Hall. As she came closer, he saw his big opportunity to finally meet his idol. Before he could get a word out, a drunken Russell stopped Cahill cold and, while still walking, said, "I know honey, I love you too," and strode past him.

WILLIAM SAROYAN

William Saroyan wasted no time when writing his plays. His first play *My Heart's in the Highlands* was written in three weeks in 1939. It wasn't a success though it received both good and bad reviews. But that didn't deter him. He set to work on his next play vowing to write it in one week. Since he had some time on his hands after the week of writing, he decided to also direct the play. He made good on his promise, *The Time of Your Life* was a success, running six months on Broadway and receiving the Pulitzer Prize for drama, as well as the Drama Critics' Circle Award. Saroyan accepted the Pulitzer but he refused to take the $1,000 prize, saying that "wealth shouldn't patronize art."

Saroyan, like many playwrights (make that, like many people in the theatre), was an odd guy. During the production of *The Time of Your Life*, Saroyan asked the producer Lawrence Langer, manager along with Armina Marshall of the Theatre Guild, to cast his cousin in the show. Langer demurred, telling Saroyan, "You can't just give someone a part." Saroyan simply responded that he would then write a part for his relative, and so the part of the newsboy was played by Ross Bagdasarian, making his one and only appearance on Broadway.

While bored, sitting on the tour bus during the play's out-of-town tryout, Saroyan and Bagdasarian teamed up to write a nonsense song with lyrics based on dialogue in Saroyan's novel *The Human Comedy*. The song was "Come On-a My House," and it was recorded to great success by Rosemary Clooney. In addition to many accomplishments, Bagdasarian, as David Seville, wrote the song "The Witch Doctor" and was the inventor of the popular Chipmunks characters: Alvin, Theodore, and Simon.

GEORGE C. SCOTT

George C. Scott was one of the great men of the theatre. Sadly, he's not remembered today except for his performance in the film *Patton*, for which he won an Academy Award. But Scott was truly a man of the theatre and he gave many memorable performances, especially at the Circle in the Square Theatre.

Scott had a unique way of learning his lines. He wouldn't read the script, but he would have it recited to him, and in that way he would immediately remember his entire role. And when the lines would change when his shows were out of town, the same thing happened, and he was unerring in his memory having only heard his lines and the changes made in the script.

HASSARD SHORT

The lighting designer-turned-director set the stage literally for the Broadway theatre we know now. It was Short who, for the show *Three's a Crowd*, eliminated footlights from the stage and put the lighting instruments on the balcony rail. Short also used a revolve not merely to change scenery behind a curtain while the action continued "in one" (i.e., in front of a shut curtain). Instead, *The Band Wagon's* double revolving stage allowed more fluid staging and opened up the stage to new effects, some presaging the current filmic types of dissolves and cross fades.

When the show *Roberta* was in trouble out of town, producer Max Gordon convinced composer and show supervisor Jerome Kern to let him bring in Short to take over the direction from Kern. One of Short's first tasks was to line up the chorus girls on the stage and try out different lighting on them. He hit one of them with a pink spotlight and the effect was dramatic. Kern exclaimed, "That man is a genius!" And from then on, a baby pink spot has been used to put women in a more favorable light.

ALEXIS SMITH

Alexis Smith and Dorothy Collins went to Dallas to see a production of *Follies* starring Juliet Prowse, Shani Wallis, Ed Evanko, and Harvey Evans. At the curtain call, Alexis Smith grabbed Collins, yanked her out of her seat, hauled her into the ladies room, and said, "I never realized how great you were in the part."

MAUREEN STAPLETON

One Saturday, Stapleton decided to go home between the matinee and evening performance of *Caesar and Cleopatra*. Asleep on her couch, she woke up to see the stage manager standing over her. "Maureen, it's thirty minutes to curtain, you've got to get up." She roused herself, threw on a coat, and they jumped in a cab. On the way to the theatre, she took off her dress under the coat. The cab driver, looking in the rearview mirror was enjoying the impromptu striptease. Stapleton snapped at him, "You keep going, I'll do the acting!" When she was introduced to Danny Kaye, he remarked, "Maureen Stapleton, oh yes, I've heard of you. You're the one who says 'fuck' in front of Helen Hayes.'" Actually, Hayes didn't mind coarse language. She explained that she was used to it; her husband Charles MacArthur used language much worse than anyone could imagine.

Stapleton played Dick Van Dyke's mother in the film version of *Bye Bye Birdie*. One day, when standing around the set, she exclaimed, "I'm the only person in this film who hasn't wanted to fuck Ann-Margret."

CHARLES STROUSE

Charles Strouse was called "Buddy" for most of his life. In fact, early sheet music of songs he wrote credited him as Buddy Strouse. But Charles's wife Barbara insisted that he change his name, feeling that Charles sounded more mature than Buddy.

So when Happy Bacharach who was a schoolmate of Charles was on his way to making it big, Charles told him he should use his real name Burt.

JULE STYNE

Visitors to Jule Styne's office in the Mark Hellinger Theatre would find Styne sitting with his assistant Dorothy Dicker, playing Yahtzee, with his false teeth on the table next to the board.

Styne had so much nervous energy, when the phone rang, he'd say "Hello" first and then pick up the phone.

Styne was a gambler, and he would bet on the horses along with Ira Gershwin and Ira's mother Rose. They'd pool their bets based on Styne's handicapping of the races. One day, Jerome Kern asked Styne to come to his house for breakfast. Styne imagined that Kern had a script that he wanted Styne to write the music for.

After breakfast, Kern and Styne went into the study and Kern brought out a sheaf of papers. Styne could hardly wait to see what project Kern had in mind. Kern handed Styne the papers and said, "Will you pick out some winners for me?" The papers were not a script but a scratch sheet of the day's races.

When Sara Zahn was performing her cabaret act devoted to the songs of Carolyn Leigh, Styne was in the audience. Zahn was a few months pregnant and her breasts were growing. She appeared onstage in a blouse and when the show was over, Styne came up to her and said, "Honey, you were wonderful. Just one constructive comment. For your first number, you should come out with a jacket on cause for that first number I didn't know what the hell you were singing 'cause I couldn't stop looking at your tits."

DAVID SUSSKIND

David Susskind had produced the legendary Broadway musical bomb *Kelly*. The score was written by Moose Charlap and Eddie Lawrence. Years later, Charlap died leaving his widow, the singer Sandy Stewart, with a baby (Bill Charlap, now a great jazz pianist). Stewart was at the playground with Bill when along came Susskind who said to Stewart, "I'm glad Moose died."

Susskind was staying at a hotel in New York. When he opened his door to pick up his newspaper, Lena Horne happened to be walking by. Susskind looked up and told her he'd be leaving the room in an hour and she could make it up then.

MAE WEST

It should be no surprise to you if you know anything about Mae West that she invented herself. A provocateur, West liked to stir things up both on-stage and off. She prided herself on flaunting tradition and pushing the moral envelope.

Producer Leonard Sillman went to see West in her show *Diamond Lil* and was immediately smitten. When Sillman's mother came to town, he insisted she meet the great Mae West, and before the show he took his mother to see West backstage. West was charming. She discussed things like cooking and keeping house, subjects dear to the heart of someone like Mrs. Sillman. West had Sillman's mother sit next to her at the dressing table while she put on her makeup for the evening show. It was a remarkable visit. Sillman's mother was speechless as they left the dressing room, not because the great Mae West treated her so kindly, but because all through the interview, West was naked from the waist up.

KURT WEILL

When Kurt Weill was asked why he did his own orchestrations, he replied, "I've had the meal. This is dessert."

Nanette Fabray was walking down the street with Kurt Weill after a rehearsal of *Love Life*. They were standing on the corner when Fabray heard Weill humming to himself. "What's that tune? Is it a new song for me?" He replied, "No, I'm singing the street. See that woman and child over there? They're doing this." And then he hummed a little tune. "And do you hear that couple talking to each other? This is their tune." And he hummed another little tune. He said, "Everything in life is music."

While the chorus of *Love Life* was rehearsing, Weill sat in a corner writing the orchestrations for another number in the show. Lys Symonette watched him and said, "How can you do that with all of this noise?" He said, "What noise?"

TENNESSEE WILLIAMS

Kenneth Pressman's hero was playwright Tennessee Williams. Pressman went to a party where Williams was surrounded by acolytes. Pressman finally gathered up his nerve to go over to his idol. Williams was alone and Pressman introduced himself. "Mr. Williams, I'm an actor and I'm also a playwright." Williams took Pressman's hands in his and said, "Poor us."

Williams used to come to Maureen Stapleton's walk-up apartment in the West 60s to have tea. Stapleton served the tea in cups from a beautiful teapot. However, the tea was actually bourbon.

One day, Williams brought his terribly obese cousin to the apartment and had to literally push her up the stairs. When they left and Williams had to repeat the process going down the stairs, Stapleton asked what the cousin did for a living. Williams replied, "She's a ballerina."

DWIGHT DEERE WIMAN

Dwight Deere Wiman was a successful producer of such shows as *Gay Divorce, By Jupiter, Street Scene* and a covey of plays. He was the heir of the John Deere Company, makers of tractors, reapers, etc. Wiman owned a wickerwork Rolls-Royce (a car that had a bar in the back and was made entirely of wood). Howard Dietz reported that the car was eventually beset by termites.

FLORENZ ZIEGFELD

Ziegfeld arrived in Chicago by train. Not one person from the press was there to meet him. He wired his press agent Will Page: "Thanks for sneaking me into town."

Nothing would stand in the way of Ziegfeld opening a show. When his star Anna Held became pregnant, Ziegfeld ordered her to have an abortion so his show (the all too ironically named) *Miss Innocence* would open on time.

Toward the end of his career, Ziegfeld was chronically broke. His press agent Bernard Sobel called Fanny Brice and told her about Ziegfeld's predicament. From then until the end of Ziegfeld's life, unbeknown to the great producer, Brice contributed $500 a month to his bank account.

NAME CHANGES

Many performers have changed their names for various reasons. Sometimes because another Actors' Equity performer has the same name or they just don't like their own name. Here are some stories about Broadway players who have changed their names for various reasons.

Kaye Ballard appeared in the hits *Golden Apple* and *Carnival* and the flop *Royal Flush*, which closed out of town. She went to a numerologist who promised her great success if she'd drop the "e" from the end of her first name. Her next Broadway appearance as "Kay" was in the musical *Molly*. It flopped.

Ada Rehan was the greatest of all leading ladies in her time. Her real name was Ada Crehan but a mistake in the program named her Ada C. Rehan. She got rid of the C. and the rest was Broadway history.

When Ruth Gordon asked George S. Kaufman what the "S." stood for, he replied, "Listen, if Al H. Woods, Charles B. Dillingham, Henry B. Harris, George C. Tyler, William A. Brady, Sam H. Harris, George M. Cohan, J. J. Shubert, A. L. Erlanger, B. F. Keith, Sam S. Shubert, and H. H. Frazee need a middle initial, why not me?" Perhaps that explains the following story.

People have wondered for years what the "P." stood for in *Of Thee I Sing*'s presidential hopeful's name John P. Wintergreen. George S. Kaufman admitted to Ira Gershwin that it stood for "Peppermint."

In today's politics, candidates emphasize what ethnic groups they dislike. But Wintergreen's platform included the statement that he "loved the Irish and the Jews."

David Braham, composer of the Harrigan and Hart early musical comedies, changed his last name from Abraham to avoid the anti-Semitism that occurred during the nineteenth century.

CHAPTER 2
The Idea

Gwen Verdon: "My initial interest in *Chicago* started way back in 1953, when I was doing *Can-Can*. I had seen Ginger Rogers playing Roxie Hart in the movie, and my performance in *Can-Can* was pretty successful and producers were telling me 'anything you want to do, we'll do it.' Then in 1973/4 Watergate was underway and I was attracted to it once more because it was all about political corruption. The play had been written as a graduating thesis, and the only copy I could find was in the New York Public Library. I also got the trial transcripts from the original case. Beulah Allen was the actual woman who shot her husband. Bob (Fosse) said, 'Let's do it like a vaudeville show, and at the Palace.' Jerry Orbach was magnificent."

Verdon had revisited the idea in the early '60s after *Little Me* had opened and Fosse had appeared at the New York City Center in *Pal Joey*. Verdon suggested they work on *Chicago*, but Fosse was leaning toward a musical based on the films *Big Deal on Madonna Street* or Fellini's *Nights of Cabiria*. Producer Robert Fryer wanted their next show to be *Breakfast at Tiffany's*. The rights to *Chicago* proved problematic, so Fosse started writing what would become *Sweet Charity*. Then Fryer secured the rights to *Breakfast at Tiffany's* and Fosse began work on that. But Truman Capote didn't see Verdon in the lead and withdrew the rights. Fryer suggested Christopher Isherwood's *Berlin Stories*, but Fosse and Verdon couldn't visualize that as a musical. Then Fosse was hired to work on another new musical, *Funny Girl*. After meetings with composer Jule Styne, Fosse left that show to Jerome Robbins. Fosse then went on to work on the Frank Loesser musical *Pleasures and Palaces*, which closed out of town. Finally, things calmed down, sort of, and Fosse began work on what would become *Sweet Charity*.

New Faces of 1937 starred Jerome Cowan and Milton Berle as two shysters who decided to put on a show that was sure to fail. They sold their backers 85% of the show . . . each. When the Cowan character goes on the lam, Berle has to decide if it's better to have a hit and go to jail or have a flop and bilk the investors. Sound familiar?

Producer Robert Whitehead and Bob Fosse wanted to do a musical version of *The Madwoman of Chaillot* with Alfred Lunt and Lynn Fontanne, with Lunt as the Rag Picker and Fontanne as the Madwoman. In addition, they dangled the directing job before Lunt. When that idea fell through, Whitehead and Fosse moved on to a new project, a musical version of Preston Sturges's film *Hail the Conquering Hero*. With the deletion of the word "Hail," the show opened and closed quickly on Broadway.

The Phantom of the Opera, *The Hunchback of Notre Dame*, and *The Most Happy Fella* are all variations of another story made into a successful musical, *Beauty and the Beast*. For *Passion*, the roles were reversed, with a handsome soldier falling for a repugnant woman.

Moss Hart had invited a bunch of friends over to his country house to spend the weekend. Among them was his collaborator George S. Kaufman and the dyspeptic raconteur Alexander Woollcott. When Woollcott was leaving, he wrote in the guest book, "I will think of this as being one of the most unpleasant weekends I've ever had." Hart turned to Kaufman and wondered what would have happened had Woollcott stayed for longer than the weekend. A light bulb went off over Kaufman's head and he said to Hart, "That's our next play!" The result was *The Man Who Came to Dinner*. Amazingly, Woollcott actually played the part during an out-of-town engagement.

Rodgers and Hammerstein got the idea for "Soliloquy" in *Carousel* when John Raitt auditioned with the "Largo al Factotum" aria from *The Marriage of Figaro*." Only half of the song was written when Rodgers suggested to Hammerstein that they expand the song by having Billy Bigelow wonder what it would be like to have a baby girl.

CHAPTER 3
Naming The Show

Charles Strouse, Lee Adams, and Michael Stewart were writing a new musical that had been titled *Let's Go Steady* and then *Love and Kisses*. They were having trouble coming up with a new moniker when the producer Edward Padula told them they had better come up with a title right away as he had to order the posters immediately. So, without too much enthusiasm, the team came up with *Bye Bye Birdie*.

George Abbott came up with the name *The Pajama Game* while walking up Fifth Avenue.

Sideshow became *Anyone Can Whistle*. When they announced the original title, people thought the show was a freak show.

When Feuer and Martin decided to make Brandon Thomas's classic play *Charley's Aunt* into a musical, they knew they had to come up with a different title. Director George Abbott came up with *Where's Charley?* but Feuer and Martin hated it. Abbott simply said, "If you can come up with something better . . . ," but no one could, so the name stuck.

Harold Arlen, Ira Gershwin, and E.Y. Harburg were working on a new show, but what to name it? Everyone had an opinion, but none sounded suitable. John Murray Anderson was the director and the bestseller *Life Begins at Forty* was on his foyer table. Ira Gershwin saw the book and suggested the title *Life Begins at 8:40*, which reflected the time the curtain would go up. Lee Shubert didn't like the name, so Gershwin suggested *Calling All Stars*, but that was rightly deemed too trite. Since no one else could come up with a better name, *Life Begins at 8:40* it was.

In the 1920s, naming shows after women characters was all the rage. There was *No, No, Nanette, Yes, Yes, Yvette, La! La! Lucille, Billie, Adrienne,*

Fioretta, Betsy, Mary, Angela, Irene, Betty Lee, Bye Bye Barbara, Elsie . . . well, you get the idea. So one smart team of producers named their show after three of the biggest hits of the time, *Sally, Irene and Mary*.

"Girl" was another favorite word for titles of both plays and musicals. There was *The Girl from Brazil*, . . . *Brighton*, . . . *Broadway*, . . . *Dixie*, . . . *Home*, . . . *Kay's*, . . . *Maxim's*, . . . *Montmartre*, . . . *Nantucket*, . . . *Paris*, . . . *Rector's*, . . . *Texas*, . . . *Up There*, . . . *Utah*, and . . . *Wyoming*. The point was, there was GIRLS in them thar bills!

Many shows have attempted to gain an advantage by how they chose their names. It's said that the name *A Chorus Line* was chosen so it would be first in the *The New York Times* alphabetical list of theatre offerings.

When Moss Hart offered Gertrude Lawrence the lead in his musical *I Am Listening*, the actress asked that the title be changed. In all her previous musicals, she had been the title character. So the show was renamed *Lady in the Dark*.

The Firebrand of Florence was named *Much Ado about Love* when it played out of town pre-Broadway.

Fade Out—Fade In was originally titled *A Girl to Remember*, then *The Idol of Millions*, and finally *Fade Out—Fade In*.

No Sirree! was a pun on the Russian revue, *Le Chauve Souris*.

Lady, Be Good! was originally titled *Black-Eyed Susan*.

Funny Face was originally titled *Smarty*.

Hello, Dolly! was originally named *Dolly: a Damned Exasperating Woman*.

The word *Follies*, in relation to a musical show, didn't start with Florenz Ziegfeld. In fact, the term was first used in England around 1906 by producer H.G. Pelissier who had a troupe of pierrots touring with that name.

The Vincent Youmans show *Smiles* underwent several name changes: *Six-Cylinder Love*, *The Spinning Wheel*, and *Tom, Dick and Harry*. *Six Cylinder Love* was also the title of a 1921 play, but it has no relation to the plot of *Smiles*.

The title *The Spinning Wheel* was also suggested for another Fred Astaire show, *The Band Wagon*. In this case, it was more appropriate since one of the show's main features was the use of a turntable.

Via Galactica was going to be titled *Up*, but it was playing at the Uris Theatre. They changed the title fearing that the ads would read *Up Uris*.

The Desert Song was originally titled *My Fair Lady*.

My Fair Lady was originally titled *Lady Liza* but Rex Harrison thought if the ads said "Rex Harrison in *Lady Liza*," it would sound dirty. Frederick Loewe thought the title should be *Fanfaroon*.

An early title of *Anything Goes* was *Hard to Get*.

Robert Anderson got the title *Tea and Sympathy* from a friend who once said to him, "I live in a rooming house where the woman has us down every once in a while for tea and sympathy."

FOUR STORIES ABOUT IRVING BERLIN

Irving Berlin came over to Moss Hart's apartment to play him the score of *As Thousands Cheer* for the first time. The great composer played number after number, singing along in his high voice. As each number was played, Hart slumped lower in his seat. The songs were terrible. What could Hart say to the great Irving Berlin?

When Berlin was finished, Hart asked him to play one of his greatest songs, "Blue Skies." Berlin played the song and it sounded terrible too. Hart sat up with a big smile on his face and told Berlin, "Irving, we're going to have a big hit!"

During the preproduction of *Annie Get Your Gun*, director Josh Logan, producers Rodgers and Hammerstein, and songwriter Irving Berlin were going through the show and figuring out where songs needed be placed. Logan decided that a new song was needed for the second act—specifically, a duet between Annie Oakley and her love interest Frank Butler. Berlin wasn't sure about writing another song; besides, what could it be? Rodgers suggested some sort of argument or challenge number. Berlin picked up on the idea immediately and left the meeting. With Berlin gone, Logan returned home to find the phone ringing. It was Berlin on the other line. He began singing the new song, "Anything You Can Do I Can Do Better." The director, thunderstruck, asked, "But when did you have time to write it?" Berlin responded, "In the taxicab. I had to, didn't I? We go into rehearsal Monday."

Berlin was playing "There's No Business Like Show Business" for Josh Logan. He loved it. Berlin performed it for Richard Rodgers. He loved it. Berlin performed it for Oscar Hammerstein. He loved it. Every time they would review the songs in the score, he'd play "There's No Business Like Show Business."

One time he left the song off the list. Richard Rodgers asked, "Where's 'Show Business'? Where's the song?" Berlin said, "The last time I played it for you, you didn't seem so enthusiastic for it so I took it out of the show." Rodgers replied, "We can't be equally enthusiastic every time you play one of the songs. Put it back in." So Berlin called his assistant Hilda and told her to find a copy of the song because it was going back in the show. She tore the office apart but couldn't find it. It was finally found under a stack of phone books, basically tossed away.

Harold Prince was the second assistant stage manager on Irving Berlin's newest musical *Call Me Madam*. One day the backstage phone rang and Prince answered it. Berlin was on the line and asked for producer Leland Hayward. Hayward was not there. "How about Ethel Merman?" asked Berlin. Nope, she wasn't there either. Berlin tried another name, "How about Russel Crouse?" Also not around. "Well," Berlin inquired, "Who's this?" "I'm Hal Prince, sir, the second assistant stage manager." "I see. Tell me Hal, what do you think of this?" And Berlin played his new song, "You're Just in Love," to Prince over the phone. Luckily, Prince liked the song or Berlin might have cut it.

SHOWS WRITTEN FOR THE MOVIES AND TELEVISION

Li'l Abner, the hit musical by Johnny Mercer, Melvin Frank, and Norman Panama, was originally conceived as a film musical. Not a surprise since Frank and Panama had contributed many successful screenplays to Paramount Pictures, and Mercer also had a contract with the studio.

Originally, Burton Lane and Alan Jay Lerner were set to write the score. When the material proved too difficult for them to crack, Mercer was brought in and the project proceeded beautifully. It was finally decided to use the Broadway show as a kind of tryout before filming. That's why practically the entire cast of the show appears in the film. Edith Adams, who was replaced by Leslie Parrish for the film, was pregnant and so couldn't do the film. There is only one other example we can think of when a show was staged with the express purpose of filming it later.

Similarly, the Mary Martin *Peter Pan* was initially planned as a television spectacular, and the show was mounted and toured so the kinks could be worked out. The producers ended up making money on the theatrical engagements and helped build word-of-mouth for the broadcast.

TWO STORIES ABOUT WRITING IN AND ON WATER

Maxwell Anderson's play *Elizabeth the Queen* was in trouble when it tried out in Philadelphia and received horrible reviews. The Theatre Guild members, the producers of the show, were frustrated with Anderson's putting off making the necessary fixes. He'd respond that he didn't feel like writing. So Theresa Helburn and Lawrence Langner the heads of the Guild, decided to close the show.

Alfred Lunt and Lynn Fontanne, who were starring in the show, offered to buy the property from the Guild. Seeing the confidence of the Lunts, the Guild decided to extend the pre-Broadway tour. The next stop was Baltimore's Ford's Theatre. When they got to the city, rain was pouring down with no end in sight. Opening night went as usual, with not much response from the audience. Langner went to Anderson's hotel room to report on the opening and to see if Anderson had done any work at all. Imagine the producer's surprise when Anderson handed him a completely revised script. Langner was speechless though he did manage to ask Anderson when he wrote all this material. Anderson replied, "Well, Lawrence, I really only write well when it rains." Helburn stated later that whenever she and Langner produced one of Anderson's plays, they prayed for rain, as it seemed that he really could only write when it was raining. And luckily for *Elizabeth the Queen*, it rained in Pittsburgh, Cincinnati, and St. Louis, and the revisions kept on coming.

Cole Porter, you might have heard, was a millionaire who lived a lush and lavish life. When it came to writing his new musical *Jubilee*, he invited Moss Hart to join him and his wife, another couple, and a valet and a maid on a cruise through the South Pacific. Hart was sure that no work would be accomplished, but by the time the ship was through the locks in Panama, the basic outline of the show was written. And by the time the cruise was over, the entire show was completed.

FOUR STORIES ABOUT DANCE A LITTLE CLOSER

When writing with Frederick Loewe, Alan Jay Lerner sat by the piano while Loewe was composing. Loewe never liked composing, so Lerner would instruct him to just noodle on the piano and when a worthy tune came up, Lerner would alert Loewe and they'd try to fashion it into a song. So, when Lerner was writing with Charles Strouse on *Dance a Little Closer*, he asked Strouse to do the same since he was in the habit of working that way.

Strouse found himself in a rowboat on the bay of Naples going out to see Alan Jay Lerner on his yacht for a working session on the show. As he approached the yacht, Strouse asked himself, "What am I doing here?"

Both Sondheim and Bernstein had warned Strouse about working with Lerner.

Strouse had two rules about collaborating: (1) Never take drugs; and (2) never get involved when the director or coauthor is married to the leading lady.

While writing *Dance a Little Closer*, Strouse broke both his rules. He was stricken with a bad back and was in great pain. Lerner was constantly on speed supplied by Max Jacobs, aka Dr. Feelgood, so he offered Strouse a drug to alleviate the pain. Strouse soon found himself in a fetal position on the floor of the bathroom wanting to die and asking that his family be brought in one by one so he could say goodbye. And rule number two? Alan Jay Lerner was married to the show's leading lady, Liz Robertson.

SHOWS THAT HAVE CONTINUED WORK AFTER THEIR OPENINGS

About six weeks after *Guys and Dolls* opened, director George S. Kaufman called a brush-up rehearsal with the cast and then informed librettist Abe Burrows that he also needed to do some work. Kaufman gave Burrows six parts of the show that needed more jokes. Burrows was surprised: "George, I thought we were finished with the script." Kaufman's answer was brief and to the point, "We're rehearsing on Thursday at two o'clock." Burrows showed up promptly with six more jokes.

The Harold Rome, Arthur Kober musical *Wish You Were Here* got bad reviews. The artistic staff knew it could be better and so they closed the show, reworked it to make the leading lady more sympathetic, and then reopened. They were reviewed again more favorably and the word of mouth was positive. The show became a hit.

The night after *Damn Yankees* opened, George Abbott called a rehearsal for two o'clock in the afternoon. Although the show got raves, Abbott knew there was work to be done. The act-two song "Not Meg" was cut. Abbott and Harold Prince went over the script and cut twenty minutes out of the show and cleaned up the ending.

Hallelujah, Baby! cut songs and put in new numbers. *Subways Are for Sleeping* made changes in the libretto to streamline the show and cut two songs. *Hello, Dolly!* had one song cut after opening.

After *Illya Darling* opened, some songs were cut, and new numbers were added. Because of the government coup in Greece, the show's star Melina Mercouri and her husband, director Jules Dassin, couldn't return home. Dassin was bored so he kept the show in rehearsal and changed songs and scenes. Five or six months into the run, they put in a whole new opening. Stephen Sondheim helped doctor some of the lyrics.

Kean had a lavish scene that took place in four bathtubs. "Social Whirl" was a very expensive number (what with all the soapsuds), so it was decided to delete it from the show to bring down the running costs.

Apparently, the music for *The Wiz* was not written by Charlie Smalls. He was a front for a bunch of songwriters who all contributed songs to the show.

Martin Charnin wrote most of the material for the revue *Girls Against the Boys*, but he did not receive credit.

Charnin was called by Bob Fosse to coauthor a new musical based on Federico Fellini's film *Nights of Cabiria*. The piece would be the first half of a new musical. Charnin would take Fosse's somewhat amorphous ideas, add his own, and give them structure and dialogue. When the first ad appeared in *The Sunday New York Times* on October 31, 1965, the only person credited was Bob Fosse (using the pseudonym Bert Lewis). The second ad in the *Times* credited Neil Simon who was hired to punch up the script.

Charnin and Fosse lawyered-up, as they say. The opening night at the Palace Theatre, the front row of the balcony was filled with Charnin's lawyers, his agent, and a stenographer who was transcribing the script. That script was then compared with an early script printed by Studio Duplicating Services, the company that copied most of the scripts on Broadway. Indeed, most of Charnin's script remained. Now, Charnin and Fosse had only written a one-act, but about 80% of what Charnin wrote was there onstage.

The case was settled with Charnin receiving a royalty for the original Broadway production, but not any subsequent productions or the film version. In addition, he couldn't speak about this for twenty-five years.

One day, at the Museum of the City of New York, the elevator door opened, and there was Fosse animatedly talking to some friends as Charnin entered. All of a sudden, the temperature in the elevator plummeted to zero.

Years after Fosse's death, Gwen Verdon walked up to Charnin and whispered in his ear, "Bob forgives you."

CHAPTER 4

Writing The Show

During the nineteenth and early twentieth century, most playwrights subscribed to formulas in writing their shows.

At the turn of the nineteenth century, dramas tended to be melodramas. Just as in commedia del arte, there were strict rules for how plays were to be constructed and played. Before the drama started, there had to be two laughs to allow the audience to get settled in. Just as in musical comedy, an opening number featured the chorus. And in vaudeville, the opening act featured minor acts while audiences got settled and latecomers could be seated without distracting the rest of the audience.

Early melodramas prohibited the leading man and lady from kissing and embracing until the final curtain, after overcoming obstacles. Playwright Owen Davis said that before any sentimental line, there must be two laughs to relax the audience.

Oklahoma! broke the mold of previous musicals by not starting with a big opening number. It did, however, include a ballet that served the same purpose as the songs: introducing character, advancing the plot, and revealing psychological underpinnings. Of course, the success of *Oklahoma!* ensured that its own new set of rules would be followed by subsequent musical comedies. Every show seemed to need a dramatic lead couple and a comic secondary couple.

The theatre had been through much of that before when *The Black Crook* combined a dramatic company with a ballet company; succeeding shows had to have ballets even if, like the songs themselves, they had little if any connection to the storyline.

George Abbott had his own strict rules. When *Where's Charley?* was being written, Frank Loesser wrote an opening number. But Abbott was against it. He told producers Cy Feuer and Ernie Martin, "This is a farce. That means you must establish the premise. Later on you may break out in song, but not before you establish the premise." Ernie Martin demurred, "But the opening is not funny." Abbott stuck to his guns, "You must establish the premise; funny is not essential while you are doing that."

Abbott eventually lost that argument, but years later the same problem cropped up. When *A Funny Thing Happened on the Way to the Forum* opened at the National Theatre in Washington before Broadway, the show opened with the song "Love Is in the Air," a sweet, romantic tune. But Jerome Robbins was brought in to doctor the show and he explained that the problem was that "Love Is in the Air" set the audience up to expect a light, romantic comedy. So Stephen Sondheim wrote the knockabout opening "Comedy Tonight," and what hadn't work before worked like gangbusters from then on.

Writing revues wasn't as easy as just throwing some songs and sketches together and gathering a cast. There was a formula for putting a revue together, just as there was a formula for putting a vaudeville bill together. In vaudeville, nobody wanted to be at the top of the show since audiences would still be coming into the theatre and settling down. Likewise, in a revue, stars wouldn't appear in the opening of the show. As with musical comedies, the opening number of a revue was usually a chorus number. After the opening, the secondary star would make an appearance and the third slot would fall to the star of the show, presuming that the chorus and secondary star would have warmed up the audience and built up their expectations for the star's turn. In fact, Beatrice Lillie, a veteran of revues in London and Broadway, had a clause in her contract stating that "Miss Lillie will not appear onstage before 8:50."

Abe Burrows's first job as a director on Broadway was the musical revue *Two on the Aisle* with a score by Jule Styne, Betty Comden, and Adolph Green. The stars were Dolores Gray and Bert Lahr. Problems arose in rehearsal when the running order of the show was posted. First up would be the traditional spot for an opening chorus. Then Dolores Gray was slated to perform in the second spot. And in the third spot was Bert Lahr's turn. Gray was incensed. She had just been a big hit in London and she felt she was Lahr's equal, so she demanded the third slot. There was an impasse and no one would budge.

Burrows left the theatre and considered quitting, which gave him an idea. He put on a snazzy blue suit, as opposed to his usual relaxed attire, and went down to the theatre. The cast was understandably surprised and confused, wondering why he was wearing a suit. Burrows announced he was going back to New York. Just then producer Anthony Farrell came backstage. Farrell was not only the main backer of the show, he also owned the Mark Hellinger Theatre where the show was slated to open. "Why the suit, Abe?" he asked. "I'm going back to New York, Tony. Nobody wants to start the show. Dolores doesn't want the number two spot. Bert is set to do the number three spot. Somebody has to do the number two spot or we have no show." Farrell thought a bit and then told the company, "If Abe goes back to New York. I'm going to close the show." And he left, followed by Burrows. Gray backed down for the good of the show and things returned to sort of normal.

After that, whenever things were going bad with a show, Burrows would say to his wife Carin, "If we can't straighten out this mess, I'm going to put on my blue suit."

Writing a show in a hotel room while on the road has become a cliché in the American theatre, but it does happen. Somehow, the pressure of being absorbed by only one thing, the show, gets everything moving like clockwork. The intensity can either bring a songwriter to new heights or destroy them completely.

Jerry Herman loved working on shows, rewriting them and working on the road. While out of town with *Milk and Honey*, Herman came up with "Chin Up, Ladies." "I Don't Want to Know" was written for *Dear World* on a piano in a hotel. For *Hello, Dolly!* Herman wrote "So Long, Dearie," as well as "Before the Parade Passes By," on hotel pianos.

Press agent extraordinaire Harvey Sabinson was in Detroit in 1963 when *Hello, Dolly!* was having tryout troubles there. After the opening night, Harvey headed back to New York City. As he parted, he asked David Merrick if he wanted anything from New York that Harvey could bring back on his next trip to Detroit. Merrick replied, "Bob Merrill."

There was a lot of controversy about the writing of "Before the Parade Passes By." Here's the true story. Strouse and Adams were asked to come to Washington, D.C., to take a look at *Hello, Dolly!* They wrote a song titled "Before the Parade Passes By," but it was rejected by Gower Champion. When Jerry Herman heard that they had written a song for the show (which he never heard), he decided he would write his own "Before the Parade Passes By," and that's the song we all know. Also in D.C., Strouse and Adams restructured the entire end of the first act as an act of largesse and gave it to Michael Stewart with whom they had worked on *Bye, Bye, Birdie* along with director Champion. Stewart basically dismissed what they had done and never thanked them. But when Strouse and Adams saw the show in New York, they realized that Stewart had used all of their ideas and never said thanks. So they sued for royalties on "Before the Parade Passes By," which they otherwise wouldn't have done. And they got them.

And when the producers of *Ben Franklin in Paris* asked Herman to contribute two songs for their score by other composers, Herman wrote, "To Be Alone with You" and "Too Charming." Having songwriters contribute to other people's scores is more common than you think. In fact, it happened to Herman too. David Merrick liked to put pressure on his artists and he brought in Bob Merrill to help Herman on two songs, "Elegance" and "Motherhood." Merrill gave Herman the idea for "Elegance," the same idea he had used in *New Girl in Town*. Merrill started the lyrics, and Herman finished the lyrics and music. And Merrill wrote most of the lyrics to "Motherhood" while Herman wrote the counterpoint. Herman wrote three songs for the Alexander Cohen production of *A Day in Hollywood, A Night in the Ukraine*. The esteemed Richard Rodgers, producer of *Best Foot Forward*, gave Hugh Martin a gift of the music to the song "The Guy Who Brought Me" and took no credit.

John Kander's first Broadway musical was *A Family Affair*, which he wrote with James and William Goldman. The three of them had met in summer camp when Kander was ten years old. They came to New York together and shared a nine-room apartment. There they started writing the musical.

Kenneth Jacobson and Rhoda Roberts adapted the play *Picnic* into a musical they titled *Hot September*. Since Josh Logan had directed the original play, they had an appointment to meet him at his apartment to see if he'd be interesting in directing the musical. At the appointed time, they were shown into the living room where Logan was waiting for them. The meeting went well with the writers explaining the show to Logan and Logan offering his opinions. When the meeting was over, Jacobson and Roberts got into the elevator and broke out in laughter. Though nobody mentioned it at the time, Josh Logan had been completely naked all through the meeting.

It was a snowy day in New York City when Frank Loesser finished the score for *Guys and Dolls*. Not letting the bad weather deter him, he brought the score to Margaret Whiting's apartment. Though he was an extremely successful songwriter, Loesser was nervous about hearing his score played for the first time. He had known Whiting since she born. She was a great singer in her own right and also the daughter of songwriter Richard A. Whiting, Loesser's contemporary at Paramount Studio. For the audition, Loesser had hired a terrific pianist, but because of the snowstorm, he couldn't make it. So they got a neophyte who couldn't play the music. Loesser was so frustrated he grabbed the score and threw it out the window. When they realized it was Loesser's original handwritten score, they ran downstairs and gathered up the pages from the snowdrifts.

Many Broadway composers couldn't actually transcribe music. They would record their tunes and an assistant or arranger would write down the melodies. Bob Merrill played the toy xylophone, Lionel Bart whistled, Harvey Schmidt couldn't read or write music and only played in the key of C. Noel Coward couldn't read or write music and could only play in the key of E-flat. Irving Berlin couldn't read or write music and could only play in the key of F-sharp.

Jerry Herman couldn't write music but could play by ear beautifully. Mel Brooks had no musical ability when he wrote *The Producers*. Mitch Leigh did take music lessons, but the rumor was that employees of his advertising company Music Makers Incorporated wrote the score to *Man of La Mancha*. And nobody who ever worked with Leigh saw him play the piano.

Here's a story that is very well known but a few of you may not know it. Alan Jay Lerner was having dinner with Andrew Lloyd Webber. They were discussing collaborating on a musical. At one point in the evening, Sir Andrew asked Lerner, "Why do people take an instant dislike to me?" Lerner's reply: "It saves time."

Herbert Kretzmer had only six and a half weeks to write the lyrics to *Les Miserables*. Boublil didn't want Kretzmer to get credit for the lyrics though only one-half of a line was based on Boublil's French lyric. Kretzmer was forced to say, "I want proper credit or I withdraw my lyrics." They grudgingly gave it to him.

How to Succeed in Business without Really Trying was saved by the Bay of Pigs invasion. The show went into rehearsal without the last two scenes. Librettist Abe Burrows couldn't figure out how to end the show. Then the horribly botched invasion of Cuba happened, and Burrows noticed that everyone blamed everybody else. And that's what happens at the end of *How to Succeed*. The television show *The World Wide Wickets Treasure Hunt* is a huge disaster: Biggley blames Finch; and Finch becomes buddies with the chairman of the board and gets a promotion, while the hapless Bud Frump takes the blame.

Arthur Schwartz was a lawyer yearning to be a Broadway composer. Schwartz admired the lyrics of Howard Dietz and through their mutual friend Bennett Cerf, Schwartz asked Dietz to collaborate on some songs. Dietz had worked with Jerome Kern on the show *Dear Sir*, which was not a success. But when Dietz got Schwartz's letter, he replied, "As I have written a first show in collaboration with a well-established composer, I don't think that our collaboration is such a good idea. What I would suggest is that you collaborate with an established lyric writer. In that way, we will both benefit by the reputation of our collaborators, then when we both get famous, we can collaborate with each other."

Dietz's next project was filling in for Ira Gershwin when he got sick during the tryout of *Oh, Kay!* The librettists of the show, Guy Bolton and P.G. Wodehouse, offered to fill in, but George Gershwin nixed them knowing they would ask for a sizable royalty. George asked Howard Dietz to fill in thinking he'd work for practically nothing just for the credit. Dietz supplied the title for "Someone to Watch over Me," as well as the lyrics for "Oh, Kay" and "Heaven on Earth." He wrote the verse to "Clap Yo' Hands" and a lyric for "That Certain Something You've Got" which Ira changed and called "Oh, Kay, You're OK with Me." Ira gave Dietz the credit for the entire lyric.

George didn't want Ira to lose any of the royalties from the show, so he gave Dietz only one cent for every copy of sheet music. Dietz's first check was for ninety-six cents. Ira then wrote Dietz and asked him to forgo his royalty entirely since the bookkeeping for such a small amount was a bother. Dietz once wrote that he would have done the job for nothing just to work with the great George Gershwin. Well, he did!

Finally, Arthur Schwartz and Howard Dietz got together to work on 1929's *The Little Show*. They worked on their songs in hotel rooms and despite their best efforts at muting the pianos, neighbors who were trying to sleep complained to the management and the songwriters had to move on to The Warwick, the St. Moritz, and the Essex House; one by one the nomads crossed the city. Schwartz took it personally: "They don't like what I'm playing." Dietz responded, "That must be it. They never complain about the lyrics."

The Little Show tried out in Asbury Park, New Jersey. Dietz and Schwartz missed the first performance because their train broke down on the way. When they arrived as the curtain fell, producers Dwight Deere Wiman and Tom Weatherly met them and announced that the show was a flop and would close at the end of the week. The next night, the show was sparsely attended, but the show was in better shape and the audience reaction was more positive. It ended up playing almost a year on Broadway.

The hit tune from the show was "I Guess I'll Have to Change My Plan," but it took three years for the song to catch on. One day, Dietz and Schwartz went to the Place Pigalle nightclub in New York to see the team of De Lys and Clarke, who had had some success in London. De Lys came over to

Dietz and Schwartz's table and told them that they discovered a great song that was thrilling audiences in London. They called it "The Blue Pajama Song." Dietz asked who wrote it, and De Lys replied that they didn't know, "Someone like Noel Coward." De Lys sang the song and asked Dietz and Schwartz what they thought. Schwartz answered, "I think it's the best song someone like Noel Coward ever wrote."

The song became a great success and people were asking the music publisher if he had a copy of "The Blue Pajama Song." The publisher didn't know the song and asked Schwartz if he knew anything about it. Schwartz informed the publisher, "Dietz and I wrote it. You published it three years ago, and I want to congratulate you on the effortless way you go about making a song a hit."

George S. Kaufman had a ritual when he started each project. He set a deadline for himself for finishing the work. He had an opening date set for the Broadway opening and that kept the pressure on to get the job done in a timely manner. Before beginning work each morning, he would scrub his hands thoroughly, symbolically starting the writing fresh.

Arthur Laurents once said that after a while, writers aren't reviewed on their works but on their reputations.

Jerome Robbins wanted *Gypsy* to begin without an overture. It's a terrific idea to start with Madame Rose in the back of the audience yelling at Louise to "sing out." But, oh, that overture! It would be a real shame not to hear that masterpiece.

Ruth Gordon was desperate to do a new production of Ibsen's *A Doll's House*. But Thornton Wilder told her that no one would sit through the old, tired version. Wilder passed on the offer to do the writing himself. So did Noel Coward, S.N. Behrman, Lillian Hellman, and the list went on. Gordon was out of possible adaptors and called to Wilder to give him the news. After some time, Wilder agreed to adapt the play although he was in the middle of writing his new play *Our Town*.

Later, Wilder was at Amherst appearing as the Stage Manager in *Our Town*. One day he asked if he could take a day's leave to go to New York to see Olsen and Johnson's rambunctious musical *Hellzapoppin*. Upon his return, he told *Our Town*'s director Harold J. Kennedy what a transformative experience it was. "I have just found my new play. I am going to write the story of man's survival in a *Hellzapoppin* technique." The resulting play was *The Skin of Our Teeth*.

Rock and Roll, the First 5,000 Years and *Leader of the Pack* were the first jukebox musicals. While not perfect, they were as good as most of today's shows. Sadly, they were ahead of their time. Madonna was cast in *Rock and Roll* but quit after the first rehearsal.

The musical version of *Gigi* on Broadway in 1973 was perhaps the first to be based on a film musical. While there were some problems with the production, the show was criticized because it was based on a film musical, and that hurt it at the box office.

The first day of rehearsal for *Destry Rides Again*, Andy Griffith and Dolores Gray walked into the room and songwriter Harold Rome immediately realized that they had no chemistry. Rome recalled, "We had two options, either to not go into rehearsal and recast the show or spend our entire out of town tryout trying to build a show that these two people could star in. We chose the latter. That's what separates the men from the boys." Griffith and Gray had only one song together, a reprise of "Once Knew a Fella."

House of Flowers had a strange start. Harold Arlen, the composer and co-lyricist, was in New York while his lyric-writing partner Truman Capote was in Rome. Arlen would make acetate recordings of music and lyric suggestions and send them across the ocean to Capote who would add his own lyrics to Arlen's.

The show's score turned out to be wonderful, but the director Peter Brook had no experience directing musicals and even less experience with people of color. Diahann Carroll wrote that the cast found him condescending and that he treated them like little children. This demoralized the cast and ultimately proved fatal to the show.

When the show was in Philadelphia, Marlene Dietrich (then having an affair with composer Arlen) met Truman Capote and his boyfriend, set designer Oliver Messel and his boyfriend, and Noel Coward and his boyfriend. "I'll tell you what's wrong with this show," opined Dietrich. "I'm the only one here with balls!"

Then things really went bad. Pearl Bailey had Josephine Premice fired—too much competition in the talent department. Choreographer George Balanchine quit and Herbert Ross came in. Then Peter Brook left the sinking ship and the directorial reins were handed over (uncredited) to Herbert Ross.

Frederick Loewe was in one of his periodic breakups with Alan Jay Lerner and began writing a show with Harold Rome titled *Saints and Sinners*. One day, Loewe called up Rome and excitedly told him, "I have some really good news." Rome couldn't wait to hear the good news. Loewe boasted, "I'm writing *My Fair Lady*." Rome answered Loewe, "That's good news for you but bad for me."

Charles Strouse spent so much time working on shows during out-of-town tryouts, he said, "I see myself always writing in men's rooms."

Many a show was written and rehearsed in men's rooms. And a few orchestras have also played among the porcelain. In the 1950s and '60s, the musician's union specified that a minimum number of musicians had to play at every performance, even plays. At the National Theatre in Washington, when plays were on the stage, there was a quintet of musicians playing polite versions of show tunes as the audience entered. David Merrick was so incensed about this union rule he had the musicians play in the smoking rooms next to the restrooms.

One day, Martin Charnin was talking to Stephen Sondheim about the news that he was going to write the lyrics to Richard Rodgers's new musical *Two by Two*. Sondheim was practically apoplectic. "If he doesn't like what you wrote and you hand it to him on a yellow pad, he'll do this!" And with that, Sondheim took a piece of paper, balled it up tight, and threw it at Charnin.

Often, a show will open with a large orchestra that is then cut back after the critics come. Likewise, many an original cast album has an orchestra that is augmented for the recording. *Say, Darling* and *Little Mary Sunshine* both had only piano accompaniments but were orchestrated for their albums.

When Styne, Comden, and Green wrote "Better than a Dream" for the movie version of *Bells Are Ringing*, they liked the song so much, they put it into the show two or three years after the show opened.

While *Camelot* was out of town, Moss Hart was in the hospital. When he was released a few months later while the show was playing on Broadway, he went back to it and cut "Then You May Take Me to the Fair" and "Fie on Goodness" and tried to put the show into better shape.

Lucille Ball was so exhausted performing *Wildcat*, they cut two numbers, including the title song, to lighten her load. But the title number stayed in the overture.

Gwen Verdon cut "Charity's Soliloquy" from *Sweet Charity*. The number was just too exhausting for her to perform eight times a week. Verdon got a letter from an angry theatergoer who felt cheated that she hadn't seen the complete show. So Verdon prorated the amount of time the song took from the show against the price of the ticket and sent the woman a check.

When Raquel Welch went into *Woman of the Year*, Kander and Ebb wrote her a new number.

Jerry Herman originally wanted Ethel Merman for *Hello, Dolly!* and wrote numbers especially for her. When she turned down the part, they were cut from the score. But when Merman joined the company at the end of the show's run, those two numbers, "Love Look in My Window" and "World Take Me Back," were put back into the show.

Harold Arlen was originally to be the composer of *Where's Charley?* and Frank Loesser was to be the lyricist. But Arlen's house in Beverly Hills burned down, and his wife Anya had a nervous breakdown. So Arlen was forced to drop out of the show. Loesser suggested that he could also write the music, and *Where's Charley?* became his first Broadway score.

When *Guys and Dolls* was being put together, Frank Loesser wanted a reprise of "I'll Know," but producer Cy Feuer thought it would hold up the action. Director George S. Kaufman solved the disagreement. Kaufman told Loesser, "I'll tell you what, we'll agree to a reprise of a first-act song in Act II, if you'll agree to let us reprise a few of the first-act jokes." Loesser laughed and agreed to nix the reprise.

Probably since the ancient Greeks, cast members and the public have invented puns on the titles of shows.

When Max Gordon opened the mega-production *The Great Waltz* at the Center Theatre, wags dubbed it *The Great Waste*. But the show became a sellout and would have run longer had Gordon not misjudged its staying power and booked a national tour before the Broadway audiences fell off. Though it played just 269 performances, the Center Theatre was so large that over a million people saw it.

Here are some more titles and their satirical variations:

Annie Get Your Gun revival with Ethel Merman—*Granny Get Your Gun*

Anya—*Anya Get Your Crown*

The Bunch and Judy—*The Bust and Judy*

The Color Purple—*The Colored People*

Dance a Little Closer—*Close a Little Sooner*

Great Day was so beset with problems on the road, they nicknamed it *Great Delay*

The King and I with Celeste Holm—*Annie Get Your King*

Strange Interlude—*Strange Intercourse*

The World of Suzi Wong—*The World of Woozy Song*

Richard Rodgers asked John Morris if he'd like to do the dance arrangements for *Pipe Dream*. Rodgers gave him a choice. He could either get paid or get credit. Morris had a family to support, so he chose the money. Eventually, he did get credit for his work.

Donald Pippin had to redo the vocal arrangements for *110 in the Shade* because Robert de Cormier had arranged the songs as if they were for a concert choir and not for specific voices in a dramatic setting. Pippin received no credit for his work.

Fred Werner was responsible for the dance arrangements of *Sweet Charity* in addition to conducting the show. When it came time to mount the Debbie Allen revival of the show on Broadway, composer Cy Coleman asked Werner, who also conducted the revival, if he would take his name off the arrangements so Coleman could get credit for the work. In the end, nobody was credited.

Sandy Wilson, best known as the songwriter for *The Boy Friend*, wanted to make a musical out of Christopher Isherwood's stories. He spoke to Julie Andrews, the star of *The Boy Friend*, and she agreed to play Sally Bowles. But then his librettist Beverley Cross (*Half a Sixpence*) got a movie assignment and dropped out, and Andrews was cast in the film version of *The Sound of Music*.

While on a trip to New York, he had dinner with Hal Prince and the two of them discovered they were working on the same project. Wilson didn't have the rights and Prince was close to tying up the rights for himself. Prince also had Joe Masteroff hired for the libretto. Wilson auditioned his score for Prince and Masteroff, but the latter told Wilson he didn't think the songs were right for his libretto.

CHAPTER 5
Songs

K ander and Ebb claimed that they wrote sixty songs for *Flora the Red Menace* and a similar number for *Cabaret*.

When Jones and Schmidt wrote their first Broadway show *110 in the Shade*, they were so nervous that they'd be unable to write songs at the last minute, they wrote one hundred or so songs. Even with all that material, they still had to write three new songs out of town. Over half were cut by the time the show opened in New York. Musical director Don Pippin reported that all the songs were really good.

Galt MacDermot and Gerome Ragni wrote fifty songs for *Dude*.

Bob Merrill wrote fifty songs for *Breakfast at Tiffany's*, and the show still closed in previews.

Bock and Harnick wrote almost fifty songs for *Fiddler*. *Fiorello* had almost three times as many songs. *She Loves Me* had fifty or so songs written for it and *The Rothchilds* had almost as many.

Jule Styne knew that Sydney Chaplin, the male lead in *Bells Are Ringing*, had a very small range to his singing voice. So he wrote a tune that centered around three notes and a simple phrase that repeated over and over again. Vincent Youmans told Styne that's what he needed to do to have a successful song. Comden and Green had a difficult time setting the tune to the lyric. Styne would go around to parties playing the music and at one such soiree, the title was provided by Frank Loesser. He told Styne to call it "Just in Time."

Jerome Kern originally wrote the melody for "Smoke Gets in Your Eyes" in a march tempo as the theme for a radio show. The show never materialized and when Kern's show *Roberta* needed new numbers, he played it for lyricist Otto Harbach and others on the creative staff. They thought it was indifferent and, as a march, not suitable for the show. Kern was about to throw out the melody when he had an idea. He slowed down the tempo and Harbach gave it a sentimental lyric.

Arthur Schwartz was following his father's orders when he went to law school, and he eventually became a lawyer, but he soon quit to become a Broadway composer. He was taking a class in preparation for the bar exam when he started whistling. That should have told him something. That tune eventually became the song "Shine on Your Shoes."

The opening notes of "The Ballad of Sweeney Todd," under the lyric "attend the tale of Sweeney Todd," are the notes of "Dies Irae" backward.

Alan Jay Lerner collaborated with Andre Previn on the musical *Coco*. One day, Lerner came to Previn's office and told him he had five different lyrics for one line of music in the score and couldn't decide among them. Previn insisted that Lerner choose which was better. Lerner prevaricated. Previn asked when he'd make up his mind. Lerner answered, "Later." So Previn locked Lerner in his office and threw the key out the window. Lerner wasn't falling for that. "You've got a spare key," Lerner said to the composer through the locked door. But Previn did not. The song was finished that evening.

When Bob Fosse was going to work on *Funny Girl*, Jule Styne played through the songs. When it came to the song "People," Fosse told Styne, "Well, it's a beautiful song, no doubt about it. It's a very beautiful song. But I'm afraid we can't use it." His logic was that the character of Fanny Brice didn't actually need anyone. After some arguing, Styne exploded and told Fosse in no uncertain terms that the song would stay in the show because it would be a number-one hit on the hit parade and Streisand would sing the bejeezus (he didn't actually use the word "bejeezus") out of it. Fosse thought for a second and laughed and agreed that the composer had a valid point. Soon afterward, Fosse was out of the show. The show's director Garson Kanin also wanted the song deleted from the score. Styne begged Kanin to keep the song in for the first performance out of town, and if it didn't get a strong reaction, he would cut it from the score. At that first performance, the song stopped the show and Styne never removed it from the score.

Richard Rodgers never complimented Oscar Hammerstein on his lyrics. While writing *The King and I*, Hammerstein slipped his lyric for "Hello, Young Lovers" under Rodgers's door. It was Hammerstein's most personal lyric, and he hoped Rodgers would like it as much as he did. The next day, Rodgers didn't mention the lyric and Hammerstein finally asked if he got the lyric. All Rodgers said was "Yeah. I set it in an hour."

During the writing of *Call Me Madam*, Jerome Robbins told Irving Berlin that they needed a song to open the second act. Berlin asked Robbins to explain just what kind of a song would fit the spot. Robbins thought and replied, "I don't know but it should be something to dance about." And that's exactly what Berlin wrote: "Something to Dance About."

Berlin's "Let's Take an Old-Fashioned Walk" was originally written for Fred Astaire and Judy Garland to sing in the film *Easter Parade*. But it wasn't deemed snappy enough, and so Berlin wrote "A Couple of Swells," and "Let's Take an Old-Fashioned Walk" went into the score of *Miss Liberty*.

John Kander and Fred Ebb auditioned to write the score of *The Unsinkable Molly Brown*. Among their songs was one titled "Belly Up to the Bar, Boys." They didn't get the job, but Meredith Willson loved the title so much, he asked to use it in his score.

The story goes that Elaine Stritch thought that "a piece of Mahler's" meant a piece of cake. But the truth is that Sondheim was making a joke when he told her that Mahler wasn't a cake. Stritch knew who Mahler was.

When Jerome Robbins first heard the song "Everything's Coming Up Roses," he said, "I don't get it. Everything's coming up Rose's what?"

Gertrude Lawrence was in rehearsal for *Lady in the Dark* singing "My Ship" and came to the lyric "I can wait for years till it appears one fine day one spring." She stopped and said, "Why four years, why not three?" Ira Gershwin agreed with her and changed the lyric, which is now "I can wait the years till it appears one fine day one spring."

The wonderful Arthur Siegel thought this lyric by Irving Berlin for *Annie Get Your Gun* was terrible: "Her nails will be polished and in her hair she'll wear a gardenia and I'll be there." Siegel said, "Her nails are in her hair? And I'll be there. Where, in her hair?"

When the remarkable Nancy Andrews of *Little Me* and *Plain and Fancy* fame was out of town with the Sammy Fain future flop *Christine*, the second act was so lugubrious, they decided to write an up-tempo number, "Ireland was Never Like This." Andrews was sitting in the rehearsal room watching Maureen O'Hara singing "Ireland Was Never Like This." The lyric went: All the boys are blowing me . . . (clap hands twice) a kiss . . . (pause).

Andrews was aghast. She went over to Cy Feuer who had taken over the direction and said, "All the boys are blowing me . . . a kiss?" And he looked at her and said, "Jesus!" The hand claps were taken out of the number.

CHAPTER 6

Producing The Show

Rodgers and Hammerstein often told the story that when Gertrude Lawrence died during the run of *The King and I*, Yul Brynner burst into tears, not because of Lawrence's death but because he would finally get top billing.

When *The Diary of Anne Frank* opened at the Cort Theatre, Joseph Schildkraut had sole billing above the title on the marquee. When Susan Strasberg received raves, it was decided to put her name alongside Schildkraut's. The star definitely didn't like the idea, but Merle Debuskey suggested to the actor that a photo be taken of him at the top of a ladder leaning on a marquee holding Strasberg's hand as if he was leading her up into stardom. He bought it since, in his mind, it was all about his generosity in sharing the space above the title.

Carol Channing's only appearance on Broadway had been in the revue *Lend an Ear*. Author Anita Loos saw the show and immediately knew that Channing was the girl to portray Lorelei Lee in the musical version of her book *Gentlemen Prefer Blondes*. Since Channing didn't have a saleable name on Broadway, Loos went to show business associates to raise the money. The Lunts, Rodgers and Hammerstein, Joshua Logan, and Leland Hayward were among the angels.

Producers would ask anyone to invest in the days before backers were consolidated into larger entities. The Theatre Guild had a terrible time raising money for *Oklahoma!* despite the great success of its authors, Rodgers and Hammerstein. It finally took two years before the show was mounted.

Among those they asked for money was the playwright Phillip Barry, who had made a good deal of money from Guild productions of his plays. After the tremendous success of *Oklahoma!* Barry had saved two telegrams. One, from the Guild, read, "Would you like to invest in a wonderful new play?" The other one, from Barry to the Guild, read, "Forget it." Barry never forgave himself for turning down the offer to invest.

Kermit Bloomgarden would read prospective scripts while sitting in his office's bathroom.

Tharon Musser, one of Broadway's greatest lighting designers, was raised in West Virginia in a home without electricity. Musser brought in the first computerized lighting board with *A Chorus Line*.

Lionel Bart couldn't write music; he actually whistled his tunes into a tape recorder and a secretary transcribed them. Eric Rogers took Bart's "music," filled it out, and orchestrated it for thirteen instruments and musicians. In London, *Oliver!* was an intimate show. The New York musician's union had a minimum of twenty-four players at the Imperial Theatre. If David Merrick had to pay twenty-four players, he was going to have twenty-four players in the pit. So, musical director Don Pippin asked Rogers to write around the original thirteen instruments and whenever Pippin wanted to bring in more, he could. The audience would hear the thirteen instruments in the center of the pit and then the music would spread as if it was in stereophonic sound. Most of the vocals were only with the original thirteen instruments. If all twenty-four musicians were playing at one time, the sound would have been too thick.

The first mechanized sets were used in *Oliver!* Sean Kenny's set was built on two turntables that continuously revolved to change the scenes and give perspective to the action. In those days, the turntables were hand-cranked by a stagehand. Merrick didn't want to pay extra stagehands, so he had the turntables mechanized. They didn't work perfectly; sometimes they'd stop just short of where they should be or overshoot their marks. At one first-act finale, the turntable wouldn't stop revolving, and the actors had to navigate getting on and off without injuring themselves. During intermission, the problem was solved.

Sometimes plays and musicals seem destined for the scrap heap of history until they get before an audience.

An invited preview performance of *Arsenic and Old Lace* is a case in point. Joseph Kesselring wrote the play, but producers Howard Lindsay and Russel Crouse doctored the script.

Following the last preview, playwright Marc Connelly gave some free advice to Crouse and advised him that if he'd postpone the opening by two or three weeks, the show might have a chance to run. Crouse didn't listen to Connelly. The show opened the next night and ran for over three years and returned 1,800% to its investors.

Honestly, the producers didn't have faith in the show themselves. A week's worth of tickets cost $40 to print. Lindsay and Crouse had two other plays opening soon thereafter, *Snafu* and *Harvey*. They thought that *Snafu* would be the big hit, so they ordered weeks of tickets for that show. When *Arsenic and Old Lace* opened to rave reviews, thousands lined up at the box office to buy tickets. But there was only a week's worth printed. By the way, *Snafu* ran only twenty weeks, and *Arsenic and Old Lace* ran ten times that.

Herman Mankiewicz was the assistant to George S. Kaufman, *The New York Times* drama editor. Both would find greater success as authors. Mankiewicz wanted to become a producer (who didn't?) and decided on a play titled *Love 'Em and Leave 'Em* written by John V.A. Weaver. When the show opened in Asbury Park, New Jersey, Mankiewicz found himself short of funds. No money for the cast, no money for transportation back to New York, and no money to pay the author his $500 advance. But Mankiewicz was a smart fellow. He borrowed the money from actress Peggy Wood. Why her? Wood was the wife of . . . John V.A. Weaver. As Sheldon Harnick once wrote, "Oh it's grand how the money changes hands."

Bernie McDonald is not a name known today, and even when he was in his heyday on Broadway, few people knew his name. But he was extremely important; it was his company that built the sets for Broadway shows. And his sets were impeccably built. One day, McDonald was at the famed writers/ policemen/Wall Streeters/etc. hangout and dive bar Bleeck's (pronounced "Blakes"). Read any biographies of noted rapscallions and alcoholics, and you'll find Bleeck's mentioned. So McDonald is at Bleeck's and runs into Richard Maney, the greatest publicist in Broadway history. McDonald shows Maney a watch and asks Maney how much he thinks it cost. Maney guesses around $250. "Wrong," says McDonald, "this watch cost me $50,000. It's what Ziegfeld gave me instead of what he owed me."

Billy Rose was extravagant in his tastes and in his producing. He had an idea for an intimate revue titled *Corned Beef and Roses*. Rehearsals spanned across Broadway occupying no fewer than three theatres. The intimate revue was ready to open in Philadelphia in October of 1930, except for one small problem. All the scenery wouldn't fit into the theatre. Come the dress rehearsal and the intimate revue's first act ran five hours.

After Philadelphia, the show went back into rehearsal in New York, performers were replaced, and the title was changed to *Sweet and Low*. The show played for a few months and closed.

Then Rose revamped it a third time and reopened on Broadway as a new intimate revue, this time titled *Crazy Quilt*, again with some new performers (including The Three Stooges) and some new songs. When the weather turned uncomfortably hot, the show closed and went on a profitable tour of the sticks. By the end of the whole affair, Rose managed to net a quarter of a million dollars from the show.

George Jessel found himself the sole producer of the Bert Kalmar and Harry Ruby musical *Helen of Troy, New York* by default. His supposed producing partner skipped out on his part of the fundraising. Jessel went to Nick the Greek for money, but the gambler said he was broke. Nick the Greek went up to Yonkers to meet a bunch of bootleggers who might invest in the show. When he got there with the songwriters and the playwright George S. Kaufman, a Mr. Butch Fink implored them to sing some of the score while his friends were taking the booze out of the vats and sticking labels on the bottles. Kalmar and Ruby sang and then, with no more score to sing, Kalmar did some magic tricks. Somehow the bootleggers got into a fistfight and the Broadway boys hightailed it back to civilization. Kaufman, who had written the libretto, came out of the failure intact. He used the whole ridiculous goings-on as the impetus to write his comedy *The Butter and Egg Man*.

Phil Silvers was helping to raise money for the musical *Top Banana*, a slightly disguised parody of Milton Berle and his fantastically successful television show. Berle didn't realize he was the one being sent up, and in fact he invested in the show and told everyone how great it was.

A rich tycoon who made his fortune in the wicker basket industry was in the lobby waiting for a rehearsal to end. Silvers was onstage singing along with the cast when he heard a strange howling coming from the lobby. Every time Silvers raised his voice in song, the howling commenced. And when Silvers stopped singing, so did the strange sound from the lobby. Silvers went out the auditorium doors and met Mr. Wicker Basket there with his Airedale dog. Silvers inquired, "Will he sing when I sing?" The owner responded, "I don't know. He sings with me."

Silvers had an idea. The dog, whose name was Ted (Sport) Morgan, was integrated into a sketch and Johnny Mercer wrote a song, "A Dog Is a Man's Best Friend" to go along with it. Whenever Silvers sang, the dog would join in and upstage him. The audience was in stitches, and the bit became a highlight of the show. It's unknown if his master invested in the show, but what he gave the show was more valuable than money.

Coda: At opening night, Silvers was onstage with Sport on a leash. Milton Berle had finally wised up to the fact that he was being lampooned and so, on opening night during the curtain call, he ran out on the stage toward Silvers and yelled, "I'll sue! I'll sue!" Sport, not recognizing that Berle was a great star but only that he was yelling at his friend Silvers, tried to get at Berle's throat. Luckily the leash held, and Berle was saved from a second mauling on opening night.

A famous producer had a lot of shows on the boards but few of them ever made money. A friend of mine, Denny Martin Flinn, asked the producer's assistant why the producer never produced an off-Broadway show. The assistant answered, "When you're going to skim a few hundred thousand off a production, you can't produce a show that only costs a few hundred thousand dollars.

Jule Styne was living in Hollywood across the street from novelist Stephen Longstreet who had just written a well-received novel, *The Sisters Liked Them Handsome*. Styne inquired if there was a musical in the book and Longstreet replied, "I don't know." Sammy Cahn, who was going to write the lyrics with Styne, started working on a treatment that followed the novel closely. It wasn't very good. Then Mrs. Longstreet came up with a title for the musical, *High Button Shoes*. That got everyone excited.

Someone thought that the show should revolve around a hoodwinker named Harrison Floy, a minor character in the book. Phil Silvers was made for the role. Joe Kipness, from the garment trade, decided he'd become a producer with the show and then George Abbott came in as director. Abbott also agreed to write the libretto. Longstreet felt he wasn't needed anymore and, in fact, never saw the show until the final performance of the second L.A. company.

Sadly, the show's book wasn't working, though Jerome Robbins's "Bathing Beauty Ballet" was a hilarious hit. Then, Silvers got laryngitis so he was forbidden to talk except when onstage for the show. Silvers would write notes to Jule Styne, who would answer them while screaming loudly. Silvers wrote in response, "I am not deaf—I just can't talk!" Finally, having recovered his voice, Silvers told Abbott that he would be ad-libbing but always within the parameters of the show. So, Silvers and Robbins rewrote the script. By the time the show opened in New York, it was a smash hit.

Once it was a success, Stephen Longstreet went around town bragging that he was responsible for all the dialogue, including the ad-libs. Silvers got wind of this and threatened Longstreet by telling him, "If you don't stop, I'll play the show you wrote."

Here's a small coda. Kipness was forced to become co-producer with a fellow named Monte Prosser. When Prosser saw that the show was not succeeding in Philly, he figured he'd get at least some of his investment back, so he sold all his house seats to a guy named George Solitaire for a few bucks per ticket. When the show became a hit in New York and started selling out, Solitaire was able to sell the house seats for $50 a pair, a huge markup. He made a killing since the show ran for 727 performances.

And another brief story. Robbins ran the "Bathing Beauty Ballet" so many times, the actor in the gorilla costume told his fellow cast members, "If he runs this one more time, I'll go out and rip his face off."

Max Gordon was the producer of a play by Clare Kummer titled *Her Master's Voice*. Roland Young was starring, returning to Broadway from Hollywood, and the director was Worthington Miner, a well-established Broadway director/producer/actor who directed the original production of Rodgers and Hart's *On Your Toes*.

Miner and Young didn't get along practically from the first rehearsal and Young finally said he wouldn't continue in the play under Miner's direction. So Miner dropped out with the parting shot that he never really liked the play anyway. Gordon stepped in as the director before the play went on to the Plymouth Theatre.

Miner requested that a letter be sent to the critics announcing that he was no longer the director and therefore not responsible for any failure of the play. Gordon felt that since practically all the work was Miner's, there was no reason to take his name off the program or alert the papers. Come opening night, the play was a big success, with the *The New York Times* giving an extremely favorable review to Kummer's work as well as Miner's.

Gordon summoned Miner to his office and said, "Well, how would you like it if I released the letter to *The New York Times*? That would be fine, wouldn't it? You getting all the great notices, and this letter saying you had nothing to do with it!" Miner gave a sheepish grin and agreed that the letter should not go out.

When Charles Frohman was given J.M. Barrie's play *Peter Pan*, he almost rejected the manuscript. But he did finally decide to produce it, and it premiered in London in 1904. A New York production followed that made a star of Maude Adams. In 1911, in a reversal of the usual process, Barrie wrote a novel based on the play. If Frohman had not decided to produce the play, would we have had the subsequent novel, movies, musicals, etc.?

In the 1920s when the stock market was soaring, a producer had only to call a couple of millionaires, tell them who was starring in the show, and a check would appear on his desk the next morning. But after the Wall Street crash of 1929, raising money became more and more difficult. Even twenty years later, *Kiss Me, Kate* had to hold over one hundred investor auditions during the course of a year. And that wasn't even the record for such auditions.

With the advent of the original cast recording, record companies would invest in a show and get the rights to release the cast album. It was a good deal for both the show, which got money and a cast recording, and the record companies, which didn't just pay for the rights to the album, but also got a stake in the show.

The most notable investment by a record company was Columbia Records' Goddard Lieberson, who put up $375,000, the entire capitalization of *My Fair Lady*, plus another $40,000 for producing the original cast recording. It's estimated that the LP alone earned over fifty million dollars.

When Leonard Sillman was trying to produce his first *New Faces* show in 1934, he needed only $15,000 to present a show with no known performers, songwriters new to Broadway, and a decidedly non-lavish production.

Sillman realized he needed some sort of name to associate with the production. So he turned to the great producer Charles Dillingham, who had produced such notable productions as *A Bill of Divorcement*, the original American production of *Peter Pan*, and *Watch Your Step*, Irving Berlin's first book musical. But, Dillingham had hit hard times, which was especially galling for a man of his stature. He spent his days in a small room at the Astor Hotel looking out the window onto Times Square. Sillman approached Dillingham to be a figurehead for the production in exchange for which he'd get a guaranteed fee for the use of his name and a royalty.

The show started off slowly at the box office, and Sillman asked the cast to take a cut in salary. After much bickering, everyone agreed except for one person. When asked why he didn't go along with the rest of the cast, he explained that when he came and left the theatre, everyone ignored him. No one ever said hello or goodbye. Sillman brought the cast together and ordered them to greet the actor when he arrived and wish him a good day when he left. They agreed, and the cut was approved.

The show ran for only 134 performances because of competition from bigger, more lavish shows, the summer heat, and Henry Fonda's leaving the cast for Hollywood. But, in addition to Fonda, the show gave the cast a foothold on Broadway, and several of them, including Imogene Coca, went on to have exemplary careers.

And as for Charles Dillingham, he had a ball being the producer of a successful show. He attended every performance and greeted old friends and well-wishers in the lobby. He'd personally wave in friends who were down on their luck. It was a golden capper to a golden career.

Sam H. Harris was one of the great producers in Broadway's early years. In 1904, Harris wandered into a vaudeville theatre and saw an act that mesmerized him. The performers were billed as The Four Cohans, and it was the youngest Cohan, George M., who especially caught Harris's eye. He went backstage and offered to put up his entire bank account of $25,000 to produce a show featuring Cohan and his family. George M. was thrilled at the proposition. However, they had bookings for the next six months, so Harris would have to wait.

Harris did wait for them but during that time, he produced a few failures and lost his entire bankroll. Harris tried to figure out how to raise another $25,000 when he recalled a gambler in Philadelphia who might spot him some money. He spent three days getting his courage up to ask the man for some cash. Harris finally asked him, and the man agreed, asking in what denominations Harris would like the money. Not knowing how much the gambler was willing to loan, Harris asked for small bills. Harris left Philadelphia with $25,000 in fives and twenties.

Finally, he had the money to produce his show, which turned out to be *Little Johnny Jones*, a smash hit on Broadway. It was so big that one of its scenes is recreated in the Cohan biopic *Yankee Doodle Dandy*. The show propelled Cohan to the highest ranks on Broadway, gave us "Give My Regards to Broadway," and set the stage for a new kind of musical on Broadway that shunned the European-influenced operetta tradition. It also led to the producing team of Cohan and Harris, which ended up putting on fifty shows on Broadway over the next fifteen years.

Guys and Dolls with its marvelous Frank Loesser score just wasn't working. Jo Swerling's book was not up to snuff, so Abe Burrows was brought in to rewrite the script, . . . well, actually write a new book. Producer Cy Feuer later stated that not one word of Swerling's book remained in the show.

Burrows had never written a musical so the investors were, understandably, nervous. One of them was Billy Rose, the producer, songwriter, and all-around character. Rose would have been right at home as a character in the show. He had invested $10,000 in *Guys and Dolls* and though Burrows was a great friend of Rose's, the investor didn't trust that Burrows could pull it off. So Rose withdrew his money from the production.

Since the score was practically completed, Burrows's libretto was written for the songs rather than the other way around.

Part of the job of producing a show is choosing the right show to produce. It seems obvious, but history has shown that the task is very difficult. The list of notable producers who have turned down subsequent hits is long.

When Thornton Wilder's *Our Town* was in Boston, audiences stayed away. They just couldn't grasp a play with no sets, a narrator, and a non-linear story. Producer Jed Harris had to cancel the second week in Boston. Luckily, he still believed in the play and opened it in New York. It won the Pulitzer Prize and seems to have been produced since by every high school and college in the country.

So it's amazing that Wilder's play *The Skin of Our Teeth* almost didn't get produced. Harris was given the first shot at the show, but he couldn't make up his mind because it was just too unconventional. After considering the script for six months, he passed on the production.

Wilder got producer Michael Myerberg, but he needed a partner to make up the budget shortfall. So he was out. Howard Cullman rejected it. Gilbert Miller couldn't even get through the play. Likewise, Vinton Freedley couldn't figure out what was going on. The Theatre Guild didn't quite believe that Wilder was serious about the play.

Obviously, *The Skin of Our Teeth* was produced, and successfully so, by Myerberg on his own. And it got rave reviews and won the Pulitzer Prize. But the successes of it and *Our Town* were due in part because both shows went against what was then the status quo on Broadway. Think about recent successes like *Cats, Rent, Avenue Q, The Book of Mormon*, and today's smash hit *Hamilton*. They all broke the mold, just as *Show Boat, Oklahoma!* and *The Fantasticks* were unique in their time.

Of course, artists can also be wrong. Such eminent songwriters as Rodgers and Hammerstein, Harold Rome, Frank Loesser, Cole Porter, Burton Lane, Jule Styne, and Comden and Green all turned down the job of writing the score to *The Pajama Game*. So Richard Adler and Jerry Ross, two unknowns, got the job (after Rosalind Russell urged George Abbott to give them a try). But look at the above list of shows that broke the mold. With the exception of *Cats* and *Hamilton*, they were all written by newcomers. Remember, even Jerome Kern and the Princess Theatre shows, Rodgers and Hart and *The Garrick Gaieties*, Frank Loesser with *Where's Charley?*, and Strouse and Adams with *Bye, Bye, Birdie* were all Broadway neophytes.

Strike Me Pink marked the end of the songwriting team of Lew Brown and Ray Henderson. Along with B.G. DeSylva, they had written some of the greatest Broadway scores of the 1920s. DeSylva decamped to Hollywood, and Brown and DeSylva kept on writing together, until *Strike Me Pink*. Lew Brown had some relations with shady characters. Henderson and Brown were the nominal producers of the show, but it was really Irving Wexler who was in charge, a multimillionaire who produced the show and was the main backer. When the show started slipping at the box office, Harold Arlen's agent A.L. "Abe" Berman contacted someone and was told to take a seat in an aisle in the back row of the theatre. In the dark, a figure approached him and asked, "Are you Abe Berman?" Berman said, "Yes," and a paper bag was put in his lap. Inside the bag was cash. Not enough to keep the show open for long.

It turned out that Irving Wexler was also known by the moniker Waxey Gordon, as a bootlegger, gangster, and operator of many gambling establishments. Wexler/Gordon lost about $150,000 on *Strike Me Pink*, and Lew Brown was advised to leave town until things cooled off.

Albert Hague and Arnold Horwitt were having backer auditions for their new show *Plain and Fancy*, which told the story of two lost New Yorkers who interact with an Amish community in Pennsylvania. Frankly, the reception wasn't great. In fact, few people were excited enough to invest money. Hague and Horwitt discussed the problem and concluded that what the show needed was a big, funny number. But somehow this beautiful and modest show didn't lend itself to a song with big laughs. Still, they figured, "Why don't we write a funny song that sounds like it could be in the show but won't be in the show?" After all, songs come and go during rehearsals and previews. So they wrote an extremely funny song about Wanamaker's and other Philadelphia department stores. The number went over like gangbusters, and the money finally started flowing into the production. When the show opened to good reviews, several of the backers asked what happened to that terrific song. And, as the songwriters had agreed, they told the investors that the song just didn't fit in with the show's score and had to be eliminated. Since the show was a hit, nobody worried about the song.

The Pajama Game had a hell of a time raising money. In fact, the producers Harold Prince and Robert Griffith gave up their salaries. They offered shares in the show for $35 each to the cast members of *Me and Juliet*. They even signed themselves on to be the stage managers of the production. And when prospects did not improve, the cast and crew were asked to forgo a week's salary.

George Abbott, who could be ruthless when it came to fashioning a musical, wanted to cut the number "Steam Heat" because it didn't advance the plot. But the standing ovations that spontaneously erupted when it was performed led Abbott to restore it before the show opened on Broadway.

Jerome Robbins had been given a pair of gold cufflinks by his father. On opening night of *The Pajama Game*, the grateful director gave them to Bob Fosse as a present. Fosse was greatly touched, and from then on, whoever had the cufflinks would pass them along on opening nights.

David Susskind, best known as a television personality and producer, decided to become a Broadway producer. He chose *A Very Special Baby*, a play by Robert Alan Arthur, as his first venture. The gods smiled on Susskind when he landed Ezio Pinza making his dramatic debut after becoming a huge Broadway star in *South Pacific*. Sylvia Sidney was cast as his daughter.

Things were going great. The advance ticket sales, as you might imagine, were tremendous. Theatre parties put in their orders, and the Shuberts gave Susskind a prime theatre. Then Pinza had a brain hemorrhage. The theatre parties vanished, and so did the Shubert house.

Luther Adler replaced Pinza and the show was booked into the Playhouse Theatre. The problems grew for Susskind, as no one seemed to know that Adler and Sidney had recently undergone a tremendously nasty divorce. To director George Abbott's consternation, the two fought constantly during rehearsals, even to the point of physical confrontation.

The show only ran for thirty-four performances, though the reviews weren't half bad. Susskind did have one piece of luck; he sold the movie rights to Kirk Douglas, and so the show closed in the black.

Costume designer Patricia Zipprodt was hired to design the costumes for *Pippin*, which was to be directed by Bob Fosse. When she asked Fosse what his concept for the costumes was, he answered, "Magical!" Zipprodt thought about it and prompted him with this: "Besides magical?" He answered, "Anachronistic." Zipprodt went home and started sketching, but she didn't know where to go with the designs. She called Fosse again and asked him what "magical" and "anachronistic" meant to him. Fosse thought a bit and came up with the answer, "Jesus Christ in tennis shorts."

That was exactly what Zipprodt wanted to hear, and she had no problem sketching out her ideas. But that wasn't the end of the story. At the dress rehearsal, both Fosse and producer Stuart Ostrow told Zipprodt that the women's costumes just weren't sexy enough. So Zipprodt figured she'd just go for broke no matter how sleazy or campy, and then she thought of Frederick's of Hollywood. As she later said, "It was horrendous, but I thought, what the hell?"

TICKET BROKERS

In the early years of Broadway, producers did all they could to guarantee at least some audience and income in the first weeks of a show's run. What they would do is go to a ticket broker like Conoli's Opera and Theater Ticket Agency at 41st and Broadway. The producers would tell the agency that their new show was terrific and that tickets could be bought for a steep discount. This presale of tickets, especially for shows with a big-name star or writer, could finance a show or guarantee that the first month or two of a run would be sold-out prior to the show's opening. Then, if the show was good, the broker could mark up the ticket prices and make back his investment.

In 1894, Joe Leblang invented the discount ticket idea in his tobacco shop on 30th Street. Shopkeepers who displayed Broadway posters in their windows would receive comp tickets as a reward. Leblang bought the tickets from the different brokers and sold them at a 50% markup. As Broadway moved uptown to what became Times Square, Leblang moved his operation to Broadway and 42nd Street in the basement of Gray's Drugstore, and in 1908, he made the first bulk purchase of discounted theatre tickets for the show *Polly of the Circus*. Producers came to depend on Leblang, and they'd send over unsold day-of-performance tickets just as the TKTS booth in Times Square does today. He would also sell full-price tickets to popular shows with a fifty-cent markup, the same markup for his discount tickets.

Those fifty-cent markups made Leblang a millionaire. He made over twenty million dollars in his career with his discount tickets, real estate holdings, and investments in Broadway shows. *Rose Marie*, *Abie's Irish Rose*, and *The Cat and the Canary* were among the shows that Leblang saved by buying up tickets.

NOBODY KNOWS ANYTHING

It's said that, in show business, nobody knows anything, even the old hands. Adolph Green was walking down the street and ran into David Merrick. Green inquired, "What's going on?" Merrick replied, "I'm producing the greatest show of my career, *Destry Rides Again*. And I've got some other show starring Ethel Merman—it's going to be a bomb." That "bomb" was *Gypsy*.

Joseph Papp saw a rehearsal of *A Chorus Line* and thought it too was going to flop badly.

A BOXING MATCH

When *West Side Story* opened on Broadway, the producers agreed to put a box around Jerome Robbins's credits whenever they were printed. Arthur Laurents, the book writer for the show and an egomaniac, was miffed. Why didn't he get to have a box!

When the two worked together again on the musical *Gypsy*, Laurents saw to it that Robbins's contract specifically stated that he would not have a box around his name. Everybody was happy until *Redhead* opened. There in the credits, director/choreographer Bob Fosse had, you guessed it, a box around his name.

Robbins said something to the effect of "damn the contract, I want my box back." Laurents simply wouldn't stand for that. If Robbins got a box, Laurents threatened to pull his libretto and shut down the show. So there! Finally, after a long, acrimonious negotiation, Robbins got his box and Laurents got a bigger percentage of the royalties, a pretty fair draw.

CHAPTER 7

Casting

Anita Gillette was performing at the Winter Garden Theatre in the show *All American*. Irving Berlin had his offices in the Winter Garden, and every Wednesday matinee, he'd come down and watch Anita's performance.

He was working on a new show, *Mr. President*, his first show since *Call Me Madam*. Berlin had suffered for years from writer's block, and *Mr. President* was his return to Broadway.

When they sent out a casting call for the role of the daughter in *Mr. President*, they asked for an Anita Gillette type. Gillette's agent called up the casting director and asked, "What about Anita Gillette?" The reply was "Fine, when can she come to audition?" It was funny that they wanted an Anita Gillette type and then, when they had the real thing, they still made her audition, twice; she got the part.

When *Golden Apple* was auditioning, every actor in the city wanted to get into it because they all felt it would be a hit. But, as everyone knew, the only way to get a job was if the producers thought you didn't need it. Kaye Ballard went to her friends and borrowed their furs. Every time she went in to audition for the show, she wore a different fur to give the impression that she was doing really well and didn't need the job. Finally, it was between her and Lisa Kirk for the part. Ballard was convinced that the fur she wore that day got her the job.

Patricia Morison appeared in *The King and I* as Anna opposite the original King, Yul Brynner. She acted opposite him on Broadway and then on tour. Morison knew of his reputation as a womanizer. "When I first was going to be interviewed—going to meet him—somebody had asked him what he thought of me. He said, 'I don't know, I haven't been to bed with her yet!'"

"When he finally showed up, I was rehearsing and he was watching and doing all kinds of acrobatics," Morison recalled with a smile. "He said, 'Would you have lunch with me?' I said, 'Sorry.' He said, 'Will you stop by my dressing room on your way out?'" Morison thought about it and decided to see what would happen.

"I knocked on the door of the dressing room and he says, 'Come in.' He's sitting in front of the mirror naked! I looked him in the eyes and said, 'Mr. Brynner, you wish to see me?' He said, 'I have to stain my body [for the role].' I said, 'I understand.' We ended up the best of friends."

Frank Sinatra's agent asked that he be considered for the original production of *Fiddler on the Roof*.

Charles Nelson Reilly loved Uta Hagen, and in 1980, he had the chance to act onstage with her at the Belasco Theatre in the play *Charlotte*. It was basically a monologue for Hagen, so friends asked Reilly why he took such a thankless role. He responded, "I always wanted to see Uta up close and what better way than to share a stage with her." The play only lasted five performances, but for Reilly it was worth it.

Jule Styne wanted to produce *Pal Joey* with a black cast. Harry Belafonte, Sammy Davis Jr., and others turned him down. Styne finally settled on Sugar Ray Leonard, the boxer. Musical director Buster Davis worked with Leonard on his singing, which wasn't bad except for some problems with the high notes. But Leonard had to audition for Richard Rodgers and that made Leonard, one of the most poised and self-assured men, very nervous; when it came time for him to sing, he just couldn't handle the pressure. He could go into a ring with a brute who was intent on knocking him out, but he couldn't sing in front of Richard Rodgers.

Vernon Duke and Howard Dietz wrote a musical version of the play *Rain* by Somerset Maugham. Their show was titled *Sadie Thompson*. Dietz wanted Ethel Merman to star in the show, and she was interested.

Years before, Dietz had wanted Merman to make her stage debut in *The Little Show*, but producer Dwight Deere Wiman couldn't see her talents, and so she was snatched up by Vinton Freedley for *Girl Crazy* and the rest, as they say, is history. Merman was all set for *Sadie Thompson*; in fact, sheet music was published with her name on it. But Merman's husband Robert Levitt decided he was a lyric writer (he was a newspaper executive) and rewrote Dietz's lyrics. Dietz, of course, objected, but Merman sided with her husband.

She suggested that her agent at William Morris, Sammy Worblin, make the decision. So Dietz made up two folios of the lyrics and gave them to Worblin. The agent perused them and, amazingly, decided that Levitt's were far and away better. Dietz pressed him on his decision, but he was unyielding in his praise of the neophyte's work. It was then that Dietz admitted he had put his name on Levitt's lyrics and vice versa.

But still Merman would not give up on her husband, so June Havoc took over the role. The show might have been a success with Merman, but Havoc, though talented, was not a star and couldn't save the show.

George Abbott was the first person to have actors read for parts in an audition. Before that, they'd simply have an interview with the producer.

David Merrick offered the part of Dolly Gallagher Levi to Jack Benny, the idea being that George Burns would play Vandergelder.

Leonard Sillman's *New Faces of 1936*'s rehearsals were going along swimmingly when a handsome blonde boy came into the theatre and asked if there might be any work for him. He had been in the chorus of the Roxy Theatre and demonstrated some dance steps for Sillman. Unfortunately, the show was cast and there was nothing for the lad. He was disappointed and walked to the stage door to leave. Just as his hand touched the doorknob, fate intervened. One of the chorus boys fell and sprained his ankle. Huzzah! The boy was in the right place at the right time and joined the company. And that is how Van Johnson made his Broadway debut.

When *All American* was undergoing casting, composer Charles Strouse flew to London and played the score for Ron Moody, who was then having an enormous success on the West End as Fagin in *Oliver!* Moody wanted to do the show. But director Joshua Logan wanted Ray Bolger. Strouse then spoke to Zero Mostel, who wanted to play the part. But Logan wanted Ray Bolger. Strouse says that when Bolger was cast, it was the beginning of the end for the show.

Redhead was written for Beatrice Lillie, unbelievable as that may seem. Gwen Verdon eventually played the lead role. Of course, changes were made to suit Verdon's talents, and even the title of the show was changed when Verdon was cast.

Singer Sue Hight recalled, "It was hot, hot, hot, August or late July. I went to the *Gentlemen Prefer Blondes* audition and I was the only brunette; all the rest were blondes or bottle blondes. There were ninety-seven girls there. I was only in New York for four or five weeks. David Baker and I worked up four songs, 'Take and Take and Take,' 'Who Cares,' 'He Loves and She Loves,' and 'Last Night When We Were Young.' David said 'Sing "Who Cares?" because it really shows off your voice.'"

"The first audition was an open call and I was selected for the next audition that was in the Ziegfeld Theatre. I was wearing a navy blue sun dress and stage manager Biff Liff said, 'You know, Mr. Levin will be here for the audition and, er, do you have any . . . it might be good. . . .' And I said, 'Are you talking about falsies?' He said, 'Do you mind?' I didn't mind. I didn't have any but I went and bought some. I took them to my aunt's house and showed them to her. She said, 'They're not big enough. If he wants falsies, we'll get him falsies.' And though she was bedridden with arthritis, she got up, sat in her wheelchair and we went down Madison Avenue where she bought me the biggest falsies they had."

"I put on a white orlon sweater buttoned up to the neck. There were two other girls there. The first was dancer Pat Birch, the wife of the lead dancer, Peter Birch. June Reiner, Anne Jeffries understudy in *Kiss Me, Kate*, was also there but she had a cold. Then it was my turn, with my sweater still buttoned up to the throat and me struggling to keep things in place, as it were. Just as I went to sing, the little pearl buttons gave up the fight and I burst through in all my padded glory."

When Herman Levin asked Hight what she was going to sing, she replied, "Who Cares?" Levin answered back, "I care."

"I got the part."

Liz Sheridan, who wrote a wonderful book named *Dizzy and Jimmy* about her relationship with James Dean, was a wonderful dancer, but she didn't have a lot of luck getting hired. It was surmised that she didn't get cast because she was so beautiful and more talented than anyone else on that stage. When Michael Bennett saw her, he picked her out of the chorus for *Ballroom*. He took her off to the side of the stage and said, "I'm not supposed to tell you this but you're in the show. You're not supposed to tell anyone 'til the auditions are over."

Bye, Bye, Birdie was written for Carol Haney, but she was too ill to do the show. Then Eydie Gorme was cast, but she got pregnant. Finally, they settled on Chita Rivera. Though the part was written for a Polish girl, they rewrote it with a Hispanic slant.

Neil Simon and director Herbert Ross had the bright idea of casting movie star Tony Curtis in their new production of *I Ought to Be in Pictures*. Curtis's agent, Irving "Swifty" Lazar, actually advised Simon not to cast Curtis.

The first preview out of town went as well as could be expected, and Simon and Ross congratulated Curtis. But then Simon told Curtis that the show would be even better after rewrites, and Curtis was thunderstruck. "What do you mean, rewrites? I thought this was the play. I thought what I learned was the play we were going to do." Simon tried to explain that was how shows worked, but Curtis would have none of it. "No. No way. I learned one play, that's all I can learn. Either we do this or we forget about it."

The pressure built up on Curtis and, during a matinee, while still in character, he lashed out violently at Dinah Manhoff, who was playing his daughter. Yelling obscenities, Curtis scared Manhoff, who didn't know how to respond. The curtain came down on the first act and the stage manager went to summon Curtis for the second act. He was dressing to leave the theatre, which he did. Manhoff was too upset to go on with the second act, and so their two understudies went on. Curtis was replaced by Ron Liebman.

But the story does not end there.

In his autobiography, Curtis told his side of the story, admitting that he was on drugs and in a bad place, but he still called Simon and Ross some extremely insulting names.

Benay Venuta was leaving the cast of *By Jupiter*, and a replacement was being sought. Richard Rodgers was walking down 44th Street when an agent came up to him and recommended one of his clients to take over the part. Rodgers explained that the girl was very tall and she would tower over the star, Ray Bolger. Still, the agent wouldn't give up. He asked Rodgers, "Have you seen her lately?"

John Cleese auditioned for the original Broadway production of *Half a Sixpence*. He decided to do it as a lark, thinking he'd have a good story to tell his mates. At the audition, Cleese read some pages and got a positive response. But when it came to singing, he claimed to not know any songs. He knew songs, of course, but he also knew that he didn't know how to sing. Finally, he gave an interesting rendition of "God Save the Queen." He went home and bragged that he got the part. Of course, they didn't believe him and neither did he, since it was an outright lie. But, the next morning, he got a phone call telling him he had the role. In his own words, he was "flabbergasted" beyond all belief.

Moss Hart recalled the great star Marilyn Miller. "Irving Berlin and I were in Bermuda just finishing writing *As Thousands Cheer*. They were insisting we ought to use Marilyn Miller but Irving and I were doubtful. The parade had passed, we thought, for Marilyn. We wanted someone refreshing, vibrant, youthful. Well, I got back to New York and was at a party and next to me sat, of all persons, Marilyn. She was beautiful—I cannot remember when she was more beautiful—and all the thrill of the days I used to sneak up to the balcony of the New Amsterdam and watch this lovely dream girl on the stage below came back to me. I think I was very much in love with her, and very much in awe, too, at the time.

"Well, she was gay. She seemed the most alive person in the place. She talked about many things. Her eyes danced, and I fell in love with her all over again. I thought maybe I should wire Berlin—perhaps we were making a mistake in not considering her. Then she began telling me about something that had happened some few days back. Seems she was on 42nd Street, and passing the New Amsterdam. She had the impulse to drop in. There was only an old doorman, and she had quite a time before he would let her wander backstage.

"She told me she went into her old dressing room and sat there and recalled when she had been the star and the room had been crowded with flowers and gifts from admirers. Then she went out on the stage.

"It was empty, of course. There was just a little pilot light throwing down a blueness. She walked down front and looked out on the empty house and fancied for a few seconds that the seats were occupied with the gay, well-dressed audience of those Ziegfeld years, and now she was one of the stars again and these people were waiting to cheer her.

"So she danced a few little steps, and then realized this was just an empty house and never again would there be for her those thrilling moments of opening-night triumphs.

"Well, as she told it to me, she stared out at those dusty, empty seats and the tears began to come. On that fine old stage of the New Amsterdam, Marilyn Miller, alone, in the path of a faint blue light, slumped down and sobbed. Then, she said, she ran out, hailed a cab, went to her apartment and cried for the rest of the night."

Moss Hart and Irving Berlin did cast her in *As Thousands Cheer*, and she was a triumph. However, she and co-star Clifton Webb treated cast member Ethel Waters terribly.

When the Harold Arlen and E.Y. Harburg musical *Hooray for What!* was having auditions, a young singer named Ralph Blane tried out. He didn't make the cut so he came back and tried out as a dancer; still no dice. Blane really needed the job and found out that the Kay Thompson Singers were rehearsing for the show. He joined the rehearsal and Thompson didn't seem to mind. The next day, the singing group came to audition for the Shuberts' manager Harry Kaufman, who noticed Blane. "Didn't I throw you out of here twice yesterday?"

Blane owned up and Kaufman kicked him out again. But Thompson told Kaufman that he was part of her group and that was that. Kaufman insisted that Blane leave but Arlen, Harburg, and stager/designer Vincent Minnelli stood up for him and he was part of the show. Blane had a job and met his songwriting partner Hugh Martin, who was also part of Thompson's singing group. Thompson and Kaufman would fight with each other throughout the rehearsals.

Things didn't go well for the musical. Choreographer Agnes de Mille was replaced by Robert Alton, Kay Thompson was replaced by Vivian Vance, and the romantic leads Hannah Williams and Roy Roberts were also replaced.

When Thompson was fired, she called up de Mille and told her that though she was fired, she had some good news: "Harry Kaufman fell off the stage and broke his back!"

"You're just telling me that to make me feel good," said de Mille.

Polly was a 1929 musical comedy of no great importance except for a performer who was ultimately fired. One of the stars of the show was a woman with the single moniker June. And she wrote the following: "My leading man was tall, dark and handsome but, as far as I could see, he was completely lacking in talent or skill as an actor, singer or dancer. Furthermore, he had a Cockney accent, and his name, Archie Leach, was hardly prepossessing. I liked him personally and he worked hard, but I felt sure he would have to be replaced before our New York opening."

Leach's contract was sold by Arthur Hammerstein to the Shuberts, who put him into a few desultory shows before he went to Hollywood where he changed his name to Cary Grant.

Teri Ralston would play the part of Ann when there were sing-throughs of the score of *A Little Night Music* at Stephen Sondheim's apartment. But when it came to casting the Broadway production, she was given the part of one of the lieder singers. She was also asked to be the understudy for Petra. She refused the job. Then the woman playing Petra was fired and Teri realized she could have had the role.

When Michael Crawford was leaving *Phantom of the Opera*, the powers that be met to discuss who should replace him. Strangely, they were interested in having Sammy Davis Jr. do the part. The arguments were hot and heavy until the general manager Alan Wasser said, "Wrong eye."

It seems obvious now when we associate a star with a certain role. Take Zero Mostel in *Fiddler on the Roof.* It's hard to think of someone else playing the part, but the casting wasn't easy. As lyricist Sheldon Harnick said, "We approached Danny Kaye but his wife turned us down saying he was too young to have marriage-age daughters." Television star Danny Thomas was considered for Tevye as was Tom Bosley, the star of the previous Bock-Harnick hit *Fiorello!*

Harnick remembered, "Jerry (Bock) and I wanted Howard Da Silva, another alumna from the cast of *Fiorello!* But Jerry (Robbins) said Tevye was a figure who is larger than life and Howard is wonderful but he's life-sized and that's why we should go to Zero." Librettist Joseph Stein sent Mostel the script, which was then titled *Tevye.* Mostel didn't care for it and politely told Stein he'd pass. So the search was on for other actors to play the part.

Walter Matthau was reading for the show when he stopped in the middle of his audition and said, "You know who you should get to play this part, don't you? Zero!" From out of the auditorium someone shouted, "If we could get Zero, do you think you'd be reading for it?"

If you'd like to read Mostel's wife Kate's reaction when she heard that he was turning down the part, go to the "Quotes" chapter.

Joel Grey was cast in *A Funny Thing Happened on the Way to the Forum* because he was short, and Karen Black, who was cast as Philia, was tall, and George Abbott thought it would be funny. But the audience didn't agree.

Abbott took a shine to Karen Black. But after she had a fitting for a white costume, it was dirty when she took it off. When the show was going out of town for its tryout, the stage manager offered to drive her to Pennsylvania Station to get the train. But Black said that she'd catch the train herself. The next day, she was nowhere to be found at Penn Station, and the train left without her. She had been waiting at Grand Central. She missed the show and Abbott had to fire her.

Betty Garrett was cast in the Leonard Sillman show *All in Fun.* During rehearsals, she would sometimes hear a voice in another room singing the same song she was rehearsing. It turned out that Actor's Equity had a rule that an actor could be fired after five days of rehearsal without pay. Sillman had cast four girls in the same role and had them line up on the stage and sing the song. In the end, he fired three of the girls, including Garrett, and kept the fourth.

Garrett also was cast in a road company of the show *Meet the People*. One of the women not cast was Shelley Winters, but she decided to travel with the show anyway. The night before the show was to leave for Detroit, an actress had appendicitis and Winters, who had spent her time learning everyone's part, got the job.

Of course, actors find out about roles and make it known that they're interested in being considered for a role if not actually hired on the spot. Ann Miller heard that there was a new musical titled *Ari* about to be cast. She wasted no time in calling her agent, urging him to put her name up to play Jackie Kennedy. After all, who better to play the former first lady than a brash, energetic tap dancer? Her agent regretted to tell her that *Ari* was not the story of Aristotle Onassis, but rather a musical version of the Leon Uris bestseller *Exodus*.

Ari did make it to Broadway, albeit without the thespian contributions of Ann Miller. David Cryer and Constance Towers were the leads in the roles played onscreen by Paul Newman and Eva Marie Saint. Even the usually reliable Jewish audience failed to support the show. It contained a concentration camp ballet danced by a black performer, Pi Douglas. *Ari* closed after only nineteen performances at the Mark Hellinger Theatre.

Phyllis McGuire of The McGuire Sisters was told by her agent that the Broadway musical *Dreamgirls* was coming to Las Vegas. Phyllis's ears perked up. "My sisters and I should do the show!" Her agent replied, "But they're black, Phyllis." She thought a bit and shrugged, "Well, just make them white."

William Daniels was sent the script of a new show about the Continental Congress and the signing of the Declaration of Independence, titled *1776*. Since this was during the Vietnam War while the country was wracked by protests and demonstrations, with hawks and doves literally fighting in the streets, Daniels didn't have much hope that the time was right for a show celebrating the founding of our country.

But his wife Bonnie Bartlett insisted that the part of John Adams was right for him so Daniels reluctantly made his way to the 46th Street Theatre (now the Richard Rodgers Theatre) only to find that the stage door was shut. Aha! He had his out. While walking to the bus stop, his conscience brought forth images of his wife berating him for giving up so soon. Daniels went to a pay phone (yes, that's how long ago it was) and called his agent who was understandably angry. "Where are you? They're waiting for you!"

she screamed. "They're at the Ziegfeld Theatre waiting to hear you sing. Take a taxi, I'll pay for it!"

When he arrived at the Ziegfeld, the producer and director told him that they just wanted composer Sherman Edwards to hear him sing. Daniels sang "Wait 'Til We're Sixty-Five" just as he had done in *On a Clear Day You Can See Forever*, except that he forgot the words. Well, no matter. He was cast, but he still had his doubts.

Come the first day of rehearsals and the cast is rehearsing the beginning of the show with Daniels as the lead. They're all singing in harmony when Daniels thought, "Jesus, guys, this sounds good. This may be something."

When auditions were held for the original production of *Cabaret*, songwriters John Kander and Fred Ebb would tell each of the women who auditioned for Sally Bowles, "Don't tell anyone but you were the best Sally." Penny Fuller, Lee Lawson, and Nancy Dussault were all promised that they would be starring as Sally. Imagine their surprise when they looked in *The Sunday New York Times* and saw a full-page ad trumpeting the show with Jill Haworth as the lead. Apparently, librettist Joe Masteroff said to producer/director Harold Prince after the auditions, "Why aren't we casting a British girl?" Since Jill Haworth was the only British woman to make the cut, she was immediately cast.

Penny Fuller was given the consolation prize. She was cast as the understudy for Sally when the show came to New York. She went on in the part after only three rehearsals and with a terrible hangover. Fuller was terrific in the role and played it over one hundred times. When Haworth left the show, Fuller was offered the role, but she decided that she had done it enough and was going to the West Coast to be in television and movies. So they hired Anita Gillette to be the standby while Haworth completed her run, and then Anita took over and was in the show for two years.

The practice of promising people they had a part when they didn't was quite usual in the theatre. Kaye Ballard was told by the producers not to tell anyone that she was cast in the title role of *The Unsinkable Molly Brown*. But the Monday paper announced that Tammy Grimes had been cast.

Did any other show ever go through as many casting machinations as *Mack and Mabel*? We don't think so. The men had it easy. Jerry Orbach was originally signed, but when Robert Preston showed up, Orbach was unsigned.

But the women had it bad, really bad. Gower Champion called Penny Fuller on her birthday and said, "I'm in the office of David Merrick and we want you to be Mabel in our new musical *Mack and Mabel*. We'll be in touch." Six months later, Champion called again and said, "When can you come in and audition?" She did and didn't get the part.

Marcia Rodd was signed to the part without auditioning, but Champion told her they had to go through the motions of seeing bigger names. Then Champion attended the Rodgers and Hart revue *Words and Music*, loved Kelly Garrett, and fired Marcia Rodd. Poor Kelly Garrett, how could she know that her joy would be so short-lived? While rehearsing, Champion brought Bernadette Peters into the rehearsal room. Garret asked Champion what Peters was doing there, and he replied, "Oh, she's here just checking out the space. Garret went on her lunch break and when she returned, she was notified that she had been replaced by Peters. Garrett was severely traumatized. Is it any surprise that the Broadway community dubbed the show *Mack and Maybe*?

Another David Merrick extravaganza went through similar upheavals. *The Baker's Wife* seemed like such a good idea. And it was. However, Topol, the leading man, was fired. Then Joe Hardy, the director, was fired. The choreographer was fired. Merrick fired the leading lady Carole Demas and replaced her with Patti LuPone, who was happy the show closed in Washington, D.C.

Merrick hated the song "Meadowlark" and asked Stephen Schwartz to take it out of the show. Schwartz refused, so Merrick snuck into the orchestra pit and removed the sheet music from all the orchestra books. At the next performance, when the musicians came to that part of the show and turned their pages, there was no music. At that moment, Schwartz ran up to Merrick and asked what had happened. Merrick just shrugged as if he didn't know.

When it was time to cast *Funny Girl*, the first choice was Mary Martin, who turned it down. Then came Anne Bancroft. Then came Carol Burnett, who told the authors, "Get yourself a Jewish girl." They did.

Anita Gillette was told to audition for the part of Tilda Mullen in *Do Re Mi*. She was instructed to meet Jule Styne at his apartment. So Anita's husband drove her over to Styne's apartment and waited for her downstairs. He didn't have to wait long.

As soon as she entered, Styne started chasing her around the apartment. Anita was pregnant at the time and lactating. Every time Styne grabbed her breasts, milk would squirt out. So there they were running around the apartment with the great composer squeezing Anita's breasts and milk soaking her blouse. After a few laps, Anita managed to grab her coat and run down to the car with her husband waiting inside.

She didn't get the part.

Sometimes a creative team has an idea for who they want for a part, but somehow it doesn't work out as planned.

The creators of the raucous musical *I Had a Ball* wanted to cast zaftig comedian Totie Fields in the lead as a crooked fortuneteller. When she didn't work out, they turned to the brilliant English comic Beatrice Lillie. But she had just played a psychic in the musical *High Spirits* and didn't want to be typecast in another show. So the leading character was rewritten as a male and Buddy Hackett was cast in the part.

The producers of *I Can Get It for You Wholesale* wanted Nancy Walker to play the secretary Miss Marmelstein. The role went to an unknown, Barbra Streisand.

Charles Strouse wanted Jack Lemmon to play Albert Peterson in *Bye, Bye, Birdie*.

Finally, sometimes an agent succeeds in getting an actor a part in a show, but it doesn't quite work out as planned. A William Morris agent worked hard to get a client of his a starring role on Broadway, replacing Molly Picon in Jerry Herman's first musical *Milk and Honey*. The show's producers liked the actress, and the agent was quite pleased with his work. He called the actress only to discover that she had been dead for months.

Deborah Kerr was offered Robert Anderson's *Tea and Sympathy* and turned it down. Elia Kazan, the director, didn't want Deborah Kerr for the play. But Anderson begged Kazan to at least meet with her and after a genial tea, he wrote to Anderson, "You are absolutely right, and she's going to do it."

At the third rehearsal, Kerr wouldn't come out of her dressing room. So Kazan went in and told her how good she was going to be, and how proud they were to have her in the play, and she had done her hair beautifully, and she was going to be "damn good in the part." Kazan was right; she was magnificent.

Tea and Sympathy's audiences were very quiet as they watched the play, though some people giggled in embarrassment at certain points. The giggling threw the cast, but Kazan explained to them, "You are talking about things onstage in front of a thousand people which husbands and wives don't talk about in the intimacy of their own bedrooms."

When the play was deemed a success, the giggling stopped, and that bothered Kazan, "Audiences respect success, unfortunately. It is one of the problems in the whole country, that the whole country respects success a lot."

When offered the role of Pseudolus in *A Funny Thing Happened on the Way to the Forum*, Phil Silvers just couldn't see any wiggle room to provide his own magic in case the show would be in trouble on the road like his other shows. So he turned down the part though he did act in the show when it was revived on Broadway. Next the producers solicited Milton Berle. He thought the show was terrific as did his wife Ruth, on whom Milton relied for guidance. Ruth didn't laugh once during the presentation by Larry Gelbart and Stephen Sondheim, but that was because she had just had plastic surgery on her eyes and couldn't move her face. Sadly, Berle turned down the role when his lawyers got into the act.

Before they were even finished writing their new play *To the Ladies*, George S. Kaufman and Marc Connelly and their producer George Tyler approached Helen Hayes to star in it. Connelly said to Hayes, "Of course you play the piano?" She responded, "Why, certainly." "Good," replied Connelly. "We have an idea for one of the acts—and it will help immeasurably if you play the piano."

And when the show opened, Hayes played the piano beautifully, as promised. Months later Connelly learned that Hayes started piano lessons the day after their conversation.

When Billy Rose was in Texas conducting auditions for his show at the Fort Worth Fair, in came the unknown, untested, and nonprofessional Mary Martin. She was dressed in men's clothing: a full dress suit and a silk high hat. Rose asked her to sing and she came up with a rendition of "Gloomy Monday." Rose asked, "Can't you sing anything else?" Martin replied that it was the only song she liked. She further told him that she was married and had a child. Rose gave her the following advice, "Forget show business, go home and take care of the dishes and the diapers."

Years later, when she was a star, she appeared in a show put together by Rose to celebrate New Year's Eve 1949. Rose had taken over the New Amsterdam roof for the occasion and dubbed the room "Chez Eleanor" in honor of his wife, the Olympic swimmer Eleanor Holms. Martin stood up and said, "And now, I would like to introduce 'diapers' in person. There he is!" Rising from his seat was Martin's son Larry Hagman.

Leonard Sillman was a remarkable person. He was in love with the theatre at a very young age and is best known today as the producer and brains behind the *New Faces* series of revues. Many a future star was discovered by Sillman, including Henry Fonda, Eartha Kitt, Inga Swenson, Maggie Smith, Paul Lynde, Imogene Coca, and many others.

Sillman got his start in the theatre when producer/director Ned Wayburn told him that a job was in the offing. Wayburn was offering Sillman the chance to work in stock in Philadelphia. This engagement would give Sillman a chance to act with such stars of their time as Gus Shy, Marie Dahm, and Edna French, the latter two being former beauties on the New Amsterdam stage working for Florenz Ziegfeld.

Sillman would have the opportunity to play several character parts, roles that were usually played by a number of actors but the budget would not allow for a large cast. That was the good news. The bad news was that there would be seven shows a day. Each show would last one hour and a half. Wayburn further illuminated Sillman when he told the novice, "The most you'll have to appear is twenty or thirty times in each show." And for that work, Sillman would receive the munificent sum of $20 per week.

Sillman was in heaven during the rehearsals and even when the show opened. Sillman talked about his many roles in the play *Honeymoon Cruise*. "I played twenty-three parts. The first was the Shah of Persia and my entrance consisted of stepping into the midst of twenty harem girls. Then I played the eighty-year-old man. Then I appeared in a succession of crowd scenes and mass meetings. I danced in a chorus and sang in a choir. I was a sailor, a beggar, an Indian, a chiropractor, an aviator, a Western Union boy, a chicken farmer from Utah." Ah, youth!

J.P. McEvoy was a well-known writer who contributed the phrase "Cut to the chase" to the English language. He also wrote sketches for the musical revue *Americana*. Humorist Robert Benchley wrote a monologue, "The Treasurer's Report," and was looking for someone to recite it in the show. When he met McEvoy's chauffeur, he knew he had found his man. Charles Butterworth, who had never acted before, was a great success and had a long career on Broadway and in Hollywood.

Another notable casting occurred in *Americana*. Composer Phil Charig had a girlfriend whom he thought would be great in the show. So he brought her to the producer Richard Herndon. Herndon signed her but when the show opened in Atlantic City, it was clear that she wasn't right for the part. Herndon fired the young girl, and she and Charig were distraught.

The show moved to New York and a week before the opening night, Charig told Herndon that he had written a song especially for his girlfriend. If Herndon would just give her a chance, he wouldn't regret it. So on opening night, Charig's girlfriend sat on the edge of the stage with her legs hanging into the orchestra pit, just like Judy Garland would later do. She addressed the audience, "My name isn't in the program but I'd like to sing a song called 'Nobody Wants Me.'" She sang the song and became that legendary thing, an overnight sensation. Her name was Helen Morgan.

Lightning would strike twice for Herndon. His next musical, *Merry-Go-Round*, played the Klaw Theatre in 1927. Leonard Sillman insisted that Herndon listen to his friend sing. He promised that she was the most fantastic singer. So an audition was arranged. It took place, believe it or not, in the basement of the Holy Cross Church on 47th Street while upstairs Mass was proceeding.

The singer had an off day, no makeup, a ratty dress, and she sang flat, really flat. But Herndon saw something special in her and signed her for the show. On opening night, she came out to sing "Hogan's Alley." She leaned against the proscenium and started to sing. But, as in her audition, she was flat. Sillman was just around the corner of the proscenium with a pitch pipe. He was there in case of such an emergency. But the singer didn't hear her note. So Sillman sang the song, and she found her pitch. Her name was Libby Holman.

When producer Guthrie McClintic announced he was mounting a revival of *Playboy of the Western World*, Maureen Stapleton called his office. McClintic himself answered the phone. The anxious actress jumped right in and said, "Mr. McClintic, my name is Maureen Stapleton and I played Pegeen Mike in stock this summer and I wondered who was going to play her in your production?

McClintic told her that he didn't know who was going to play it, and besides he didn't think he needed to tell her in any event. This got Stapleton's dander up, and she told the producer, "Well, I don't give a goddamn who's going to play it, so you don't have to tell me!" She started to put down the receiver when she heard McClintic say, "How would you like to come and see me, Miss Stapleton?"

This took her by surprise but she agreed to come to his office. She showed up and, by Stapleton's own account, didn't shut her mouth for over three hours. They never mentioned *Playboy*, but Maureen told him the entire story of her life, bad and good, ups and downs, ins and outs. He concluded the meeting, telling her she'd hear from him before the week was over.

On the following Saturday, he asked that she come down. She had finally gotten her audition! But when she got there, she was shocked to find out that she did not have an audition. It was the first rehearsal, and she had the part.

As an aside, McClintic's wife Katherine Cornell was one of Broadway's greatest actresses, so great that she actually took part in understudy rehearsals, something no other actress would consider doing.

Directly after *Playboy* closed, Stapleton was hired by McClintic and Cornell to tour with them in *The Barretts of Wimpole Street* and when that tour was concluded, she joined them in *Antony and Cleopatra* on Broadway.

Antony and Cleopatra featured Lenore Ulric, who was a great actress in her time and had also been the mistress of producer David Belasco. Ulric was playing a supporting role, but she didn't mind. Katherine Cornell was so kind, she gave Ulric the star dressing room when they were on the road.

The set had a large turntable that revolved to bring on the cast and set pieces. At one performance, the spear carriers, which included a young Tony Randall, stood in place in their Roman soldier garb. The turntable revolved while Ulric and Stapleton watched from the wings. As the men revolved past them, Ulric remarked to Stapleton, "See anything you like, dear?"

The turntable also created a bit of a problem. Sir Cedric Hardwicke played Caesar and a young Charleton Heston was making his Broadway debut in a minor role. Hardwicke was to make his entrance on the turntable. Heston would then come on saying, "Hail Caesar, I have dispatches," and hand scrolls to Hardwicke. The turntable moved, but there was no Caesar. Heston, seeking to save the situation, made his entrance, scrolls aloft in his hand. He strode across the turntable to the stage right wings, calling "Ahoy, Caesar!" Perhaps he mistook the turntable for a boat.

One day someone suggested to Tennessee Williams that Leonore Ulric might make a good Amanda in *The Glass Menagerie*. Ulric was aghast. "Why, that's a mother role!" she exclaimed, thereby taking herself out of the running for one of the greatest dramatic roles.

Stapleton made her mark on Broadway as Serafina in the original production of Tennessee Williams's play *The Rose Tattoo*. She was only twenty-four-years old. She herself wasn't sure she could pull off the part. As she told Williams, producer Cheryl Crawford, and others, "Look, I don't know about this. I can't promise you that I can do this part, 'cause I don't know. I'd like to play it, but I can't promise." To which Williams responded, "I don't care if she turns into a dead mule on opening night. I want her for the part!"

Speaking of Tennessee Williams and *The Rose Tattoo*, after Stapleton was cast, it was time to cast the children. The first child came on all bravado and declared, "My name is Judy Ratner and I don't go to school." Daniel Mann, the director, asked her why not. She replied, "I have a tutor." Mann said, "Oh, so you have a tutor." She replied, "Yeah." "And what does he do?" To which little Judy Ratner replied, "He toots." She got the part even though she wasn't really right for the role. But Williams loved her attitude. When she left the stage, Williams exclaimed, "Did you see? She has no neck! That child has no neck!" Those of you who know Williams's plays know that four years later in *Cat on a Hot Tin Roof*, Williams used the phrase "no neck monsters."

Williams had a fourteen-year relationship with Frank Merlo, who handled the nitty-gritty for him. Merlo had a dry wit of his own. When he and Williams were meeting in Hollywood with Darryl Zanuck of 20th Century, the studio head inquired of Merlo, "And what do you do?" Merlo grinned at Zanuck and replied, "I sleep with Mr. Williams." That was telling him! (Note: Some sources credit the conversation to Frank Merlo and Jack Warner.)

Williams himself had a similar sense of humor. He didn't quite trust reviewers. He once wrote, "I do not say 'fuck the drama critics' because fucking is too good for them."   *what a charmer*

When Jack Gilford's wife Madeline was a young girl, she heard that there was a part open in Maxwell Anderson's play *The Eve of St. Mark*. She put on her best outfit, very chic and beautiful, but she didn't get an audition. The next day, she figured she'd try again. This time, she wore a red dress slit low . . . as low as propriety allowed. She got the audition and the part.

When Jack Gilford was just starting out, someone saw him performing at a benefit and told him that he should be in the revue *Meet the People*, which was trying out in Los Angeles. Gilford took the train to L.A. but was unable to get seen for the show. A while later, he was invited to a party and, like most show-biz parties at the time, people got up and performed. Gilford did his bit and Elliott Sullivan, who happened to be in *Meet the People*, asked him if he would be interested in joining the show. He was, and that went on to become his first Broadway show.

Betty Garrett had a friend Gussie Kirschner who would go up to complete strangers and strike up a conversation. One night she was at Carnegie Hall and started talking to one of the ushers. She asked what he did when he wasn't ushering. He explained that he was the stage manager for Orson Welles who was then in the middle of directing *Danton's Death*. Gussie said to the usher, "I have a young actress friend and I want you to get her a job with him."

Garrett went down to the rehearsal, which was a madhouse, as was usual with Welles at the helm. She tapped Welles on the shoulder but he was otherwise engaged. Without really looking at her he said, "Okay, you're cast." She had a little scene as a maid but the part was soon cut. Still, she was among the rabble underneath the stage that made crowd noises. She wasn't actually seen in her Broadway debut, but she was heard, sort of.

Finally, Garrett got her big chance, a part in the Cole Porter musical *Something for the Boys*. She had her own song, "I'm in Love with a Soldier Boy," and was the understudy for Ethel Merman. When Garrett finished the number, Merman came right out on the stage for her next scene. Since the audience was still applauding Garrett, Merman called her back onstage to take another bow.

One day, Merman got laryngitis and couldn't go on. Garrett was nervous as hell. Merman told her the line that became one of her best-known quotes, "Listen, kid, if they could do it better than you, they'd be on the stage and you'd be in the audience." The producers wanted to close the show that evening, but Merman convinced them to keep it open and give Garrett her break.

Fred Ebb recalled that a seventeen-year-old Liza Minnelli was recommended to him by a friend. Minnelli came to Ebb's house and asked what he was working on. He played her some of the songs from *Flora, the Red Menace*, and she got very excited. She sang a few of them and Ebb was excited too.

Ebb told director George Abbott about Minnelli, but Abbott had seen her in the off-Broadway revival of *Best Foot Forward* and didn't like her. Abbott was waiting to hear from Eydie Gorme. Abbott finally told Ebb, "I don't like the girl but bring her in." Minnelli learned "A Quiet Thing" to sing for Abbott, but when she came on the stage to sing, she overheard him say, "Well, this is a waste of time!" Her audition suffered. Abbott stuck fast to his decision, and Ebb had to call Minnelli and tell her she didn't get the show.

But then Eydie Gorme decided not to make her Broadway debut in the show and Minnelli was hired. Eventually, Abbott came to see just how talented Minnelli was. When the show flopped, Abbott blamed himself for the failure. He liked Minnelli so much that he protected her from playing anything negative.

Edie Adams went to an audition for the role of Eileen in *Wonderful Town*. There were almost 400 girls auditioning and Adams didn't even get to sing. The receptionist told her that her blonde hair and hazel eyes didn't fit the role. After a few weeks, the role was still not cast. Director George Abbott was getting nervous. Abbott called Richard Rodgers to see if he had anyone to suggest for the role. Rodgers turned to his assistant John Fernley, who nominated "the one that refused to be an understudy for *South Pacific*." That girl, the one who turned down the understudy role for Mary Martin, was Edie Adams.

Adams was called in and told to bring along shorts and stockings. She dressed as demurely and young as she could, sang her song, and was asked to go to a dressing room and put on the shorts and stockings. Adams was skeptical about having to change and asked why it was necessary. She was told there was a part in the script where she and the star Rosalind Russell swap stockings. So Adams changed and read the scene. When she was finished, someone said, "Thank you," which usually means that you didn't get the part. So she stomped up to the dressing room in a snit. She changed and went home.

Meanwhile, in the theatre, George Abbott was waiting for her, wondering why she was taking so long getting into her street clothes. Finally, Hal Prince, the second assistant stage manager, called her at home and reported to Abbott that she left because she thought there wasn't any use coming down the stairs only to be told she didn't have the job. Abbott said to Prince, "Well, that's our Eileen, all right."

While she was rehearsing, she'd get direction from George Abbott, from the lyricists Comden and Green, from choreographer Donald Saddler, and from the librettists Jerome Chodorov and Joseph Fields, who wanted the blocking and performance exactly as in the play version. Needless to say, she was a mess.

Rosalind Russell's pianist Lou Kessler told her not to give up her day job. What did that mean? She then found out that other girls were auditioning for the part. So she called up George Abbott and explained the situation with the five directors. The next day, he told everyone to lay off her, that only he was to give the actors notes. The other auditions stopped. But there was to be one more director on *Wonderful Town*; Jerome Robbins came in at the request of George Abbott.

The great thing about having so many plays opening, touring, and in rehearsal somewhere was that almost any good actor could find work. And there was enough regular work for actors to go from one play to another and thus hone their craft.

Even in the 1940s and '50s, there were enough musicals coming through the pipeline such that chorus singers and dancers would give their notice on opening night and have work the next day in a new show coming along. And that's why they were called "gypsies."

Naturally, it was also difficult to cast shows when there were over 200 shows opening in one season all competing for the best talents. Some performers got lucky breaks. James Cagney, Cary Grant, and Wallace Beery all came from the chorus to become big stars in Hollywood.

The Shuberts solved their casting problems by being intensely loyal to their chorus members. The head of casting for chorus roles was a gentleman who was known by the nickname "Ma." He could shuffle his girls and boys from show to show, ensuring that there was never a lack of talent for chorus roles. As the years rolled on, some of these folks grew old in the employ of the Shuberts. And those who were once attractive, fresh-faced youths when they started might be in the umpteenth revival of *Blossom Time* still singing the same chorus roles in middle age. When they aged out of usefulness on Broadway, the Shuberts would farm them out across the country in the same shows since the sticks weren't so discerning.

When Liza Minnelli came to her friend Fred Ebb and asked if she could be in *The Rink*, he told his collaborators, "We can have Liza in the show, but my vote is against it." Of course, she did get the part, but her representatives were terrible with arguments about billing, the number of songs, etc., and the Liza that the audience came to see wasn't the character she played. Finally, Ebb admitted, "The show was tough, and I think the casting of her was a fatal mistake."

The Earl Carroll Vanities of 1932 was closing in New York, and there was a part for an English straight man. Brice Hitchens was cast alongside Milton Berle who had starred in the show on Broadway. Berle was curious about the Brit. Something about him seemed not right. He cornered the singer backstage and asked him outright who he was. After a little back and forth, Hitchens admitted he was actually Charles Clarence Robert Orville Cummings. He'd already been on Broadway briefly in a flop play, *The Roof*. In that show, he was billed as Blade Stanhope Conway and played an Englishman, the Hon. Reggie Fanning. Hitchens's secret was safe with Berle. And he played again in *The Ziegfeld Follies of 1934* where he introduced the song "I Like the Likes of You." After that, he went back to the name that would follow him from Broadway to television, Robert Cummings.

Richard Kiley went down to the Majestic Theatre to audition for *South Pacific*. The other auditioning actors had great operatic voices, and that intimidated Kiley. Just before he was to sing, the guy before him belted "The Song of the Open Road," the song that Kiley was going to sing. Kiley thought about just leaving the theatre, but when his name was called, he announced, "You've just heard the definitive version of that song. Here is the comic version." He didn't get the job. But Richard Rodgers did cast Kiley in *No Strings* and Kiley reminded Rodgers about his audition. Rodgers responded, "Jesus Christ, was that you? Oscar and I would often say to each other, 'Whatever happened to that poor son-of-a-bitch?'"

Albert Marre wanted Kiley to play the Caliph in *Kismet* opposite Joan Diener and Alfred Drake. When they went into rehearsal, Drake realized that both he and Kiley were baritones. So when Kiley would rehearse a song, Drake would suggest he sing it in a higher key. This went on so often that Kiley was singing tenor by opening night. And from then on, the role of the Caliph has been sung by a tenor.

Don Pippin really wanted the musical director job on *Oliver!* He called David Merrick's office and Merrick's secretary Helen Nickerson advised Pippin that he wouldn't get the job. Pippin told Nickerson that he'd like Merrick himself to tell him. So he was given an appointment to see the great man. Pippin had his nerve up: "I walked into his office, all red and black. His desk was on a platform and he really looked like the devil. Merrick didn't even look up. He just said, 'Yes.'" It startled Pippin, but he didn't speak until Merrick looked up. "I had a lot of chutzpah and said, 'You're bringing over *Oliver!* and I want to be musical director of that show.'" Merrick was really shocked. He looked down at his papers and wrote some things. "Why should I give it to you?" That floored Pippin, but he walked right up to the desk and said, almost nose-to-nose with Merrick, "Because I love that show and I love the music and nobody can do it as well as I can." Merrick was stunned. He looked at Pippin and said, "All right, I'm going to give you this show. But you better be as good as you say you are." On his way out, Pippin told Nickerson that he got the show and Nickerson said, "You're kidding!"

During the run of the show, at one intermission, the PR person walked up to Pippin in the orchestra pit and told him he was nominated for a Tony. Pippin looked at her confused and asked, "A Tony what?" He had never heard of the Tony Awards. Pippin won the award and when he got back to his seat, Merrick put his arm around Pippin and said, "You're as good as you said you are."

At an audition onstage for the musical *A Doll's Life*, an actress came in wearing period dress, a wig, and full makeup. She started her monologue and from the audience, director Hal Prince said, "What is that shit on your face? Wash it off and come back in later!"

Actor James Spahn got an audition for the Norman Wisdom musical *Walking Happy*. On the day of the audition, he woke up early, made himself a healthy vegetable smoothie, went to the gym to work off some of his nerves, and then went to his vocal coach to make sure his voice was in top shape. He got to the theatre in plenty of time. Finally, he was called up on the stage to sing his audition song, Cole Porter's "So in Love" from *Kiss Me,*

Kate. The pianist played the intro and Spahn sang "Strange dear . . ." and then was told that was enough and was excused.

Ken Kantor was auditioning for George Abbott's production of *Damn Yankees.* Abbott was a very decisive fellow. They asked Kantor to sing "You've Got to Have Heart." Kantor sang "You've gotta have heart, miles and miles of heart" when Abbott stopped him. Then they asked Kantor to read the line "Joe, you've been a fine boy this last six months." Abbott had him read the line again, only with the emphasis on the word "you." Kantor did so and was dismissed from the audition. Kantor was positive he didn't get the job, but he did. That's all Abbott needed to make up his mind.

Director George S. Kaufman was late for *Guys and Dolls* auditions. When he finally arrived, actor B.S. Pully's temper was getting shorter and shorter. Finally, he called out, "Are we going to fucking audition or what?" When Kaufman heard that he cried, "That's our Big Jule!"

Jack Klugman was called in to audition for *Gypsy* but he demurred, saying he wasn't a singer. They asked him to sing "You'll Never Get Away from Me" to Ethel Merman. Klugman agreed but told the men behind the table, "If Merman belts, I'm walking out." So Merman sang so softly and sweetly that her voice cracked. When that happened, it gave Klugman such courage that he felt he sang like Ezio Pinza.

Bob Fosse's auditions were famous because 200 or 300 people would show up at the open calls, and that was for only men or only women. The first thing Fosse did was talk to the dancers and explain that he had to eliminate some of them although they were all excellent dancers. He felt so bad about cutting dancers from auditions. For those who were left, he'd have them do a little combination and then say to them, "Please wait upstage" or "Thank you very much." When he got down to twenty men or twenty women, he always taught a routine to the song "Tea for Two," a scene that is recreated in the film *All That Jazz.* In that movie, the director asks the performers to please leave their bags off the stage and wait either in the wings or in the audience. Our next anecdote explains why.

Joe Layton auditioned 500 women for twenty parts in *No Strings.* One of the women was told "Thank you," and she hit the roof. "Is that all I get for ten fuckin' years of training? A thank you? Who the fuck do you think you are, talking to me like that?" And she went on and on before stomping out. One of the other dancers auditioning told Layton that he was lucky. At the auditions for *Little Me,* the same dancer had hit Bob Fosse with her rehearsal bag and knocked him into the orchestra pit.

Richard Kiley was so nervous auditioning for *Redhead* that both director Bob Fosse and star Gwen Verdon sang along with him. He got the part.

Lisa Kirk, Nanette Fabray, Dolores Gray, Kaye Ballard, and Alice Ghostley were all considered for the leading role in *Mame*. But something about each of them didn't seem quite right. The producers wanted Judy Garland for the part, and she would have been terrific, but she was too, shall we say, undependable for a huge musical. Jerry Herman saw a Playbill for *Anyone Can Whistle* and was reminded of just how terrific Lansbury was. The producers were not convinced. So Herman secretly rehearsed Lansbury at his house and taught her two of the songs from the show, "It's Today" and "If He Walked into My Life." Herman even gave her some blocking for the numbers. She had only two days to learn the songs, and the day of the audition, another plan was hatched. For, unbeknown to the production team watching the audition, it was Jerry Herman himself in the pit accompanying Lansbury.

FOUR STORIES ABOUT JOSH LOGAN CASTING

Auditioning by singing for the creative team as William Daniels did is the usual way to get cast. Early one morning around seven o'clock, a bleary-eyed Elaine Stritch went to walk her little dog. When the elevator arrived to take her to the lobby, the door opened and there was Jack Cassidy coming down from an upper floor. Cassidy, grinning, said to Stritch, "Guess what, Elaine! I just got cast in *Wish You Were Here*!" It wasn't until she was on the street with her dog that she realized that the show's director Joshua Logan lived on a floor above hers.

The chorus of *Wish You Were Here* was cast in a different way. The show had what's known as a coup de theatre (i.e., something extremely bold or inventive that sets it apart from other shows). In this case, there was an actual swimming pool on the stage of the Imperial Theatre. One day, Thomas Tryon, who later wrote the novel *The Other*, auditioned for a part in the show. Auditioning actors were told to bring a swimsuit to the tryout. While waiting on line outside the stage door, a truck driver pulled up and asked what was going on. Tryon told him they were having auditions for a musical. The driver asked, "Can anybody try out?" and Tryon said, "Sure." So the guy got on line.

When the truck driver was called onstage, Josh Logan asked him if he had a swimsuit. And they guy said, "No." So he stripped down to his briefs. Tryon was cast in the show and so was the truck driver.

When auditioning actors for *Picnic*, Logan had the male actors wear jeans. During the auditions, they were hosed down so Logan could see exactly how their pants fit and what was "emphasized."

Josh Logan made sure that he had attractive casts in all his shows. And he loved to have guys with their shirts off whenever he could. It's not a surprise that directors want to cast beautiful women and handsome men for sex appeal. It's what used to be called "casting for the tired businessman." We think it was Abe Burrows who said, "If you don't want your musical to fail, the audience must know who they want to fuck."

GWEN VERDON'S AUDITIONS

Mitzi Gaynor was the first choice to play Lola in *Damn Yankees*, but she turned it down.

After her smash success in *Can-Can*, Gwen Verdon was offered the role. Even though she had almost no experience playing an acting role, Harold Prince and Robert Griffith believed in her and desperately wanted her.

Verdon remembered, "My audition for *Damn Yankees* was for singing only—not dancing." She still didn't know if she got the part when Harold Prince came up to her and asked her to meet him and the director George Abbott at Roseland. "He loves to dance, and he'd like to get to know you," said Prince to Verdon, but she knew it was still an audition.

"I almost blew it," Verdon later recalled. "Halfway through the evening I told Mr. Abbott he was on the wrong beat. And he stopped right there, and he made me sit down. And then he hired one of the hostesses to dance with him for the rest of the night, while Hal held my hand. I figured that was that for me."

Of course it wasn't, but Verdon was plenty scared. Though she was an unexpected smash in a supporting part in *Can-Can* (to leading lady Lilo's chagrin), this was her first starring part in a musical, so a lot was riding on it.

The next obstacle came when choreographer Bob Fosse had misgivings about working with Verdon, and she had her doubts about him. She was an unproven singer and actor, and Fosse only had one Broadway credit to his name. The two of them met in a rehearsal hall and they tried each other on for size. Luckily, everyone agreed to work together on the show.

Verdon recalled how hard it was to learn Fosse's choreography. "For the number 'Lola' Bob told me it had to be sexy and said 'I'll show you—I'll dance it for you.' I think I'd faint if I had to act sexy. I'd look like I needed a ham sandwich. He choreographed the dance in extreme detail, even to when I could blink!"

At a Thursday night performance, one of Verdon's songs was not landing with audiences even though everyone connected with the show thought it was a sure thing. Director George Abbott said, "The audience doesn't know who the character is. We'll need another scene and a new song to introduce her. And we need it for Saturday matinee." Richard Adler and Jerry Ross wrote the song the following day, played it for Verdon, who said she loved it but would never be able to learn it by Saturday. Abbott said, "No problem." The song was performed in front of a drop; a stage manager was behind it whispering the lyrics to Verdon. At that performance, "Whatever Lola Wants" stopped the show.

Gwen again: "I auditioned four times for *New Girl in Town*. When Marilyn Monroe couldn't sing and Shelley Winters couldn't dance, I got it."

CHAPTER 8
Rehearsals

Judy Holiday was very afraid she'd be a bomb in *Bells Are Ringing*. She went up to Jule Styne before rehearsals and started to say she had changed her mind. Styne told her, "That's fine. But we will sue you."

The day before the first rehearsal of *Fiddler on the Roof*, Jerome Robbins sent Harold Prince a note that he would be bowing out of directing the show. Hal Prince, in turn, sent Robbins a telegram telling him that it was fine; he'd just have to cover the cost of the production.

The morning of the first rehearsal of *Follies*, Harold Prince awoke to find that his eyes were yellow. He thought he might have jaundice but it dawned on him that it was simply fear.

When Diahann Carroll met Joe Layton before rehearsals began for *No Strings*, she told him that she absolutely could not dance. For nine weeks he rehearsed her. On opening night out of town, she stood there and did not dance during the first number. Layton was angry and told the entire company to come downstairs after the performance. Carroll was scared; although Layton didn't get angry easily, she felt he was going to chew her out in front of the company. So she decided to lead with humor, and not only humor, but racial humor. She proclaimed, "Joe, I guess this proves to you that we all do not have rhythm. So don't ask me to do any of that shit anymore." Layton choreographed the entire show around Carroll, and his staging was revolutionary.

During *On A Clear Day*'s rehearsals, Burton Lane came out into the lobby where he found Robert Lewis, the director. Lane asked Lewis, "What are you doing in the lobby?" Lewis replied, "They're doing choreography." Lane retorted, "I thought you were the director of the whole show."

In the Nathan Lane revival of *A Funny Thing Happened on the Way to the Forum*, Bill Duell was playing the old man Erronius who has to run seven times around the Seven Hills of Rome. Duell was an older man who, amazingly, was still looking after his very elderly mother. He was the first guy to show up at rehearsal. Duell had a routine when he got to the rehearsal room. He first hung up his coat, then ate a snack, got his props, and waited offstage right for his first entrance. At one rehearsal, before they got to his part in the show, they broke for lunch.

Duell returned to the rehearsal room, hung up his coat, got his props, and waited offstage right for his cue. Finally, at 4:30, they got around to his entrance. He got his cue, went out onstage and said, "Line." It had taken so long to get around to him, he had completely forgotten his first line. The company broke up and couldn't stop laughing even when they started the scene over. Director Jerry Zaks had no option but to cancel rehearsal for that day.

During rehearsals of *The Music Man*, the producer Kermit Bloomgarden and Robert Preston himself were unsure whether he was truly musical theatre material. In the roles he had previously played in the movies, he had never done a musical. So they mutually agreed that if it wasn't working out, at the end of two weeks, they would part as friends.

Likewise, when *How to Succeed* was in rehearsals, they hired an actor to learn all of Rudy Vallee's part. He waited around until the producers were sure Vallee could do the show. By the way, Vallee drove them all crazy throughout the run.

Ann Shoemaker took over from Charlotte Rae when *Half a Sixpence* was still in rehearsals. Shoemaker was not a fun gal. In fact, another of the show's actors, Carrie Nye, quipped, "Apparently, when you break the ice with Ann, there's a lot of cold water underneath."

George Abbott was directing *Damn Yankees*. One of the actors had to make a phone call in the scene, but the scene wasn't working. There was something wrong. Abbott's solution was to tell the actor that he was dialing the wrong number. The actor was perplexed. What did that mean he was dialing the wrong number? Abbott explained that the performer needed to dial all seven digits. The audience didn't believe the scene because the actor was dialing only two or three digits.

The Boston reviews came out for *Prettybelle* and they were fiercely negative. Gower Champion told the company, "I have to get back to New York but I'll come back right away and we'll put in changes." He never returned.

Burton Lane and his wife Lynn went to Philadelphia to see Noel Coward's *Sail Away* and *How to Succeed*. *Sail Away* had completely sold out its out-of-town engagement and *How to Succeed* was doing middling business. They went backstage after the performance of *How to Succeed* and met Frank Loesser. Burton said to Frank, "The show is just wonderful." Frank said, "Yeah, but that Noel Coward thing is going to clobber us. We don't stand a prayer next to *Sail Away*." Lane said, "Trust me, my boy, you have nothing to worry about."

Mary Martin followed her success in *The Sound of Music* with the Dietz and Schwartz show *Jennie*. Martin had taken the Rodgers and Hammerstein show more seriously than the critics and was hanging out with nuns and priests. Several of them would show up at rehearsals of the new show and give her theatrical advice. One of the nuns in particular took offense to some of Dietz's lyrics. In the song, "Before I Kiss the World Goodbye," Martin refused to sing the lines: "Before I go to meet my maker, I want to use the salt left in the shaker."

Life with Martin was difficult. All the many years she was in shows, she was saving her voice for the stage, so she communicated with her son Larry Hagman only by writing notes. Hagman resented his mother's devotion to her career, and for years he wouldn't talk to her.

David Belasco had a habit of thinking for long periods of time while the cast sat by waiting. At other times, he'd huddle with the lead actress and whisper directions to her. One actor, John Cope, had enough. He said, "I get goddamned sick of hanging around here watching the old man think."

Adele Astaire was thought by most people to be more talented than her brother Fred. She had a mischievous nature and began arriving late to rehearsals for *The Band Wagon*. Lyricist and director Howard Dietz told her that if she came late one more time, he'd spank her with the cast watching. She did and he did.

Ezio Pinza had one of the greatest voices of his time. But when he was rehearsing *South Pacific*, director Josh Logan had to keep berating him, "They'll never understand you. You've got to say the words!"

During rehearsals for *Chicago*, the show was becoming lewder and lewder. Jerry Orbach decided to come to the rescue of the show since Fosse refused to listen to anyone, let alone the producers and writers. Orbach was a smart guy and he thought hard about what to say to Fosse, so he gave him all this Brechtian mumbo-jumbo about the "alienation effect" at the end of "Razzle Dazzle" and how Fosse needed to build to the alienation at the end, and blah, blah, blah. This was all explained in the most tortured way. Fosse, insecure about Brecht and all that, bought it all and thanked Orbach. The next day, Fosse got rid of all the over-the-top sexuality as if it was his own idea.

Actor Jim Brochu talks about when he went to the dress rehearsal of Martha Raye in *Hello, Dolly!* Raye didn't have much time to learn the part, and when Dolly made her entrance on the trolley car, Raye stepped off, opened her purse, and said, "There's nothing in here but a mirror and a dildo."

Actress Maude Adams is now best known for her turn as Peter Pan in the original Broadway production of J.M. Barrie's play. Producer Charles Frohman disagreed with the way that Adams was saying a line in another Barrie play, 1914's *The Legend of Leonora*. Frohman decided to settle the argument by asking Barrie what he intended. Barrie was living in London, so naturally Frohman took a ship there to talk to the great playwright himself.

Adams made a specialty of acting in Barrie's plays. And he returned the compliment by adapting his novels into plays especially for her. As she did with Frohman, Adams preferred her own ideas about acting. When she was appearing in Barrie's *What Every Woman Knows*, she and actor Dick Bennett quarreled relentlessly and loudly. The next season she was about to open the London production of the play *Chantecler*. On opening night, she received a telegram from Bennett. The telegram read, "How happy you must be to be your own leading man."

Remarkably, Adams had a successful second career after her retirement from acting in 1916. She worked at General Electric on stage lighting and with Kodak in the development of color film. She briefly returned to acting before teaching it at Stephens College.

Jane Fonda had a difficult time on Broadway. Though her personal reviews were good, the plays for the most part were failures. One of the successes was Arthur Laurents's play *Invitation to a March*. Fonda appeared alongside some terrific actors including Eileen Heckart, Madeleine Sherwood, and James MacArthur, oh, and Shelley Winters who slapped Fonda within the first five minutes of rehearsal. We don't know why. Winters was subsequently fired from the show and replaced by Celeste Holm. The cast was surmising that Fonda was cast only because she was Henry Fonda's daughter. Fonda noticed they didn't ask that question about MacArthur who was Helen Hayes's son.

Jane Fonda appeared in the play *There Was a Little Girl* even though her father thought she shouldn't take the part. The play was beset by troubles from the start. Director Joshua Logan had a nervous breakdown during rehearsals and was out for over a week. Then, during a performance in Boston, Louis Jean Heydt died offstage. The play closed after only sixteen performances, but to everyone's surprise, Jane Fonda received a Tony nomination for best featured actress in a play.

The original Japanese version of the play *Rashomon* concerns a bandit who kills a samurai and rapes his wife. The story is told through the eyes of four witnesses. The American adaptation by Fay and Michael Kanin starred Rod Steiger and Claire Bloom. Steiger was a method actor and that proved to be a big problem during rehearsals. In Philadelphia, Steiger started wildly slapping his arms. Peter Glenville asked him what the hell he was doing. The actor replied that he was swatting flies that were biting his arms. Glenville offered to have the theatre fumigated, but Steiger explained these were imaginary flies in the forest. The director told him that he was not to continue swatting under any circumstances. But Steiger was not to be dissuaded from his methods. In fact, in addition to the distraction of the imaginary flies, he was also tearing at his costume. It seems that the imaginary flies were also drawing imaginary blood. He calmed down when the show hit Broadway.

Producer David Susskind received a telegram on opening night assuring him that "... *Rashomon* will be the most successful rape of the season." Brooks Atkinson wrote in *The New York Times* that the show was "a perfectly imagined microcosm of sense, sound and color." Not exactly a rave. In fact, George Abbott, the associate producer of the show, said, "No one knew what the fuck that meant," explaining why the show closed despite a good story and script.

After a production closed, Ted Mann of Circle in the Square would always take home a piece of furniture from the set. At one rehearsal of *Anna Karenina*, there was a sofa on the set and a little boy in the cast stood on the sofa with his shoes on. Mann screamed at the boy and that's when the cast knew Mann was taking the sofa home.

Josh Ellis tells this story: In 1981, Lena Horne was rehearsing *The Lady and Her Music* on the eighth floor at the 890 Studios (Michael Bennett's place).

Down the hall, Chita Rivera was rehearsing *Bring Back Birdie*, costarring Donald O'Connor.

One morning we had "press meet-and-greet day" for Lena, with lots of TV crews, radio interviewers, print media and photographers scheduled to attend. I was the full press agent of *The Lady and Her Music* and helping out on *Bring Back Birdie*, so Chita vaguely knew me from a few previous meetings.

When I passed the *Birdie* rehearsal room, the door was shut and Chita was in the hallway. She was wearing no makeup and her hair was unkempt. I told her that lots of press was about to descend upon us and if she wasn't "camera-ready," perhaps she'd want to stay in her rehearsal room to avoid unwanted photo-ops.

Chita explained, "They're working with Donald this morning. I have nothing to do. Do you need help?" Help, I thought, what can Chita Rivera DO? Help with what? I asked. "Anything you need," was her reply.

Would you consider escorting the press from the elevator to Lena's rehearsal room? And when they get there, could you help us hand out press releases? "Sure," she said.

Can you imagine the delight the members of the press got when the elevator door opened and Chita Rivera greeted them with, "Hi, I'm Chita. Welcome to Lena Horne's rehearsal." Of course she didn't need to identify herself. Everyone knew who she was! That morning Chita never put on makeup. She never combed her hair. She was just having fun. And so was everyone else.

Peter Gennaro choreographed the number "America" in *West Side Story*, as well as the Sharks' steps in "Dance at the Gym." But Jerome Robbins had Gennaro sign a contract giving up all rights to the dances. And when Robbins accepted his Tony Award for the choreography, he neglected to mention Gennaro.

While in rehearsal for *A Little Night Music*, Glynis Johns came down with hypoglycemia and had to go to the hospital. Harold Prince didn't want to postpone the production, which was days away from opening. He contacted Tammy Grimes to see if she wanted to take over the part. But Grimes made such onerous demands, Prince turned her down. Johns recovered and opened the show.

When she turned one hundred, Patricia Morison told the following story. At the age of eighteen, she was cast in the 1933 Broadway comedy *Growing Pains*, which lasted twenty-nine performances. "I was so bad in it they fired me in rehearsals," said Morison, a warm, witty woman with an amazing recollection of her storied life. "I cried so hard they gave me a walk-on. I have forgotten what it was about, honey."

At the first orchestra rehearsal of *West Side Story*, the music was so new, fresh, and extremely difficult that the orchestra members asked to take their parts home with them so they could work on the rhythms before the next rehearsal.

Sue Hight was cast in her first featured singing part on Broadway in the musical revue *Two's Company*, which was especially tailored to Bette Davis's talents by songwriters Vernon Duke and Sammy Cahn. The day of the first rehearsal the cast sat expectantly on the stage waiting for Ms. Davis to arrive. Suddenly, the doors at the back of the house were flung open. Down the aisle and up onto the stage strode the star herself. She threw her mink on the floor, sat down, took a carton of cigarettes from her bag, put them decisively on the table, and said, "Let's start!" From then on she was just one of the company and they loved her.

When Ann Miller was rehearsing "I'm Still Here" for the Paper Mill Playhouse production of *Follies*, she asked Stephen Sondheim if she could cut some of the verses. He refused. Then she asked if she could at least pep it up since it's so slow. Again he refused. Nonetheless, she did a great star turn in the show. Sadly, her feet were in such bad shape, two stagehands had to carry her onstage for her numbers.

When Ben Vereen was rehearsing *Jesus Christ Superstar*, he was having trouble being understood, so director Tom O'Horgan asked actress and acting teacher Helen Gallagher to help him. After listening to him, Gallagher told the star that he had to decide exactly how black he wanted to be so that he could be understood.

When comedians Olsen and Johnson's laugh riot *Hellzapoppin* was opening at the Winter Garden in 1938, the musicians were very grateful to have work, as jobs were scarce. The man who played the tuba hadn't worked in a while and was always busy spit-polishing his instrument. In fact, it was so shiny that if one of the stage lights caught it, the audience would be blinded by the reflection. One day, one of the Shubert brothers asked the conductor, "What is that shiny big thing on the end of the pit that's reflecting all the light?" Well, the conductor was very nervous. He was worried that this tuba player would be fired after being unemployed for so long. He said, "Why, that's the tuba." He was surprised when the producer said, "It looks fantastic, can we get one for the other side as well?"

The 1970/71 season saw a number of shows open that featured casts of advanced age. First came *No, No, Nanette*, then *Follies*, and eleven days later, *70, Girls, 70*. When *Follies* was about to open on Broadway, producer/director Harold Prince told Harvey Evans, "They better get the ambulances ready on Broadway." In fact, during the pre-Broadway tour of *70, Girls, 70* in Philadelphia, David Burns dropped dead during a performance.

One of the octogenarian performers in *70, Girls, 70* was sitting backstage next to Fred Ebb and watching the rehearsal. He told Ebb, "That's a swell number." Ebb replied, "Well, you better get the hell out there, you're in it."

Joseph Fields wrote a wartime comedy titled *The Doughgirls* and George S. Kaufman directed it. Kaufman kept complaining to Fields that the actors weren't punching up their exit lines and therefore weren't getting their laughs. Kaufman was a strong proponent of funny lines at actors' exits and wrote his shows accordingly. While waiting for a rehearsal to continue, a cleaning woman walked across the stage with her mop and pail. Fields said to Kaufman, "Jesus, George. She got off without a laugh."

Gillian Lynne would come to the mega-hit *Phantom of the Opera* every once in a while to check up on things and put the company through their paces, cleaning up any sloppiness and changing the staging. At one rehearsal for the song "Masquerade," she had the cast glide across the stage. After they reached the other side of the stage, she called out Ken Kantor, a fine singer and actor but certainly not a dancer. She then asked Ken to step forward and repeat the glide. Ken agreed although he knew that he was terrible. After he completed the step, he went up to Lynne and asked, "Did you have me repeat it because I was so good or because I was so bad?" Lynne batted her eyelashes and looked warmly into his eyes and said, "I did it because you're you."

Rehearsals for the musical *Two By Two* took place up in the Bronx in the Feller Scenic Studios. Lyricist Martin Charnin would come to composer Richard Rodgers's office and share a ride up to the Bronx. As Charnin tells it, "Every time we passed 96th Street we would see people in abject poverty. I asked Dick, 'How do we drive through all this poverty and pestilence?' Rodgers replied, 'You look straight ahead.'"

While in rehearsals for *The Bird Cage*, the women of the cast swore in such bad language that even the male cast members were shocked. Eleanor Lynn, Kate Harkin (Zero Mostel's wife), Rita Duncan, and Jean Carson were so rude, Melvin Douglas told director Harold Clurman, "I've been in the Army and I've been in show business all my life, and I've never heard such language." Clurman was about to have a run-through with some guests present and thought it prudent to tell the cast, "Now, we'll read this for the backers, and ladies, please, watch your language; there'll be gentlemen present."

While rehearsing "Luck Be a Lady," Frank Loesser yelled at his actors about singing loudly and stormed out of the theatre. He came back a few minutes later with an ice cream cone and as they were singing loudly, he smiled and continued to eat it.

Loesser knew that loudness meant energy. He also had a sign backstage at rehearsal of *The Most Happy Fella* that read "Loud is good." He'd have a big problem today when microphones do the work and shows miss that energy.

Larry Blank tells this story about a rehearsal of *Copperfield*, a very short-lived musical in which a lot of the chorus members were Jewish. There was no particular reason; it just turned out that way. Also in the cast was a young Christian Slater (Mary Jo Slater, his mother, was a noted casting director).

At one point in the show, Slater, playing the young David Copperfield, was supposed to be tossed off a set piece into the arms of the male chorus. Slater hesitated, nervous about being caught. Down below was Richard Warren Pugh waiting for the leap. Losing patience, Pugh shouted as loud as he could, "Throw Christian to the Jews!"

When George S. Kaufman directed a show, he wanted no one unrelated to the production in the theatre watching him work. But his sometime-collaborator Marc Connelly was quite the opposite. Connelly enjoyed having masses of people sitting in the theatre watching him work. When Connelly was rehearsing the operetta *Two Bouquets*, he invited more than the usual number of friends to sit in and watch the proceedings. Around that time, Kaufman was walking down Broadway when a friend passed by and asked him, "How are Marc's rehearsals coming?" Kaufman replied, "Fine. The balcony's fallen off a little, but it's still crowded downstairs."

By the way, Kaufman had the same trouble with George Gershwin when he directed *Of Thee I Sing!* Gershwin liked to invite all his friends to rehearsals, and that maddened Kaufman.

Kaufman was punctual, extremely punctual. He'd call a rehearsal from 12 noon to 4 p.m., say. At two minutes before noon, he'd arrive and call the cast together. At 4 p.m. on the dot, he'd disappear without a word.

Just a week into rehearsals of *Happy Hunting*, Ethel Merman proclaimed that the Broadway neophyte, composer Harold Karr, could never speak to her again. It seems that while rehearsing Merman's numbers, Karr criticized Merman's phrasing, saying, "Miss Merman, if I wanted the song sung that way, I'd have written it that way." They never spoke to each other again. Note: Some people credit lyricist Matt Dubey and not Karr.

In 1973, Abe Burrows was rehearsing the play *No Hard Feelings*. The show's title was ironic because during one rehearsal, Burrows stepped off into the orchestra pit of the Martin Beck Theatre and broke several bones. His son James took over rehearsals until Burrows could recuperate. James Burrows grew up to be the co-creator of *Cheers* and one of television's greatest sitcom directors.

When *Dude* was rehearsing on the stage of the Broadway Theatre, the stage (which occupied the place where the orchestra seats once were) was covered in dirt. When the actors came out onstage the dirt flew up and the actors all started coughing and couldn't get through the script. So they dampened the dirt so it wouldn't get stirred up. And you know what happens when dirt and water mix—mud. Then square textile pieces were put down to simulate dirt and, finally, there was plastic on the stage floor.

Josh Ellis saw a matinee of *Half a Sixpence* and during one dance, a chorus boy lost his hat and, without missing a beat, another chorus member threw it back to the boy who caught it with aplomb. It was a remarkable testament to the talents of Broadway chorus dancers. Ellis loved the show so much, after the matinee, he went right to the box office and bought a ticket for the evening show. During the same number, wouldn't you know it, the same chorus boy lost his hat, the same chorus boy who picked it up picked it up again and threw it to the other dancer exactly as he did in the matinee. Ellis was disappointed, but in fact, the trick had been an accident during a rehearsal and it was so fantastic it was put into the show. The bit was so tricky and difficult, two hats were actually dropped and the one in the best position was the one thrown and the second one was kicked offstage.

Josh Logan wanted to see *South Pacific* onstage because they had been rehearsing in a room. At the end of "A Wonderful Guy," Mary Martin performed a cartwheel, but in the new surroundings, she couldn't judge how much room she had, so she cartwheeled directly into the orchestra pit. Her fall was broken by Trude Rittman who was playing at the rehearsal. Rittman was sent to the hospital.

The next day, Rittman received a bouquet of flowers from Martin contained in a football helmet.

TWO ACTORS WON'T LEARN ONE MORE WORD

Ethel Merman earned the nickname "Miss Birdseye" when she refused to learn a new set of lyrics while *Call Me Madam* was in the final preopening performances. During *Gypsy*, Merman had told the team that she'd learn anything up to a week before opening, at which point her performance was fixed. Sondheim wrote an introductory verse to "Some People" that he wanted Merman sing, and gave it to her two weeks before opening, but she didn't like it and refused to learn it. Sondheim quietly inquired about his rights to force the issue and was told the "Miss Birdseye" story and how Berlin's dummy lyrics for "The Hostess with the Mostest on the Ball" ended up being used throughout the run. As a result, he dropped the issue.

Harold Rome said that during *Fanny*, Ezio Pinza had it in his contract that he would not sing more than twenty-five minutes the entire evening, and he had to have all his music six months before the first performance. When they were out of town, there was a moment in the show that, according to Rome, just wasn't working and he realized it needed a song. He spent two weeks writing the song "Let's Talk about a Woman."

He went to the piano in Pinza's dressing room and played the song. When he was finished, Pinza said, "That is one of the most beautiful songs I ever heard. Too bad I can't learn it. I told you I needed to have all my music six months before we started. It's not going to happen."

So Rome put the song into *Destry Rides Again* for the villain played by Scott Brady. Rome had been told by Scott Brady's agent that the actor had a beautiful singing voice. Brady showed up for rehearsal and turned out to be tone deaf, so the number was also cut from *Destry*.

DIRECTORIAL ADVICE

Barnum's rehearsals were literally a circus, and at the end of the previews, they decided to make the show into one act instead of two. Glenn Close was increasingly stressed out. She would make her entrances with Jim Dale as her husband through one set of doors. She would ask director Joe Layton, "Excuse me, Joe, but what is my motivation for coming through these doors?" Layton wasn't a motivation kind of guy; he'd just try ideas and see what worked. During the final rehearsal, he decided to make a change and have Close come through a different set of doors. "What's my motivation?" Now, Layton lost it and told her, "You're coming from the fucking toilet. Now, just get out there!"

During a rehearsal of *Once Upon a Mattress*, Joe Bova asked, "What's my motivation?" George Abbott replied, "Your paycheck."

Ruth Gordon was rehearsing for the road company of the play *The First Year*. When she came to a line that got one of the biggest laughs in the show, she played around with different ways of saying it. Winchell Smith was directing the show and said to her, "No, no, dear. If you've got lines that don't go, then you can fool around with them. But when you get lines that do go, just say it, dear, just simply say it."

The stage doorman of the theatre in which they were rehearsing told George Abbott that Smith was "the best of them all. When Winchell Smith gets through explaining a line to an actor, if he can't get it into his head, he'd better go back to driving his truck."

CHAPTER 9
The Race Issue

Today, blacks and whites occupy the same stage in the same play, but it was not always so. Today, we even have as great an eminence as James Earl Jones playing the patriarch of an otherwise-white family in a revival of *You Can't Take It with You*. And multiple characters in *Hamilton* are played by white, black, and Hispanic performers regardless of historical accuracy, and nobody minds.

Noble Sissle and Eubie Blake and the producers of 1921's *Shuffle Along* were nervous about the chances for the show. Would white audiences accept two black characters falling in love and singing a serious, non-stereotypical love song, "Love Will Find a Way"—just like white characters? Colibrettist and costar Flournoy Miller learned that "a newspaper man told Mr. Cort (the theatre owner) that the public would not stand for Negroes acting romantic on a stage and suggested that the entire love plot be excised." The idea of blacks as capable of having romantic feelings—as opposed to the "animal" sexuality associated with jazz music—was controversial for white audiences. It implied an equality of the races that few were ready to accept.

An African-American critic writing for *New York Age* commented on this prejudice among white audiences: "White audiences for some reason do not want colored people to indulge in too much love-making. They will applaud if a colored man serenades his girl at the window, but if, while telling of his great love in song he becomes somewhat demonstrative . . . then exceptions are taken. It may be the general impression prevails that Negroes are only slightly acquainted with Dan Cupid; or maybe it is thought they have no business being ardent lovers."

Actually, there had been earlier black shows that honestly portrayed love between a black man and a black woman. Cole and Johnson's *The Red*

Moon (1909) was perhaps the first. The most notable example was James Weldon Johnson's *My Friend from Kentucky* (1913), which was produced at the Lafayette Theatre in Harlem. As its composer stated, "'Rock Me in the Cradle of Love' ... had been sung by the Negro tenor to the bronze soubrette in a most impassioned manner, demonstrating that the lovemaking taboo had been absolutely kicked out of the Negro theatre." But *My Friend from Kentucky* was an aberration. Although white audiences came up to Harlem to see it, it was primarily aimed at a black audience.

Shuffle Along's great success was a watershed event for black performers and the black theater. Not only did it mark a highpoint for blacks on stage, it broke the color barrier in the audience as well. *Variety* noted that blacks were seated in the orchestra section of the house and not forced to sit in the balcony as in many other theatres. True, the paper noted that "the two races rarely intermingled," which made its white readers less nervous at the possibility of being seated next to a black patron. In fact, the orchestra section had a line of demarcation between the three-quarters of the downstairs reserved for whites and the rest offered to blacks. But even that small step proved to be historic. *Shuffle Along*'s desegregation policy, as tentative as it might have been, was the first step in an eventual true opening of theatre seats to all races. By 1930, critic, social activist, and songwriter James Weldon Johnson proudly wrote, "At the present time the sight of colored people in the orchestras of Broadway theatres is not regarded a cause for immediate action or utter astonishment."

Bert Williams was one of the biggest stars of his day and the first black man to have his name in lights over the marquee. At one performance at the St. Louis Orpheum, Lionel Barrymore exclaimed to the stage manager, "Isn't he great!" The manager had to admit it: "He's a good nigger and knows his place." Just then Williams came offstage and said as he walked by, "Yes, he's a good nigger and he knows his place and his place is dressing room Number One."

When Eugene O'Neill's play *All God's Chullun Got Wings* was about to hit Broadway in 1924, hackles were raised at the announcement that the white actress Mary Blair would play the wife of Paul Robeson, a black man. One would have thought the sky was falling. Robert Benchley, critic for the old *Life Magazine*, wrote about the "threatened insult to Nordic purity." It was odd, he noted, that "no protests are ever received against a white actress' playing on the stage with a white actor who may be degenerate, criminal, or unclean. If there is such a jealous watch to be kept over the honor of our white womanhood, we should not limit it to the cases of diverse pigmentation."

When *Porgy and Bess* was to play the National Theatre in Washington, it was the show's star Todd Duncan who insisted that the theatre open its seating to blacks and whites alike. Duncan had another experience with *Porgy and Bess* that lifted his spirit.

In the late 1940s, Duncan played the Royal Opera House in Copenhagen in the show. While there he heard about another production of *Porgy and Bess* during the war. Duncan told Berthe Schuchat in an interview, "The Gestapo wanted more music and allocated for that. The Danish staged four new operas. They chose *Porgy and Bess* to show how they hated the Nazis. After all it was performed by Negroes and written by Jews. They thought the Nazis would veto it. Money was poured into *Porgy and Bess*; people were sent to America to get real Negro wigs. At the premiere, 200 Nazis were in the audience. They enjoyed the first act, but during intermission they got up and walked out. They allowed the Danish to do the next two performances because they were sold out.

"But the Danes gave forty more performances underground during the war. The Germans would always find out that it had been done the night before, but they never knew when it was going to be done. The Royal Opera was dark on the outside. And that was the Danish performers' fight. They performed fearing they'd be blown up or killed by the Nazis. The Danes used, 'It Ain't Necessarily So' to jam Gestapo radio lines. That became a symbol of resistance."

LOST IN THE STARS NATIONAL THEATRE STORY

Porgy and Bess wasn't the only black show to have trouble with racism. When Kurt Weill and Maxwell Anderson's musical drama *Lost in the Stars* went on tour, black performers weren't always welcome in white hotels. And the theatres were no different.

When they were booked in Baltimore's Ford's Theatre, the local NAACP and the Committee on Non-Segregation in Baltimore Theatres asked the actors not to play in the segregated theatre. Todd Duncan, the same great actor who had gone through a similar situation with *Porgy and Bess*, demanded that the engagement be cancelled. The producers agreed.

The American Theatre in St. Louis was also segregated, but it was decided to play that theatre since the message of the play, anti-apartheid in

South Africa, was important to be heard by white audiences. So the show went on despite picketing outside the theatre.

When the tour was over, playwright Maxwell Anderson sent a telegram to the cast. It read: "I believe we were engaged in a great cause together, that we benefited that cause extraordinarily and that our country will be a better place in which to live because of what we were trying to do."

Three musicals had interracial love stories and found themselves the targets of racism.

When *Golden Boy* was playing in Philadelphia, word got out that the show featured a white woman having a romance with a black man. Racists bombarded the theatre with death threats against Sammy Davis Jr., Strouse and Adams, and others. Police were called in to protect Davis. Actors were accosted as they exited the stage door by people who were there strictly on principle—they had probably never seen a live show.

In Boston, Davis was again under attack. Only this time, it was from fans. They climbed all over his car trying to get him to stop and give them autographs. It was insane. But when the show hit Broadway, there were people shooting at the marquee of the theatre.

In Richard Adler's musical *Kwamina*, Terry Carter was paired with Sally Ann Howes. Hate mail flooded the theatre both before the show opened and even after it had closed. Sally Ann Howes was sent a present, a piece of used toilet paper. Classy!

A month after *Kwamina* closed, Richard Rodgers and Samuel Taylor's musical *No Strings* opened with Richard Kiley paired romantically with Diahann Carroll. This time it was a white man in love with a black woman. While it ran, a few people would walk out during every performance. Some did so quietly, while others would make comments as they headed for the exits. One time, a man stood up and, dragging his wife up the aisle, turned and yelled, "Nigger lovers!" It threw the actors off. Richard Kiley came to the front of the stage and told the audience, "We're very sorry for this interruption. With your permission, we would like to start the scene over where Miss Carroll enters."

It should be said that *Golden Boy* made no bones about Davis and Wayne sleeping together in the show, whereas in *Kwamina*, there was no touching or kissing. And in *No Strings*, any kissing was done in silhouette.

CHAPTER 10
Out of Town

We start with our earliest story, one that should silence the modern-day whiners and loafers who constantly complain about the theatres, rehearsal schedules, their fellow actors, etc.

Joseph Jefferson was one of the greatest stars of the American theatre. He made his stage debut at the age of four in 1833 and acted throughout the United States, Australia, and England. Jefferson's most famous character was Rip Van Winkle. We're telling you all this to perhaps whet your appetite for his autobiography (aptly titled *The Autobiography of Joseph Jefferson*), which is perhaps the greatest theatre biography ever written. Every actor should read it, especially the later chapters about the acting profession.

Bringing theatre to people who had never seen a live performance of any kind was a mission and way of life for Jefferson, his family, and their acting troupe. As an example of the dangers that awaited the valiant thespians, here is a brief summery of part of their journey.

Jefferson and company traveled to Chicago in 1838 by packet boat on the Erie Canal, earning passage by giving a percentage of the receipts to the captain of the boat. After Chicago, he and his family went west to Galena in open wagons over the prairie. From there, they went to Dubuque by sleighs on the frozen river. Though the performers made the trip unscathed, their baggage, scenery, props, and curtains (and horses) crashed through the ice into the Mississippi. Luckily, the sleigh rested on a sandbar and everything was recovered and dried out. Where there wasn't a theatre, they would perform in a warehouse, courthouse, barn, and even a pork house, the pigs having been removed temporarily. All through the performance of *Clari, the Maid of Milan*, the pigs vociferously expressed their disappointment in being driven from their home and being unable to watch the hams on the stage.

When they decided to spend an entire season in Springfield, Illinois, they were forced to build their own theatre. Once it was built, however, another calamity ensued. A religious revival was in town and the fathers of the church pressured the local government to levy a hefty tax upon the sinners and their new edifice.

Traveling by flatboat down the Ohio, sometimes the current would slow down. The solution was to cut a hickory pole out of a nearby tree and hoist the drops upon it to act as a sail. Farmers and their families, passersby, and passengers on the steamboats that plied the river were treated to an odd spectacle. Down the river came a canvas castle with a forest painted on the reverse side. When they passed these impromptu audiences, the captain would swing the sail around from forest to palace and back again. In good spirits, the intrepid company decided to put on a pantomime, and sword-fights and battles would float by past the fields and towns.

Patricia Morison on *Kiss Me, Kate*: "Before opening night in Philadelphia, we all got together and said, 'If we get good personal reviews out of this show we are lucky.' And then opening night happened. We couldn't believe it. I was stunned. You never know what an audience is going to do."

While out of town in Detroit, Bob Fosse was trying to get Neil Simon to take over writing the libretto of the Frank Loesser musical *Pleasures and Palaces*. Fosse finally convinced Simon to do it and the playwright received a telegram from him: "Meet you at the airport at six p.m." So, Simon continued to pack when, a half hour later, he got a second telegram: "You're fired." In the interim, Loesser had decided to close the show. Fosse, Sam Spewack, and Loesser had discovered they were working on three different shows.

Audiences can also be rude, especially audiences that aren't used to attending the theatre. Eartha Kitt was out on the road with the play *The Owl and the Pussycat*. The audience kept talking during the performance. Eartha, who took no guff from anybody, broke character, came down to the foot of the stage and addressed the audience thusly, "May I remind you the curtain is UP!"

Before *The Grand Tour* hit San Francisco, the song "I Want to Live Each Night" was set in a brothel beautifully designed by Ming Cho Lee. On the set was a portrait of the "Rape of the Sabine Women," a pink piano, and nude etchings. The female chorus was dressed as prostitutes. It was decided that the whorehouse wasn't quite the right setting, so the powers that be went 180 degrees in the opposite direction and changed the setting to a convent! The song was cut (it turned up later in *Miss Spectacular*), the "Rape" painting was changed to a Madonna and child, Ming Cho Lee covered the etchings with drapery, and the whores came out dressed as nuns.

The first performance of *Come Summer* in Boston wasn't well received by the audience. The show had sets by Oliver Smith based on the artwork of Grandma Moses, but the audience was unprepared for that style of painting, and the audience was laughing at what seemed to them to be bad artistry.

At the curtain call, Ray Bolger came downstage and addressed the audience. He told them, "Don't worry, unlike *Hair*, we won't resort to nudity."

Gertrude Lawrence was appearing at Cape Cod's Cape Playhouse. While chatting with one of the theatre's apprentices, she learned that he had never learned how to drive. Here he was in Cape Cod for the summer and a car would definitely be useful.

The next morning, the boy was awakened by the sound of a car insistently honking outside his window. He looked out to see Gertrude Lawrence demanding he get behind the wheel. The great actress and her chauffeur sat in the backseat with a bottle of champagne and two glasses while the neophyte took his place behind the wheel and drove the three of them around the theatre's parking lot.

Chu Chem was in the Goodspeed Opera House 1965 season along with *Purple Dust* and *Man of La Mancha*. The plan was to share the casts and creative team for all three shows. Mitch Leigh wrote the music for all of them. The first, *Purple Dust*, was a failure at Goodspeed even with Richard Kiley, Joan Diener, Ray Middleton, Robert Rounseville, and others who were also in *Man of La Mancha*. Next up was *Man of La Mancha*, which of course was a great hit that was held over. Since *La Mancha*'s run was extended, *Chu Chem* was sent out on a pre-Broadway tour. For those of you who wondered why Sancho Panza had a distinct Yiddish accent in Spain, it was because Irving Jacobson who played Sancho was also supposed to be in *Chu Chem*.

Menasha Skulnik and Molly Picon were big stars in the Yiddish theatre, on Broadway, and movies. They both were in *Chu Chem* in Philadelphia's Locust Street Theatre prior to Broadway. Josh Ellis was there and remembers everything. During one performance, "Skulnik comes out and quiets the audience, 'Ladies and gentlemen, I want to make an announcement before the show starts. There's a character on the stage who is not in your program. He is holding a big book in his hands. He's the prompter and any time we do not know a line, we'll ask the prompter for the line, he'll give it to us, and we'll go on with the show.'

"In the middle of the first act, the orchestra strikes up the vamp to a song and Skulnik breaks character and comes out to the front of the stage and says, 'Ladies and Gentlemen, we beg your indulgence. Right here is a song from the show. It's not a very good song. Would you mind terribly if we skip it and go right to the scene? Okay, mister conductor?' The vamp stops and they go into the scene.

"At the end of the first act and during the intermission there are two sumo wrestlers who perform for the audience even though the set doesn't need to be changed.

"After the intermission, Skulnik comes out again and says, 'Ladies and Gentlemen I beg your indulgence one last time. I bear good news and bad news. First the bad news. Molly Picon, who played my wife Rose in the first act has taken ill.' 'Oyyyyy,' goes the audience; she was the main reason people came to the show. Skulnik continues, 'But bad news is followed by good news and in the second act my wife Rose will be played by a great lady of the Yiddish theatre, Henrietta Jacobson! Come out, Henrietta.' Now, Henrietta Jacobson weighs twice as much as Molly Picon who was very tiny. And clearly there was no time to prepare a costume for Henrietta Jacobson; the costume being a tiny kimono. So what do they do? They put Henrietta Jacobson in a long black robe and pin Molly Picon's tiny kimono to the front of it. And that was the Saturday afternoon performance and the show closed after that evening's performance. Molly Picon was never in the show again. She had quit the show during the intermission of the matinee!"

Chu Chem got the following review: The King and Oy.

While *Silk Stockings* was trying out in Philadelphia, Sherry O'Neill, the understudy for Yvonne Adair, told Gretchen Wyler who was in the chorus that she was going to New York for an audition, but not to tell anyone. Meanwhile, Ernest Martin, producer of the show who was having an affair with Wyler, let Wyler know that Yvonne Adair was going to be out of the matinee that same day. Keeping her promise to O'Neill, Wyler didn't tell Martin or the stage management that O'Neill was going to be out of town. Wyler knew that she was next in line if the understudy didn't go on.

So there she was sitting in the dressing room just biding her time until the stage manager made the announcement: "Sherry O'Neill, please come to the stage manager's desk." Wyler continued to powder her nose and waited 'til everyone figured out that she had to go on in the role. She went on, stopped the show, and they gave her the part.

Rita Metzger, cast in the important role of the Leader in *Zorba*, had gone to attend a friend's wedding when *Zorba* was out of town. There was a storm and Metzger couldn't get back to the theatre. Loraine Serabian went on for the matinee performance and that was it. Metzger finally made it back and was informed that the role was no longer hers.

If it weren't for Jean Arthur leaving *Born Yesterday* two weeks before the show premiered in New Haven, we might not have had Judy Holiday as a big a star.

If Jack Pearl, a radio comedian, had not quit *Yokel Boy* with only four days left in Boston before coming to New York, Phil Silvers might not have left burlesque and developed his fast-talking shyster character that he honed in shows (*High Button Shoes*), television (as Sgt. Bilko), and films (*It's a Mad, Mad, Mad, Mad World*). *Yokel Boy* was a Lew Brown (producer, director, librettist, lyricist, and composer) musical mess; such a mess that $65,000 of scenery was left in the alley of the Majestic Theatre on Broadway—nobody knew where it was meant to go in the show!

Silvers was so nervous on opening night that before the curtain went up at the Majestic, he walked over to the Gaiety Theatre on 47th Street and did a few burlesque bits for the audience there to build up his confidence. Then he went back and opened the show.

Meanwhile, lyricist Sammy Cahn went to his seat in the theatre and promptly fainted from nerves. The show was raked over the coals by the critics but Silvers got good notices. So he and the star of the show, Buddy Ebsen, decided to rework the show without telling Lew Brown. Business picked up! The show started to make money. Then Lew Brown placed a full-page ad in every New York paper. The ad read: "I'm sorry." Then, below the quote, Brown reproduced all the bad reviews. The show quickly died.

One good thing came out of the show. Louis B. Mayer saw a performance and signed Silvers to a Hollywood contract.

Bob Fosse always wanted to push the envelope with his choreography and direction. When *New Girl in Town*, the musical version of *Anna Christie*, was in New Haven, Fosse choreographed a whorehouse ballet that ended with an onstage rape. After opening night, the word got out through critics' reviews and the stage door was padlocked by the local police. Either the dance had to go or the show could not reopen. Producer Hal Prince and librettist/director George Abbott made Fosse clean it up, though he snuck in pieces of the dance here and there. Fosse hated not having the final word, and it spurred him on to having his own way by directing, choreographing, and sometimes even writing the books of his shows.

Smiles should have been a big hit. It starred Marilyn Miller and had Fred and Adele Astaire in leading roles. Vincent Youmans wrote the score and Florenz Ziegfeld was the producer. William Anthony McGuire rewrote the original script but things fell apart relatively quickly. Youmans was lying on the floor drunk during much of the rehearsal period. McGuire was either drunk or trying to pick up ladies from the chorus. Marilyn Miller wanted the big song of the show, "Time on My Hands," cut. She finally agreed to sing the song but only one chorus. Miller also demanded that Harriette Lake's two dance numbers and songs be cut before opening in New York. Harriette Lake later became better known as Ann Sothern.

Gus Schirmer staged a revival of Rodgers and Hart's *Pal Joey* that would play summer theatres around the Northeast. Bob Fosse would play Joey, Carol Bruce was given the role of Vera, and the show was a big hit wherever it played. Schirmer was so sure of this production, he asked composer Jule Styne, who was also a producer, to come down and see if he'd consider mounting the show on Broadway. Styne saw the production and raved about it. He knew the time had come for audiences to accept such a great story. Styne met with Schirmer, Fosse, and Bruce and told them that the show was perfect for the Great White Way and, in fact, Harold Lang would be perfect as Joey and Vivienne Segal could reprise her role as Vera. Then he said goodbye and drove off leaving the thunderstruck trio with their jaws agape and their dreams shattered.

Bob Hope's career on Broadway was slow to gather traction. He was fired from his first show and then was cast in *Ups-a-Daisy* and then *Ballyhoo of 1932*. It was during the out-of-town tryout of that show in Atlantic City when, during the performance, there was a short circuit and the entire theatre went dark. In order to stop the audience from panicking, producer Lee Shubert buttonholed Hope and sent him out onstage to calm the audience while the problem was fixed. A natural ad-libber, Hope was again called to help the show when it was in Newark. This time, the opening number was held up by the dancers, so Hope was again sent out by Lee Shubert to entertain the audience. Hope told them, "Ladies and gentlemen, this is the first time I've ever been on before the acrobats," making reference to his usual low place on a vaudeville bill. "But seriously, folks," Hope continued, "We're doing a new number tonight and we rehearsed late. Things aren't quite set up, so please be patient." Then he pretended to notice someone in one of the boxes. "Hello, Sam!" He explained to the audience, "That's one of our backers up there. He says he's not nervous, but I notice he's buckled his safety belt." At one point his monologue was interrupted by a candy seller going up and down the aisles selling sweets. Hope asked him what he was doing. The man replied that he was making his living by selling candies and added that he was making $100 a week. "What did you say you make doing this?" asked Hope. "$100 a week," answered the man. Hope said, "Give me that basket and you get onstage!"

The bit went over so well, writer Al Boasberg had the idea for Hope to open the show by sitting in the box and introducing himself as the head of the complaint department. A couple of stooges were placed in the audience and Hope was off and running.

HOPE: Ladies and gentlemen . . .

STOOGE: My God, is this show really going to open?

HOPE: Well, if we waited a couple of weeks longer, that tuxedo of yours would be in style again.

STOOGE: I hope your gags are as new.

HOPE: Ladies and gentlemen, tonight we are inaugurating a new idea to the theatre . . . the complaint department. Of course, we know there'll be no complaints because this show is as clean and whole-some as the magazine.

STOOGE: Well, so long.

HOPE: You leaving?

STOOGE: Yeah, I'm going over to Minsky's.

Hope then asked the orchestra to start the overture but got no response. He then yelled at them, "Hey, fellas wake up." Snores emanated from the pit. Hope then fired a pistol in the air. Nothing. Finally, he rang a cash register and the conductor and musicians woke up and began playing the opening.

Though *Ballyhoo* was not a success, his next show was a big hit and again, Hope ad-libbed. In 1933, Hope was spotted by producer Max Gordon while performing at the Palace Theatre. Gordon thought Hope would be perfect for a new musical he was presenting titled *Gowns by Roberta* (the title was later shortened to just *Roberta*). Gordon brought composer Jerome Kern over to the Palace and Kern agreed to have Hope join the show. It was his big break. The great performer Tamara played a Russian princess in the show and Hope was in the scene with her as she sang the hit song from the score, "Smoke Gets in Your Eyes." The lead-in to the song was Tamara saying, "There's an old Russian proverb, 'When you're heart's on fire, smoke gets in your eyes.'" Hope felt the scene needed some levity and wanted to reply, "We have a proverb in America too. Love is like hash. You have to have confidence in it to enjoy it." Librettist and lyricist Otto Harbach rejected the idea, but when the show was having troubles in Philadelphia he asked Kern what he thought and the gag went into the show. It was a huge success. Even Harbach finally saw that the joke worked.

Hope was emboldened by his success and added more jokes ("Long dresses don't bother me, I have a good memory"), even hiring a gagman to give him new material. This time, Harbach put his foot down and put a stop to Hope's antics.

Hope's final Broadway show was Cole Porter's *Red, Hot and Blue*. The show was technically a book show like *Roberta* but with Ethel Merman and Jimmy Durante above the title, ad-libs flew fast and furious. And the stars weren't above breaking the fourth wall on purpose. In one scene, Hope and Durante were duck hunters. They'd shoot and ducks would fall from the flies. Even when they didn't pull the trigger, ducks would fall. At one performance, Durante forgot his lines and asked the prompter to "throw me the book." It got a big laugh from the audience, but when he pulled the same joke the next performance, Hope realized that Durante was just jockeying for more laughs.

When Desi Arnaz was in Boston with the show *Too Many Girls*, he got a terrible infection in his foot that made it impossible to stand or walk. It was so bad he had to be admitted to the hospital. This left the show in a bad position. Arnaz's understudy was strawberry blonde Van Johnson, as far away in looks from the Cuban Arnaz as a person could get. Johnson was in a panic as were the show's creators. Arnaz asked the doctor if his foot could be numbed for the three hours it took to do the show. The plan worked and for the next three days, Arnaz sang and danced in between bouts of treatment at the hospital. By the fourth day, the infection had healed.

At the out-of-town opening of *Wonderful Town* in Boston, Edie Adams asked where the makeup man was. She'd only been in television and didn't know that stage actors did their own makeup. Everyone thought she was kidding except for Rosalind Russell who helped Adams apply her makeup.

While *How to Succeed* was out of town, Charles Nelson Reilly had an idea that he was certain would bring the house down. He pitched the idea to Abe Burrows who just shook his head and said it wouldn't work.

Reilly was like a dog with a bone. Over and over again, he kept approaching Burrows with it. Finally, he wore him down and Burrows said, "Fine, try it at the matinee today and I'll be at the back of the house."

So when the golden moment came, Charles Nelson Reilly unfurled his comic gem. Sixteen-hundred audience members sat in complete silence. The only thing that Reilly heard was the booming voice of Abe Burrows at the back of the house shouting, "Nothing!"

Being on the road can be a real hardship unless you are Lillian Russell. When she played a whirlwind tour of over fifty towns and cities in *The Butterfly*, her inamorata Diamond Jim Brady set her up with a private train car. It had a drawing room, three bedrooms, two servants' bedrooms, bath, kitchen, dining room, and a small conservatory. The drawing room had a baby grand piano, writing desk, and lounge chairs.

Today the musical *Kelly* is known as one of the biggest flops in Broadway history. Herbert Ross was the director and, before rehearsals began, his wife, the dancer Nora Kaye, asked him, "Herbie, why are we doing this piece of shit?"

The show told the story of Steve Brody who, in the nineteenth century, claimed to have jumped from the Brooklyn Bridge and lived. That was the climax of the musical. At one performance, Don Francks, the actor playing Brodie, jumped from the grid in a harness attached to a rope held by a stagehand. As he jumped, Anita Gillette heard a man in the audience shout, "I thought that mother would never jump."

As rehearsals and then out-of-town performances continued, it seemed like every day new numbers were written, scenes were cut, Don Francks's hair color changed, anything to make the show better—which, of course, made it worse. Ella Logan, returning to Broadway following her great success in *Finian's Rainbow*, found her role entirely eliminated. Producer David Susskind rehired her. Then she was fired again. Mel Brooks and his writing partner Leonard Stern came in to doctor the script. Susskind, meanwhile, was either sleeping with or attempting to sleep with practically every woman in the company. The New York critics killed the show and following the opening night, only four people were on line at the box office. And they were asking for their money back. But the worst insult came from a writer with the *Saturday Evening Post* who followed the show through the rehearsal and out-of-town tryouts. He dined and drank with the cast, palled around with them, and then eviscerated them and the show in the article. It's now a collectors' item among Broadway fans.

The day after the opening, the cast was called to the theatre where Susskind gave a speech as the set was taken out and the costumes packed up.

Jerome Robbins hated the song "Little Lamb" from *Gypsy* and wanted it cut. The song was sung by Sandra Church, whom Jule Styne was "dating."

At one Saturday matinee, the song was cut. Between shows, Styne came to the theatre and said, "Mr. Robbins, I just spoke to the Dramatists Guild and if 'Little Lamb' is not reinstated in the score immediately, I will pull my score."

Charles Nelson Reilly was called in to replace Victor Spinetti in *Skyscraper*. Reilly had two days to learn the part. At the first rehearsal, he was nervous acting opposite the great star Julie Harris. She was getting so many re-writes, she was fried. At the rehearsal, she went up on her first line. Reilly strode to the footlights and yelled to the producer Cy Feuer, "Cy, where did you get this girl?" Harris looked at Reilly and burst into laughter and told him, "You and I are going to be great friends." Harris and Reilly developed a great friendship, professionally and personally. He later directed Harris in fourteen plays, including her Tony Award-winning show *The Belle of Amherst*.

Allegro was out of town. While Lisa Kirk was singing "The Gentlemen is a Dope," she fell off the stage into the orchestra pit where she was caught by the musicians and hoisted back on stage. All the while she never stopped singing. The audience went crazy! The next night, she thought, "That was kind of wonderful." So she repeated the stunt. Richard Rodgers or Oscar Hammerstein (depending on who tells the story) came backstage and pulled her aside and said, "Oh, no. You're never doing that again!"

When *Finian's Rainbow* was in its infancy, Burton Lane was rehearsing the chorus on one of their numbers. Lyricist E.Y. Harburg entered the room and instructed the cast members to pay no attention to what Lane had taught them. Harburg explained, "He's only the pianist." That was the beginning of a great rift between Lane and Harburg. In fact, Lane stated, "It was a good thing we didn't have to change one song. What we opened with out of town was basically the show that opened on Broadway." On opening night, they sat on opposite sides of the theatre. Lane didn't speak to Harburg until three years after the show opened.

As the lights came up after the opening night performance of *Finian's Rainbow*, Irving Berlin came up the aisle toward Lane. He said, "Hi Burt. Where's Yip?" Lane had no answer.

Harburg was not only the lyricist but also the coauthor with Fred Saidy and the de facto director of the show. Perhaps his bluster was because he was actually insecure about taking on such a big project. Harburg couldn't be criticized about anything in the show except his lyrics, and he was absolutely confident about those.

During the tryouts, Lane asked a performer why he gave such a lackluster performance. The actor replied, "How would you be if your replacement was in the audience watching you?" Harburg was so nervous about the show he had called agents in New York and had them send down replacement performers. None of the original actors were replaced.

When "The Begat" and "Necessity" were falling flat, Harburg wanted to cut the numbers. Musical director Milton Rosenstock thought Lyn Murray's vocal arrangements weren't up to snuff, so he asked Harburg to wait until he had time to work with the cast on the numbers. Rosenstock and the performers worked in the lower lounge of the theatre before and after the show and revised the vocal arrangements. And, of course, they made it into the show.

At some performances of the show, Ella Logan was fooling around with the tempos of the songs, changing notes, giving the score a jazzy feel, and using back phrasing, etc. Lane told her to stop but she didn't. So Lane told Milton Rosenstock to take the performance off. Lane conducted the show and Logan was shocked to see Lane conducting when she made her entrance. She never changed any notes or rhythms again.

Maude Adams was the favorite actress of playwright J.M. Barrie (see "Rehearsals"). She was out of town with Barrie's play *The Ladies' Shakespeare*. One day Barrie had an idea for a scene and scribbled some new dialogue. The cast and crew were staying at the Traymore Hotel in Atlantic City, and Barrie sent over the text to the director who looked at the page and then asked the stage manager what he thought. Maude Adams came out of her dressing room and examined the pages for a long time. She finally admitted that she couldn't read a word Barrie wrote. The director and stage manager also couldn't make heads or tails from Barrie's scratches. So they summoned the playwright himself. Upon arrival, Barrie took the pages and everyone was silent. Finally, he gave a smile and proclaimed, "I can't either."

When the musical *Oh Captain!* was playing in Philadelphia, the show was about a half-hour too long. The easiest thing was to cut some musical numbers and adapt the script accordingly. Unfortunately, one of the actors had his entire part deleted.

This happens more often than you would think. Jean Fenn disappeared from Noel Coward's *Sail Away*; Ella Logan's parts were cut from two shows, *Drat! the Cat!* and *Kelly*. Christine Andreas's role disappeared before the opening night of *Legs Diamond*. *Chicago* lost David Rounds and his song "Ten Percent" during previews. The Vietnamese kid was cut from *Woman of the Year*. The prostitute, who was the third female character in *1776*, was cut out of town.

Marian Winters who played Mrs. Kolowitz in *So Long 174th Street* was informed at the airport when the cast was boarding a plane to Philadelphia that she was not wanted on the trip. The musical *The First* had three characters who sat in a bar and opened acts one and two. They were cut. The three included Patricia Drylie, who had made a comeback in *Ballroom*.

The role of Jerry Ryan's wife Tess Ryan was played by Amanda McBroom and never saw the opening night of *Seesaw*, thanks to play doctor Neil Simon's advice. Johnny Desmond was in *Sugar* out of town when his role was changed from a singer to a tap dancer. Michael Dunn was relieved of duties when his role (and we use the word extremely loosely) was eliminated from *Dude* during the second round of previews.

Claiborne Cary and Mitzi McCall, as the Potter Sisters, were cut from *Little Me* and so was their song "Smart People Stay Single," which they sang with the Buxbaum Brothers. After the first preview in Philly, Cary walked out to the parking lot and saw Patrick Dennis, author of the original novel, vomiting. She didn't have to ask him what he thought.

The Bruckner family was wiped out in Boston during the tryout of *On a Clear Day You Can See Forever*. Dr. Bruckner's brother and his mother were cut in Boston. One brother lived to act another day. As we mentioned a few pages ago, Anita Gillette quit *Carnival* to go into *The Gay Life* only to find her part cut out of town.

And the show *Something Different* had its entire third act cut.

As everyone knows, the Shuberts have their own eponymous alley alongside the Shubert and Booth Theatres. Alexander Cohen's musical revue *Hellzapoppin* was due to open at the Minskoff Theatre on the west side of Shubert Alley. Jerry Lewis was starring in the show, which was about to go on a pre-Broadway tour. Cohen decided he'd name the arcade that stretched in front of the Minskoff's lobby between 44th and 45th streets "The Jerry Lewis Arcade."

Alas, *Hellzapoppin* never made it to Broadway. But certain people, namely, this author and the press agent Kevin McAnarney, still refer to the passageway as The Jerry Lewis Arcade. And we urge other theatre aficionados to do the same and make Alexander Cohen's dream come true.

During a show at the Kennedy Center, two chorus boys, while onstage with their backs to the audience, texted on their cell phones.

Before Broadway, Eugene O'Neill's epic play *Strange Interlude* was banned from Boston. So the show was booked in the nearby suburb of Quincy.

During a meal break between acts, audiences went to the closest restaurant. The restaurant was failing and was about to go out of business when the show's audiences came to eat there on the dinner breaks. The boost in business kept the restaurant afloat and it soon became successful. The name of the restaurant was Howard Johnson's.

When O'Neill's *The Iceman Cometh* was having one of its revivals on Broadway, it also had an intermission for meals. Near the theatre was the Gaiety Delicatessen (made famous in the musical *Skyscraper*). They advertised an "INTERMISHNOSH."

James Kirkwood's play *UTBU* opened in Boston to terrible reviews. The cast pleaded with producer Lyn Austin to close the play. No dice. But when they arrived at their next engagement in Philadelphia, there was a line at the box office and around the block. Hopes rose; maybe the critics were wrong and people really wanted to see this play. Then hopes fell; the line at the box office consisted of people who had heard about the Boston reviews and wanted refunds.

When the show *Glad to See Ya* was in trouble out of town, Jule Styne told lyricist Sammy Cahn that George Abbott had seen the performance and advised that the ending of the show should actually be the beginning. Cahn was confused; it just didn't make sense, but Abbott was a great play doctor so he must be right. Flash-forward a few years to the show *High Button Shoes* written by Styne and Cahn and directed by George Abbott. One day Cahn remembered Abbott's advice on *Glad to See Ya* and asked Abbott what he meant. Abbott replied that he had never seen that show. What! Cahn rushed over to Styne and told the composer that the director had never seen the show and had never advised putting the ending at the beginning. Styne looked Cahn in the eye and said, "If *I* had told you that's what we should do, would you have listened to me?"

Robert Preston had what he felt were his two greatest performances in *We Take the Town* and *The Prince of Grand Street*, which both closed out of town. He thought the theatre betrayed him and never came back to Broadway.

The Angela Lansbury revival of *Gypsy* was in Chicago and one of the newsboys didn't have a boyfriend. So after one of the performances, Lansbury went to a gay bar with other members of the cast and that night there was a knock on the cast member's door. There was Angela Lansbury with some guy whom she pushed into the room and said, "Have a good time." grotesque

During a performance of *Annie Get Your Gun* in Philadelphia prior to New York, the show was not well received. At the curtain call, Ethel Merman came down to the footlights and addressed the audience saying, "I'm sorry the show didn't go well, it's the boots costume designer Lucinda Ballard gave me to wear."

When *Camelot* was trying out in Toronto, the creative staff was thinking about having Bruce Yarnell replace Robert Goulet as Sir Lancelot. When the star Richard Burton got wind of the discussion, he absolutely forbade the change. After all, Yarnell was 6'4" and would have towered over Burton. So Goulet kept his job and became a star as Lancelot. However, Yarnell played the role of Sir Lancelot many, many times around the country.

During rehearsals of *Mr. President*, songwriter Irving Berlin told everyone how he couldn't sleep at all. He was a terrible insomniac. So they're in Boston with *Mr. President* and it's the middle of the night; the fire alarm goes off in the hotel and they're all ushered out to the street and they can't find Berlin. After the fire alarm is called off, Josh Logan goes to Berlin's room and he's sound asleep.

Mr. President was written with librettists Howard Lindsay and Russel Crouse. Josh Logan was the director and the show featured Nanette Fabray, Robert Ryan, and Anita Gillette. When the reviews came out, the *Boston Globe*'s headline was "Knee Deep Amongst the Corn." It was decided that the negative reviews wouldn't be discussed with Mr. Berlin. That morning, Berlin, Lindsay, Crouse, Logan, and Gillette were walking across Boston Common to the theatre talking about anything but the reviews. About midway through the park, Berlin inquired, "Did any of you see the reviews?" Logan hemmed and hawed while everyone else didn't know quite what to say. Berlin broke the silence and said, "'White Christmas,' 'Blue Skies,' 'God Bless America,' I know my songs are corny. But so is 'My Old Kentucky Home.'"

When *The Act* was trying out on the road, Martin Scorsese was the director. He was having an affair with Liza Minnelli, which was more important than the fact that he had never directed a musical. He would film sections of rehearsals and then go home and edit them so he could redirect them the next day. Once he showed up and asked John Kander who one of the dancers was. It turned out that the dancer was a swing boy who had been on for a week while another dancer was out with back trouble. Kander realized that Scorsese hadn't been coming to the performances. He spent his time in Liza Minnelli's dressing room enjoying cigars. Gower Champion took over the direction although he was not credited. And he even substituted for Barry Nelson, the show's leading man, for a week in New York.

Alfred Drake was the premier musical theatre star of the 1940s. Late in his life, he said, "I really would have had a career if I had been a few inches taller." Since his career included such hits as *Kiss Me, Kate, Oklahoma!* and *Kismet*, it was a sad statement. It is true that Drake never made it in Hollywood, but then Mary Martin, John Raitt, and Ethel Merman didn't have Hollywood careers to match their talents either.

Ken Kantor was walking outside Sardi's Restaurant and noticed the great actor. "Aren't you Alfred Drake?" he asked. "Well, I used to be," responded Drake.

The superb singer Joan Weldon was starring with Drake in the Robert Wright and George Forrest musical *Kean*, starting out in Boston. The show, as you might have surmised from its title, was a biographical portrait of the great English actor Sir Edmund Kean. The opening night audience in Boston stood up and cheered as the curtain fell. As soon as Weldon changed and took off her makeup, she ducked into a limo where the songwriters Wright and Forrest and the director Jack Cole were already ensconced. The writers were patting each other on their respective backs, savoring their triumphant success with the Boston audiences. Just then, Weldon asked, "Should we be working on the show?" They all looked at her as if she were crazy. As she related later, she knew the show was in big trouble because there wasn't any incentive to work on the show's many problems; the show's success in Boston led to its failure on Broadway.

One other reason for the failure of the show in New York was that Alfred Drake was ill. Wright later said that they knew Drake was sick when they went into rehearsal, but they didn't want to postpone because they might lose the theatre. After the New York opening, Drake missed many performances. The only solution was to close the show.

David Merrick didn't make the same mistake as Wright and Forrest; before *Do Re Mi* had its opening night in Washington, he met with *Washington Post* critic Richard L. Coe. Merrick admitted, "I had him come in and give a bad review so the creators would get to work on it."

Some shows like *Hello, Dolly!* may not have had as long runs if it weren't for the stars in the lead roles. So when stars miss performances, the box office suffers.

Liza Minnelli missed performances of *The Act* even though the show kept cutting back the number of performances per week.

Carol Burnett's extended hiatus from *Fade Out-Fade In* made audiences wary of purchasing tickets for what had been a huge hit before Burnett's absence.

Madeline Kahn was missing performances of *On the Twentieth Century* and though she was the star, her replacement, the unknown Judy Kaye, was remarkable in the role. But audiences wanted to see the star, not an understudy.

The same thing happened with *American Idiot*, and when Nathan Lane and Matthew Broderick would miss performances of *The Producers*, audiences wanted their money back.

Chicago was in terrible shape in Philadelphia and Bob Fosse was taking it out on members of the cast, as well as Kander and Ebb. One day, Kander said to Ebb, "Why don't we get on a train and go back to New York. This isn't worth it. No show is worth dying for."

The Conquering Hero, based on the Preston Sturges movie *Hail the Conquering Hero*, had an especially rocky tryout. Nothing was working and the director/choreographer was desperate to make the show work. In fact, he decided that he himself should replace the leading man Tom Poston. The producers Roger L. Stevens and Robert Whitehead saw no other choice but to fire him. He was replaced by Albert Marre as director and Todd Bolender as choreographer. But when the show finally opened, no one was credited in either role. *The New York Times* review stated, "Whoever mixed the ingredients failed to produce freshness or excitement." This is surprising since the original director and choreographer was none other than Bob Fosse.

The Conquering Hero did make theatre history, however. It was the impetus for one of the most-quoted quips in Broadway history, a line that is misquoted constantly. Here's what librettist Larry Gelbart actually said while out of town with the show, "If Hitler's alive, I hope he's out of town with a musical."

Another line that has been misquoted and misattributed over the years was from Larry Kert, rehearsing in London for *Company*, who said during an especially grueling tech rehearsal, "Who do I have to screw to get out of this show?" In the back of the audience, composer Stephen Sondheim called out, "The same person you screwed to get in!" (Note: Ethan Mordden claims this happened at Larry Kert's birthday party.)

Directorial students at the Yale School of Drama had a free pass to go down to the Shubert Theatre anytime they wanted to drop into rehearsals. Joseph Hardy went down to watch the final dress rehearsal of Eugene O'Neill's

Long Day's Journey into Night. Frederic March and Florence Eldridge were the stars. At the end of the performance, an old woman came up on the stage and went to the director Jose Quintero. She took off her wedding ring and gave it to Quintero. It was Carlotta O'Neill, the author's widow.

When they didn't like a show, the Yale students didn't mind letting the cast know. When Michael V. Gazzo's play *A Hatful of Rain* opened in New Haven, the Yale crowd, two balconies full of them, hooted and hollered. Of course, it did run almost five hours! The dean of the Yale Drama School apologized for the students' behavior in an ad in the newspaper. Overnight, Frank Corsaro cut the play down to a manageable size and the second night audience's appreciation buoyed the entire company.

The show had other rocky moments out of town on the way to Broadway. At the end of the Philadelphia tryout, Tony Franciosa suffered horrible stomach pains and was taken to the hospital where it was determined that he had kidney stones. His illness meant that he missed the Washington, D.C., opening and so Harry Guardino, his understudy, took his place on opening night. As you may know, understudies don't get a lot of rehearsal before an opening. At the very end of the play, Guardino was so nervous when he went to punch actor Frank Silvera, playing his son, that he actually clocked Silvera on the jaw and knocked him out. Shelley Winters poured a pitcher of water on him and he finally came to in time for the fourth bow of the curtain call.

Marshall Barer doctored a lot of shows. Once when he was approached to write a show, someone told him that he should turn the job down. And then, if the show was in trouble, he could step in as a play doctor. The reasoning went that if the show were a hit, Barer would be a hero. And if the show failed, Barer wouldn't be blamed. After all, he had tried his best with bad material.

During the short run of *Rex* at the Lunt-Fontanne Theatre, most of the bumps were caused by Nicol Williamson's mercurial personality. In fact, Williamson actually slapped one of the actors during the curtain call. The actor had said, "That's a wrap," but Williamson thought he heard "This is crap." The papers picked up on the story and it made headlines. When costar Penny Fuller saw the papers, she was apoplectic. She took the papers, barged into Williamson's dressing room, threw the papers at him, and yelled, "You son of a bitch, now we'll run for years!" It didn't.

Nicol Williamson struck again when he was starring in Paul Rudnick's play *I Hate Hamlet* alongside Evan Handler and Jane Adams. Williamson had been rambunctious (actually, drunk) all through the rehearsal period, but one performance was the cherry in the Manhattan. James Freydberg, one of the show's producers, recalled, "In the middle of the scene Nicol suddenly said to Mr. Handler and Ms. Adams: 'Put some life into it! Use your head! Give it more life!' He felt the scene was too slow." Then came the final scene of the act where Handler and Williamson were meant to duel. Mr. Freydberg continued: "In the first movement of the fight, when the swords are supposed to hit, this time they missed. Nicol later said he thought that Evan was pulling something on him, and Evan felt that Nicol was pulling something on him. It's a very intricate choreography, and the truth is, it really may have been an innocent miss on both their parts." Well, Williamson became quite rowdy and slapped Handler on the ass with the broad edge of his sword.

Freydberg again: "When that happened, Evan walked straight through the door on the set, and out." Williamson was left without a partner to terrorize, so he turned to the audience and said, "Well, should I sing? It seems someone who has missed a few parries has elected to leave the stage, which unless one is very, very sick is an unprofessional thing to do. Please excuse us. We'll begin the second act as quickly as possible."

As the run continued, sans Handler, during curtain calls, Williamson would lead the audience in a rousing chorus of "Happy Days Are Here Again" and exhort them to "head home and enjoy a nice juicy slice of sexual intercourse!"

When the ill-fated musical *Sheba* was having its tryout in Chicago, Kaye Ballard went to the front of the stage during the curtain call to address the audience. She said, "Thank you very much for coming to our show. I also want to thank our director, Bill Francisco, who left after the opening night and was never seen again." She then went on to castigate almost everyone else in the production.

When the revival of *Oh, Kay!* was at the Kennedy Center before Broadway, and dying a horrible death, standing in the back of the house watching a performance was producer Cyma Rubin, who said to director Donald Saddler, "I know what's wrong with the show, the chorus girls' shoes."

Rubin's daughter Loni Ackerman was in *No, No, Nanette*, which was also produced by Rubin. But it wasn't nepotism that got her cast. She's a marvelous singer and actress but, of course, people thought that's how she got cast, though she had already appeared in *George M!* and *Dames at Sea*. When she won a portable TV in a raffle, the cast went around telling everyone that her mother rigged it so Loni would win. Loni proved to everyone just how talented she was when she had the lead in the L.A. company of *Evita* and blew everybody away with her fantastic performance.

Mitch Leigh, composer of *Man of La Mancha*, fancied himself a producer, and in 1983, he mounted a revival of *Mame* at the Gershwin Theatre. The show was originally to be produced by Joe Kipness, but he was busy with *Woman of the Year* and other shows, and so Leigh stepped in. He sent it on a two-year national tour before Broadway. But Leigh was a cheapskate and cut corners on the set, costumes, and lighting. The poster had a horrible caricature of Angela Lansbury. Lansbury referred to it as "a picture of the woman. Whoever she is."

The first booking for the show was at the massive Academy of Music in Philadelphia. It opened on the Fourth of July and many people decided to decamp to the newly revitalized Atlantic City with its gleaming, if tacky, casinos. At one performance, the audience was sparse. Angela Lansbury called the cast together and gave a pep talk: "There are 270 people who paid good money and really want to see this show. So, I want each of you to give the best performance you can and let's do the best show we can." The cast did, and the audience went wild. Lansbury's husband Peter Shaw came backstage after one performance and said to his wife, "I'm sorry there weren't so many people in the audience." To which Lansbury replied, "Yes, but they were so enthusiastic!"

Sadly, tickets sales didn't pick up and Leigh decided to just bring the show to New York and take a tax write-off. The problem was that several of the actors had sublet their apartments for two years and were now homeless. The revival lasted a month.

Once it was clear that the show wasn't going to be a smash hit, Leigh wanted it to close. But Jerry Herman, Angela Lansbury, and Jimmy Nederlander each put up $25,000 of their own money with the understanding that, when the show became profitable, they would be paid back. The first week, the show lost $10,000. The second week, the show only lost $5,000. The third week, the show had a profit of $5,000. Leigh immediately closed the show to guarantee that he could take the write-off. To add insult to injury, Leigh said he was planning to reopen it, in his own words, "with a nationally recognized star." Obviously, Leigh didn't like Lansbury, who was adored by everyone who ever met her. Leigh would refer to her with a certain four-letter word that started with the letter "c."

When the show opened in New York, Leigh was so cheap, he chartered a city bus to take the cast to the opening night party instead of supplying limos.

Leigh also filmed the show during its New York run for a television special, but because he hated Lansbury (who hated him back), it was never broadcast and has never been found.

Two years later, Leigh presented Yul Brynner at the Broadway Theatre in *The King and I*. That revival ran for a year, but the show didn't always sell out. Leigh refused to put the show up at the TKTS discount booth because he thought it would diminish Brynner's value.

When *Carousel* opened in Boston before heading to New York, Richard Rodgers had severe back pains, so he was strapped on a stretcher and put in a box seat behind a curtain. The drape muffled the sound and Rodgers could barely hear the music and none of the applause. He assumed the show was a failure.

Cole Porter had to be carried into the theatre to see his shows after his legs were severely damaged when a horse fell on them.

Here's a story you probably already know, but it bears repeating. When *A Funny Thing Happened on the Way to the Forum* was in Washington, D.C., at the National Theatre, the show wasn't quite working.

Abbott turned to one of the writers: "I don't know what to do. Call somebody in. Maybe George Abbott."

They decided to bring in Jerome Robbins to help fix the show. Robbins had already turned down the direction of the show, resulting in author Larry Gelbart sending him the following telegram: "Your cowardly withdrawal is consistent with your well-earned reputation for immorality."

Robbins had been a friendly witness at the House Un-American Committee hearings that resulted in the blacklisting of *Forum* star Zero Mostel and another member of the cast, Jack Gilford. Gilford's wife Madeline was also named by Robbins. But Mostel and Gilford took the high road and decided that they would not stop someone from working on the show due to their politics. As Mostel was quoted as saying, "We of the left do not blacklist."

But when Robbins met the cast, things became tense. As he went down the line shaking everyone's hands, Mostel was at the end. What would he do? Would he deign to shake Robbins's hand? Mostel turned to Robbins and bellowed, "Hiya, loose lips," and the tension was broken. Mostel would never talk to Robbins again. If he had a question, he would ask another actor, "Would you ask Mr. Robbins. . . ."

This story is not about a tryout but rather a national tour. As her husband Charles MacArthur recalled, his wife Helen Hayes was going to play New Orleans with *Victoria Regina*. Instead of residing at the Roosevelt Hotel, she decided on a small hotel in the Latin Quarter. She was delighted with her accommodations and she enthused about her domicile in every interview. Reporters seemed surprised that she was staying at that hotel and that she liked the ambiance so much because, as it turned out, the inn was a beautifully appointed bordello.

Leonard Sillman's revue *Fools Rush In* was playing in Port Washington, Long Island, at an outdoor theatre. There was rain forecast for that evening so a makeshift tarpaulin was erected over the audience. At the start of the show, there was a slight drizzle, but as the show continued, the rain became a deluge. The sound of the raindrops hitting the tarp nearly drowned out the shenanigans onstage. But worse, the rain did not slide off the tarp but gathered in the center creating a gigantic bulge only a few feet over the audience's heads.

But the audience was mesmerized by what was happening onstage. Elizabeth Morgan was singing her heart out on the chorus "I'm so bored with it all—j'ai ennui." She repeated this several times though the audience could barely hear her. Four or five verses of the song later, Morgan, at the top of her lungs, raised her voice to the skies and shrieked, "J'ai ennui." The tarp gave way and about five gallons of water plunged down onto her face and into her mouth.

The audience finally recognized the situation and ran out into the storm.

When *The Pajama Game* was in New Haven, nerves were on edge. To the neophyte composers Richard Adler and Jerry Ross, the show looked like it would never come together. Scenes and songs were switched around, given to different characters, and sometimes taken right out of the show. Janis Paige was nervous because it was her first musical, and she took out her stress on Lemuel Ayers and his costumes. She was getting more and more worked up when Rosalind Russell came on the scene. She took Paige by the arm and sat her down in her limousine. She then corralled the show's three producers, Harold Prince, Robert Griffith, and Frederick Brisson, and ordered them to get in the backseat. Russell then got behind the wheel and drove them to downtown New Haven. There they went from store to store buying new clothes for Paige. At the end of two hours, calm was restored and so was the team's good nature.

Park Avenue was playing in Boston at the Colonial Theatre. The show's second act just didn't work. Arthur Schwartz recalled, "Just before the audience gathered on opening night Ira Gershwin, George S. Kaufman and I were standing around in the back of the audience looking at the lovely wooden ceiling. Ira said, 'Look at those wooden beams.' I said, 'My god, this place is a fire trap.' George Kaufman answered, 'It'll make our second act.'"

When Neil Simon's *The Gingerbread Lady* premiered on Broadway, a woman got up from her seat in the middle of the show and started pacing in the back of the auditorium. It was Elaine Stritch, and she was angry. Simon walked over to her and she told him in no uncertain terms, "That's my play. That play belongs to me. I should be up there right now doing this goddamn play." She eventually did appear in the play in the London production.

The show *Beggar's Holiday* was in deep trouble in Boston. Despite the talents of the songwriters Duke Ellington and John Latouche, and director John Houseman, the show just wasn't working. Lines were changed constantly to no avail. So George Abbott was called in as a play doctor. He asked that they go back to the original script, before all the changes were made, to see what they started out with. But nobody could find the original script. It just didn't seem to exist. Thus the show was doomed.

This is a story that's been told and retold so many times, it seems apocryphal. But here's what really happened.

Jack Gilford was playing in a tent theatre production of *Finian's Rainbow* in Flint, Michigan. Tent theatres were usually in the round with entrances and exits up long aisles. One part of the plot of *Finian's Rainbow* is when a racist white senator is turned black. At this theatre, when the spell was put on the senator, there was a blackout and the actor playing the senator quickly ran up the aisle and had blackface applied by a stagehand. At one performance, the actor lost his sense of direction and went up the wrong aisle. At that exact moment, an audience member decided to sneak out during the blackout. He went up the aisle usually used by the actor and found himself covered in blackface, disoriented, blinded by a spotlight, and calling out "Harriet . . . Harriet. . . ."

The Little Dog Laughed was a Harold Rome show that was a lefty musical fable. The producer cast his girlfriend in the female lead. "As soon as she walked out onstage, I visualized the closing notice being posted. I knew we couldn't bring the show to New York." And the producer refused to fire her. Rome said, "She must have been good for something. It just wasn't singing or dancing or acting." The show never made it to New York.

Where's Charley? opened in Philadelphia with Ray Bolger as the star. He was what was known as an "eccentric" dancer. Bolger put so much energy into his performance he collapsed in his dressing room after the curtain came down. A doctor came and said he was suffering from exhaustion and who knows when he would be able to rejoin the show. When they asked director George Abbott what they could do without Bolger, he declared, "We close the show. Ray Bolger is not just the star—he is the show." Luckily, three days later, Bolger returned and learned how to conserve his energy when onstage.

Cy Feuer and Ernest Martin had a great hit with *Where's Charley?* and later with *Guys and Dolls*. But when Cole Porter's *Silk Stockings* was out of town, they became tyrants, insisting that Kaufman, director and coauthor with his wife Leueen MacGrath, put in more and more corny jokes. Kaufman left the production for two weeks in protest. And the female star Hildegard Neff wrote in her diary, "George Kaufman refuses to go on rewriting and adding the crude gags that Cy and Ernie insist on. He is more taciturn than ever. Cole Porter doesn't leave his hotel room." Abe Burrows was brought in to doctor the show. Neff wrote, "The 'play doctor' is slicing through the play like a snow plow, peppering it full of rancid Capitalist-Communist corn, strangling Ninotchka with mouthfuls of partyese." Kaufman finally couldn't take it anymore, apologizing to the cast at his departure. Feuer took over the direction. When the show reached Boston, Kaufman and his wife returned to the production expecting to be greeted with open arms. But Feuer informed them that they had been fired, and their services were no longer wanted.

The Odd Couple was in rehearsal in Boston when Walter Matthau objected to a line in the scene with the Pigeon Sisters, two British ladies who lived in the same building as Felix and Oscar. The sisters suggested that Oscar and Felix take them out on a double date. Felix said, "What's wrong, Oscar? You didn't like doubleheaders?" Simon himself didn't like the line but didn't know what to substitute. While Simon's concentration was on bigger problems with the play, Matthau kept badgering him about changing the line.

The following day, Simon received a letter from an audience member who had seen the show and liked it a lot, except for that one line. The letter was signed "Morton Cantrow, Ph.D., English Dept., Harvard University." Simon was impressed and decided it was time to write a new line, which he did.

When the cast inquired about the line change, Simon showed them the letter. When Matthau read it, he smiled. Simon's antenna went up, "You bastard, you wrote the letter, didn't you?" Matthau gloated, "It worked, didn't it?"

When *The Happy Time* was in Los Angeles trying out, director Gower Champion told Kander and Ebb to expect that producer David Merrick would come to them at some point and warn them that, if they didn't make changes, he would close the show. What happened? Merrick came to Fred Ebb and said, "I'm ready to close the show. Gower won't make the changes I want, and I'm closing the show unless you can influence him." Ebb didn't and Gower didn't and Merrick didn't. It was all part of the Merrick act.

Of course, Kander and Ebb had their own problems with Champion. They were barred from the theatre during rehearsals of *The Happy Time*, as Jerry Herman was with Champion on *Hello, Dolly!*

When it first opened out of town, the posters for *Do Re Mi* had hyphens between the words, and then they were removed. Before the first previews, librettist Garson Kanin's wife Ruth Gordon was outside painting out the hypens in the title.

During rehearsals of *Hello, Dolly!* Carol Channing would put lettuce leaves in her pockets during rehearsals and pull them out for a snack.

One thing that Gower Champion would not abide during rehearsals was any noise. During rehearsals for *Carnival!* he berated the entire cast, threatening to fire anyone who made any noise whatsoever. Dancer George Morrisey took a safety pin out of his bag and dropped it to the floor. Champion whirled around and demanded, "OK, who let that pin drop!" The entire cast broke into laughter.

Bob Fosse loved the rehearsal process and loved his dancers. When the Frank Loesser musical *Pleasures and Palaces* put up a notice in Detroit on a Tuesday announcing the show would close after the Saturday evening show, Fosse and the dancers had a rehearsal of the "Tears of Joy" number even though the curtain would come down in a few days.

Likewise, Gower Champion kept rehearsing *Hello, Dolly!* long after the show opened. When Ginger Rogers came into the show in August 1965, Champion replaced the song "Come and Be My Butterfly" with a dance number called "The Polka Contest."

When Gwen Verdon was out of town with *Sweet Charity* just before it came into the Palace Theatre on Broadway, disaster struck. The show had a scene where Verdon hid in a closet. A feather boa was hanging in the closet, and Verdon inhaled a feather that got stuck in her throat. She had trouble breathing and her voice was raspy until one day she had to go to the hospital and have the feather removed. But she was laid up until her vocal chords *cords* recovered. Her understudy Helen Gallagher took over the part and for a while, it looked like Verdon wouldn't open the show on Broadway. But she recovered in time to give a brilliant performance on opening night.

When *Gypsy* was out of town, it was the Easter/Passover season. Jule Styne decided to throw a Seder for the company. Ethel Merman was nervous about what she would have to eat, and Arthur Laurents assured her that she would probably have chicken. When the day of the Seder arrived, Styne gave her the seat of honor at the head of the table. She sat down and pulled out a ham sandwich from her purse. Styne grabbed the sandwich and threw it on the floor. "Ethel," he said, "You're insulting the waiters!" Then he turned around and started laughing so Merman couldn't see him.

George S. Kaufman and Ring Lardner's play *June Moon* was trying out in Atlantic City, the premiere tryout town in the 1920s. Kaufman kept cutting down the play. Cuts in the script were made daily. Lardner was strolling on the boardwalk taking a break from the craziness when a friend bumped into him. "What are you doing down here, Ring?" inquired the friend. Lardner took a breath and said, "I'm down here with an act."

The original Broadway cast recording of *Oliver!* was taped at the old NBC Radio Studios at Hollywood and Vine while the show was on tour before going to Broadway. The show was such a hit even before it opened on Broadway that producer David Merrick made sure to have the album ready while the show made its way to Broadway.

The Roar of the Greasepaint, The Smell of the Crowd was not a success in its premiere in London. When Merrick brought it to the States, he had such faith in the score that he also recorded the cast album before the pre-Broadway tour. He was correct, and the show and its songs were tremendous hits.

JOHN RAITT

Very early in the national tour of the musical *Shenandoah*, a young actor had to perform a dance number. But he wasn't a dancer; he was a singer, so the dancing was very hard for him. But at one performance, he executed the dance perfectly. He ran into the wings, feeling very proud of himself, when he realized that he missed his bow in the curtain call. So without thinking, he ran onstage to take his bow. Well, at the exact same moment, the star John Raitt was walking forward to take his bow, and the actor cut him off.

After the curtain came down, Raitt called the actor over and asked what the hell he was doing. The actor apologized and told Raitt it wouldn't happen again.

Raitt threw the cast a party in Detroit because his daughter Bonnie was appearing on *Saturday Night Live* for the first time. It was around his birthday and the cast watched the performance. After she sang, she looked at the camera and said, "Happy birthday, Dad." It was a very sweet moment. This was a case where a rocky relationship between a star and his daughter ended up working out just fine.

In *Shenandoah*, Raitt played the role of Papa Charlie, and one of his sons gets shot by a sniper. Papa Charlie was supposed to pick up a gun and shoot the sniper, and this was the lynchpin for further plot developments. Raitt was a Quaker; he didn't want to play the scene. And so he changed the dialogue where he has the sniper in his sights. Just when he was about to pull the trigger, he said, "No, I'm not going to kill you though I want to. I want you to go home to your family and for every day for the rest of your life, I want you to remember that you killed my son." In a way, it was a more powerful statement.

Raitt was one of the nicest stars. He loved being John Raitt, but not in a vain way. He just really enjoyed his talents and sharing them with audiences. During the tour, the cast kept asking Raitt to sing "Hey, There" from *The Pajama Game* or one of his other great songs like the "Soliloquy" from *Carousel*. But he kept turning them down, saying he would do it when they had a party. The cast was performing in Nyack, New York, in a theatre that used to be a shoe store in a strip mall. It was dubbed the Helen Hayes Theatre.

Because the theatre was so small, for that engagement, the company was put on a stock contract and the understudies were let go for the week. Nyack was close enough to New York, so the cast was told to take the train to and from the theatre. Well, one day, there was a terrible snowstorm and the boy playing the slave boy couldn't get to the theatre. Now, that role was very important. Between the scenes, he would come out while the sets were changed. And he had one big song in the show, "Freedom." Without an understudy there was a big problem. Raitt stepped in front of the curtain before the show and explained to the audience that one of the cast members could not make it to the theatre, but if they were very good, there'd be a surprise for them at the end of the show. After the curtain call, Raitt went up to the front of the stage and sang "Hey There" and "If I Loved You." The audience was thrilled, the cast was thrilled, and what could have been a disaster was turned into a night to remember.

Raitt was the original baritone-tenor with a great range. There was no break when he went from head voice to chest voice. He could sing pianissimo or fortissimo with great ease. He probably had the greatest theatre voice of the modern era.

FIVE DAVID MERRICK STORIES

Gower Champion was very insecure, so when *Carnival!* opened in D.C., it was in perfect shape; but he didn't trust himself, so he started changing everything. When Merrick saw it with the changes, he made Champion put everything back the way it was originally.

Merrick liked to pit writers against each other. When he was producing the musical *Do Re Mi*, Merrick told lyricists Betty Comden and Adolph Green that Jule Styne's music was ruining their lyrics. Merrick then went to Styne, saying that Comden and Green's lyrics were no good. He thought that antagonism got the best out of his writers.

When Styne and Bob Merrill's musical *Sugar* was trying out in Washington's Kennedy Center, Gower Champion asked Jerry Herman to look at the show. Styne spied Herman in the lobby and told him in no uncertain terms that he was to take the next train back to New York. Herman complied. Gower then screamed at Jule Styne, "You ruined everything!"

Tom Jones recalled: "When *I Do! I Do!* was out of town for tryouts, I happened to be reading *The Rise and Fall of the Third Reich*. Perhaps because of that I couldn't help seeing many similarities. I saw Harvey and me as Czechoslovakia and David Merrick as Hitler." Jones told Peter Filichia that, in the musical *Celebration*, he based the character of the money-grubbing, avaricious Mr. Rich on Merrick.

Nicol Williamson was appearing in the play *Inadmissible Evidence* in Philadelphia Arguing whether the play should be kept in its original three-act form as it was produced in London, or whether it should only have two acts, the actor and the producer got into a fight in the alley by the stage door of the theatre. Williamson won the fight if not the battle when he punched Merrick and sent him reeling into a trashcan.

During the out-of-town tryouts of *110 in the Shade*, Merrick was unhappy with Inga Swenson's performance. He thought she was too teary-eyed and weepy, feeling sorry for herself all the time. "It's killing the show," he insisted. In fact, it was director Joseph Anthony's direction that made her do this. Before one performance, Merrick walked into Swenson's dressing room while she was putting on her makeup and told her, "Tonight during the first act if I see one tear or hear one thing of self-pity from you, your understudy is going on in the second act." Inga asked musical director Don Pippin, "Oh, my god, what do I do?" Pippin told her, "I suggest you do what he said." She did, and the show started working for the first time.

The male lead Robert Horton wasn't a stage actor though he had a good voice and was a talented actor. He had made his fame on the television western *Bonanza*. In his performances, he tended to overcompensate for his insecurity by being overly macho. Perhaps he was trying to hide his homosexuality.

[handwritten margin note: might be better & others followed his lead]

At the same time that *110* was in Boston, Noel Coward's *The Girl Who Came to Supper* was at the Colonial Theatre. Pippin bumped into Coward on the street and invited him to see *110 in the Shade*. After the performance, he and Pippin went to the Ritz to have dinner. Pippin asked Coward what he thought. "Well, my dear," said Coward, "the vagabond queen has to go," referring to Robert Horton. Noel Coward later told Marlene Dietrich, "Robert Horton's idea of acting the cowboy is to push his pelvis forward and swagger. I wanted to shout, 'Show us your cock and get on with it!'"

[handwritten margin note: typical civilized remark]

At the orchestra reading in Boston, orchestrator Hershy Kay was being hounded by Merrick on every number. "I want the melody in the woodwinds. There's no melody!" Kay stayed up all night rescoring the songs, and it turned out that Merrick was right.

Merrick said to Pippin, "You know, this show's too much of a musical. Agnes (de Mille) has done all those beautiful dances. We don't need them. They just get in the way of the show." The next morning, he called a production meeting and said, "Agnes, your work is brilliant. Absolutely superb. But Agnes, I've had to make a very serious decision. We have to cut them. This show isn't really a musical but really a play with music." De Mille pulled herself together and said, "David, no one has ever told me that about my work." "Well, maybe it needed to be said," replied Merrick. And de Mille made the cuts.

On *110 in the Shade*, director Joe Anthony was unhappy with the third opening they tried. He asked de Mille if she could work on something that would set the scene. She did and showed it to Anthony. But in the end, she told Anthony, "Joe, look up there. It's supposed to be hot and they're dancing. It's wrong." And she herself cut the dance.

LAURETTE TAYLOR

A young writer was under contract to MGM and among his duties was to write material for Margaret O'Brien. He tried to get the studio interested in a new play he wrote. No dice. Finally, someone picked up the play for production, but the road to Broadway was not easy. Tennessee Williams's *The Glass Menagerie* went on to become a tremendous hit. Starring in that play was Laurette Taylor, one of the greatest actresses in theatre history. But even the tryouts were rocky and whether the show would come into New York was doubtful.

The Glass Menagerie opened in Chicago with only a $400 advance. Why take a chance on a playwright and a play no one's heard of, with an unreliable actress? Taylor was an alcoholic and her performances could be spotty. But her acting was so electrifying, it was worth the gamble to give her the lead.

Opening night came and the stage manager knocked on Taylor's dressing room door. "Half hour, Miss Taylor." "Better hold it," was the reply. "Hold it, Miss Taylor?" The stage manager was now getting nervous, very nervous. "Anything wrong?" he asked, trying to keep his heart in his chest. "No." "Anything I can do?" Taylor replied, "Come in. I'm dying my Blue Mountain Casino costume. I told them it looked too good." There was the great actress with her costume in a washtub and her arms blue from the dye.

At the curtain call that first night, Julie Haydon, Taylor's costar, ignored the audience and bowed to Taylor. "Don't ever do that!" Taylor instructed Haydon. "But you're so *great!*" "Don't ever do that!" repeated the actress. The next night, the same thing happened, only Haydon dropped to one knee and kissed Taylor's hand. "Don't do that, Julie! I warn you! "But you're so *great!*" "I warn you!" The next night, the same thing happened again, except as she was kissing Taylor's hand, Taylor clocked her on the chin and knocked her out! Needless to say, the audience, stage manager, and the rest of the cast were shocked. The curtain went down slowly, as if it itself couldn't believe what had just happened.

And did you know, the Chicago critics returned the second night to see the show again? Has that ever happened in the history of the theatre? Well, yes, it did. When Maxwell Anderson's *Winterset* opened at the Martin Beck Theatre in 1935, the critics returned for another performance and some asked to read the script before writing a second review.

For the entire run, Haydon said goodnight to Taylor every evening after the performance. On one night, Taylor said, "Julie, this is Mrs. Cas ..." She was cut off by Haydon. "Oh, Miss Cassidy, *thank* you for that bad notice." Haydon replied, "No, Julie, this is Mrs. Cas ..." Again she was cut off by Haydon. "It will help me to learn! *Thank* you for all the dreadful things you said about me." Finally, Taylor was able to finish her sentence. "Julie! This is *not* Claudia Cassidy, this is Irene Castle!"

On opening night at the Playhouse Theatre on West 48th Street, people were still worried about Taylor's drinking problem. Would the stress of opening on Broadway get her off the wagon? Gifts filled Laurette Taylor's dressing room: flowers, presents, telegrams, and a bottle of scotch, the last from critic George Jean Nathan. After the performance, Nathan came backstage to congratulate Taylor. The actress pointed to the bottle of booze and said to Nathan, "Thanks for the vote of confidence."

MATA HARI

During the ill-fated tryout of *Mata Hari* at the National Theatre in Washington, Marissa Mell played the title character opposite Pernell Roberts who, like Robert Horton in *110 in the Shade*, was one of the *Bonanza* Cartwright brothers trying to break out from television into Broadway. The big news before opening was that Roberts would not appear in his toupee during the show. This was a much discussed story at the time.

At one rehearsal of *Mata Hari*, director Vincente Minnelli asked to have a scene rerun. This required ten minutes of changing the set back to its original position, changing the lighting cues, and getting the cast back in place. The cast started running the scene and almost immediately Minnelli stopped them. He went up to one of women in the chorus and told her how he wanted her to hold her purse. That was it. All through the rehearsals, he was obsessed with costumes and props.

One of Mell's costume changes was very quick and the dress was flown in on a batten. If she stood in a specific spot, the dress would come down and she'd step into it just before the lights came back on. At one performance, she was standing in the wrong place. The lights came up and there she was in her bra. She screamed and tried to cover herself and the lights went off again.

The gala opening-night charity performance for the Women's Democratic Committee of the show in Washington was, in fact, the first dress run-through of the show. At the end of the show, Mata Hari is shot. Mell is lying on the ground, dead, with her hands tied behind her back. The curtain was halfway down when Mell, wearing white gloves, reached up and scratched her nose. There was no curtain call that night.

NOW YOU SING THE SONG, NOW YOU DON'T

When Marilyn Miller heard Harriette Lake sing "Blue Bowery" and "More than Ever" during the Boston tryout of *Smiles*, she insisted that the songs be cut from the show. Miller, by the way, wasn't an especially good judge of material. She hated the song "Time on My Hands" and refused to sing it. Paul Gregory sang it to Miller instead and she sang one verse of the song with a new lyric by Ring Lardner.

When Pearl Bailey heard Diahann Carroll sing "Don't Like Goodbyes" in *House of Flowers*, Pearly Mae insisted that the song be given to her, even though it didn't fit her character. She got it.

During the Boston run of *John Murray Anderson's Almanac*, the titular director Anderson heard from several people as well as critics (who are people, no?) that singer/dancer Elaine Dunn should be given more to do in the show. Cast member Kenneth Urmston recalled, "They gave her a number titled 'Going Up.' It was an elevator song. And they put in the song in Boston, and it stopped the show cold. And so what was told to me was that Polly Bergen said, 'That is the last time she'll be doing that. I'm the singer in the show. She's supposed to sing and dance with Carleton Carpenter.'" And Bergen got the number.

ALL IN FUN—OR NOT

The musical revue *All in Fun* opened on December 27, 1940, and closed the next day after three performances. But it might have done better if producer Leonard Sillman hadn't made some mistakes while the show was out of town.

Sillman was approached by a pianist who was looking for a place in the revue. He played for Sillman and Phil Baker, the co-producer. His performance was not impressive. When the show opened in New Haven, the same performer sent a telegram saying that he'd like the chance to sing one number in the show with no pay. If they were satisfied with him, he would work for whatever salary they deemed fair. Sillman ignored the telegram, which was written by a Danish performer named Victor Borge.

Producer Jed Harris urged Sillman to listen to a German composer who had just arrived in the United States. The composer demonstrated some of his songs. Sillman kindly told him that American tastes were different and maybe he should give up the dream of becoming a composer in the States. That man was Kurt Weill.

FOUR STORIES ABOUT *ANNIE* AT THE GOODSPEED OPERA HOUSE BEFORE BROADWAY

When *Annie* was out of town, the girl playing the title character was miscast. It might not surprise you to hear that every little girl in the show knew each other's lines perfectly. That's what kids can do. In fact, it was a big problem that the other girls were silently mouthing Annie's lines. So, at one performance, Martin Charnin went up to one of the orphans and told her that she'd be going on that evening as Annie. That girl, as you may have guessed, was Andrea McArdle, and she brought the perfect amount of toughness to the part.

Jay Presson Allen, the playwright and author who is perhaps best known for *The Prime of Miss Jean Brodie*, saw a performance of *Annie* and was immediately struck by it. She called Mike Nichols up and said to him, "Get your ass down here." He saw the show and liked it but told Charles Strouse and Martin Charnin, "I don't usually produce shows." The next morning at 7 a.m., Martin Charnin got a call from Nichols who said, "We'll do it. I'm going to be the producer I never had," referring to Saint-Subber who had produced Nichols's early hits.

Strouse insisted that the billing read "Mike Nichols presents" because of something Harold Prince had told him during their show *It's a Bird, It's a Plane, It's Superman*. Prince said, "If it's a children's show, nobody will come. But if it's a show that's an adult show that parents can bring their children to, you'll be a hit."

In one scene, there was a fight with some boys against a fence in the background. Then the scene changed to the orphanage. Martin Charnin needed an extra forty seconds for the set change, so they wrote a new song for Annie to sing while the change was made. It was a simple song just written to pass the time. The song was "Tomorrow." (Note: Martin Charnin told Peter Filichia that the first words he wrote for the show were "The sun will come out tomorrow. Bet your bottom dollar that tomorrow there'll be sun.")

SEX ON THE ROAD

If you were married or had a partner, the rule was that if you were on tour with a show and cheated on your partner, "Drunk and on the road don't count."

There was another rule that if you went out of town either pre-Broadway or on a national tour, you had to have sex with somebody. One young guy went out of town with a cast of only four people, all of whom were elderly. He was very, very concerned that he hadn't gotten laid. But when he got to Boston, he figured out that he didn't have to sleep with an actor and so he found someone else associated with the production and fulfilled his "duty." But if you had sex while on the road, the rule was that you could never talk about it to anyone. Yet another rule was that you had to buy donuts for the entire company. So if you went down to breakfast and there were donuts, you knew that someone had hooked up the night before. Sadly, this tradition has not continued.

And, if you were a play doctor, part of the agreement was that you had your choice of chorus members to sleep with, male or female.

CHAPTER 11

Theatres

The Alvin Theatre's name came from the two producers who built it: Alex Aarons and Vinton Freedley. The theatre is now named the Neil Simon Theatre.

In the "Quotes" chapter, there are two examples of how badly the Shubert Brothers Organization kept up the Majestic Theatre. Today, theatres have a different problem that keeps them from being in tip-top shape: Shows simply run too long. In the past, when a show closed, theatres would be cleaned, and repainted if necessary. Improvements to the electricity or plumbing could be attended to. But now, with no downtime, many theatres are disturbingly filthy or downright dangerous.

Sometimes, architects just screw up. Often, they have no background of theatre design, so they build huge barns with lousy acoustics, bad sight-lines, and inconsistencies of design and style. The Shuberts employed the esteemed designer Herbert J. Krapp to design most of their theatres, and he was a marvelous designer. But he did screw up on one project. The Forrest Theatre in Philadelphia didn't have dressing rooms in the design. So the building across the alley had to have dressing rooms put in. At first, the actors had to run outside in heat, rain, or snow to get from the stage to the dressing rooms. Now, an underground tunnel connects the two buildings.

The opening night of the Biltmore Theatre didn't have all the drama on the stage. Elizabeth Marbury, the famed agent, attended the first performance along with decorator Elsie de Wolfe and Anne Morgan. De Wolfe and

Morgan went down the aisle and Marbury took the aisle seat, which fell through the floor of the theatre.

Of course, no show could match the record of the original London production of *Me and My Girl*. It ran 1,646 performances, certainly a notable run for its time. But what made the run so spectacular was that the show was bombed out of two theatres during the war, but nevertheless went on.

Old theatres were sprayed with disinfectant not only because of body odor, but also to kill bed bugs, lice, and other unwanted pests.

The Cotton Club had no bathrooms in the dressing rooms for performers. Instead, they put cans under the dressing room tables that the performers could dump out in the alley. The Marquis Theatre, when it was first built, was also missing bathrooms in the dressing rooms. But they did not put cans under the dressing tables.

When the Marquis opened, there were many, many problems with it. For one thing, the box office was in a very small space on the street level. Then audiences had to take an escalator to a very small landing and make a sharp u-turn to another escalator that brought them up to the auditorium level. There was often a dangerous crowding between the escalators. There were other problems with the theatre. The exhaust from the cars that traveled through the enclosed driveway entered the ventilation system and went right into the dressing rooms.

The Marquis Theatre was built in the new Marriott Marquis Hotel, one of the most controversial buildings in Times Square history. The hotel took the place of the Morosco, Bijou, and Helen Hayes theatres, and the Astor and Victoria movie theatres. Some problems have been solved, but many remain. The bathrooms are the same ones that the hotel's guests use, so they can be extremely busy, and theatergoers have to show their stubs to use them. Stagehands hate the theatre because there is no freight elevator, so sets have to either be carried upstairs or be brought up on the public elevators.

When it first opened, the stage area was sometimes so cold that the cast could actually see their own breath. Marriott spent half a million dollars to give the theatre its own heating, ventilation, and plumbing systems. Before the renovations, fumes were seeping into the backstage areas. There was an exterior vent for the sewer system, which was located only thirty feet from the theatre's air intake, and the system sent the air right into the women's dressing room. Ten drains in the floor of the theatre spewed sewage that backed up through the system.

During the war years, London had an ingenious way for people to reserve seats. On your way to work, you'd go to the box office and pay thruppence (three pence) for a reserved spot on the box office line for returns or seats that would be released later. Just before showtime, stools lined up outside the theatre had copies of patrons' ticket receipts in the order in which people had visited the box office. Then, the box office would sell the seats to the line in the order in which the spots were reserved.

Since we're in London, while *South Pacific* was playing at the Drury Lane Theatre, the stage area was so immense that there was still room behind that show's set for the complete scenery of *Guys and Dolls* to be set up for rehearsals when *South Pacific* wasn't in performance.

In the 1940s and beyond, theatres would announce in their programs that a certain perfume was used to scent the theatre. During the *Ziegfeld Follies of 1936*, the program announced: "The Winter Garden is perfumed with Charles of the Ritz' Spring Rain." During *The Firebrand of Florence*, the Alvin Theatre was perfumed with Prince Matchabelli's Stradivari.

a convicted Jewish felon

Garth Drabinsky talked his way into knocking down the beautiful Lyric and Apollo Theatres, merging them into the barn known as the Ford Center, er, Hilton, er, Foxwoods, er, Lyric. The Apollo and the Lyric were beautifully restored theatres by their owners, the Brandts, but Drabinsky had his way. But it wasn't just those two beautiful theatres that Drabinsky ruined. Next door was the Times Square Theatre, and Drabinsky had plans to make that into a store selling his theatrical merchandise. So he ran some sound tests and convinced the 42nd Street Redevelopment Corporation to promise that the Times Square would never again be an operating theatre. To this day, the Times Square sits empty while Drabinsky's theatre hosts flop after flop.

CHAPTER 12

Previews

During previews, Neil Simon wrote three hysterical scenes for *Seesaw*, the musical version of William Gibson's hit play, *Two for the Seesaw*. The creative staff thought the show needed a stronger emotional impact at the end of the second act, given what the main character, Gittel Mosca, had gone through. Composer Cy Coleman and lyricist Dorothy Fields wrote a new scene that bookended the song "I'm Way Ahead." On the evening before the scene went in, Coleman sat in a taxi with Michele Lee and went over the whole sequence. They then went upstairs to a rehearsal room and rehearsed the song. That evening, the scene and the song were already in the show. Lee had cue cards in the orchestra pit since she had never done the song before onstage, let alone with the orchestra.

There was a scene where Gittel was originally going to meet Jerry Ryan's wife, but Neil Simon said, "She can't meet the wife. She can talk to her on the phone but it's wrong for the audience to see the wife." Simon wrote a monologue for Gittel talking to her mother on the phone, and it went in the same night. That's the kind of pressure that went on in that show.

As Michele Lee noted, "They made the show better but they also made it good. Sometimes when something doesn't work, the scene or song is out immediately instead of giving the cast and writers a chance to work on it."

One of the greatest turnarounds in the history of Broadway theatre was the production of Kurt Weill and Paul Green's *Johnny Johnson*. The first preview was a disaster, with people beginning to leave after only ten minutes. By the time the curtain fell on Act Two, fewer than twenty audience members remained in the house for Act Three. But the work continued and on opening night, the reviews were good, especially for Weill's music. Audiences also responded enthusiastically with standing ovations (before they became a cliché) and multiple curtain calls. But the show proved too esoteric for Broadway audiences at large, especially with such larks as Rodgers and Hart's *Babes in Arms* and Cole Porter's *Red, Hot and Blue!* on the boards at the same time, and it closed after only sixty-eight performances.

At the first preview of the rare Jule Styne flop *One Night Stand*, two friends lingered in the theatre to listen to the exit music. An usher noticed them sitting alone in the house and asked them, "Are you with the show?" When they answered, "No," she asked, "Then what are you doing here?"

At the first preview of a show, people would walk in past the ticket taker, even though they didn't have tickets. The ushers and staff assumed they were with the show.

Here's a personal story. Theatre lovers who could not afford tickets to all the shows on Broadway, people who didn't want to pay for a show and were content to see just the second act, as well as those who saw a show and wanted to see it again without buying a ticket would second-act a show (i.e., go into the theatre as the audience was returning from intermission). Sometimes second-acters would carry a program from the show and waltz into the theatre as if they were coming back.

My friend Carl Earl Weaver, a Broadway performer in *The Wiz* and other shows, talked me into second-acting the musical *Merlin* at the Mark Hellinger Theatre. I was nervous but I agreed, knowing that I'd never pay to see the show. So Carl and I walked into the theatre with the rest of the audience and stood in the back. The lights dimmed and the orchestra struck up the Overture. Apparently, we had first-acted the show but must have either gotten lost in the crowd going in or looked like we knew what we were doing and so bypassed the ticket takers.

Once, Carl second-acted *The Little Prince* and stood in the back of the Alvin Theatre watching the show. The director, assuming he was with the production, asked him what he thought should be changed and Carl gave his opinion.

(Note: This is sometimes impossible today since many theatres check ticket stubs of audience members coming back for the second act.)

CHAPTER 13

Opening Night

In the days before theatres were air conditioned, shows opened in the fall or in December just before the Christmas holidays. Today, shows try to open as close to the Tony Awards as possible, with the idea that voters' memories are short and shows that open early in the season won't be remembered in the spring.

The show that broke the fall opening routine was *South Pacific*, which opened in April of 1949.

Speaking of openings, most shows want to open on a Thursday night so the review will appear in the Friday papers' entertainment sections. If a show is thought to be a failure, it might open on Friday evening so the review will be printed on Saturday, the day when the fewest papers are sold.

At the opening night of Rodgers and Hart's musical *Dearest Enemy*, Richard Rodgers conducted the orchestra. Whether he was simply exhausted or extremely nervous we don't know, but we do know that he fainted.

When Phil Silvers opened in the 1972 revival of *A Funny Thing Happened on the Way to the Forum*, he came onstage for the prologue in which he was meant to say: "Playgoers, I bid you welcome. The theatre is a temple, and we are here to worship the gods of comedy and tragedy." But when Silvers entered, the audience cheered. It threw him so off-track that he was confused and forgot his lines. He quickly pulled himself together and haltingly said, "Welcome playgoers! The theatre is a-a-church?" Librettist Burt Shevelove turned to composer Stephen Sondheim in the back of the theatre and said, "If a nice Jewish boy like Phil Silvers can't remember 'temple'—we're in for a rough evening!"

Hello, Dolly! opened at the St. James Theatre after only two previews. That's right. Two previews. Shows today can have weeks of previews. *Sarava* and *Spiderman: The Musical* are two shows that seemed to never want to open. But *Dolly!* had only two previews before the opening night. The day after the opening, David Merrick called up Jerry Herman and said, "Get out of bed, jump in a cab, and get down here. You are going to see something that only happens once in a lifetime." Jerry did as told, and there was a line around the block waiting to buy tickets to the biggest hit on Broadway. It was such a great day, even curmudgeonly David Merrick handed out hot coffee to the crowd.

Ethel Merman's opening night in *Hello, Dolly!* was remarkable. Obviously, when she came out, she got a tremendous hand. But when the title song began, the audience was on its feet. And when the chorus started, the audience sang together at the top of their lungs, put their hands behind their backs, and swayed in time with the music. When the song was finished, everyone sang along in a brief encore. Merman waved at the audience, imploring them to sit down so the show could continue.

Here's another Jerry Herman anecdote: At the opening night of *Mame* at the Winter Garden Theatre, the orchestra was conducted by the brilliant Don Pippin. As Pippin came into the pit, he looked at the audience and gave his father a wink. Pippin's father was bursting with pride and turned to the man next to him and boasted, "That's my son conducting." To which the other man replied, "He's conducting my son's music."

A writer from *The New Yorker* wanted to interview lyricist Ira Gershwin about his new show *Of Thee I Sing*. Gershwin suggested the writer meet him at intermission. As they stood talking, a dapper man came up to congratulate Ira. "That's my brother-in-law," explained Ira. Soon, a woman came up to Ira to congratulate him. "My sister," he explained. Then a couple bounded over to let him know how terrific the show was. "My brother Arthur and my sister-in-law." Finally, the lights flickered and Ira and the writer started toward their seats when a woman grabbed hold of Ira and told him how much she was enjoying the show. The journalist just looked at Ira who responded with a shrug, "My mother-in-law."

Gwen Verdon never wanted to be a star. She was a dancer, and a great one at that, but she was interested in the process of putting a dance together, first with choreographer Jack Cole and then with Bob Fosse. Producer Cy Feuer saw Verdon performing with the Jack Cole Dancers in a nightclub and was struck immediately by her talents. He was producing the musical

Can-Can along with his partner Ernie Martin and saw Verdon's potential as the lead dancer in the show. Lilo was the star of the show, brought all the way from Paris to sing the Cole Porter songs. Verdon had three big numbers in the show: a can-can number, the "Garden of Eden" ballet in the first act, and an Apache dance in the second act. And it was during that dance when her life changed. On opening night, she finished the dance, went to her dressing room, took off her costume, and put on a robe. Meanwhile, back in the auditorium, the audience was cheering, and they wouldn't stop until she came back to take a bow. Producer Feuer ran up to her dressing room, took her by the hand, and led her onto the stage. A star was born; Lilo was not happy.

Out of town with *Can-Can*, the show's librettist and director, Abe Burrows, arrived at the theatre only to find actor Hans Conreid up on a ladder measuring the size of his billing.

The dress rehearsal of *The Guardsman* seemed to be going well. The Lunts were starring for the Theatre Guild for the first time. After the show, Maurice Wertheim came up to Alfred Lunt and bluntly informed him that he wasn't good in the show. Now, this was the great Alfred Lunt, and the criticism took him aback. Wertheim was on the board of the Guild. What had the rest of the board thought? In the taxi, at home, and getting into bed, he kept repeating, "He didn't like me." In the middle of the night, his wife Lynn Fontanne heard a noise. And there was Alfred with a bag sneaking out the window and going down the fire escape. Where was he going? What was he thinking? As you may know, *The Guardsman* was one of the Lunts' triumphs. So the next time an actor asks you what you think of his performance, be kind.

At the opening of *Promises, Promises* on Broadway, David Merrick handed Neil Simon an opening night present, a framed telephone bill with the charges for Simon's telephone calls while he had been in Hong Kong.

When *Promises, Promises* opened in London, David Merrick came to the opening and introduced Neil Simon to a woman he called "The future ex-Mrs. Merrick."

The young Ethel Barrymore was excited to be appearing opposite Sir Henry Irving and Ellen Terry in *Peter the Great* at the Lyceum Theatre in London. Though she was in only one scene, her part was strong and, besides, the critics and the haute monde would see her London debut. She was only eighteen years old but she was a Barrymore, and her reputation and that of her family preceded her. Barrymore was in the wings anxiously waiting for her cue to enter when Ellen Terry skipped right over the cue. Terry had no idea what she had done until Sir Henry brought it up after the show.

Ethel Barrymore wasn't perfect either. When she was in *The Constant Wife* in Cleveland, she kept going up on her lines. Luckily, future screen director George Cukor was hiding in the fireplace feeding her the dialogue. Afterwards, she hugged playwright Somerset Maugham and said, "Willie, I ruined your beautiful play tonight, but it will run a year." She was correct.

When she opened at the Empire Theatre in Barrie's *The Twelve Pound Look*, the audience gave her a standing ovation upon her entrance. They stood, cheered, and clapped until their hands hurt. When they calmed down, Barrymore addressed them: "You make it very tempting." Then she began the play.

George S. Kaufman was the mentor of producer Saint-Subber. After the opening of *Kiss Me, Kate*, Kaufman told the neophyte producer, "You've started your career at the top and you'll end it at the bottom."

By far the worst opening night in theatre history took place on November 25, 1895, at the opening of *Excelsior, Jr.* The show opened the brand new Lyric Theatre, part of the giant Olympia complex on Broadway. Oscar Hammerstein I was the force behind the opening night. Between 4,000 and 10,000 tickets had been sold or given away, a vastly larger amount than could actually fit into the theatre.

On the night of the opening, the crowds were drenched in a cold rain. The potential audience members stormed the theatre's entrances; it was every man and woman for themselves. As *The New York Times* reported, the scene was like a football scrimmage: "A modern gridiron, with nobody to retire the injured from the field and nobody to count the yards of gain or loss." The police called for reinforcements to try to shut the theatre doors. At 10 p.m. more than 5,000 patrons, as the *Times* put it, "slid through the mud and slush of Longacre back into the ranks of Cosmopolis."

Hammerstein had private rooms for his guests, but unfortunately the paint was still wet and several of the elite found their clothes ruined. The next day Hammerstein's troubles continued. A steam pipe burst in the cellar; two workers were killed and others were badly injured.

The show finally opened four days after the melee.

When the Dutch comics Weber and Fields decided to offer Lillian Russell a part in the opening production of their new Weber and Fields' Music Hall, the actress told them that they simply couldn't afford her. But they did sign her because they had a plan for raising the $1,250 a week guaranteed her for thirty-five weeks and the cost of her expensive costumes. The producers decided to auction off seats in the boxes to New York's most eligible bachelors. Stanford White, William Randolph Hearst, and Diamond Jim Brady were among the bidders. The publicity was tremendous, but it paled in comparison to the $10,000 in box office they earned from the auction.

For everyone involved, the opening night of *Little Me* on November 17, 1962, was fraught with tension, and not simply because nerves had been stretched to the breaking point during rehearsals and tryouts. They also had concerns about the audience that night. A vast portion of the house had been filled with a theatre party, which meant that some theatergoers would be late and, worse still, some might have over-imbibed at the dinner preceding the show.

Simon described the scenario: "The house was half-filled as the overture started, two-thirds filled as the curtain went up, and the final three hundred stragglers filed in feeling for their seats in the half-darkened theater all during the first scenes." After this, it wasn't long before one tuxedoed theatergoer roused himself and began to stagger up the aisle in search of a men's room, and as he passed Coleman, Simon, and Fosse at the back of the theater, he screamed, "This is the worst piece of crap I've seen since *My Fair Lady*."

The creators' worries were compounded by what was happening on the stage. Caesar was delivering an erratic performance, mangling laugh lines by changing words and coughing. As this happened, Simon recalled how Fosse reacted to the problems that were happening throughout the rehearsal period: "[Fosse] very simply put his arms down at his sides, closed his eyes, and fell backward, every part of his body hitting the floor simultaneously."

Casper Roos, a very nice guy, as well as a wonderful performer, was feeling very sick with a bad cold during the previews of *Here's Where I Belong* at the Billy Rose Theatre (now the Nederlander). On opening night, he struggled not to cough or show the audience that he was sick. By the time the curtain fell, he felt terrible and immediately went home to bed. The next afternoon, still feeling poorly, he went to the theatre only to find it locked. The show had closed after that one performance. Roos had to find someone to let him in so he could clean out his dressing room.

Florenz Ziegfeld was constantly worried on opening nights that his shows weren't good enough. Still, he had a remarkable track record of successes. But nothing could dissuade him from the thought that his latest show would be a bomb. On the eve of the opening of the musical *Rosalie*, Ziegfeld told the librettist William Anthony McGuire, "This is going to be my biggest flop ever." And he really meant it. McGuire gave Ziegfeld a look of pity and told him, "Please accept my condolences, in this, your darkest hour of success." *Rosalie* was a success, running over 300 performances, a fine run in 1928.

The revival of *Journey's End* that opened at the Empire Theatre on December 18, 1939, couldn't have picked a worse day. The show, a harrowing look at war, had gone over brilliantly during previews, and expectations were high. Ten minutes before the curtain went up at 8:30, radio reports came in that Hitler had taken Poland. The next day all the critics commented only on what was happening in Europe.

There was a certain segment of the population that had never seen Liza Minnelli perform. They assumed she was cast in *Flora, the Red Menace* just because her mother was Judy Garland. On opening night, Garland came backstage. In the show, Minnelli sings the song "You Are You." One of the lyrics is "You are not Myrna Loy, Myrna Loy is Myrna Loy." Garland suggested to Ebb that Liza instead sing "You are not Judy Garland, Judy Garland is Judy Garland." Needless to say, the change did not go into the show.

On every opening night, George Abbott would have a glass of wine and a dance with a chorus girl, and if the show was a success he'd say, "Well, it worked out this time." If the show was a failure, he would have a glass of wine and a dance with a chorus girl and say, "Well, this time it didn't work out."

It's a rule that if you receive a free ticket to a critics' performance or opening night, you cannot leave before the show is over. Well, at one opening night, Milton Berle couldn't stand it anymore. During intermission, he went to the coat check and retrieved his overcoat. Just then, the producer came up to him. Berle didn't miss a beat as he put on his coat, saying, "God, it's so cold in there!" Then he returned to his seat.

Some shows seemed poised for success on opening night. Others await their fates but have enough in the coffers to try to weather bad reviews if they come. But for *The Pajama Game*, it was a make-or-break opening night. The show had only $15,000 in the bank from advance sales. You know the rest, but the creators sure didn't, and they were worried as if their very careers were dependent on the nine critics of the daily papers. And they were right. Who knows what would have happened had the reviews been bad? On the day after the opening, Harold Prince was overjoyed: "Think of it. This morning we had $15,000 in the box office. That was enough to run the show for three days. And look at what happened. Isn't it a wonder? Isn't it a limitless wonder?" And that's why people go into the theatre: Dancing on a precipice and surviving is the greatest feeling in the world.

THREE STORIES ABOUT *PIPPIN*

At the time *Pippin* was about to open on Broadway, critics were asked to choose among three previews in the days right before. This left the writers more time to collect their thoughts and write reviews. But it also put stress on the performers having to give their all knowing that their futures were in the hands of the people sitting in the audience for three performances.

During previews, the fog machine spewed out so much fog, the star John Rubinstein found it difficult to breathe, let alone sing. So the fog was dialed back. But the heavy fog was back for the critics' previews, and so he performed them in terrible voice.

When Michael Rupert took over from Rubinstein during the run of the show, he started having nightmares about swimming through black water while trying to reach a white house on the shore, but he could never, try as he might, escape the black water and reach the house. He finally went to a psychoanalyst who helped him get over the feeling of fear and oppression that came with doing the show.

LIONEL BARRYMORE—TRY, TRY, AGAIN

Lionel Barrymore had his share of woeful openings. The first opening night of his career was among the worst. He made his stage debut in a production of Sheridan's *The Rivals*. He was terrible, more than terrible, horrendous by his own account. He was so embarrassed that after the opening scene of the play, he took off his makeup and fled the theatre. After walking the streets of Kansas City for a few hours, he went up to his boardinghouse room and found a note from his grandmother, Mrs. Drew, on his bureau:

"My Dear Lionel: You must forgive your Uncle Sidney and me for not realizing that when Sheridan wrote the part of Thomas he had a much older actor in mind. We feel that we were very remiss in not taking cognizance of this—although we are both happy that you are not at the advanced age you would have to be in order to be good in this part.

We think, therefore, that the play as a whole would be bettered by the elimination of the front scene and have decided to do without it after this evening's performance. Sincerely and with deep affection, your Grandmother, Mrs. Drew."

Barrymore was fired after another opening night, this time in the play *Sag Harbor*, which was the opening play for the brand new Republic Theatre on 42nd Street (now the New Victory Theatre). James A. Herne was the actor-manager of the company and by all accounts, including that of Barrymore, he was an exceedingly good actor and a very kind man. After the opening, Herne fired Barrymore in the kindest way: "Lionel, this is a disaster for which only I can be blamed. I have done you a disservice for which I hope you can forgive me. Due to my own ineptness and for no other reason at all, you have been cast in an impossible part.

"Oh, you have created a brilliant role out of it, but it is of course not for you and gives you no scope whatsoever for your talents. I should be ruining your career, which is going to be brilliant, if I did not urge you at once to drop this very poor role and take a vacation.

Yes, that's it, what you need is a vacation, my boy. You just take a vacation. Do not, I beg of you, hold this lapse against me."

Another bad opening night for Barrymore was in a production of *Oliver Twist* in Minneapolis. He was still not the professional that he would become, but he had no problem memorizing the two parts he played in the drama, Toby Crockett and Joey. At the dress rehearsal, everything was proceeding apace until the last scene of the show. Barrymore was onstage as Toby Crockett when Joey was to enter and the two would have a conversation. Barrymore was understandably confused since he was playing both parts. Seeing a window in the set, he, as Toby, walked to it and while looking outside, had a conversation with Joey, with Barrymore switching voices between the two parts. The producer McKee Rankin, who was thrilled that he wouldn't have to hire another actor, kept the scene as it was for the remainder of the run.

Barrymore finally made it on Broadway in *The Mummy and the Humming Bird* with his uncle John Drew in the lead. Barrymore played a hot-headed Italian, or rather he overacted. His character was meant to build up to a white-hot anger, pull a knife out of his belt, kiss it, and scream, "Vendetta! Vendetta!" after which he was to fall onto a chair, wracked with sobs. At rehearsal, however, he pulled out the knife, kissed it, and fell down, completely missing the chair. Director-producer Charles Frohman softly addressed him, "Now, I'm glad you did that tonight, Barrymore. Because you will never do it again."

Barrymore did not do that again, but his acting remained, shall we say, vibrant. When a friend asked John Drew how Barrymore was doing, Drew replied, "Well enough, thank you, considering that every night I have to play second fiddle to that preposterous nephew of mine."

THE MORNING AFTER OPENING NIGHT

When Harold Prince opened a new show, whether it got good reviews or bad, he gathered his staff together the day after and started on the next show. It was something Prince learned while working with George Abbott.

Nick and Nora was savaged by the press. The next morning the phone rang. When librettist Arthur Laurents picked up the phone, it was Jule Styne calling. He said but one word: "Next!"

When Jule Styne's musical *The Red Shoes* was savaged by the press, the next morning the phone rang. When Styne picked up the phone, it was Arthur Laurents. Before he could speak, Styne interrupted: "I've already started."

CHAPTER 14

Critics

"You've heard of Johnny One-Note. Let's welcome Jerry One-Note."—Brooks Atkinson, writing about Jerry Herman's off-Broadway revue *Parade* in *The New York Times*.

"The lowest point of the evening came when Richard Kiley stood up and sang an awful song called "The Impossible Dream."—Edwin Newman on NBC television.

Merrick refused to allow NBC newsman and drama critic Edwin Newman to attend the opening night of *We Have Always Lived in the Castle*, claiming that theatre was the same as any of the products advertised on television. "After all," Merrick explained, "they don't constantly criticize General Motors or General Foods, do they?" Newman was blasé, stating, "That's all right, I'll attend the next night and see the closing." Ironically, NBC was a subsidiary of RCA, which had invested heavily in the show.

In *The New York Journal-American*, Robert Garland complained that Orson Welles's massive musical production of *Around the World in 80 Days* had "everything but the kitchen sink" in it. The next performance, Orson Welles came out for a curtain speech with a kitchen sink.

When *Oklahoma!* opened in New Haven, Walter Winchell's gal Friday, Rose, went up to see it and wired back, "No legs. No jokes. No chance." This has also been attributed to producer Michael Todd, who wired back, "No legs. No tits. No chance."

Cy Howard offered this advice over a nosh after the show to department store owner and producer Alfred Bloomingdale when his show *Allah*

Be Praised was opening out of town in Boston: "My solution for the entire problem is to close the show and keep the store open nights."

Fredric March and his wife Florence Eldridge were in the Theatre Guild production of *Home for the Harvest*. The reviews were bad, really bad. This wasn't a surprise to the two performers, and in the next day's papers, they took out an advertisement with a drawing of a trapeze artist missing the trapeze. And below the cartoon were the words "Oops! Sorry!"

Critics might be right in their opinions, but that doesn't mean those opinions are necessarily a barometer of what will run. When George Jessel opened in *The Jazz Singer*, the critical reception was harsh, to say the least. *The Journal-American*'s Alan Dale opined, "Among the openings last week was *The Jazz Singer* with the vaudeville actor George Jessel. It is needless for me to write about this play, since the magazine will not be out for two weeks, and, in all probability *The Jazz Singer* will be closed by then." Dale might have been right about the merits of the show but it had a healthy run until the summer heat forced it to close. And, of course, the film version, starring Al Jolson, was also a hit.

Dale got his comeuppance of a sort during another show. Fannie Hurst, best known today as the author of *Imitation of Life*, was sitting in a box on opening night. She let her arm fall languidly over the side of a box and her heavy bracelets fell off her arm onto the head of Alan Dale. He was knocked out. Alexander Woollcott announced in his column the following day, "The evening was uneventful for the audience, but one critic was carried away, not so much by the entertainment as by Fannie Hurst's bracelets made of Portland Cement."

When British comedienne Hermione Baddeley saw *Oh, Calcutta!* she commented, "The sketches are too long and the cocks are too short!"

Cole Porter knew that whenever one of his shows would open, the critics would write that the score was "not up to his usual standards."

When *The Rink* opened, *The New York Times* critic Frank Rich was not kind. Liza Minnelli was distraught. "He dismissed me in two sentences," she cried. Librettist Terrence McNally replied, "You're lucky. He dismissed me in two very long paragraphs."

A critic described Rosalind Russell's singing in *Wonderful Town* as "the Ambrose Lighthouse calling for its young."

Appearing in the operetta *Polonaise*, Jan Kiepura and Marta Eggerth (married in real life) were lambasted by Robert Garland in *The Journal-American* as "Ham and Eggerth."

Percy Hammond was considered a poet of criticism. Disgusted with the blatant semi-nudity in a musical revue, he wrote, "The human knee is a joint and not an entertainment." Some of the audience members might have differed. When Hammond saw an especially old and hoary sketch, he wrote, "They've played it so often that they can play it in their sleep, which they did yesterday."

He was excellent in recognizing new talents and was among the first to extol Helen Hayes, Walter Hampden, Ruth Gordon, and others.

Many of today's critics know nothing of theatre history or styles of performance. After all, for many of them, their first show might have been *Mamma Mia*. So they've never had the opportunity to see the great shows that were acted, produced, directed, and designed by masters in the field.

When a revival of a show comes to Broadway or is presented by Encores or one of the other concert producers and the production is less than stellar, critics often blame the underlying work rather than the production. The show is usually the scapegoat because of the ignorance of the critics. Likewise, so-so shows get good reviews because they seem good by current standards.

That brings to mind former-theatre-critic-now-movie-critic Michael Phillips's criticism of a summer theatre production of *Paint Your Wagon* in San Diego with less-than-wonderful acting. He wrote: "When the cast sang 'There's a Coach Comin' In,' I hoped they meant an acting coach."

David Merrick had a longstanding gripe against Walter Kerr, who was then writing for *The Herald-Tribune*. In 1963, Merrick sent out a poem titled: "Elegy Written in Shubert Alley" with apologies to Thomas Gray. The opening lines were:

The Kerr-few tolls the knell of parting play.
The Weeping way, and leaves the street to darkness and to me.

Today it's standard practice for critics to attend the last preview performances before the opening night and their reviews. But when *Philadelphia, Here I Come* was in previews, Stanley Kauffmann, the lead critic for the *Times* announced he was attending a preview so he might have more time to write his review, Merrick was determined not to let that happen. Kauffmann showed up but Merrick closed the show that night, claiming that a rat was in the Helen Hayes Theatre's generator. Somehow, the rat was never caught. Though Merrick lost that performance's box office, he more than made up for it in publicity.

Charles MacArthur absolutely refused to read the reviews of his latest collaboration with George S. Kaufman, *Johnny on a Spot*. Of the critics, Kaufman reported to MacArthur, "Truthfully, none of them was constructive. Perhaps the word should be 'destructive.'"

MacArthur said, "I always felt that a playwright with a bad play is like a ballplayer who has just struck out—only in this case the umpire throws a bat at him."

The show opened one month after the attack on Pearl Harbor, a fact that figures in the dénouement of this story. MacArthur ran into critic George Jean Nathan at the Algonquin Hotel. The scribe didn't like the play but didn't hold it against MacArthur. The playwright went up to Nathan and angrily waved a newspaper in his face. The headline read "MacArthur Expects Vicious Attack!"

Sometimes, critics make mistakes that are then corrected later in their career. Brooks Atkinson writing for *The New York Times* famously said about the original production of *Pal Jocy*, "Although *Pal Joey* is expertly done, can you draw sweet water from a foul well?"

Twelve years later when the show was revived, Atkinson penned, "Mr. O'Hara's night-club tout has begun Broadway's new year auspiciously."

Of course, times change, and the original production of *Pal Joey*, featuring an antihero, was radical at the time.

Jimmy Valentine, a critic for the *Cleveland Plain Dealer* wrote of Betty Garrett in *Plaza Suite*, "In the first act of *Plaza Suite*, Betty Garrett walks funny. In the second act, she talks funny. In the third act, she *finally is* funny."

When Maureen Stapleton was starring in *The Emperor's Clothes*, one critic opined, "Maureen Stapleton played her part as if she hadn't yet signed the contract with the producers."

A critic of another kind skewered Stapleton. It was the second night of the 1973 revival of *The Rose Tattoo*. Just before the curtain rose on Act One, one of the children in the cast asked Stapleton if she had read the reviews. "No!" "Well," the dear child reported, "they said you were too fat and too old." With that the curtain went up.

Bob Hope had a successful career on Broadway but it took a little time to flower. He was in 1927's *Sidewalks of New York* but his part was cut down before the show reached Broadway. One critic wrote, "Ray Dooley has something, Ruby Keeler has something, and Bob Hope has something too, but you won't notice it if you sit back about five rows."

Walter Kerr was a horrible critic when it came to musicals. When *Fiddler on the Roof* opened, he wrote, "It takes place in Anatevka in Russia, and I think it might be an altogether charming musical if only the people of Anatevka did not pause every now and again to give their regards to Broadway with remembrances to Herald Square."

Dorothy Parker was a famous quipster. When Robert Benchley would take a vacation, Parker would fill in for him. The end of her reviews would often contain the line, "Dear Mr. Benchley: Please come home. A joke is a joke." At the end of one review while filling in for Benchley, Parker wrote, "All is forgiven."

Parker made more than her fair share of bon mots, often at the theatre's expense. Of Katherine Hepburn, no less, she wrote that the actress ran the gamut of emotions from A to B. About a new drama, she wrote, "*The House Beautiful*, for me, is the play lousy."

Show people sometimes resent what they perceive to be the grandstanding of critics at their show's expense. So, once in a while, producers will ban critics from their shows. The Shubert Brothers were the most thin-skinned of the producers. When Heywood Broun was banned from an opening night, he bought his tickets. He was still barred, so he sued the Shuberts.

Walter Winchell, the noted columnist whose power for a time was absolute, was denied entrance to one of 1928's most anticipated shows, the Marx Brothers musical comedy *Animal Crackers*. The house manager, the ticket takers, and the box office personnel were all at the ready to catch Winchell coming through the front doors. He fooled them by having Harpo Marx let him in through the stage door. Winchell reviewed the play from the wings.

And there were a lot of shows to review. In the 1926/27 season, there were 263 openings. The next season beat that record by one show. That 1927/28 season holds the record for most productions opening. The 1928/29 season saw a drop; only 225 shows opened. Then came the Crash, with a capital C; the depression hit and the 1930/31 season was comparatively lackluster with only 187 openings.

Obviously, no one critic could cover all the different openings, so the lead critic would have to guess which show opening on the same night as another would be the bigger hit. Heaven forbid he should choose a flop while a second stringer got to review the success. A few times, two critics weren't enough to cover all the evening's openings, and then newspaper editors assigned everyone from the sports pages to the guy who wrote the want ads to cover the opening nights. During the 1927/28 season, in one week, seventeen plays opened, eleven of them on Monday night! They must have had copy boys reviewing that evening.

Richard Ouzounian is the chief theatre critic for the *Toronto Star* and a noted director. When he was at university, his school was selected to compete on the television show *G.E. College Bowl*. His classmates put together a team that would cover all possible questions. Categories like science, history, mathematics, and others were reviewed. But they needed someone for the arts. Ouzounian was chosen because of his wide knowledge. At the competition, the score was tied, and the final question was "Who discovered heavy hydrogen?" To the shock of his teammates, Ouzounian buzzed in. He proudly answered, "Harold Urey." The answer was correct, and they won the game. Afterward, they asked him how he knew the answer. He explained that Urey and his discovery are mentioned in the song "Revenge" in the musical *It's a Bird, It's a Plane, It's Superman.*

Not all critics are professional. Producer/playwright John Golden was tired of people coming backstage after shows they disliked, spouting meaningless compliments. "Very interesting!" "Darling, people loved it!" You get the idea. Golden found that he could hear what they honestly thought if he criticized his own work.

Similarly, Estelle Winwood had a friend beg her to come to a show in which she was going on for an ill actor. Winwood came to see the show. The friend was terrible, really terrible. Now Winwood was in trouble. She didn't want to just spout inanities like the ones mentioned above. So she thought for a while and finally said, "My Darling, if only you could have been out front with me."

At the opening night of *Evita*, the *Times* cultural critic Bill Honan asked Gerald Schoenfeld of the Shubert Organization if he could be introduced to Hal Prince. When that was accomplished, Prince asked Shoenfeld, "Why do you guys kiss the ass of *The New York Times*?" Shoenfeld's answer was "So you don't have to."

Lillian Russell was a great beauty in her day. Many considered her the most beautiful woman in the world. But as she grew older, her body changed. When she appeared in Offenbach's *La Belle Helene*, Alan Dale of *The New York Journal* wrote, "Lillian has no beauty beneath the chin. She could not possibly wear three quarters of a yard of silk and corset lace with the confident effrontery of Edna Wallace Hopper (the costar of the piece), and she moved with the soft heaviness of a nice white elephant."

Not everyone in the theatre was obsessed with the critics and their reviews. When Oscar Hammerstein II decided to go to bed before the reviews came out for *Flower Drum Song*, his son James asked him why he didn't stay up to read them. Hammerstein replied, "The newspapers will say the same thing tomorrow as tonight."

George Jean Nathan perhaps went overboard in his criticism of Kurt Weill and Ira Gershwin's *The Firebrand of Florence* when he wrote: "The ladies of the ensemble resemble Mr. David O. Selznick, and many of the males would provide perfect illustrations for the tales of the Brothers Grimm." Nathan seemed obsessed with the physiology of cast members. When reviewing *Carousel*, he was perturbed about "the protrusion of (John Raitt's) sweatered chest."

ROBERT BENCHLEY

Robert Benchley, the droll humorist, was for a time the drama critic for the first *Life Magazine*, not the one we now know. His bête noire was *Abie's Irish Rose*. He wrote, "On the night following *The Rotters*, residents of Broadway were startled by the sound of horses' hoofs clattering up the famous thoroughfare. Rushing to their windows they saw a man in Colonial costume riding a bay mare from whose eyes flashed fire. The man was shouting as he rode and his message was: *The Rotters* is no longer the worst play in town! *Abie's Irish Rose* has just opened!"

Benchley wasn't alone in panning the play. It was a fairly unanimous knockout by his fellow referees of the drama. But the play outsmarted them by running for five years.

Benchley's criticism sometimes took a backseat to his role as a humorist. The Apollo Theatre and the Times Square Theatre shared a sidewalk on 42nd Street. In 1921, two shows opened on the same night, *Love Birds* at the Apollo and *The Right Girl* at the Times Square. Intermissions of both shows occurred simultaneously, and according to Robert Benchley, he and his party accidently entered the wrong theatre and saw the second act of the neighboring show. And so he killed two birds with one stone by reviewing both shows the same night. As he wrote, "Aside from the fact that there wasn't so much of Pat Rooney and Marion Bent, there was really no way of telling that this was not the second act of the same show we had started out with. It might have been the second act of any musical show."

Benchley also had a fond regard for coughers in the audience. "Laurels for the evening must go to the gentleman sitting in the neighborhood of G-115. No only was he in excellent voice, but he picked his pauses with great cleverness, coughing only when impressive silences were being indulged in on the stage. Good work was also done by the people sitting in C-111, M-13, G-7, and L-114. The rest of the house was adequate."

TALLULAH BANKHEAD

Tallulah Bankhead's performance in *Antony and Cleopatra* was not a success. It's a safe bet that most agreed with critic John Mason Brown's assessment: "Miss Bankhead barged down the Nile last night as Cleopatra— and sank." Furthermore, he wrote, "As the serpent of the Nile she proves to be no more dangerous than a garter snake."

Richard Watts Jr. opined that she seemed "rather more a Serpent of the Sewanee than of the Nile." Even her pal Robert Benchley wrote that she seemed "to wax unintelligible in the clinches, a fault shared by several of her team-mates, all of which is too bad, considering the hard work that Shakespeare must have put in on his wording." George Jean Nathan opined, "Miss Bankhead played the Queen of the Nil."

Bankhead herself could be a critic. She was taken by Alexander Woollcott to a production of Maeterlinck's *The Burgomaster of Stilemonde*. At the end of the first act, she commented to her date, "There's less in this than meets the eye."

CHAPTER 15
Box Office

When *Porgy and Bess* was recently revived at the Richard Rodgers Theatre, it was advertised as *The Gershwins' Porgy and Bess*. Hundreds of ticket buyers called the box office, only the number they called was the one for the Gershwin Theatre box office where *Wicked* was playing. It took a while for the Gershwin Theatre to figure out why they were getting calls from people who wanted to see Audra MacDonald.

When the farce *Three Men on a Horse* opened at the Playhouse Theatre on Broadway, it got rave reviews. But somehow, the front mezzanine seats were not selling. Press agent Alex Yokel decided to fix the situation by charging as much for the mezzanine seats as the orchestra seats and it worked. The show was soon a sellout.

When Harold Prince decided to keep balcony prices extremely low for *It's a Bird, It's a Plane, It's Superman* in order to give students and people with less means a chance to see the show, the experiment failed and the tickets did not sell.

There was a ticket broker who had a variety of websites, each named after a theatre. Thus, there was a RichardRodgersTheatre.com, a GershwinTheatre. com, etc. People would book tickets through the sites and then, if there were problems, they would call the theatre box offices where they were told that they hadn't bought tickets through the box offices. This only served to confuse patrons further.

A couple living in Brooklyn received a pair of tickets to *Oklahoma!* the hottest ticket in town, without any note or explanation. They went to the theatre and enjoyed the show immensely. When they returned home, they found that their apartment had been robbed.

When Charles Nelson Reilly was touring his one-man autobiographical show *Life of Reilly*, people would call the box office and ask who was playing in the show. The box office would reply, "Charles Nelson Reilly." The patron would respond, "He's dead. You know, the tall one with the bald head." "You're absolutely right madam, he's dead but he still manages to come in and perform every night."

CHAPTER 16

Audiences

Audiences can certainly be outspoken, or even worse. Robert Alan Aurthur's play *Carry Me Back to Morningside Heights* boasted Sidney Poitier as its director. Poitier was at the forefront of all the publicity, in advertising as well as interviews. So it was understandable that in the middle of the first act, an audience member, justifiably confused, stood up and shouted, "Where's my man Sidney?" The show lasted only seven performances at the John Golden Theatre.

The off-Broadway musical revue *Berlin to Broadway with Kurt Weill* was having a great success, even though some audience members thought the show consisted of songs by Irving Berlin as sung by Kurt Weill.

When *Rent* hit Broadway, it inspired zealous fans to see it again and again. They were dubbed "Rentheads." As you might know, fans sometimes record the show on their phones. *Rent* had one actor who covered a number of roles. One of the Rentheads had recorded a number of shows and in each of them the actor had played different parts. So the fan spliced the tapes together in such a way that it seemed that this one performer played the entire show, with himself in almost all the male parts.

Groupies are not a new phenomenon. Fred and Adele Astaire were playing in *Funny Face* in London when one man saw the show over and over again—over one hundred times in fact. When Astaire asked him if he had seen any other shows, the young man replied, "Well, I don't know if I'd like them or not, and I know I like this one."

During the Chicago run of *The Elephant Man*, Philip Anglim was getting annoyed by noise coming from the audience. The title role he was playing was a physical and mental ordeal. At one performance, he faced the audience, broke character, put his hand out in a beseeching manner, and walked down to the edge of the stage. He said, "This is a very difficult and demanding play to do and we cannot compete with the rattling of candy wrappers. Thank you!"

At the curtain call, he came downstage and turned his back on the audience and refused to take a bow.

Audiences sometimes forget that actors can see them from the stage. When Constance Towers was starring in *Show Boat*, there was once a man masturbating in the front row.

Once when John Stamos appeared with James Earl Jones in *The Best Man*, while taking their curtain call, Jones whispered to Stamos, "There are some nice boobies in the third row."

In the 1950s and 1960s, theatre parties were an important element in any show's box office. The "theatre party ladies," as they were dubbed since they were invariably women, would come to matinees from the suburbs. Their representatives would be wooed by producers to buy blocks of tickets before the box office opened to the general public. The first show to sell to theatre parties was Cole Porter's *Kiss Me, Kate*.

The revue *Two on the Aisle* has a song about the show train, a train that specifically came down through Connecticut on matinee days to carry theatergoers to Broadway shows.

Many professionals of today don't listen to the audience when their shows are out of town or in previews. They think of every excuse for the audience's lackluster response. One songwriter, who has recently had many shows on Broadway but has never had a hit, came up to his leading lady and yelled at her, "I wrote you a showstopper and you didn't stop the show." His ego just couldn't believe that it was the song that was bad. He had to blame the singer.

There was a guy who, if he didn't like a show, would just get up and walk out. As he continued to see shows, his patience grew increasingly short. When he went to see *Her First Roman*, the overture began with the sound of a gong. That's when the guy picked himself up and left the theatre. Other audience members may have wished they did the same.

Today's audiences seem to think that standing ovations are expected. Sometimes, this phenomenon of standing ovations gives the wrong message to the cast. Brian Matthews, who starred in the title role in *Copperfield*, couldn't understand why the show had closed after thirteen performances. After all, audiences were giving it standing ovations. Unfortunately, it was his only Broadway appearance.

The Phantom of the Opera began the practice of lining up audiences outside the theatre as if they were in elementary school. For hundreds of years, audiences could find their own way into theatres, but after *Phantom* many theatres continued this custom, herding audiences in like cattle.

Katherine Hepburn in Boston at the opening of *West Side Waltz* stopped the show when a woman in the audience snapped a flash photo. She walked down to the lip of the stage and berated the woman, "You up there, get out of the theatre. Beat it! I'll pay you twice the cost of the ticket. This is an outrage." The woman was escorted out of the theatre weeping.

Shortly before the play ended its run, she berated a man in the front row for propping his feet on the stage. She yelled at him again during the curtain call.

During the run of the Nathan Lane revival of *A Funny Thing Happened on the Way to the Forum*, a man was sitting in the front row behind the conductor, sound asleep. The cast was singing "Everybody Ought to Have a Maid," which has several encores. With each additional encore, Lane sang louder and stomped the stage floor harder in an attempt to wake the sleeping man. Nothing worked. So he whispered in Ken Kantor's ear during the applause for the last encore, "Don't start your line." Lane then stepped downstage when the applause ended and whispered to the audience, "There's a man in the front row sound asleep." The audience chuckled and Lane stood there, folded his arms, and waited for the man to wake up. When the poor man woke up, he had 3,200 eyes staring at him. Later, in the second act, during the chase scene, Lane came running out of Senex's house with a cup of coffee from a diner and he thoughtfully passed it to the conductor who then passed it to the man who had slept through Act One.

Lin Manuel-Miranda saw an audience member texting repeatedly during a performance of *Hamilton*. It was Madonna; he didn't let her backstage to say hello. Then he tweeted about it, and the comment went viral.

During *Grace*, an audience member vomited over the balcony railing.

And during *Ragtime*'s original stint on Broadway, seat cushions had to be frequently replaced because patrons were peeing in their seats.

One night, Helen Mirren saw a man sleeping in the front row during *A Month in the Country* at the Roundabout. She walked to the edge of the stage and flicked him with her shawl, waking him up, and continued her speech as if nothing had happened.

During the recent revival of *A Delicate Balance* while George Grizzard was in the middle of a big speech, a cell phone went off in the audience and a woman answered it and proceeded to have a conversation. Without missing a beat in his monologue, he growled, "Lady, if you don't hang up right now I'm going to come off this stage and take it out of your hand." Then he continued the speech.

Alec Guinness was in the final scene of *Dylan* out of town; his character is drunk and is making a pyramid out of shot glasses. Right in the middle of this, a little old lady in the front row decided to put on her rain hat, gather her umbrella, and get a head start walking up the aisle. She no sooner stood when Guinness in perfect character asked her to kindly sit down and he would continue.

When a revival of *Cat on a Hot Tin Roof* played in Los Angeles in 2014, things turned ugly. During one performance, an audience member catcalled whenever the actress playing Maggie was onstage and yelled insults to the other actors. Things got really bad (as if that wasn't enough) when the insults turned homophobic. When Brick, a repressed gay character played by Anton Troy rejected Maggie in a scene, the heckler reportedly shouted out "because he's a fag."

That's when John Lacy who played Big Daddy lost it. Lacy explained: "Brick tried to respond and the audience member said it again. I just said, 'What did you say, motherfucker?' I went through our fake stage door, took off my vest, went into the audience as he stood proudly to stare at me with a stupid grin on his face. I pushed him, and he was drunk so he easily just collapsed. I knew better than to start throwing punches, I had made my point. I silenced the heckler and thankfully one of the audience members, this enormous, 6'5", 280-pound filmmaker named Tim Sullivan, who happened to be gay and was not at all happy about what was happening, reached over and picked this guy up by his shirt collar and carried him out of the theatre." Though the actors resumed their places and finished the show, Lacy was summarily fired and Troy immediately quit in solidarity. With both lead actors gone, the production was forced to close early.

After *Gypsy*'s Overture plays, the show opens with the actress playing Rose entering from the back of the house and yelling to Louise to speak up. At one performance, a woman tried to shush Bernadette Peters when she entered from the back of the house. "Would you be quiet? This is a Broadway show!" One of her neighbors replied, "She knows dear, she's the star."

In 1977's *Miss Margarida's Way* with Estelle Parsons, the audience was encouraged to write rude things on the blackboard during intermission. After the second act started, someone threw a wad of wet toilet paper, which narrowly missed Parsons's head. She froze in place and said, "Miss Margarida does not like that nor does Miss Parsons and she won't continue 'til that person is removed."

At another performance, someone took chewing gum and put it on her desk during intermission. Parsons broke character and said, "I will not touch this. Will whoever did this please come up and take it away." The audience member did and the show continued.

During previews of *Dr. Zhivago* on Broadway, the show had many long romantic duets. In the second act, during a particularly long duet, a woman in the mezzanine yelled out, "Stop! You have to stop!" So the actors and the orchestra stopped, and the woman was removed from the theatre. Another audience member commented, "It's too bad, I thought that was the best one."

During the drama *Disgraced*, a woman showed up late and had a big conversation with her friend. It was so disruptive the audience could not hear the play. The curtain was brought down and the woman was ejected. The play started again from the beginning. The first line was something like "I've done this before." It got a huge laugh from the crowd.

Enemy of the People was playing at the Manhattan Theatre Club and a cell phone went off three times during Boyd Gaines's big scene. Finally, an usher escorted the woman out. During the curtain call, Gaines came out pretending to talk on his cell phone.

In the original Broadway production of *The Mystery of Edwin Drood*, George Rose was playing around with the audience as the Chairman. A woman in the front row threw her program at him and he said, "Thank you madam but no autographs 'til after the performance."

A stalker jumped onstage when Farrah Fawcett was in *Extremities*.

Barry Kleinbort was at a production of *Waiting for Godot* when one woman turned to another during intermission and asked, "Do you think that Godot is going to show up?" Her friend answered, "I don't think so, he isn't listed in the menu."

Arlene Francis was in a taxi, and a driver, who had a thick Jewish accent, recognized her and asked what her husband Martin Gabel was doing. She told the cabbie that Gabel was in *King Lear*. The driver was taken aback. "Tell me," he inquired, "is it any good in English?" *King Lear* was one of the mainstays of the Yiddish theatre, and many audience members at one of the many Yiddish theatres downtown were unaware that the play was actually written in English.

AUDIENCES ONSTAGE

Wanda Cochran, a singer in the chorus of the original production of *Brigadoon*, told this story. The best set in the show was almost at the end of the evening. Oliver Smith designed a bar that was quite realistic. And there were steps on the side of the Ziegfeld Theatre's stage that led down to the audience. During a very important scene where the leading man has to make up his mind about returning to Brigadoon and the woman he loves, a man got up out of the audience, walked onto the stage, sat at the bar, and ordered a drink. The actor playing the bartender pretended to make him a drink. During the blackout after the scene, two stagehands came and dragged the man off the stage.

While the pre-show music for *Hand to God* was playing at the Booth Theatre, an audience member climbed onto the stage and plugged his cell phone into a fake electrical jack on the stage. A member of the stage crew had to come out and unplug the phone and give it back to the, shall we say, idiot. And then they made an announcement about why you can't do that.

The miscreant issued an apology (we won't mention his name), blaming alcohol and citing a misunderstanding of stage magic. No harm was actually done, and the twittersphere was, for a few days, a better time than actually watching the show.

Over at Lincoln Center a day or so later, a young woman sitting in the front row of *Shows for Days*, spent the first act texting and sharing those texts with the young man sitting next to her. During intermission, the cast talked backstage about how rattled they were by this woman. At the top of the second act, Patti LuPone was supposed to come down from the stage and shake hands with the patrons in the front row. She did so at the performance in question, but when she shook the young woman's hand, she also took the phone out of her other hand and exited backstage.

Similarly, at a performance of *Swingin' on a Star* at the George Street Theatre in New Jersey, a revue of Johnny Burke's songs, a big galoot almost wrecked the show. The stage was set thusly: A false proscenium was halfway toward the back of the stage and the band was placed behind it. In front of the proscenium were four cabaret tables, two on each side of the stage.

Before the show began, a patron of the arts decided his seats weren't good enough, so he took his wife by the hand and decided to sit at one of the tables on the stage. Conductor Eric Stern came out to lead the band in the overture and didn't see the identically sweat-suited couple. Now the audience was calling to the couple to get off the stage. But they were having none of it. The catcalls grew louder, but the band was too loud for Maestro Stern to hear.

During the overture, a cast member playing a waiter would go from table to table putting out plastic glasses of water. He placed two glasses on the first table and then came across the by-now belligerent husband and his embarrassed wife. The actor tried to tell the man that he needed to go back to his seat, but he wouldn't. So the actor followed his blocking and put down the two cups of water, which the husband angrily swept off the table into the audience.

Finally, Eric Stern caught on to what was happening and stepped back, knocking into the false proscenium that proceeded to sway precariously. Stern tried to steady it as the band continued to play. Now more performers entered the stage only to find that the show had taken a strange turn. So, while the band played, the proscenium wobbled, the audience screamed, "Get off the stage," and the cast looked like deer in headlights, a giant man strode up to the stage, lifted the interloper by his velour collar, and dragged him off the stage and outside the theatre while his wife still sat at the table in a daze. Finally, she followed her husband and a cheer went up in the audience. The show that followed didn't have a chance to compete with the preshow.

OVERHEARD

"My favorite opera is *Phantom of the Opera*."

At the end of *Nick & Nora* a couple were walking out of the theatre: Wife: "Well, did you figure out who did the murder?" Husband: "What murder?"

A theatergoer came up to George Abbott after a show and told him she couldn't see part of a scene from where she was sitting. He advised her, "Buy a better seat."

Brian Dennehy in *Death of a Salesman* heard a phone and a woman saying, "I can't talk right now. I'm at the theatre . . . eh."

Shirley Herz, a great Broadway press agent and the first to win a Tony Award (the second was Adrian Bryan-Brown) loved to tell this story. *Torch Song Trilogy* was playing at the Helen Hayes Theatre. Two old ladies were deciding whether to see the matinee. One asked, "Isn't that a gay play?" The other answered, "Well, I don't know, but if Helen Hayes is in it. . . ."

Two women were talking to each other and one says to the other, "What do you want to see?" And the other one says, "I don't know." "Well," opined her friend, "I heard *The Book of Moron* is good." And the other corrected her, "It's *Mormon*." And the first looked askance and said, "Really?"

AUDIENCE PARTICIPATION

Long before audiences were asked if they believed in fairies to restore Tinkerbell to health, audience participation was rife in the theatre.

In the *Follies of 1909*, the chorus girls wore baseball uniforms and played catch with the audience while they sang "Come On, Play Ball with Me, Dearie."

Ziegfeld hired designer Joseph Urban to build him a theatre over the New Amsterdam. The audience took an elevator up eight stories to the rooftop theatre. Urban copied a very special piece of architecture from the Folies Bergere in Paris. A glass runway allowed the audience below to view the showgirls from a unique vantage point. The men in the audience flocked to see what was under the chorus girls' dresses.

The shows on the New Amsterdam Roof were titled *The Ziegfeld Midnight Frolic* since they were performed after the completion of the shows downstairs in the main auditorium. In the very first *Frolic*, during one number, the chorus girls had the male audience members hold balls of yarn while the girls knitted. At another version of the *Midnight Frolic*, helium-filled balloons were attached to the chorus girls' costumes. One of the drunker audience members thought it would be funny to pop one of the balloons, and from then on, everyone joined in popping them. In 1917, when German aggression was moving America closer and closer to entering the fray, the balloons were replaced by miniature zeppelins. That same *Frolic* had a number, "Try a Ring, Dear," wherein audience members would toss large rings onto canes held by the chorus girls. The first person to do so was Lynn Fontaine!

Frolic patrons were seated at tables and instead of clapping in approval, they were given little wooden hammers called knockers that they banged on the tables to indicate their enjoyment. There were also telephones on the tables, and patrons could call people at other tables, much like the scene in the musical *Cabaret*.

A recent production of *A Little Night Music* in London gave out a bunch of free tickets to people standing outside pubs with their pints of ale. Many of them had never been to the theatre before. During one performance, a patron got up and urinated on the front of the stage.

CHAPTER 17
Superstitions

The first meeting of the cast of *A Very Rich Woman* took place onstage at the Belasco Theatre. The cast sat in a semicircle getting ready to read the play. The star of the show, Ernest Truex, got up and went to a spot on stage left. He stood there and announced to the company, "Here's where I stood rehearsing *A Good Little Devil* the day Belasco told me I was going to be a success." Ruth Gordon walked over and told Truex to move over so she could stand on the same spot. Then the rest of the company followed suit, hoping the spot onstage would prove lucky for them too.

For the opening of the 1920 musical revue *What's in a Name?* singer Charles Derickson sprinkled pounds of salt in the alley leading to the stage door.

No one is allowed to utter the word "Macbeth" in a theatre. Rather, they're supposed to say, "The Scottish Play." You also can't say "Lady Macbeth," unless, of course, you are in a production of *Macbeth*. This superstition began in England, which makes sense.

Whistling in a theatre is considered bad luck. Stage rigging, with hemp ropes and counterweights, was originally adapted from ship rigging. So it was only natural for sailors, fresh off the boat, to be hired as stagehands. As they did on ships, they communicated by a system of whistles that signaled scenery changes. An unplanned whistle from somebody else could send scenery flying, potentially causing injury or worse.

Walking under a ladder is bad luck on the stage in case a stagehand drops something.

Putting a hat on a bed is also considered bad luck in the theatre.

And saying "good luck" is verboten; you have to say "break a leg."

Theatre people also picked up the French habit of saying "merde" (shit) to mean good luck.

THREE STORIES ABOUT LUCKY CLOTHING

Fred Astaire and his sister Adele gave one of the greatest performances of their career in Bridgeport, Connecticut, while in *The Bunch and Judy*. That afternoon, Fred had gone shopping and had bought an expensive bathrobe. He attributed the great performance to the bathrobe, which from then onward was known as his lucky bathrobe. He wore it on opening night of every show and, when he went to Hollywood, on the days of the first screenings of his movies.

John Murray Anderson had his own lucky piece of clothing. He would wear his oldest suit throughout the rehearsal period. After the show opened, he would go to the roof of his apartment house and burn the suit. Anderson completely believed in the superstition. If a show happened to be a failure, he rationalized that he had put on the wrong suit.

Milton Berle loved his mother and his wife Ruth too. Milton returned to Broadway to star in Herb Gardner's new play *The Goodbye People*. At the opening night party, the reviews came in and were read out loud. *The New York Times*, the most important paper for selling tickets, panned it. It was the death knell for the show. After the review was read, Ruth Berle turned to her husband and said, "Darling, is it okay if I take off my lucky dress now?"

CHAPTER 18
Publicity

A publicist once asked how he could get his client's name in the paper. George S. Kaufman suggested, "Shoot her!"

Golden Rainbow opened in the spring of 1968 and ran into 1969. In January of 1969 they started putting out ads announcing, "Second year on Broadway." Imagine if a show opened in December and in January they advertised "second year!"

Bide Dudley, a critic and drama editor at the New York *Evening World*, explained what the job of a press agent is. "Each story should hint that the show you're publicizing is the greatest ever written, and that anyone who doesn't go to see it is a dirty son-of-a-bitch. Your rating as a press agent will depend on the degree to which you can approximate that ultimate."

A lot of famous people have tried their hand at flackery. Lillian Hellman was the press agent for the show *Bunk of 1926*. Ben Hecht, another famous playwright, was the press agent for *Captain Jinks*. Hecht was formerly a reporter in Chicago, so he had the credentials for over-exaggerating the truth. Authors, all masters of writing fiction, found work plugging productions. Russel Crouse, Channing Pollock, Jed Harris, S.N. Behrman, Brock Pemberton, Arthur Kober, all were press agents. Even humorist Robert Benchley pushed the plays of William A. Brady. John O'Hara beat the drums for Warner Brothers films.

Speaking of names of famous press agents, the most famous of his time and the most reviled was named, believe it or not, A. Toxen Worm. Naturally, he was the press agent for the Shubert Brothers.

When Richard Maney was publicizing the Rodgers and Hart extravaganza, *Jumbo*, he sent out a humorous release announcing that at the finale of the show, the title character, a large pachyderm (elephant) would be shot out of a cannon. A gullible editor at *Vanity Fair* wanted to send down a photographer and writer to cover the remarkable feat.

Anita Gillette was Anna Maria Alberghetti's understudy in *Carnival!* but she never got a chance to go on, so she signed to be Barbara Cook's understudy in *The Gay Life*. She even opened the show out of town with the song, "I Lost the Love of Anatol." When Merrick heard about this he was furious. Anita went out of town with *The Gay Life* and soon thereafter her song, scene, and character was cut. So, Anita was out of a job. Just then, Anna Maria Alberghetti was taking her vacation from *Carnival!* and David Merrick forgot being angry with Anita and hired her to perform the part of Lili until Alberghetti returned.

On Anita's opening night of *Carnival!*, *Gypsy*'s composer, Jule Styne, sent her a telegram that read, "Don't get knocked up again," referring to Anita's pregnancy during the run of Gypsy.

Producer David Merrick sent Anita a telegram that said, "Don't you dare make a fool out of me tonight."

Merrick made a big deal of Anita's debut. "A star is born!," screamed the press releases.

Merrick decided to put Gillette's name up in lights, replacing that of Alberghetti. When the marquee was ready, he and his new discovery posed for photographers. Merrick was thrilled as was his actress. The photos were carried by the news services (it was a time when what happened on Broadway was national news) and Merrick was sure that Alberghetti would be fuming.

Two weeks later, Anita Gillette received an envelope. Inside it was an invoice for $90 from a sign painter in Paramus, New Jersey. Merrick had ordered the sign painter to send the bill to Gillette, charging her for painting her name up on the sign for all to see.

TWO SIMILAR STORIES DECADES APART

Prior to going on the road, Rodgers and Hammerstein called their new musical *Square Dance*. But once they opened in New Haven, the name was changed to *Away We Go*. The producers, the Theatre Guild, had flop after flop and didn't have enough money to move the show from New Haven to the next town, Boston. The reviews in New Haven were so-so and some of the chorus girls caught the measles and the second act was rewritten but Armina Marshall and Lawrence Langner believed in the show and raised the necessary funds by selling the Guild Theater to WOR Mutual Radio.

When the New York opening could be announced, the press office printed 10,000 releases that were going to be sent to Theatre Guild subscribers all across the country, critics, newspapers, etc. But then they learned that the title of the show was going to be changed. Thrown out were the 8,000 releases that had already been printed with the name of the show: *Oklahoma*. Now, another 10,000 releases were mimeographed when word came down that the title would have an exclamation point at the end. Each release had the word "Oklahoma" three times in the text. So, instead of printing yet another 10,000 releases, Helene Hanff and her secretary, Lois, wrote in pen 30,000 exclamation points. Meanwhile, Joe Heidt, the Guild's press agent had to have all the signage, posters, marquees, etc. changed in New Haven and Boston.

During the previews of *Into the Woods*, Stephen Sondheim wrote a new number for the witch, "Last Midnight." The Playbills have been printed. Press Agent Josh Ellis asks that the 10,000 Playbills be reprinted to take out "Boom Crunch" and add "Last Midnight." The afternoon of the first critics' performance there are the new Playbills. In 10,000 Playbills, "Boom Crunch" is gone. That's good. But instead of "Last Midnight" the Playbills read "Lost Midnight." Stephen Sondheim to Josh Ellis, "Get out the Sharpies." And that's what Josh and his staff did. Each Playbill was changed by hand.

THIRD ACTS

During the run of *All American*, the cast signed a petition to get off the stage while Ray Bolger did his act after the curtain call.

John Raitt would always do a third act when he toured. While in *Seesaw*, he'd sing "Oh, What a Beautiful Mornin'" and "They Call the Wind Maria." Raitt was complaining to his wife that he didn't have any good songs in the show. His wife corrected him saying, "What are you talking about John, you have the two best songs in the show."

When Raitt performed in *Carousel* on the road, at the curtain call he'd sing, "Oh, what a beautiful evening. Thank you for coming my way."

Once in a while, Al Jolson in the middle of *Bombo, Sinbad* or whatever show he was performing, he would stop the show and ask the audience if they'd rather just hear him sing.

He'd dismiss the cast, feeling he didn't need them getting in the way of his unofficial third act. The audience agreed. Song pluggers would pay him to sing their songs so they could put "As sung by Al Jolson at the Winter Garden Theatre" on the sheet music.

Burton Lane was so incensed by Jolson doing the same thing at the end of *Hold on to Your Hats* he refused to attend the opening night. On occasion Jolson would show up late and go onstage to apologize to the audience. He would tell them about the delicious dinner he'd had next door to the theatre and how he just hadn't been able to rush through it. He would then ask whether the audience minded if he put on his makeup onstage, and instructed his dresser, Louis Shreiber, to bring on the burnt cork. He would then ask the ushers to go out and buy dozens of boxes of candy, which were then passed out to the audience while he sang. After the concert he would inform the audience that he was going back to the restaurant for dessert and if the audience would give him a half hour, they could join him for more songs around the piano.

Walter Huston would sing his great number from *Knickerbocker Holiday*, "September Song," after the curtain call even if the show was a straight play.

While in *Hello, Dolly!*, Carol Channing would make the same curtain speech. It went something like this, "Are you the people who saw me in (insert name of her previous show that played that theatre)? I thought so, you smelled the same."

When the Andrews Sisters were in *Over Here!*, after the curtain call they did a ten minute medley of all their big hits. Of course, the cast had to stand on stage smiling just as casts had to stand for Carol Channing and Pearl Bailey when they were playing in *Hello, Dolly!* and Ray Bolger in *All American*.

CHAPTER 19

Stunts

Stunts have been a mainstay of the theatre through time immemorial. For the Broadway theatre, because of its proximity to the limelight and the offices of *The New York Times*, Times Square is the location of most great publicity stunts.

Broadway columnist Louis Sobel recalled the days when newspapers and magazines went along with the joke:

> In those mellow times editors were generous and warm hearted; they regarded theatrical stories and photographs as a legitimate form of news of the day, amusing to the reader, and entitled to the space no matter how crazy the copy, especially when that copy combined a mixture of smooth writing, good humor and pseudo-truth. But that was a time for pure tomfoolery, and space was made available for it. This was true especially for pictures; there were gracious sepia-toned rotogravure supplements, a newspaper section now forgotten and almost quite unknown to many newcomers in our trade.
>
> Stunts in particular were the press agents'—and the editors'—delight; among others of my craft, I turned them out almost daily, sometimes talking over two telephones at the same time, while shouting instructions to my assistants.

Most of the early stunts following the turn of the twentieth century involved the beautiful girls who graced the early musical comedies.

Some stunts have been known to backfire. Mrs. Patrick Campbell was involved in a stunt in which it was claimed that the noted actress had won a lot of money while playing bridge with society ladies. However, the backlash from moral-minded readers and religious leaders made the publicity all the more damning.

Anna Held was the most exploited performer in her time. Florenz Ziegfeld had imported her from Paris and drummed up interest in her meager talents through a series of outrageous stunts, the most famous of which was her milk baths.

During the run of the *Ziegfeld Follies*, Mae Daw, an unknown at the time, decided to challenge dancing star Ann Pennington to a cow-milking contest. She had no reason to do so except to get her name in the papers. It worked; papers the next day pictured the two women at the Long Island home of boxer James J. Corbett. Mae Daw also spent months practicing the saxophone for a "surf jazz" party with the *Follies* girls.

Jean Stewart traveled with a baby lamb as a pet.

Pearl Eaton almost drowned the entire chorus line when she crashed her team's boat into another boat during a Central Park boat race. Fortunately, the stage door Johnnies who lined the shore could swim, and they pulled the soaked girls from the lake.

Gilda Gray, best known for her shimmy, became a star when an enterprising press agent arranged for a suitably handsome man to wrap a $100,000 diamond necklace around a bouquet and toss it onstage during her number. The same exact stunt was used for actress Julia Sanderson. This time, the bouquet, thrown by a "German baron," contained an $18,000 necklace. The press bought the story again.

Press agent Will A. Page was the mastermind behind many of these stunts, but his personal favorite was the "strip golf game." The idea grew out of an argument between chorus girls Shirley Vernon and Nellie Savage. The girls' dates insisted on their naming a day for the unusual match. The men were so insistent that plans were made to drive to Long Island and play that very next day. Before leaving, Miss Vernon had the foresight to phone Will Page and ask him to serve as referee. He agreed and made some phone calls himself, ensuring press coverage. The rules of the game were simple. If the hole was halved or tied, the girls would remain as they were. If the hole were lost, however, the loser would remove one piece of clothing. All eighteen holes were to be played.

Midway through the match, quite a crowd had gathered and the women were reduced to their underthings. Fortunately, someone came to the aid of Miss Vernon at the last minute and supplied her with a barrel. It did nothing for her game, but it did make her a star. The photo of her strange garb was printed all over the world, and offers for Miss Vernon's services came from Hollywood and Broadway. Ziegfeld was forced to raise her salary again and again until she replaced Marilyn Miller in *Sally*.

The 1910s and '20s were filled with stunts, usually built around famous actresses: Valeska Suratt's Fourth of July Christmas tree; Olga Nethersole's "Sappho" kiss; and Ruth Urban's banquet for thirty, which featured a pig as the guest of honor. Harry Reichenbach put a live lion in a midtown hotel room in order to publicize the 1921 production of *Tarzan of the Apes*, but the play managed only thirteen performances.

Earl Carroll of *Earl Carroll's Vanities* produced the unsuccessful *The Lady of the Lamp* in 1920. Carroll was desperate for the show to succeed because it was his first producing venture. "I Am Gambling My Last Thousand Dollars" headlines claimed over the articles in which Carroll begged the public to support his show, which he had also written. Carroll asserted that if audience members were unsatisfied, he personally would meet them in the lobby after the show and refund their money. True to his word, Carroll was in the lobby at the end of every performance. Most people admired the producer's pluck and left after shaking his hand. The show closed after a respectable, although not profitable, 111 performances. Carroll managed to make the event a success anyway because, following one of the performances, a distinguished gentleman named William R. Edrington handed Carroll his card and asked to see him. Carroll made an appointment with the banker, which resulted in Carroll becoming owner of the Earl Carroll Theatre.

Bernard Sobel, an author and press agent who represented both Ziegfeld and Carroll, recalled one of the stunts he produced while in Carroll's employ.

"I was working for Earl Carroll, exploiting *The Blue Kitten*, and sent out a story that Lillian Lorraine, star of the show, did her own washing. Of course, down in the second or third paragraph I qualified this plebian statement by saying she didn't exactly stand over a washtub doing the heavy work, such as bath towels or pillow cases and bed sheets. She confined her 'washing' only to those dainty bits of personal apparel . . . negligees, gloves, or light lacy handkerchiefs, the things that surely could not be entrusted to the indignity of a common laundry."

Sobel also remembered a series of stunts on Ziegfeld's behalf:

When I moved into the Ziegfeld office I learned that the great Flo, as a press agent, was always one step ahead of me. The battle was violent, pleasurable, and long. He taunted me, reprimanded me and seldom praised me, but the joy of working for him, and with him, was praise enough.

Stunts made news, and each day I planned something new. I had the chorus girls from *Louis the 14th* parade in bathing suits at City Hall, as a military recruiting drive. Ziegfeld gently asked me to refrain from this kind of publicity.

Inwardly he rejoiced, since the stunt helped prolong the show's life on Broadway and launch its road tour.

Ziegfeld girls staged a monster Maypole Dance on Michigan Boulevard in Chicago, twirling long ropes of brilliantly colored ribbons. Equally successful was the stunt we staged in Central Park to herald the advent of spring in New York, an early March 21st. A bevy of showgirls shivered in bikinis of the day, to be chased by the cops: we had forgotten to get a permit for the party.

I wrote a feature column for Yale students and used the Ziegfeld byline, but he never knew about it; later it was reprinted in the *Herald-Tribune*. In Ziegfeld's name, I also wrote a preface to a Kenyon Nicholson book—"Revues." He placed so little emphasis on authorship—he had bought and sold so many authors, Ring Lardner included—that he pitched the volume into a wastebasket from which I gratefully rescued the tome once he left the room.

But the most surprising stunt I ever arranged occurred at the time *Gentlemen Prefer Blondes* was a literary best seller. Latching on to a topic that suggested a stunt was always a good tactic. In this instance, I planned a "strike."

The idea was that Ziegfeld became annoyed at the popularity of blondes created by the book's eminence, and was showing great preference for brunettes in the company. I didn't write a story, but coached Paulette Goddard, then a dream of a teen-age blonde, to lead a group of blondes to strike.

The "strikers" wound up in the editorial room of *The New York Times* to air their complaint against Ziegfeld; the first day there was a half-column story, then another the following day. We could have had plenty more, except for Ziegfeld.

I had, of course, neglected to tell him about the stunt; when the *Times* telephoned him about the strike, he had to reveal his own ignorance of the subject. He laughed about it later, admitting he had been fooled by the stunt. Later I talked it over with a *Times* reporter and expressed my own surprise that the staid newspaper had printed anything about the hoax. He said: "We knew it was a stunt, but we enjoy a bit of it when it's properly mixed with humor."

Another famous stunt was the bet by Margaret Mayo that she could write a play in one day. The actress was appearing in *Pretty Peggy*, and press agent Channing Pollock needed an idea to drum up business. The scheme worked this way: Mayo made a bet with playwright Theodore Burt Sayre that she could write a play in twenty-four hours. To prove that the wager was on the up and up, it was decided that Sayre himself would provide the synopsis, which would be delivered in a sealed envelope at the start of the day.

Pollock arranged for his stenographer to aide the actress in finishing the four-act work. The night before, a finished play of Mayo's was hidden around the room where the writing was to take place. All through the day, Pollock and Mayo pretended to be in the throes of creativity. Between visits by reporters, they enjoyed leisurely meals. Sayre, who happened to be a close friend of Pollock, assured the press that he himself wrote the synopsis. That he did, while Pollock dictated it to him over the telephone. The newspapermen were suitably impressed when, at six o'clock the next morning, an exhausted Mayo delivered the manuscript entitled *The Mart*. Mayo later became an author in her own right with successes such as *Baby Mine* and *Polly of the Circus*.

Many stunts were instigated in order to disguise the shoddiness of a production. Edward L. Bernays was a fledgling producer in 1913 with his show *Damaged Goods*. The play's title seemed entirely too apt, so a plan was hatched. Bernays happened also to be the co-editor of the *Medical Review of Reviews*. The play was somewhat racy for its time, and the producer decided to open it only to members of the newly formed Medical Review of Reviews Sociological Fund. Membership cost exactly the same as a theatre ticket. Newly enrolled members of the fund kept the play running for sixty-six performances.

Stunts have often taken the form of legal action. Performers were continually suing management and vice versa. Marion Alexander might have started the idea when she sued Sam S. Shubert for $10,000 because he stated she was not beautiful.

During the run of *Fantana* in 1905, Channing Pollock hatched a stunt in which a chorus girl's dog wore expensive diamond earrings. Neither the dog nor the chorus girl owned a pair of earrings, so Pollock was happy to supply a pair of cheap fakes and the bubble gum needed to make them stick. The press looked askance at such an obvious fraud, and a reporter from the *World* had the nerve to refuse to use the photo. Pollock was forced to defend his honor and have the dog's ears pierced, and Tiffany's was asked to supply a pair of earrings suitable for canine use. This time, all the papers used the photo.

Pollock drummed up business for the 1906 production of *Happyland* at the Casino Theatre by announcing a matinee "for women only." To ensure coverage of the nonevent, Pollock arranged for a man to crash the theatre dressed in ladies' garments. There was also a husband who insisted that his wife exit the theatre immediately if he was not allowed to attend. Pollock's window dressing was unnecessary because the event turned out to be tremendously popular, and the performance was sold out.

Pollock thought up many other stunts to please his producers. Nena Blake, a chorus girl with 1904's *The Royal Chef*, was kidnapped in costume and sent halfway across the country. Her sister Bertha kissed a man who had never been kissed before. Actor Adele Ritchie's niece had her name legally changed to Adele Ritchie Jr., and the namesake was wooed by a "Siamese millionaire."

In the days before photocopy machines, scripts had to be hand-typed with crude carbon-paper copies. In order to cut down on secretarial work, actors received "sides," which contained only their lines and a few cues. Thus, in the latter part of 1905, when producer Henry Miller claimed that his play *Grierson's Way* had to be postponed because the only complete script had been lost, the press bought into the lie. A $500 reward was announced to sweeten the story while the rehearsals continued. The press agent on the show was surprised to learn that Miller subsequently did lose the script and was panicked at the thought of having to pay the $500. Luckily, a stage-hand found the script and accepted a small reward.

Harvey Sabinson was one of Broadway's greatest PR men. When *Finian's Rainbow* was on Broadway, Sabinson joined up with the press agent of the musical *Up In Central Park* and devised a sure-fire stunt. The female choruses (it was always females in stunts by the way) would have a boat race on the lake in Central Park. The plan was to have the police break up the proceedings and arrest the cast members. Unfortunately, the police didn't seem to notice at all.

More recently, stunts have been used sparingly and with little of the panache that earlier practitioners brought to the art. When *Grease* celebrated its fourth birthday on Valentine's Day in 1976, a couple was married onstage. For 1979's *Knockout*, a staged bout between star Danny Aiello and heavyweight Larry Holmes was held. Wilbur the Pig, a cast member of *King of Hearts*, was treated to a limousine ride and lunch at Sardi's. For the first anniversary of *Deathtrap* on February 26, 1979, press agent Jeffrey Richards gave a party for psychics who predicted the future of the show and its cast. Larry Blyden, who coproduced and starred in the 1972 revival of *A Funny Thing Happened on the Way to the Forum* with Phil Silvers, decided to give a free Fourth of July performance. By 11 a.m., all the tickets were gone. Josh Ellis had a unit of the New York Blood Program in the lobby of *Dracula*. For every year of its long run, *Big River* hosted a frog-jumping contest outside its theatre under the auspices of publicist Adrian

Bryan-Brown. And none other than New York's Mayor John Lindsay appeared in a Friday night performance of *Seesaw*, zinging bon mots while the song "My City" was performed behind him. Lindsay was a dead ringer for the star Ken Howard, and a photo was taken of Lindsay, Howard, and Michele Lee with a quizzical look on her face.

John Golden produced a show called *Pigs*, which played in the halcyon year of 1924. In those days, a person could pull a stunt and be proud of it. For the show, a dozen of the title characters were shuttled between a stable and the theatre. Harry Kline was the enterprising press agent for the show and saw to it that the pigs were transported in a straw-covered wagon everyday. The driver took his squealing load up and down the streets of Times Square. On the wagon was a sign: "These Pigs Perform Nightly at the Little Theatre."

And speaking of pigs, when Josh Ellis was representing the Eva Le Gallienne revival of *Alice in Wonderland*, he realized that the production required a trained pig. So, as a stunt, Ellis decided to hold an audition for a star piglet. The entire press corps showed up and asked, "Who will train those pigs?" The regal Miss Le Gallienne replied, "I will. It's easier than working with actors."

Ellis devised another stunt that included animals. This time it was a pair of camels. The show was the revival of *Kismet*, now titled *Timbuktu*. The idea was to have two of the stars, Melba Moore and Eartha Kitt, ride down Broadway on the dromedaries. The day of the stunt, Ms. Moore did not show up, and Ms. Kitt proclaimed that she would not ride down Broadway alone. "Joshua, get up on that camel," ordered Ms. Kitt and, like the great press agent he was, Ellis mounted the camel and away they went. The next day, the ad agency sent Ellis a picture of him on the camel with the caption "The camel that broke the press agent's back."

Ellis devised a stunt that David Merrick loved. It was 1980, and Ellis suggested they hold an audition for the 1990 cast of *42nd Street*. Merrick insisted it be on the stage of the Winter Garden Theatre with the set in place and the orchestra accompanying all 350 pre-teen entrants. They were taught the routine by the dance captain and the press sat in the audience as the curtain rose to reveal the dancers. Eight years later, two of those young tap dancers got into the cast of *42nd Street*. As Josh Ellis said, "Even in Merrickland, a fake stunt can turn into the real thing."

For the most part, stunts and fakes have lost their appeal. Richard Maney once bemoaned the fact that today the authors of stunts would be "drummed out of the regiment. Hyperbole and deception no longer are effective weapons."

THREE STUNTS WITH ALICE DELYSIA

Will Page also managed to make Alice Delysia a huge star with a series of stunts. As luck would have it, the performer had a well-developed sense of humor and a desire to see her name exploited. When Page and producer Morris Gest decided to bring Delysia from Europe during Prohibition, they wrote an unusual clause in her contract. It stated that she was to have one bottle of wine available at every meal. The reason given for this request was that the actress needed the wine to keep up her joie de vivre and "without which Mlle. Delysia will pine away and her audience-value diminish."

When Delysia arrived in the United States, she was wearing a flaming-red-leather dress and an ankle watch encrusted with huge diamonds. Following that, Page kept the heat on her career with a variety of ploys. A dog was trained to attack her during a luncheon. It was planned that she would then divest herself of the canine and exclaim: "More muzzles or foreign artistes will never visit these shores again." Unfortunately, the dog didn't quite understand its part, and the actress was nearly mauled, resulting in the closing of her show for three nights.

Page also cooked up a scheme for Delysia that took its leading participant by surprise. Delysia had been receiving love notes from a millionaire suitor. She wasn't interested in him and wanted him to go away. Consulting Page, she showed him one of the missives, in which the young man stated, "You doubt my love but you are wrong. Merely to kiss your hand, I would crawl over broken glass on my hands and knees." Page arranged for the press to be present in Delysia's dressing room when the young man arrived. Little did the suitor expect to find the floor strewn with broken glass. At the end of the trail of glass was Delysia. She challenged him: "You said you would crawl over broken glass on your hands and knees to get me. Let me see you crawl." This was meant to be the end of the stunt, but the young man quickly dropped to his knees and actually crept across the room toward the velvet-clad Delysia. The actress and the other guests stared in horror as the man slowly crossed the room. When at her feet, he rose and stated, "I've made good, now what about yourself?" Delysia changed her mind about the man, and they enjoyed a long relationship.

DAVID MERRICK—KING OF THE STUNT

Fakes have passed into disfavor. Show business is more a business than a show, and newspapers pride themselves on reporting the truth. On the other hand, publicist Richard Maney doted on stunts that were obviously fake and, in fact, too ridiculous to pass up. Maney created most of his stunts while working for the master showman David Merrick. Facing an embarrassing failure with his first show *Clutterbuck* (1949), Merrick arranged to have a "Mr. Clutterbuck" paged throughout Manhattan. Every hotel and restaurant resounded with the name of Mr. Clutterbuck. Although the show was not a success, Merrick saw the value of a good stunt.

When Grace Kelly got married in Monaco, a plane circled overhead trailing a banner exhorting the wedding party to come and see the Merrick production *Fanny* (1954). Closer to home, Merrick was seen in Manhattan walking an ostrich named Fanny. *Fanny* featured a belly dancer, so Merrick placed a belly-dancer statue in the Poet's Corner in Central Park; the statue was nude. The sculptor, who perhaps saw his art on a higher plane, was insulted that Merrick would use his artwork for a stunt. Again, the newspapers reveled in Merrick's mischievousness. Even this wasn't enough to satisfy the indefatigable Merrick. He found the names of suburbanites listed in the phone book and called to invite them to see *Fanny* free, provided they brought one paying customer. When *Fanny* finally closed after 888 performances, the ledger books showed a handsome profit of almost $1 million.

Other Merrick-Maney stunts were just as colorful as those for *Fanny*. When *The Good Soup* opened in 1960, someone circulated the rumor that the playwright Felicien Marceau was a Nazi collaborator. Much newspaper coverage ensued. When Merrick's production of *The World of Suzi Wong* and the Rodgers and Hammerstein musical *Flower Drum Song* were both about to open in 1958, Merrick sent Asian-Americans to picket the *Flower Drum Song* box office with signs proclaiming *The World of Suzi Wong* as "the only authentic Chinese show." Richard Rodgers was not amused.

The Matchmaker was given the Merrick treatment when he arranged to have a chimpanzee drive a taxi around town carrying the sign "I am driving my master to see *The Matchmaker*."

When John Osborne's *Look Back in Anger* was playing at the John Golden Theatre in 1957, Merrick felt the need to get more press for the show. Kenneth Haig was accosted by a woman from the audience who jumped on the stage and repeatedly hit the actor with her fists while screaming a diatribe against men. The police were called and the woman was arrested. Haig didn't know about the stunt and his surprise was genuine. Merrick had to convince the police that the whole thing was a stunt so the woman could have the charges dropped and be released from jail.

And as a remedy for a bad critical reception, Merrick was known to prescribe some strong medicine. At the beginning of a live broadcast from outside the theatre of one of his flops, Merrick gleefully assigned a press agent to take an ax to the television cable, thereby literally cutting off the bad review.

But perhaps the greatest stunt in Broadway history began while *Subways Are for Sleeping* was having its out-of-town tryout in Boston. Knowing that the show was in trouble and would probably fail in New York, Merrick approached stage manager Robert Schear and told him to find a Manhattan telephone book. Schear thought it was a strange request but persevered in finding just such a telephone book in Beantown.

Merrick called his press agent Harvey Sabinson and mentioned that there was a Howard Taubman listed in the New York directory. A plan was hatched. Sabinson and Merrick's advertising director Fred Golden would look up people whose names matched those of the New York critics: Howard Taubman (*New York Times*), Walter Kerr (*Herald-Tribune*), John Chapman (*Daily News*), Robert Coleman (*Daily Mirror*), Norman Nadel (*World Telegram*), John McLain (*Journal-American*), and Richard Watts (*Post*).

Sabinson then brought these people to the city, wined and dined them at the Plaza Hotel's Oak Room, and transported them to the theatre. Afterward, he asked them what they thought of the show and suggested they lend their names to quotes that he composed. Golden, a Merrick favorite, made up a full-page ad to run in all the New York papers that reprinted the erstwhile quotes, names, and pictures. *The New York Times* discovered the stunt after its first edition and pulled it. However, the attendant publicity became so enormous that the *Times* was forced to run the ad when reporting the hoax. Only *The Herald-Tribune* did not catch the fraud. John McClain wrote of the incident, "The only reaction that affected me strenuously was a letter I got from somebody saying: 'I just saw your picture in the advertisement for *Subways* and then I looked at your picture in the paper and I like the one in the advertisement better.'"

CHAPTER 20

Performing The Show

Singer Sue Hight reminisced: "My first show was *Gentlemen Prefer Blondes*. On Saturday afternoon before the Entr'acte, we'd be sitting in our dressing rooms fixing our makeup, chatting, waiting for the second act. We'd get our pay envelopes and it was $55 for eight shows a week. I thought I was rich. I'd never seen so much money handed to me. At the same time Rodgers and Hammerstein were paying base salaries $125 plus I think it was five or fifteen dollars for understudies when I was in the original production of *South Pacific*. When you were a girl in *South Pacific* you were a non-person. I think we had only seventeen minutes total on stage. It was such a bore because you had nothing to do. Sit in the dressing room and do your makeup or stand around in a clump. Then you'd go onstage and do your little bit and then you were off for an hour."

Orson Welles's massive production of Cole Porter's *Around the World in Eighty Days* had thousands of dollars worth of scenery left in the alley. When the show was going to open in London, the British unions wouldn't let American-built sets be brought over, and the London production never happened. The sets ended up being thrown away.

And yet another show's sets wouldn't fit into the theatre. When *Flying Colors* was about to move into the Imperial Theatre, one of Norman Bel Geddes's sets would not fit because of a gas pipe running along the back wall. Taking matters into his own hands, Bel Geddes began sawing away at the pipe. Luckily, his assistant Tom Farrar saw him and stopped him from blowing up the theatre. The set design was revised and everything was restored to order.

Stanley Prager was a beloved performer/director/stage manager who acted in both film and stage. He was in the revue *Two on the Aisle* opposite Bert Lahr and Dolores Gray. Lahr instructed Prager never to move when Lahr was talking onstage. "If I see you move, kid," threatened the comic, "you're fired. Understand?" Prager understood, but at one performance his nose was itching fiercely. It would not be denied in its need to be scratched. Lahr was facing the audience, and Prager quickly brought his hand up to his nose when Lahr's hand shot up and grabbed Prager by the wrist. "I told you not to move!" Lahr remonstrated. The audience cracked up.

Actors have been known to mark time when in rehearsal only to come alive before an audience.

Shirley Booth was rehearsing William Inge's *Come Back, Little Sheba*, walking through the part, marking her lines, expending no energy. Inge and the director Daniel Mann wanted Booth replaced by Joan Blondell. The producers, the Theatre Guild, disagreed and Booth had one of her greatest triumphs in the role. They said the same of Laurette Taylor when she rehearsed.

Mark Horowitz of the Library of Congress came upon a carbon copy of a letter that Hammerstein presumably sent to the stage manager of *The King and I* in February 1953 when Constance Carpenter was playing Anna. The letter is four typed pages and goes into any number of details he thinks should be changed based on watching a recent performance. My favorite paragraph is this: "Please forward my suggestion to Connie that instead of imagining the young lovers being down at about where the horn section is, that it would be better if they were out, if she called out into the night, out into the front. She may answer that she has always been doing this. I don't know, but if she has I think it's wrong. I think the lovers ought to be somewhere on the first balcony. They are all the young lovers in the world she is really talking to. The song is bigger than that. She makes it small by singing down to the orchestra pit to her left."

William Snowdon, the boy who originally played Friedrich in *The Sound of Music*, had to be let go from the cast. He suffered from a terrible problem that often hits young Broadway performers; his voice changed. Arthur Warren was his replacement. One day the stage manager handed Arthur a card and told him that it was from Miss Martin. "What is it?" "Miss Martin wants your hair colored blonde." He was the only kid in the cast who wasn't in professional children's school. So thinking he'll get the crap kicked out of him if he colors his hair, he doesn't go to the stylist.

This goes on for a couple of days and he's performing in the Wednesday matinee. The stage manager calls him aside and says to him, "Arthur Warren, Mary Martin wants to see you in her dressing room after the matinee." He knocks on her door and she says come in. He opens the door and Mary Martin, one of Broadway's greatest stars, is standing there with rubber gloves on and a bottle of peroxide. She says, "Take off your shirt." And then she dyed his hair. And when he went to school, the kids didn't even notice.

During the run of *The Sound of Music*, Martin was going to tape a new production of *Peter Pan* for color television. Mary made sure that all the Von Trapp kids got to play little things in *Peter Pan*. Warren got to play one part of a tree. As he recalled, "I wasn't facially on camera but I was in the show."

The show was rehearsing in the Helen Hayes theatre across the street from the Lunt Fontanne Theatre where *The Sound of Music* was playing. Warren was in shock, "She had a rope around her waist for the flying. The guy who was controlling the rope during one of the tapings smashed her into the wall and broke her arm. We had an evening performance of *The Sound of Music*. During the show she was in agony but the audience didn't know. After the final curtain, she let them take her to the hospital and the next day she came in with her arm in a cast and nothing was said about it."

After she injured herself, she worried that the kids would be frightened to go back up on the wire. So she insisted at the very next rehearsal that they do the flying again. When they hoisted her up, she saw that a mattress had been attached to the wall of the theatre where she had hit. And below the mattress was a sign that read, "Mary Martin slapped here."

Martin had another terrible accident when flying as Peter Pan. While out of town, the cable holding her up came off of its gear and she fell six feet and was jerked so badly when it stopped, she injured her spine. Every day before the show, a doctor would use a needle to shoot a painkiller between her vertebrae.

Martin stayed at the Hampshire House during the run of *The Sound of Music*. Richard Halliday would go with Mary to the theatre every night. One day when he was out of town, she got into a cab and didn't know the name of the theatre she was playing in. So she instructed the driver, "Take me to *The Sound of Music*."

Gwen Verdon: "The dance 'If My Friends Could See Me Now' in *Sweet Charity* was Neil Simon's idea, who loved the whole concept of the Italian movie star scene. Bob sent me twenty-two separate notes, one after each performance, telling me to keep my feet together when I land, as he didn't want the audience to see my underwear. I solved that issue—I didn't wear any."

Claire Trevor saw the now legendary production of *Medea* starring Judith Anderson. Trevor went backstage to see the great actress. When she entered the dressing room, she exclaimed, "I can't tell you how I feel about the performance." Judith Anderson replied, "Try."

Richard Burton made a return to the musical stage in a new production of *Camelot* at the New York State Theatre in Lincoln Center. The show started all right. Burton came out to sing his first song "I Wonder What the King Is Doing Tonight" when he got out of sync with the orchestra and went up on his lyrics. One of the knights came out and spoke to Burton and the curtain came down. An announcement was made that Burton was too ill to continue but that the understudy William Parry would take over the role. Many patrons walked out of the theatre while others stampeded to the box office for refunds. Audience members were told they could get a refund if they mailed in their stubs. Certain cagey audience members then scoured the floor of the auditorium picking up stubs that were thrown away in disgust. In fact, several people actually made a profit that evening.

But the worse wasn't over. That night, when William Parry stepped into the role of Arthur, a chorus member had to cover Parry's original role of Sir Dinadan. When the song "The Lusty Month of May" began, it was clear that there wasn't anyone to cover the chorus member. The choreography for the number was based on couples. And each couple had a bower of flowers that they handed off from couple to couple. The problem was that there was an extra woman. So they couldn't hand off the bowers and that created a chain reaction in the choreography that resulted in a train wreck.

All together, a wonderful evening in the theatre!

Here's the cast of characters for the following story. In Neil Simon's *Barefoot in the Park*, Penny Fuller is playing Corie. Mildred Natwick is playing Corie's mother. Kurt Kasznar is playing the upstairs neighbor Mr. Velasco. Robert Redford is playing Paul, Corie's husband.

Fuller's mother came to see her daughter in the show. She got into town at 7:30 on Saturday night and went backstage to say hi to Fuller and Natwick.

There's a moment in the play when Natwick rings the doorbell from the street and Fuller opens the door to yell downstairs: "Four flights mom!" One Monday night, Fuller opened the door but standing there, out of sight of the audience, was Fuller's mother wearing Mildred Natwick's costume. It was Natwick's idea.

A few minutes later, Penny opened the door to say, "Two more flights up," and there were Natwick and Fuller's mother hurrying to switch costumes. A little later, when Fuller opened the door again to let Mildred Natwick into the apartment, Natwick was so tickled with herself she made her entrance laughing and couldn't talk for three minutes.

Later in the show, there's a scene where Corie wants to get her mother fixed up with Mr. Velasco. Natwick and Kasznar were about to go on their vacations. During the show, Kasznar had a long break so he went upstairs to clean off his dressing table for his replacement. He was so involved he got his timing mixed up and forgot to make his entrance.

The stage manager ran upstairs yelling, "Kurt! Kurt!" The stagehands playing poker in the basement thought he was saying, "Curtain! Curtain!" They ran upstairs and there's no stage manager. Then they saw Robert Redford lying on the floor. They'd never seen the play, so they didn't know it was his blocking. Thinking that Redford had fainted or was actually dead, they started bringing the curtain down. By that time, the stage manager returned, saw the curtain halfway down, and yelled to the stagehands, "Stop! Stop!"

Mildred Natwick was calmly sitting onstage watching the curtain come partway down and wondered where Kasznar was. She thinks, "I gotta get off." Kasznar was in the wings wearing only his bathrobe and shorts saying, "Let me go on. I have to help her!" By this time, the guys are pulling the curtain back up and the stage manager tells Fuller to go onstage without Kasznar. Natwick takes one look at Fuller coming on without Kasznar and says to her, "Well, dear. Say goodnight to Mr. Velasco," and leaves the stage. Fuller couldn't figure out how to get out of it but Robert Redford nonchalantly got up off the floor and continued with the next scene as if nothing happened.

Fuller was playing Madame Renevskaya in a production of *The Cherry Orchard*. In the third act, Renevskaya is throwing a ball and her brother is off selling the cherry orchard. Renevskaya waltzes in with the young revolutionary and she says, "I'm tired, I must sit." They sit on a little settee at which point her daughter Anya, played by Cynthia Nixon, comes in and says, "Mama, mama. I just heard in the kitchen that the cherry orchard has been sold." Well, that's what should happen.

At one matinee, Fuller says, "I must sit" and there's nothing. No Cynthia Nixon. Penny immediately thought of Mildred Natwick in *Barefoot in the Park*, whose mantra when things were going badly was "Get off the stage." But Fuller's legs would not uncross. It was if she was in a nightmare. She remembers thinking, "I remember, Millie, but I can't, my legs won't move." Finally, the young revolutionary improvises, "You know, before I met Anya I never danced." Fuller gave him a horrified look, uncrossed her legs, patted him on the knee and said, "You're doing very well" and got up to go off the stage. At which point, Corless Preston, playing the maid, runs on with this look on her face as if to say with pride, "don't worry I've got it all under control." And she proclaims to Fuller, "Madame, madame, I just heard back-stage that the cherry orchard has been sold!"

During the run of the Vincent Youmans show *Smile*, Adele Astaire had a date to sing on the radio. She asked Larry Adler to accompany her. Now Adler was a brilliant harmonica player and an okay pianist, but not quite good enough when Adele asked him to take the song up half a tone. This meant he'd have to play the song in C sharp, which meant using mostly the black keys, which proved to be beyond his talents. Adler himself admitted, "Even the composer wouldn't have recognized what I did." Adele was distraught, which meant that her brother Fred was more than distraught. Apoplectic is a better word. Adler described what happened next: "(Fred) left a news-paper in my dressing room, the *Herald-Tribune*. By cutting out letters and rearranging them, he had manufactured a front-page headline: LARRY ADLER IS A LOUSY CUNT. He never let me forget my disastrous perfor-mance and would introduce me to people as 'Adele's great accompanist.'"

Harvey Evans is a legendary gypsy, appearing on Broadway for over fifty years. When Harvey played Will Parker in the Jones Beach production of *Oklahoma!* he came onstage with tight jeans and a pink bandanna around his neck. One husband turned to his wife in the audience and was heard to say, "That's a cowboy?"

Richard Rodgers always had a girl in the chorus, if you know what we mean. His wife Dorothy knew about it and every opening night, she'd make a point of introducing herself to the girl.

While Rita Gardner was watching a rehearsal of Bob Fosse and Vivica Lindfors in *Pal Joey* at City Center, Richard Rodgers sidled up to her and said, "Oh, this is painful. Let's get out of here. Come on, nobody will miss us." She politely refused. Shirley Jones had the same thing happen to her and also refused Rodgers's advances.

When Anna Held opened in Florenz Ziegfeld's production of *A Parlor Match* on September 21, 1896, the gates of decorum suffered their first attack when she sang "Won't You Come and Play with Me." What would be tame in today's world was shocking in 1896. But Held was from Paris, and the French, as all Americans knew, were much more blasé about sex.

Here's the chorus:

> I have such a nice little way with me,
> A way with me,
> A way with me,
> I have such a nice little way with me,
> I should like to have you play with me,
> Play with me all the day long.

Hot stuff, no?

Year in and year out, every Christmas, one noted producer gave out exactly fifty-seven brownies to the cast, crew, and orchestra, the exact number of people backstage. So if one person takes two brownies, one person won't get any brownie and is out of luck. Through the years, some people have never gotten a brownie.

If a show has a big star, producers have always hated making the announcement that he or she will not be performing that night. People are entitled to run to the box office and get their money back. This was unacceptable for David Merrick. He had their money and he wasn't giving it back!

During the run of *Hello, Dolly!* when the actress playing Dolly would be out of the show, the stage manager made an announcement, "At today's performance, the role of Mrs. Levi will be played by Bibi Osterwald." Most of the audience didn't know Dolly's last name and as soon as the announcement was made, the house lights went black and the orchestra started up the overture leaving no time for those in the know to get refunds.

When John Gabriel went on for Robert Goulet the Saturday before *The Happy Time* opened, Merrick turned off the exit lights and brought down the house lights, making it impossible for refund seekers to safely find their way to the box office in the dark.

After Bette Davis left *The Night of the Iguana*, the producers tried the Merrick technique and gave a hasty announcement, "At this performance the part of Maxine Faulk will be played by Miss Davis's understudy, the well-known stage actress Madeleine Sherwood." Though the lights had gone down immediately after the announcement and the curtain went up, the audience still rose to get their refunds. But from the stage, Madeleine

Sherwood addressed them, "Come on, ladies! Give me a chance! I'm really very good and the play is terrific!" A few of the women were embarrassed enough to return to their seats.

But sometimes an announcement is greeted with cheers from the audience. When Liza Minnelli briefly took over for an ailing Gwen Verdon in *Chicago*, when the stage manager said, "At today's performance, the role of Roxie Hart usually played by Gwen Verdon (audience: "Awwwww") will be played by Liza Minnelli (audience: "Hooray!").

As a result, Actor's Equity demanded that a replacement notice had to appear in two of three ways: A notice on the cast board in the lobby, a slip of paper in the program, or an announcement made over the speakers in the auditorium.

Of course, some shows now have the audiences enter through the alley rather than the lobby and, besides, in the crush to get into the theatre, those who actually enter through the lobby often don't see the cast board. And many people don't look at their Playbills before the show begins, so they don't see the slip of paper announcing a replacement.

Ethel Merman's attitude toward Fernando Lamas in *Happy Hunting* is well known in theatre circles. Lamas, a Hollywood actor, was certain that Merman would blow him off the stage so he devised a way to get the audience's full attention. Lamas's endowment was larger than most, so he figured he'd emphasize his greatest asset. He asked costume designer Irene Sharaff to design his pants in a way that did this. When the pre-Broadway engagement in Philadelphia opened, he, or rather part of him, certainly got the audience's attention, which was expressed by several patrons gasping at the monument and the fact that it was essentially being trotted out on the stage. Merman was appalled, and the pants and Mr. Lamas's appendage did not appear again. But the damage was done, and Merman refused to acknowledge Lamas when they were both onstage talking to each other. She chose to deliver her lines to the audience.

But this was not the first time Merman disapproved of a leading man. During *Call Me Madam*, director George Abbott had to constantly reprimand Merman for not facing costar Paul Lukas during their scenes together.

Kim Hunter was playing opposite Marlon Brando in *A Streetcar Named Desire*, and she accidentally tore his T-shirt. They kept it in the show.

There were more mishaps during *Streetcar*. At one performance when Brando carried Hunter to the bed, the lights didn't go down. "Oh, Christ," Brando quipped to Kim Hunter, "How far do we have to go for realism?"

Boredom can easily strike long-running shows. And that's when tricks and pranks get started.

The Nathan Lane revival of *Guys and Dolls* had a spate of backstage mischief. The men's dressing room was very long with a long table along one wall. All the men dressed there. One night, Ken Kantor, sitting in front of his mirror, bent down to put on his shoes. All of a sudden, water shot into his face from under the table. One of the other performers had gotten a long piece of plastic tubing that ran the entire length of the room and ended in front of Ken. The actor, who we will not name, put water in the tube and closed it off with a cork. As soon as Ken bent over and reached down for his shoes, the actor blew into the tube, the cork popped out and the water soaked Ken. He was so flummoxed that he froze in shock.

That same mischievous actor took a performer's socks and put them in the dry ice machine during the second act. Right before the curtain call, he retrieved them and put them back in the dressing room. When it came for the actor to put on his socks, they were frozen solid and stiff as a board.

Speaking of socks, one night after the show, Ken got dressed and hailed a taxi to take him home. As he was riding in the car, he felt something icky between his toes. When he got home, he took off his sneakers to find someone had put blue powdered clothing dye in his socks that combined with the perspiration from his feet and created a thick blue paste that dyed his cuticles and calluses a bright shade of blue for many weeks to come.

Paper Mill Playhouse in Milburn, New Jersey, also has its share of childish but funny behavior.

There was a guy who was extremely anal. At his seat in the dressing room, he had a clean towel laid out with all of his dry rouges and paint-brushes in size order, perfectly lined up. Next to them was a very large jar of cold cream that he used to remove his makeup. So the cast did as casts do and moved a brush or rouge a little bit and he would always move it back exactly to the same place. One night, the jar of cream was practically empty but the actor was determined to finish it. Naturally, the cast filled it with springy snakes and screwed on the top so when he opened it, the snakes popped out dramatically. The cast had bought a new jar of cold cream for him.

But then things escalated. One night, the same actor came in and his dressing table was completely bare. There was nothing there. He got really got flummoxed. "Where are my things?" he asked his fellow thespians. The cast pointed up to the ceiling. Someone had hot-glued all his tubes and paints and brushes to the ceiling in the exact positions that he had them set on the makeup table. And there they stayed through the run of the show. To be fair, the perpetrator bought him a new makeup kit.

But the actor whose makeup was on the ceiling needed his revenge. He went to a bakery and when the woman behind the counter asked what size pie he wanted, he said, "To be honest, I'm going to throw it at somebody." And the salesperson exclaimed, "My goodness, this is the first time I've sold a pie on a suicide mission"; it was to be a kamikaze pie.

Also at Paper Mill, there was one guy, we'll call him Bob, who came in with new headshots. He had three different shots and couldn't decide among them. He was driving everyone crazy asking them to help him make up his mind. For the record, they were all lousy. Bob just couldn't decide and the actors all begged him to just make up his @#*!* mind. One of the actors, we'll call him Fred, was at the end of his rope, and during one performance, he took one of the headshots down to the publicity office and made 600 copies.

While Bob was out to dinner between shows, Fred took the copies and put them on the windshields of all the cars in the parking lot. Then he dispersed them throughout the building, on the inside of the orchestra pit, in the bathrooms, and along the halls. When Bob came back from dinner, Fred innocently asked him if he had made up his mind which picture he liked. "No," said Bob. "Well," replied Fred, "I asked some people which ones they liked. Take a look."

Fred opened the dressing room window and fluttering in the evening air were hundreds of Bob's faces looking back at him. Bob gasped and ran outside, grabbing the photos. He thought he was through until he went onstage and found more pictures. Everywhere he looked, his pictures were taped up. He couldn't avoid seeing them just as the cast couldn't avoid seeing them when he couldn't make up his mind.

Here's a kinder but no less devious prank that took place at Paper Mill. While rehearsing *Damn Yankees*, director George Abbott was having a hard time staging the courtroom scene in Act Two so that the entire cast could be seen from all angles. It had to be so exact that there were marks on the stage for placement of all the chairs. One of the ladies in the show, we'll call her Roberta, had been in a lot of shows with Fred, and it was always expected that he would pull some practical joke or another.

Her chair was blocked to be just right of center. Every night, Fred would imperceptibly move her mark a little bit farther to the right. Little by little, quarter inch by quarter inch, her seat was moved closer and closer to the wings. The movement was so slight, Roberta never noticed, even though she was always on the lookout for Fred to pull something. Actors are so agreeable, so used to following the directors' orders, they think, "If that's where the mark is, that's where I'll sit." By the end of the run, her seat was halfway offstage until only her knees were visible to the audience. On closing night, Fred moved the mark back to where it had started, many feet toward the center of the stage. Roberta immediately grasped what Fred had done, and all through the scene she was shooting daggers from her eyes at him.

Now we turn our attention to the Darien Dinner Theatre in Connecticut. *Camelot* was playing there and everyone got into the habit of baking pies, brownies, and all sorts of baked goods for the cast and crew. They did this because there wasn't a lot time between shows to get something to eat. Well, one guy in the cast, we'll call him Bob, would always take the largest piece of brownie or pie or whatever. But that's not why the cast took its revenge.

In the show, Merlin makes his entrance and as if by magic he makes a rabbit appear. The cast was very fond of this cute little rabbit. One day between shows, they heard this terrible screeching sound. They turned around and there was Bob pinching the rabbit. He wanted to see if the rabbit would make a noise. The cast members were aghast.

Revenge had to be taken, but how? One of the actors, we'll call him Fred, said, "Of course, ExLax brownies." The company loved the idea. Fred was an expert. He knew that if you put laxative in the batter, it wouldn't be effective. So, Fred frosted the brownies and cut them so that there was one piece much larger than the others. In the frosting of that single piece, he put twenty-four doses of ExLax. It was a two-show day, and the brownies were put out before the matinee.

In that production of *Camelot*, the men wore three layers of tights and were in and out of armor many times. All through the matinee, the performers watched Bob, waiting for something to happen. But nothing did. They thought, "Surely tonight," but at the evening performance, nothing happened. Dejected, they all got into their carpools and headed home. That's when it happened. Bob's car had to stop five times at the side of the road. He came in the next day and said, "What a weekend! I spent the whole time on the toilet. It must have been that Mexican food I ate between shows on Sunday."

Since we're on the subject, at one performance of *Fiddler on the Roof*, Fred was playing Tevye. In the show, Tevye gets into bed with his wife Golde during a blackout. Just before the lights came back on for the scene, the actress playing Golde whispered one word to Fred that shook him to his core—"diarrhea."

Here are some non-prank stories about that same production of *Camelot* at the Darien Dinner Theatre. Pellinore comes onstage with a large dog on a leash. The producer decided that to save money, he would replace the well-trained theatre dog that cost big bucks with his own pet who we'll call Fido. Since the switch from professional acting dog to lapdog came during the run of the show, they never rehearsed with Fido. He made his first appearance in the role before an audience. Fido so didn't want to be onstage it was unbelievable. The stage floor was covered with masonite and when Fido saw the audience, he immediately tried running into the wings. But because the floor was slippery, he couldn't get traction. So, while Pellinore is doing his scene, Fido is running, running, running and going nowhere. The audience was in hysterics.

Another night, Pellinore and Fido came on and Fido squatted and relieved himself right behind Pellinore who remained unaware of Fido's present. As the scene progressed, the audience was laughing like crazy. The actor playing Pellinore was thinking, "Wow! I am great! This scene is going so well!" He wandered around the stage with his chest puffed out. In his wandering, he came close to the pile of shit on the stage and just missed it—over and over again. And the audience was going nuts. Just before the end of the scene, he took a step back right into the pile of poop. The audience laughed for a full seven minutes. Every time they'd catch their breaths and calm down, someone would snicker and it started all over again.

That production of *Camelot* was the show that simply wouldn't close. The theatre was, like many theatres, in terrible financial trouble. And so it was cheaper to keep the show running rather than pay for a new show. They kept extending it. David Holliday was starring as King Arthur. He had made a career out of playing three parts—King Arthur, Don Quixote in *Man of La Mancha*, and Henry Higgins in *My Fair Lady*. He had played the roles so often, he brought his own costumes and props.

Holliday never really interacted with the other company members and, although they had been together for months, he never knew anyone's name nor did he do anything with the rest of the company. He would pick one cute chorus boy and invite him into his dressing room. "Won't you come to my room between shows? I have a hotplate and I'm cooking a steak."

One day Holliday was coming down the hall and as he brushed by one of the actors he wished him a good afternoon by name! The actor was so shocked and amazed he ran into the men's dressing room where the actor Gene Masoner was sitting. Masoner had seen and done it all and was one of the quickest, funniest people alive. He was very carefully putting on his makeup when the actor barged in screaming, "Gene! Gene! You're never going to believe it." Masoner barely looked up and dryly said, "What?" "I was out in the hallway and David Holliday spoke to me by name!" Masoner replied, "I don't think 'Get out of my way, tubby,' counts." Once, the same actor was next to Masoner when they were getting into armor.

Masoner looked over and said, "It's terrific." "What's terrific?" asked the actor? "It's like watching somebody put eight ounces of tuna into a six-ounce can." Masoner was one of the first actors to die of AIDS even before there was a name for it.

During that same production of *Camelot*, during the song "The Lusty Month of May,",the cast was lying on blankets and eating fake food. They asked the producers if they could bring their own food and eat that. The producers didn't care, so the cast brought in grapes. Then, for the evening show, someone got an idea to have an eating contest. They weighed out five pounds of grapes for each of the three cast members' baskets. The idea was to see who could eat the most grapes during the shortest period of time. It was "the scene be damned, give me more grapes!"

In *The Merry Widow* at the Darian Dinner Theatre, there were three comic characters. One of the actors was tall and skinny, one was of medium height and weight (we'll call him Fred), and the third was about 4'3" and weighed around 300 pounds (we'll call him Bob). It was the perfect cast for a production of *Goldilocks* (the fairytale, not the musical). Anyway, they were playing a comic scene that never seemed to work, but at this one performance, the audience was laughing up a storm. The three cast members felt great. The scene was really working! Then Fred realized that the laughter wasn't in sync with the jokes. He looked over at his fellow performers and realized that the fly on Bob's pants was open. When the audience saw the shock on his face, they cracked up again. While the audience was laughing uncontrollably, Fred pulled Bob around so their backs were to the audience. Fred said to Bob, "Get your pants closed!" Bob quickly zipped up his pants. But then Fred had a brainstorm. He unzipped his pants. They turned around. Now the audience could barely control themselves. It was a perfect save by the quick-thinking Fred.

When Marcia Lewis was asked to play Golde opposite Topol in the Broadway revival of *Fiddler on the Roof*, people strongly advised her not to since he had a terrible reputation for mistreating his fellow performers. He'd already gotten rid of three Goldes. Lewis signed on, resolute that he wasn't going to get to her. While onstage, he'd whisper things like, "I think you're so ugly. I don't understand how the audience can look at you. You're disgusting." After the run was over, Lewis had a stroke, which she attributed to stress while acting with Topol.

Bob Schear was the stage manager of the original production of *La Cage Aux Folles*. When the Minskoff Theatre revival was getting ready to go into rehearsal with Gary Beach in the lead, Bob went to talk to the director about being the stage manager again. They sat for about fifteen minutes when the director said, "You know, the problem is, Bob, we really want people to look at this show with fresh eyes." Bob said, "Okay." He wanted to say, "Why the fuck does a stage manager have to look at a show with fresh eyes?" Later, Bob was told that it was the director's way of turning someone down without being accused of ageism.

Anita Gillette was acting in a John Guare play with a well-known actor as her leading man. The actor was not getting a good response from the audience, so he threw away some of his lines. At another performance, the same thing happened. Gillette was getting angrier and angrier. After one show, she went downstairs to his dressing room. He was standing there in his briefs when Gillette reached forward and grabbed him by the balls. She looked him in the eye and said, "If you do that again. . . ." He didn't.

This story took place at the Martin Beck Theatre. Outside it was raining, but a crowd had gathered to have the star autograph their programs. Inside, the star was screaming at his dresser. Down the hall they went with the star still yelling, then to the stage door and outside. The star was still berating his dresser when a woman tapped him on the shoulder. The star whipped around and glared at the woman, "What do you want!" he bellowed. "Will you please sign my program?" the woman meekly inquired. The star turned his back on her. The woman took her umbrella and whacked the star on the back. The stage doorman watched all of this and said, "That's the first time the fan ever hit the shit."

I Had a Ball was a rambunctious musical about a fake psychic in Coney Island. Buddy Hackett was the star along with Richard Kiley and Karen Morrow. Hackett would ad-lib and generally misbehave to the consternation of Kiley, but audiences ate it up and, after all, it was a feel-good musical, albeit one with an above-average score. When Hackett decided it was time for him to take a vacation, many names were bandied about, but Hackett, who had approval, would not agree on any of them taking over. So, despite the show being a success, it had to close.

Pearl Bailey, like Danny Kaye, had a wonderful public image. She was dubbed "the Ambassador of Love." In fact, she could be a horrible person, not just mean but purposely vindictive. When she starred in *Hello, Dolly!* there was a secret system on the backstage sign-in sheet. When there was a little green flag, the cast knew that she was in a good mood. But when there was a red flag, watch out!

Bailey had just written an autobiography and at the curtain calls always plugged her book. Like Al Jolson during all his shows and like Ray Bolger in *All American*, during the extended curtain call, she'd make the cast stand in back of her. When she mentioned her book to the audience, she would ask one of the chorus boys, usually Denny Martin Flinn—the token white guy—to run and get a copy for her. The chorus member, after performing an arduous show, would have to run into the wings, downstairs, and to Bailey's dressing room to retrieve the book. When it was suggested that a copy of the book be placed just offstage in the wings, she rejected the idea, preferring to force the chorus member to run around.

But that wasn't all. During the show, when Dolly makes her grand entrance at the Harmonia Gardens, the cast performs the title number. The number always earned immense applause. When it was over, the waiters held their positions, trying to catch their breath while the applause went on and on. Bailey would turn to the audience and say something like, "Wasn't that wonderful? Wouldn't you like to see it again?" Naturally, the audience would cheer and she'd hike up her skirt, throw the train of her dress over her shoulder and climb back up the stairs. The cast would have to do the whole number again. Bailey would come across to the audience as a fun, generous actress who would do anything for you, but the cast had a completely different view of her.

At one performance, when she asked the audience if they wanted to see the number again, one man in the audience yelled out, "No!" And Pearlie Mae, the Ambassador of Love, yelled to the ushers, "Throw him out!" And the man was ejected from the theatre.

We want to say that Bailey was magnificent in the show. She was truly exciting to watch, but for the cast and crew, the run was a nightmare.

Stanley Donen, later to become one of the best directors of film musicals, got his start on Broadway in the chorus of *Pal Joey*. Coming from South Carolina, Donen had a thick southern accent, for which he was mercilessly teased. Only fellow chorus boy Van Johnson was his friend. Someone who definitely wasn't Donen's pal was Henning Irgens, who relentlessly teased him. One day Irgens said to Donen, the neophyte, "What are you going to do about makeup? Actors are responsible for their own makeup, you know." Irgens offered to take Donen to choose his makeup. They bought eyebrow pencils, pancake, and a sponge for applying it. When it came to taking the makeup off after the performance, Donen wanted cold cream, but Irgens suggested a better solution: orange marmalade. While onstage, Leila Ernst whispered to Donen, "They're all in on it and are waiting to watch. So when we're finished, whatever you do, *don't use the orange marmalade!*"

Frank Loesser had other jobs besides being a top-notch songwriter. He also had a publishing company that we discussed in the "Personalities" chapter of the book and, along with orchestrator Don Walker, founded Music Theatre International, the leading musical theatre licensing organization.

George Abbott watched a rehearsal of *Pleasure Dome*, walked up to Kaye Ballard, and said, "This show is going to make you a star." Kaye was excited and went to lunch. When she returned, she found out that the show had closed in rehearsal.

Just before *Dreamgirls* was going on the road for tryouts, director Michael Bennett's assistant choreographer Bob Avian warned producer Marvin Krauss, "Beware, sooner or later everyone gets the wrath of Michael Bennett. Don't be upset, just be prepared." In the second year of the run of the show on Broadway, Krauss was called into an advertising meeting. Krauss knew that Bennett was angry. He knew that Avian's prediction was about to come true. Krauss thought of his options; should he defend himself or apologize? The only way was to try to defuse Bennett. So Krauss climbed up on the conference table, took down his trousers, and when Bennett walked back into the room, there was Krauss mooning the great director. Krauss then took a line from *Mr. Roberts*, "Now, what's all this crap about no movies tonight?" That broke the ice, everyone talked, and there was no explosion.

Shirley MacLaine was the understudy to Carol Haney in the original production of *The Pajama Game*. She took over after Haney broke her ankle. Hollywood producer Hal Wallis saw the show and quickly signed her to Paramount Pictures. When Judy Kaye took over the lead from Madeline Kahn in *On the Twentieth Century*, she received a telegram on opening night from MacLaine that read "Watch what happens now."

When shows are written around a single star, things can get out of hand, and the star can find him or herself carrying the show without a break. When Gwen Verdon was in *New Girl in Town*, the role was so exhausting she began cutting songs. It got so out of control that at one performance, she cut seven songs!

Years later, when she was in *Sweet Charity*, she cut "Charity's Soliloquy" when she was too tired, and it was replaced with a reprise of "Big Spender" by the girls. That change went into the national tour.

When Barbara Harris was out of town with *The Apple Tree*, Sheldon Harnick warned her to pace herself so she wouldn't run out of steam while doing eight performances per week. In New York, Carmen Alvarez performed in the matinees and Phyllis Newman later took them over.

As we noted earlier, Ray Bolger collapsed with exhaustion while in *Where's Charley?*

During the run of the Vincent Youmans cursed musical *Smiles*, it was decided to insert the song "You're Driving Me Crazy" as a replacement for "Hotcha Ma Chotch." Eddie Foy Jr. and Adele Astaire had only a few hours to learn the new song, so Foy took a piece of cardboard, wrote the lyrics on it, and then placed it in front of the footlights. Before the show started, stagehands swept the stage and the lyrical cheat sheet went into the trash. When the performers entered, neither knew the lyrics and were forced to make up nonsense lyrics. There's no record of what the audience thought was going on.

Richard Kollmar, later the husband of the much-hated gossip columnist Dorothy Kilgallen, was cast in Rodgers and Hart's musical comedy *Too Many Girls*. Bets were placed around the theatre as to when Kollmar would go up on his lines. At one performance, Kollmar skipped a whole scene. Another time, he sang Marcy Wescott's verse on "I Didn't Know What Time It Was," which was clearly written for a woman. The audience was in hysterics, but all Kollmar could think was that Wescott had done something wrong. She had to decide whether to sing his lyric, which would have compounded the error, or repeat her own lyric and show what an ass he was. She decided to sing her own verse and Kollmar be damned.

Before one of the performances of *Mornings at Seven*, Maureen O'Sullivan limped into her dressing room with bruises on her body. Her costar Kate Reid asked her what had happened. O'Sullivan replied that she had gotten into an accident with a taxicab. Reid immediately asked O'Sullivan if she had gotten the cab's medallion number and the driver's name, and told her she should definitely sue the company. "Well," Sullivan sheepishly replied, "I don't think I have a case." Reid's blood started to boil. "What do you mean you don't have a case? You have to have a case." O'Sullivan explained, "The only problem is the taxi was parked."

There's a famous story about Maxwell Anderson and Lawrence Stalling's wartime drama *What Price Glory*. The play was rife with profanity, shocking for the theatre of 1924. The show's language upset certain members of the public who demanded that the "gutter language" be censored. But it seemed that no one had that power. The commander of the Brooklyn Navy Yard,

Rear Admiral Charles P. Plunkett, thought that the way to shut down the show was with a federal law that prohibited non-servicemen from wearing service uniforms in a way that demeaned the office. Plunkett tried to enlist the U.S. district attorney in his crusade, but Colonel William Hayward saw nothing wrong. Plunkett then tried to get the mayor of New York, John F. Hylan, to take action. Hylan appointed Major General Robert Lee Bullard to the task. Meanwhile, the *World* newspaper revealed that Plunkett had sent profanity-ridden letters when he was overseas. Bullard refused to take action. Hylan sent Police Inspector West to the Plymouth Theatre with three officials and a stenographer. The cast was ordered to take out all the bad language during the performance and West announced he enjoyed the play very much. Surprisingly, the clergy rallied around the show. The show went on to great success and opened the door to more realistic depictions of military life in wartime.

Al H. Woods was the owner of the Eltinge Theatre on 42nd Street. It was named for the great female impersonator Julian Eltinge and is now the lobby entrance of the AMC movie theatres. Before the show, Woods would sit in a chair tilted back against the façade of the theatre while the audience entered. But this story is about Estelle Winwood. Woods's part in it comes later.

The stage manager of Winwood's show did not get along with the actress. At one performance, Winwood's underwear had lost its elasticity and was slowly sliding down her legs. Winwood continued with her lines, crossing over behind the piano where her bloomers finally hit the stage floor. Then she walked around to her rightful spot in center stage without missing a beat. There was a hole in the stage where an electrical wire came through and the stage manager went underneath the stage, reached through the hole, and grabbed Winwood's drawers. The manager ran over and waved the offending underwear under the nose of producer Woods. "Didn't I tell you she's temperamental?" he yelled.

When Lauren Bacall took a vacation from *Woman of the Year*, Raquel Welch replaced her, got rave reviews, and did great business. Bacall was furious that anyone else could be successful in her role.

William Daniels, who starred in *1776*, had this to say: "The producers' group—all of the Broadway producers—make these nominations for the Tonys, so it came up that I was nominated in a supporting role, and I said, 'No, thank you, because who am I supporting?' I mean, John Adams is on the stage all the time. It was obviously a starring role. So Alexander Cohen called me and said, 'Bill, you're turning it *down*?' I said, 'Yes! Who am I supporting?' He said, 'Well, you came in late, we did it in the spring, and all those spots were filled for the starring role.' I said, 'So? Fine! Go ahead and remove it.' He said, 'You mean you're not even going to *come*?' I said, 'No, I'm not going to come. Take my name off it. I'm not supporting anybody!' So that was that. That was the closest I came to a Tony. [Laughs.] How ridiculous. But I don't think much of awards anyway. We just went on, and we were very successful."

When the national tour of *Top Banana* was playing Salt Lake City, the show tanked during the title number "If You Want to Be a Top Banana." Phil Silvers was perplexed since the show had just begun and the song was always an audience pleaser. The manager of the theatre ran backstage and told Silvers, "They think you're ridiculing their religion!" Silvers was even more confused. There was one line in the song's lyric that went "This must be the place!" It turned out that when Brigham Young first saw the site of Salt Lake City, he exclaimed, "This is the place!" Silvers ran around to the dressing rooms telling the cast to substitute any words they could think of for "This must be the place."

The play *Just Suppose* starred William Faversham. Leslie Howard made his Broadway debut in the show, but this story is about Faversham. After one performance, producer Henry Miller came up to Faversham and said, "Favvy, dear boy, such a good performance. What was it you were referring to in Act Two when you pointed to the panela?" Favesham, affronted, responded, "Why to the panela." "Ah, but what are panela?" Faversham responded, "Oh, you know. . . ." Miller rejoined, "No, dear boy, I don't." Finally Faversham admitted, "Well, dammit, I don't either." The stage manager brought the script over and there it was: "The marvelous old panela." Faversham told Miller, "I told you so." Miller looked at the script and then Faversham and said, "I believe that's a typographical error, dear boy. I believe that should read 'panels.'" The play had been running for months and no one had questioned the "panela."

Sometimes theatre folk don't understand the way civilians talk. The discussion was about Boston. A woman said to the actor, "My father died in Boston." The actor responded, "We died there, too. Where was your father playing?"

At the beginning of the run of *West Side Story*, the show, which usually came down around 11:20, was instead finished twenty minutes earlier, at 11 p.m.

Remember, those were the days when the curtain didn't go up until 8:30. Composer Leonard Bernstein wanted to check out why the show was twenty minutes shorter, so he came to see the show along with orchestrator Sid Ramin. The tempos of the songs were rushed and Bernstein was irate.

After the performance, Bernstein ran down the aisle to the orchestra pit and looked for the conductor Max Goberman. He was nowhere to be found. Bernstein asked the orchestra where he was. The first trumpet player replied, "Probably at Grand Central." It seemed that Goberman had moved to New Rochelle and the last train was at 11:10. By that time the tempos were set in the minds of the orchestra, as well as the dancers, and they couldn't be changed.

The play *Autumn Crocus* starred the ethereal Dorothy Gish and Francis Lederer, making his Broadway debut. When Gish had her big scene alone on the stage, Lederer would come in and dust and polish the bar, clear the tables, and otherwise draw focus. When Gish complained, Lederer explained that since his character was the owner of the bar, it was only natural that he would come in to clean it up.

Years later, Lederer was appearing in a road company production of *Man of Destiny* along with Gloria Swanson. For some reason, Lederer kept spitting on the floor. Swanson asked him to stop, and he answered in a fashion similar to what he told Dorothy Gish: "I am a soldier. A soldier would spit on the floor."

Swanson dressed him down in no uncertain terms. Lederer replied, "You are worse than Katharine Cornell. At least she had some excuse because it used to get on the hem of her dress."

Jean Barrere was the stage manager for Judith Anderson's legendary Broadway revival of *Medea*. For her first entrance, she was to come onstage screaming "Death! Death!" at the top of her lungs. To get in the mood, she'd think of all the bad things that would whip up her deepest anger.

Anderson's costars were John Gielgud and Florence Reed, the latter being Anderson's bête noire. Anderson hated Reed and vice versa.

At one performance, Anderson told Jean Barrere to take a message to Florence Reed. "You are to tell that old bitch that she is not to move a muscle, not a muscle, during my soliloquy."

Barrere told Reed the message verbatim to which Reed replied, "Tell Judith to go fuck herself!"

Now the show was about to begin. Reed entered as the curtain went up. Barrere called places for Anderson who stood in the wings ready to go on.

"Did you give Florence my message?" asked Anderson.

"Yes, Miss Anderson. Warning, you're on."

"What did she say?"

"You're on Miss Anderson."

"Tell me what she said," Anderson said from somewhere deep and dark in her soul.

"She said, Miss Anderson, that you should go fuck yourself."

"DEATH! erupted Anderson. "DEATH!" And she strode onto the stage.

Miriam Hopkins could be quite a handful on the screen and onstage, but she did have a good sense of humor. She was about to open in John Van Druten's play *There's Always Juliet* in Princeton, New Jersey. When the company got on the set for the first time, what was supposed to be an elegant house was instead full of threadbare furniture, the likes of which you've seen in a million shows, furniture that has appeared in play after play and looks it. Hopkins took one look at the furnishings and proclaimed, "I can't act on this second-hand junk!" She then called her maid and told her that a truck would be arriving at her Sutton Place apartment and instructed her to let the moving men remove all the living room furniture. She gave the housekeeper one last instruction: "If my husband is asleep on the couch, which he usually is, be sure to get him off it before they move it. We don't need him down here."

While we're on the subject of John Van Druten. . . . When Margaret Sullavan was appearing in John Van Druten's play *The Voice of the Turtle*, she got into a tremendous argument with Sammy Schwartz, the company manager. The fight escalated until Sullavan smashed a mirror over Schwartz's head. At intermission, Sullavan asked if Schwartz was going to take her to dinner after the show as always. He did.

Kitty Carlisle's costar in a Cleveland production of *Design for Living* was Herbert Berghoff. He was completely bald but on opening night, for the first time, he put on a toupee. At the top of the first act, Carlisle opened a door to let Berghoff make his entrance. But when she did, there was a strange man on the other side of the door, so she promptly slammed it shut.

Ginger Rogers was one of the not-so-nice actors. She was playing in summer stock and having a nauseatingly sweet romance with Bill Marshall. They'd speak a sort of baby talk French to each other. One day, Ginger asked him to "fermez la porte de la cuisine." He answered in baby talk. She asked him again: "Fermez la porte de la cuisine." This banter went on for so long that finally a stagehand, at the end of his rope, called out, "She said, 'Close the kitchen door!'"

A similar situation happened at the Williamstown Theatre Festival in Massachusetts. One of the young female stagehands sat down on a curb to have a smoke. Two of the actresses in the play, a mother and daughter, walked by in disgust and said to each other in Spanish what a slob the stagehand was. Unbeknown to them, the stagehand sitting on the curb enjoying a quick smoke after a long day's rehearsal spoke Spanish and heard everything. She had the grace not to respond, but she did tell everyone in the show what happened.

The theatre in the mall in Paramus, New Jersey, has more than its fair share of anecdotes. At a performance of Noel Coward's *Design for Living*, Jayne Meadows was sitting on a couch in a beautiful sequined gown. When she got up, a similarly sequined pillow stuck to the back of the dress giving her a Kim Kardashian type of look, if you know what I mean. Her costar and husband Steve Allen commented, "Don't look now, darling but I think you're being followed."

By the way, the manager of the Paramus Playhouse-on-the-Mall was none other than the future bestselling writer Robert Ludlam.

Julie Harris was one of the theatre's greatest actresses. She loved acting so much that she would go on the road anywhere at anytime just to be onstage before an audience. While other performers would only deign to be on Broadway, Harris trod the boards in all kinds of stages in towns that had rarely seen quality, professional theatre.

Unlike Tallulah Bankhead, for example, Harris had the audience so spellbound, she could make the tiniest movements have great impact. When she played Joan of Arc in *The Lark*, in one scene, she was brought up from the dungeons where she has been under the harshest interrogation for three days. She came upstairs barely able to summon the energy to lift her head. When she was at last in front of the tribunal, she yawned. And that yawn perfectly embodied the character and her will.

Saluta was a 1934 show about a bunch of gangsters who make an American composer an offer he can't refuse: travel to Italy to put on an opera that will compete with Mussolini's state opera. Somehow, the show included a song titled "Chill in the Air" with chorus girls dancing in penguin costumes. Wouldn't you like to see that on Broadway today?

Hold On to Your Hats was a musical with a score by E.Y. Harburg and Burton Lane. Al Jolson put up the money for the show and starred in it alongside his wife Ruby Keeler. Their marriage wasn't going so well and neither was the show. One day, the audience was surprised and confused when Jolson and Keeler came onstage having an argument that didn't seem to have anything to do with the plot. Something about someone's mother ruining their marriage. Keeler, defending motherhood, left the stage, for good. She was replaced by Martha Raye.

Maggie Smith was starring in *Lettice and Lovage* at the Ethel Barrymore Theatre. The Barrymore shared a back wall with the Longacre Theatre where the show *Truly Blessed* was playing. The sounds of spirituals came through the shared wall into the Barrymore Theatre. Smith complained about the sound and the stage manager decided to put up black curtains on the theatre's shared wall to muffle the sound. The next day, he came up to Smith and announced, "We hung the blacks." To which Smith replied, "Isn't that a bit severe?"

Countess Maritza was another in a long string of operettas produced by the Shubert Brothers. The show starred Odette Myrtil in the lead as a fiery gypsy who fiddled while Rome burned. Myrtil was going home to see her mother in France and told J.J. Shubert about her plans. He granted her leave and told her they'd just put in her understudy. "But she doesn't play the violin," Myrtil informed the producer. "Well," Shubert said, "you're not leaving for two weeks, are you? She can learn!"

When *Onward Victoria*, the musical biography of Victoria Woodhull, was in previews, composer Keith Hermann was asked to write a new opening number. He did so but, before the number could be orchestrated, the producers wanted him to put it into the show at the next performance. So, against his wishes, Hermann sat in the pit and played the song on the piano while the other musicians sat there. As a protest, Hermann wore a paper bag on his head while playing the number. It was subsequently orchestrated, but it did no good for the show, which suffered from the worst criticism one could say of any show: It was boring.

In *The Phantom of the Opera*, Madame Giry was supposed to say of Christine that "she has been well taught." At one performance, Sally Williams had a slip of the tongue and said, "She has been well fed."

In *The King and I*, the King is lying on his bier dying. Kneeling down before him, facing upstage, is the crown prince. The King gives him advice on how to be a good ruler and dies. Ronny Lee played the prince in the original production. As he lay dying, Yul Brynner would tell Lee an especially dirty joke. Lee would silently crack up, his shoulders shaking as he tried not to laugh out loud. The audience, seeing his shoulders shaking, thought that he was sobbing at the death of his father.

Here's the joke that Brynner told him: One day, the god Thor went down to Earth and made love to a mortal woman. When he got back to Olympus, he told Zeus about his wonderful adventure. Zeus suggested that he tell the woman who he was. The woman would be pleased at having been chosen by a God for lovemaking. So Thor went down to Earth again and met the woman. He announced, "I am Thor!" She looked at him and responded, "You're thor? I'm tho thore I can hardly pith."

Ann Miller's voice was off one night during *Sugar Babies*. She tried to warm up but couldn't do it. They implored her to do the show. She said she would if they would make an announcement that her voice was not quite right that night. They told the audience that she had throat problems ("Awwww"). Then they said she would do the show ("Yea!") and everyone cheered. This went on for three shows. After her voice had healed, the next date in the next town, Miller insisted that the announcement continue. Mickey Rooney was so pissed off, at one performance after the announcement he grabbed the mike and said, "This is Mickey Rooney. I've been divorced four times, bankrupt three times, and I'm going to do the show!"

Marsha Bagwell was in *A Funny Thing Happened* with Rooney. During a performance, he was down in the audience fooling around. She yelled at him to get back onstage and continue the show!

Songwriter/director Barry Kleinbort was standing in the back of the house during *The Secret Garden* and overheard the following. During intermission a man went up to an usher and said, "I beg your pardon. I'm having a little trouble following what was going on. Could you tell me what happened during the first act?" And the usher said, "Do you remember that last minute where the little girl meets the little boy in the bedroom?" "Yes." "Forget everything else. That's all you need to know."

Nancy Walker was a real professional and once she got comfortable in a show, she could relax backstage. During *Do Re Mi*, while she was waiting for her entrance cue, she'd sit in the wings knitting. And when her cue came, she calmly put down her knitting and walked onto the stage.

Walker told Josh Ellis a story about David Merrick approaching her one night during the run of *Do Re Mi* as she was about to make her first entrance. She was in the wings, seated solo at a little nightclub table that was about to be rolled onto the stage on a wagon. Merrick leaned over and conspiratorially whispered in her ear, "How can you do this shit night after night?"—referring of course to the musical that he himself had produced. A fraction of a second later, without giving her time to reply, the stage-hands pushed her onstage. Curtain up!

Before they went into rehearsals of *Coco* at the Mark Hellinger, Katharine Hepburn wanted to see the theatre. So she had producer Frederick Brisson take her to 51st Street. Outside the theatre, Hepburn said, "You've made a big mistake." Brisson looked at her. "Look," she said, pointing to the construction of the Uris Building. "How do you expect me to compete with that?" Sure enough, the sound was heard in the theatre during matinees. Hepburn walked into the construction site and asked the men if they wouldn't mind stopping at 3:30 on Wednesdays and Saturdays when she was singing the title song. Each matinee day, the foreman would yell, "Hey, everybody, stop work, Kate's doing her number."

For some reason, sets exact their revenge on actors.

In repertory in England and in many summer theatres, sets were painted on both sides of flats. Many an actor entering from backstage would see the set for the other show and get temporarily confused as to which show they were playing.

Elsie Randolph went on through a doorway that turned out to be a fireplace on the set facing the audience.

Maureen Stapleton had trouble with a screen door on the set of *The Rose Tattoo*. She needed to make an exit through the door, but no matter how hard she pulled, the door would not open. Finally, she just exited through the back door on the set. A little while later, Eli Wallach came through the aforementioned screen door with no problem whatsoever. The audience cracked up.

Jayne Meadows was appearing in *Tonight at 8:30* and had her lines written on a tablecloth. The cast hated her so much they would substitute another tablecloth.

One of the many *Man of La Mancha* tours was at the Kennedy Center Opera House. On the engagement's opening, composer Mitch Leigh was in the orchestra pit with a spotlight on him as he conducted the overture. The only problem was that the orchestra was in a room upstairs where the musical director was actually conducting the overture.

Dorothy Fields spoke about how musicals had evolved since she began her career in 1926 and pointed to *Sweet Charity* as an ideal example. "The curtain closes just once through the entire show, at the end of the first act," she told syndicated reporter John Crosby, adding, "Now there are all kinds of pieces of elaborate mechanical devices which eliminate the need to close the curtains to change the scenery. This also means the secondary love story—the one that always took place before the curtain—has been eliminated."

Fields's sense of humor matched Coleman's remarkably well, particularly when they hit a snag. "We'd be staring at each other so that my only recourse was to go to the bathroom," Coleman recounted while recording an interview for the ASCAP Foundation Living Archive Series. "And I'd say, 'I'm going to the bathroom,' just to break it. And I'd wait there, and I always came back with an idea. And so it got to the point where it became a joke. Dorothy would say when we were stuck, 'Cy. Go to the bathroom.'"

Desi Arnaz begged his wife Lucille Ball not to make her Broadway debut in *Wildcat*. To him, she had nothing to prove, but Ball always wanted to star in a Broadway show. Being a Broadway veteran, Arnaz knew that the toll of eight performances a week was a killer. But Lucy insisted, even to the extent of putting up most of the money for the show.

He was right. Lucy fainted not once, but twice from exhaustion. Six days following the second dizzy spell, the show went on hiatus for two months, not a good way to keep up ticket sales momentum.

But it was not to be. Nine days after announcing the break in performances, director Michael Kidd and librettist N. Richard Nash announced that the August 7 reopening was cancelled. In fact, the entire show was cancelled. *Wildcat* was officially kaput. Hoping to save face for Ball, they blamed the Musicians' Union who wanted to be paid for the nine-week layoff in performances.

Betsy Von Furstenberg on the closing of the show *Dear Barbarians* said: "It was the only show I ever did when all of the flowers I got for opening night were still alive when we closed."

During the run of *West Side Story*, in order to save money, when the cast's jeans wore out, they replaced them with store-bought jeans. They looked terrible because the originals were handmade and subtly dyed. And, most importantly, the originals were specially constructed so the cast could dance with them. The store-bought denim wouldn't give, so the actors couldn't dance well in them.

Barbara Baxley was playing in *Brecht on Brecht* and refused to go on because there was a cat up a tree outside the theatre. Viveca Lindfors said that Baxley thought she was a cat in a past life.

Michel Legrand was asked to write a new piece for *Amour*. Instead, he told the conductor that there was enough music for the conductor to take and write a new piece. Legrand was done with the show.

One couple who wrote the score to a recent musical that opened at the Palace Theatre was shocked when they were asked to write some more material. As far as they were concerned, once the show had gone into rehearsal, their jobs were over.

According to Burton Lane, Robert Russell Bennett could orchestrate a song while working on a crossword puzzle with the radio playing and a blonde on his knee.

Josh Ellis was the press agent on the Yul Brynner revival of *The King and I* at the Uris Theatre. He recalled the filming of Brynner's section of the Jerry Lewis Muscular Dystrophy Telethon: "I was there when this was done live on Labor Day Weekend, 1977 in New York City. The invasion of Normandy required fewer logistics. Brynner, who was previously a television director himself, supervised every single camera angle, demanding the use of a crane at the end to get the best angle for the polka. Every detail was given loving care and attention." After the performance, the telethon's director and his assistant went backstage to chat with Brynner, who had insisted that they bring his throne to the taping and that he needed it back for his show that evening. The director's assistant shyly and embarrassingly admitted she hadn't seen the throne onstage all night. "Well," Brynner explained with a smile, "It actually looks like a coffee table."

Jule Styne and Bob Merrill hated to go to *Funny Girl* after opening night because Streisand was cutting parts of songs and acting unprofessionally. So before they went, they'd send word that Judy Garland was coming to see the show. Streisand was at her best behavior when she thought there was a star in the audience, but she always wondered why Garland never came backstage to see her.

Gypsy has a scene that takes place in a Chinese restaurant. Madame Rose gets up from eating and sweeps the silverware into her purse. Just before that, Lane Bradbury would pick up the teapot so that it wasn't in the way of the silverware. One matinee, Lane forgot to remove the teapot and she forgot again at the evening performance. Jerome Robbins was so angry, he called her in for a special one-hour rehearsal.

Lane came to the theatre to find the table set up with the teapot and silverware and the stage manager standing there. Over and over, she would pick up the teapot and the stage manager would sweep the silverware into a bag. This went on for the whole hour— lift, sweep, reset, lift, sweep, reset.

At that evening's performance, she again forgot to pick up the teapot. Now Robbins was apoplectic. At the next performance, when Lane came out to do "Let Me Entertain You," her batons weren't set in place so she was forced to pretend she had them. Robbins figured that was the best way to illustrate how important it is to get the props right.

Julie Kurnitz was watching the musical *Happy New Year*, which was made up of scraps of Porter songs jammed into the plot of the play *Holiday*. Afterward, when Kurnitz was asked what she thought, she replied, "I tried not to hate it while I was awake."

Betty Comden and Adolph Green were performing their show *A Party with Comden and Green*, to a less-then-enthusiastic crowd. In fact, it was flop-sweat time. Green, who loved performing, came offstage with a deflated Comden and enthused, "They want more!" Comden had to physically restrain him from going back onstage.

When Gower Champion was putting Ginger Rogers into *Hello, Dolly!*, in the final scene, he told her to go up the stairs of Horace Vandergelder's hay and feed store and deliver the line about the blue wallpaper. Champion was surprised to see Rogers walking backward up the stairs. When he asked her why she was doing that, she explained, "A star never turns her back on the audience." Champion whispered to his assistant, "We're in deep shit."

During Rogers's run in *Hello, Dolly!* Merrick was cutting back the production expenses. There was nobody backstage to do Rogers's wig, so she had to style it and put it on herself. She almost went onstage with her wig on backwards.

Nick Von Hoogstraten, now owner of the Broadway poster emporium the Triton Gallery, was an intern at the Westchester Playhouse while Ann Miller was playing there. A man in the audience had a heart attack so, thinking quickly, Nick ran backstage and got Miller's oxygen tank and possibly saved the man's life. When Miller found out, she got upset.

When Adelaide Hall's mother went to see *Blackbirds of 1928*, she was shocked by her daughter doing what she termed risqué dance moves during the song "Diga, Diga, Doo." She tried to stop the show during Adelaide's performance.

The 1975 revival of *Porgy and Bess* was playing in Chicago. The actors playing Porgy and Sportin' Life hated each other. Sportin' Life bothered Porgy so much that during one performance, Porgy stood up and got up off the goat cart as if to strike Sportin' Life. Surprisingly, nobody called out, "It's a miracle!"

During the run of the revival of *The Little Foxes*, agent Lionel Larner arranged for the cast to attend a function at the White House. This was during the Reagan administration, and playwright Lillian Hellman refused to go. The show's star Elizabeth Taylor and her husband Richard Burton were all for it, so fellow cast member Maureen Stapleton convinced Hellman to forget her politics and join them.

They were on the receiving line as the President and First Lady entered the room. Nancy Reagan came down the line—"Hello, Mr. Burton, Hello, Miss Taylor, Hello, Mr. Larner, Hello, Miss Hellman. Hello, Maureen, how are you? So good to see you." When Nancy Reagan passed, Hellman turned to Stapleton in amazement. "What's with the 'Hello, Maureen'?" "Well," responded Stapleton in a voice loud enough for everyone to hear, "she fucked my husband."

Stapleton was known for her extremely salty language. One day, she and lyricist Betty Comden were sharing a taxi. Stapleton was spewing a variety of obscenities. When the cab was dropping Betty Comden off, she said to Stapleton, "Maureen, would you like to come up for a cup of shit?"

Nancy Andrews and Virginia Martin were in *Little Me*. Andrews and Martin played the same character at two stages in her life. Andrews thought Martin was very strange. At a benefit, they shared a dressing room. Martin turned to Andrews and said, "Do you want these earrings? I think they're haunted."

On the same wavelength, while in *Gypsy* at Papermill Playhouse, Betty Buckley had an exorcism performed over her costumes.

Margaret Sullavan was playing against Robert Preston in *Janus*. And I really mean "playing against." They just didn't get along. Sullavan was the reason the audiences came to the box office, but Preston had the better role. Finally, they came to a détente. As Preston put it, "Let's leave it this way, Maggie. You keep on bringing them in and I'll keep on entertaining them."

Leonard Sillman told the story of the "Isn't She Lovely" number in *New Faces of 1956* as happening by mistake. He had hoped the audience would laugh at the outrageous costumes as a takeoff on lavish movie musicals. The giant staircase was not completed until the evening of the first preview. There was no chance to rehearse. So the ladies and the famous female impersonator T.C. Jones came down the steps for the first time. That's when the ladies began to wobble as they made their way down the steps. The audience howled and they were forced to repeat it for all performances after that.

Don Ameche said that when he did *Goldilocks*, it was because Barry Sullivan had been begging the producers to let him out of the show. So Ameche had one week to learn the show and open. The first time he actually sang the score with the orchestra was on opening night.

He took the job because he knew that the Theatre Guild, who was producing the show, had fifteen weeks of theatre parties. He figured that even if they didn't get good reviews, he'd have fifteen weeks of work. The show ran exactly fifteen weeks.

Ameche loved the show. He realized one problem with the show was that audiences liked the secondary characters more than they liked the leads. Both Pat Stanley and Russell Nype won Tony Awards as best featured actors.

Dolores Gray resented performers who outshone her and in *Two on the Aisle*, she resented both Bert Lahr and Kaye Ballard. Little by little, Gray and her mother had Ballard's part cut down. Her song "If (You Hadn't but You Did)" was given to Gray. Finally, all that Ballard had left was a scene playing a Martian with Bert Lahr, a spoof on the children's TV show *Captain Video*. Ballard's costume made her unrecognizable, and her lines consisted of "Beep, beep, beep, beep."

When Ballard came out for her curtain call, the audience was confused at this woman taking a bow who they had never seen. Ballard quit the show. But not before Bert Lahr, making reference to Gray's complexion, told her, "Forget about it, Kaye, forget about it. She's got a face like a golf course; thirty-six holes!"

When *The Sound of Music* was produced at City Center, the great soprano Eleanor Steber was interested in making her musical theatre debut after a life in opera. She was cast as the Mother Abbess. Because she was so used to doing opera, English lyrics didn't come easily to her. So in "My Favorite

Things," she sang "White girls in dresses with blue satin sashes" and when she couldn't remember a lyric she'd repeat the same line over and over (e.g., "Brown paper, brown paper, brown paper, tied up with strings")

In the climactic scene in the garden of the abbey where the Von Trapp family is going to be discovered by Rolf, her line is "How will you go?" and Von Trapp says, "Don't worry mother, we have a car." Her next line is "The car will do you no good, they've put a guard at the gate." At one performance, she asked Von Trapp, "How will you go?" He answered, "Don't worry mother, we have a car." She then said, "The car will do you no good, they've hung a goat on the gate." The Von Trapp kids started to break up in laughter and Constance Towers covered their mouths so the scene could continue.

June Havoc gave her mother a ticket to the opening night of the Cole Porter musical *Mexican Hayride*. Havoc's mother, the inspiration for Madame Rose, sold her ticket.

During *My Fair Lady*, they brought the chandeliers down too far on the "Embassy Waltz" set and one of them hooked onto Rex Harrison's toupee and took it right off.

Dick Sabol, the replacement for Frid in the original production of *A Little Night Music* had to light Hermione Gingold's cigarette, which was in a little tray with a box of matches. At one performance, the matches weren't there. After the show, Gingold ripped him up one side and down the other for being so unprofessional. So the next night, at the same spot in the scene, once again the matches were not there. But Sabol had thought ahead and had a spare box of matches in the pocket of his waistcoat. He lit Gingold's cigarette. The following night, he showed up at the theatre an hour early and saw Gingold walk around the prop table, take the matches, and put them in her purse.

Director Robert Lewis told a story about actors being on automatic pilot. The actor John Granger was extremely handsome but very stupid. The play was *Cherie* and this was a scene between the handsome blonde actor and Kim Stanley who was playing Cherie. At the end of one line, Stanley picks up a cigarette and Granger lights it. At one performance, she forgot to pick up the cigarette and Granger almost lit her nose, not realizing that there wasn't a cigarette in her mouth. Lewis said, "This is what endeared him to me for the rest of his career."

Cy Coleman told the following story. *Little Me* was out of town in Philly and Neil Simon and Cy Coleman were backstage in front of Sid Caesar's dressing room. Cy Coleman said to Simon, "What's up with Sid, he was awfully slow tonight. He wasn't picking up his cues." So Simon looked at Coleman and said, "You tell him." Coleman said, "OK." He went into Caesar's dressing room, and Caesar asked him, "What did you think of the show tonight?" Coleman said, "Oh, great, great. There's just one thing. You were a little slow in picking up the cues tonight." So Caesar says, "Slow? You want it faster?" He goes to the sink in the dressing room and rips it off the wall and says to Coleman, "Was that fast enough?" Coleman backs out of the dressing room to see Simon doubled over in laughter on the floor. Simon had worked on *Your Show of Shows* with Caesar, so he knew what his reaction would be.

That's one version of the story. Neil Simon in his book *Rewrites* tells it like this. Cy Feuer, the producer of the show, told Caesar he thought the show was great but a little slow. Caesar responded, "A little slow? Really? You mean a little *slow* slow or like turtle slow? Or was it *really* slow like a glacier slow? If you want, I could speed it up a little. I could make it so fast, the audience doesn't even have to come in. They could just go to the box office, buy their tickets, and go home." And he went on and on. Caesar walked back to his hotel room muttering the whole time about the slow, slow, slow. He got to his room and ripped the bathroom sink out of the wall. "Ask Cy if that's fast enough."

You can choose which story to believe.

Connie Stevens had gone to Puerto Rico on her day off, and the next day she called the theatre in which she was starring in Neil Simon's *The Star-Spangled Girl* and said the plane had a flat tire. So her understudy went on. The next day, the same thing happened, another flat tire. So the understudy went on.

The third day, the understudy went on when suddenly Stevens showed up backstage ready to go on. The only problem was that the first two acts had already played. Stevens didn't mind. She put on her costume and went on for the third act. As Neil Simon wrote, the audience was flummoxed. Who was this girl and where was the other girl, and was this part of the show they didn't understand? And if the audience didn't know what the hell was happening, you can imagine how surprised her costars Richard Benjamin and Tony Perkins were when Stevens suddenly showed up for the third act.

When it was time for the curtain call, Stevens took her bow and then called her understudy out to take a bow. Now the audience was astonishingly confused. Just as the curtain was about to come down, Stevens said she had an announcement, that she was engaged to marry Eddie Fisher. Suddenly, the flat-tire-on-the-airplane story seemed even more dubious than before.

Gary Beach was in a show titled *Smile, Smile, Smile*. On opening night, one of the writers stuck his head into the actors' dressing room and said, "If you think of anything funny to say, say it." Everybody just looked at everybody else, didn't say a word, and kept putting on their makeup.

At the first preview, the producer had an idea. Right before the curtain call, doves would be released onto the stage. What they hadn't taken into consideration was that the ceiling of the theatre was very low and the hot lights were too close to the doves' cages. The cast was singing their last song when the doves were released, and a bunch of dead doves fell onto the audience.

The lead actor was a guy named Bobby Lee who did not have a thumb on one hand. He had lost it as a child. During the opening number of the show, they tried to borrow an effect from *Pippin*. They did a silhouette of his hands, but they didn't count on him not having one thumb. The audience shrank back in horror when he held his hands up. It was a doomed production.

After a performance, Ann Miller addressed the audience: "I'm so honored because we have two of the greatest songwriters in the audience tonight. Richard Rodgers and Oscar Hammerstein." There was a kind of pall in the theatre since Hammerstein had been dead for years. Miller walked offstage and somebody told her, "Oscar Hammerstein is dead!" She replied, "Well, what do I know, I've been on tour."

Jean Arthur was in *The Freaking Out of Stephanie Blake*. At the end of one of the few performances, during the curtain call, she said to the audience, "Help me. You have to stop them. They're making me do this." And the curtain was quickly brought down.

The Miracle Worker. The actor playing the doctor in the first scene was bombed one night and said, "Captain and Mrs. Keller, I have some bad news for you, your baby's dead." The curtain quickly fell.

Richard Burton himself told the story about one performance of *Hamlet* when he was so drunk he lapsed into a monologue from *Tamerlane the Great*. And at the conclusion of the monologue, he realized what he had done and said to the audience, "Marlowe."

In the *Sound of Music*, there were a lot of problems getting the show together. Richard Halliday, Mary Martin's husband, went up to Rodgers and Hammerstein and said, "The problem with you guys is all you care about is the show." Mary Martin and Halliday were in the Mary Martin business. Martin only cared about her role in the show.

Fred Astaire was in Detroit during the national tour of *The Passing Show of 1918*. He was in his hotel room napping when he awoke with a start realizing he didn't set the alarm. It was 8:15 and he was due on stage in eight minutes. He ran to the elevator but it wasn't around. So from the eighteenth floor, he flew down the stairs until he caught up with an elevator that took him to the street. The traffic was bad so a taxi was out, so he zigzagged through the crowds on the sidewalk the six blocks to the theatre. He ran in the stage door, threw off his coat and hat, and walked directly onto the stage. No one had noticed he hadn't returned to the theatre after the matinee.

He had another lapse in London. He left the stage and went to his dressing room to change into his street clothes when the callboy yelled that he was to be onstage in one minute. Astaire grabbed his coat, collar, and tie and went onstage carrying them. His fellow cast members were shocked but recovered quickly and ad-libbed something about Astaire's character getting into a fight.

Astaire is not the only actor to be confused as to whether a show was over or if it was just intermission or what! Gordon Connell said that deep into the run of *Hello, Dolly!* it was after the matinee and he was standing outside under the marquee. One of the girls who played the horse was out there with him, and she asked him if they were coming out of the matinee or going into the evening show.

In the same show, Sondra Lee was walking along Eighth Avenue in her costume when the stage manager caught up to her and asked where exactly she was going. She replied, "I'm going home." The stage manager responded, "Well, please come back and just try to do the second act."

Tallulah Bankhead was starring in a short-lived play titled *Footloose*. On a Wednesday afternoon, she left *Footloose* to go to another theatre to see the show *The Hottentot*, from which she'd been fired. Ann Andrews, the actress who replaced Bankhead, was surprised to see her there. "What happened?" she enquired of Bankhead. "It's only three-thirty! Why aren't you at your play?" Bankhead had left the theatre at the end of her first act thinking that she had finished the matinee.

During *Plaza Suite*, George C. Scott was one of the first actors who didn't have a run-of-the-play contract. He just couldn't stand to be in a show for a long time. As he explained, "After eight months I get squirrely. My brain goes berserk-o. I can't do it anymore, so I only sign for eight months."

Phyllis Diller was an unlikely choice to take over *Hello, Dolly!* on Broadway. Her fans came to the theatre expecting to see her over-the-top performing and hear her trademarked explosive laugh. But she decided to play the role straight, which confused many in the audience. At one performance, during the eating scene in Harmonia Gardens, something went wrong, and Diller came out with that loud, braying laugh and the audience ate it up. Finally, they got the real Phyllis Diller. But after the show, Diller called the company onstage and apologized for breaking character.

At one of Diller's first performances in the show, she completely screwed up the lyrics to "I Put My Hand In" and the conductor tried to throw her the words. She turned upstage and watched the dancers and at the end of number, she commented that she had never seen what was going on behind her. She then asked the conductor if she could start over and do it again and he said, "No, go on."

Whenever Ginger Rogers forgot a line while performing on Broadway in *Hello, Dolly!* she wouldn't try to cover it up. Instead, she'd tell the audience, "Just wait a minute." Then she'd go offstage and get her line. When she'd come back onstage, she'd report that she had the line and then she went on with the show.

Raquel Welch, like Betty Hutton before her, would also drop character in the middle of a performance when she was starring in *Woman of the Year*. During "The Grass is Always Greener," a duet with Marilyn Cooper, Welch broke up. After the song was over, she addressed the audience and complimented Cooper on her performance. Cooper was really embarrassed.

Jane Russell replaced Elaine Stritch in *Company*. She was a Christian Scientist and in "The Little Things You Do Together," she would not sing "It's not so hard to be married. And Jesus Christ is it fun." So she sang "It's not so hard to be married and my oh my is it fun." To say that it didn't get a laugh is an understatement.

During *Camelot*, Richard Burton and Robert Goulet made a bet that they could each play the show when they were drunk. So before the show and during the performance, they each polished off a fifth of vodka. And after the performance, Richard Burton went up to Julie Andrews and said, "What'd you think of the performance." And she replied, "It was better, actually."

Ruth Williamson was excellent in the small role of General Cartwright during the Nathan Lane revival of *Guys and Dolls*. Lane said, "It looks like she has a sharp knife and she's scraping every ounce of comedy off the bone of that part."

Mark Waldrop was in the original company of *Evita!* with Patti LuPone. They were out of town for a couple of months and opened in New York. Waldrop and LuPone had been sharing the same stage for a long time. Standing in the wings, LuPone said, "Tough audience." Waldrop snapped back, "I don't know, I'm getting all my laughs" and strode onto the stage.

In the original production of *Evita!* the ensemble spends a lot of time offstage doing nothing. Several members of the company invested in knitting machines. Gradually, six or seven people ended up buying these machines. Underneath the stage, it looked like a sweatshop with everyone working on their knitting.

In the 1976 revival of *My Fair Lady*, the chorus had nothing to do for the entire second act except for "Get Me to the Church on Time," so they would invite their respective boyfriends and girlfriends to visit their dressing rooms. It was a wild time.

Similarly, Jo Sullivan was in *As the Girls Go* at the Broadway Theatre, which was around the corner from the Alvin Theatre where *Mr. Roberts* was playing. It turned out that the female chorus of *As the Girls Go* was offstage while the sailors in *Mr. Roberts* also had a break. The girls would come over to the sailors' dressing rooms and make out. And the stage management for *Mr. Roberts* would make an announcement over the intercom to tell the girls that their cues were coming up.

THREE STORIES ABOUT GETTING LAUGHS

There's a scene in *Mr. Roberts* that involved a number of actors onstage. The scene contained a very large, dependable laugh. Each of the guys in the scene thought they were the reason that the laughs kept coming, whether they had the line, the setup, or the reaction. They decided that the only way to resolve the problem was that on a succession of nights, one person would do one thing and the rest of them would do nothing. They did this on six or so successive nights. And they didn't get the laughs any of those nights. So the conclusion was, of course, that it was the collective effect of all of them that was getting the laugh. Once they had determined it was the group effect, they went back to doing it the way it was originally staged. But it took them several weeks to get the laughs back. Because they had dissected it so much, it was difficult to put Humpty Dumpty back together again.

There are some actors who are instinctual, and others who work hard to achieve a certain effect. When Lynn Fontanne was appearing in *Reunion in Vienna*, there was a laugh line that always failed to get a laugh. No matter what she did or how she varied the timing or delivery, the line would not go over. Finally, after trying and trying in performance after performance, she got her laugh. It was the last show of the run, but it gave her much satisfaction nonetheless. Lunt and Fontanne, being married, usually performed together and after each performance, they'd go back to where they were staying and go over the evening's show in minute detail, always seeking ways to make their performances and the play better for the audiences.

George Abbott was directing *Damn Yankees* at the Paper Mill Playhouse. He was turning one hundred that year. Ken Kantor wasn't getting a laugh on the line "Nobody said anything about you being dumb. Exactly." But the line didn't land. So Kantor asked Abbott what he should do. Abbott instructed Kantor to say the first line then count to two and a half and deliver the word "Exactly." Being a trained actor, Ken thought the direction was nonsense. So to prove Abbott wrong, he did it exactly the way Abbott instructed and it worked every night.

Mary McCarty was in the original company of *Chicago* and after a long break, she returned to the show. To get her back in shape and teach her some new blocking, McCarty had an afternoon rehearsal with the star Gwen Verdon and Craig Jacobs, the stage manager. McCarty didn't want to learn new blocking and asked Verdon if she could just do the song as she had originally performed it. Verdon thought for a while and went backstage to call Bob Fosse from one of the dressing rooms. In a little while, Verdon returned and told McCarty that Fosse had agreed to her doing the old blocking. After McCarty left, Verdon confided to Jacobs that there was no phone in the dressing room.

Robert Morse was called into Walter Pidgeon's dressing room during *Take Me Along* only to find the actor peeing in the sink. "Don't worry," he said to Morse, "It's an old theatre tradition."

It's interesting to compare different autobiographies with each other. Mary Martin tells of the final days of rehearsal for *South Pacific* in London. She was lost with some of the changes in the show that Josh Logan made before the opening.

A meeting was held in her dressing room with Rodgers, Logan, and Martin. In her version of the story, she tearfully begged Logan to change the show back to the way it was on Broadway because she wasn't good in the role anymore.

Logan tells a different version in his autobiography. Martin had a crisis of confidence that could only be assuaged by his promising that everything would be fixed so she shouldn't be so distraught.

In Richard Rodgers's version of the meeting, Martin, through tears, begged Logan to please fix the show because she was just dreadful. Logan agreed, at which point Rodgers caught Martin's eye in her makeup mirror. Logan saw Martin wink at Rodgers, "See, I got my way."

In *Chitty Chitty Bang Bang*, there's a scene in one (in front of the curtain) that includes the song "Little Chuchi Face." Behind the curtain the dancers were warming up for their number "The Bombi Samba." Giant presents were piled up behind the dancers. Ken Kantor and Jan Maxwell were performing the scene in front of the curtain. The curtain went up too early, revealing the presents as well as the dancers warming up. In an awful, vulgar accent, without dropping a beat or character, Maxwell ad-libbed to Kantor, "Bombi, don't turn around, it will spoil the surprise."

On opening night of *Peter Pan*, Mary Martin sent a telegram to Ezio Pinza, her former costar in *South Pacific*, on his opening night in the musical *Fanny*. The telegram read "Hope your Fanny is as big as my Peter."

In Frank Loesser's opera, er, musical, er, opera *The Most Happy Fella*, Lee Cass who played the Postman sings out the names of characters who are receiving mail: "Herbie Greene, Johnson, Sullivan, Van Pelt, and Pearl." For years, musical theatre aficionados have wondered why those names. Some were easier than others to guess. Greene was the conductor Herbert Greene. Johnson was Susan Johnson and Sullivan was Jo Sullivan. Van Pelt was Lois Van Pelt who was in the ladies ensemble. But for years, no one knew who Pearl was. The lyric goes "Herbie Greene, Say who's Pearl?" It turned out that Pearl was a woman who was having an affair with Greene.

Julie Kurnitz had some trouble with her balance. During a performance of *Anything Goes* at the National Theatre in Washington, Kurnitz as the Margaret Dumont character comes through the upstage doors with a life preserver around her neck. Ken Kantor is playing the Captain of the ship and while he's facing the audience, behind him he hears a thud followed by the life preserver rolling past him and into the orchestra pit. Kurnitz had tripped and sent the life preserver flying.

Kurnitz was acting in *Peace*, an Al Carmines show running off-Broadway at St. Clement's Church. She and another actor played two characters in blackface. During one performance, a man got up and walked down to the stage and said, "I'm gonna get you. Get off the stage. I'm gonna get you if you don't get off the stage." Julie and her fellow performer were scared to death and didn't know what to do. But they finished the performance and got a police escort out of the theatre. Thereafter there was no blackface.

Lesley Stewart was Julie Harris's understudy in *Skyscraper*, and she got word that she was going on for Harris. Stewart was getting ready to head for the theatre when the 1965 New York blackout occurred. She figured that she was probably not going on. Her boyfriend Don Grilley was rehearsing at the Variety Arts rehearsal room on Eighth Avenue. So she decided to walk over there and find him. The building was pitch black. She yelled up to the rehearsal hall, "Is Don Grilley up there?" A voice came back, "Yeah, he's trying to get Thelma Pelish out of the elevator." Now, Thelma Pelish weighed over 200 pounds, and getting her out of the elevator was a massive and hilarious effort.

Audiences at the Cape Playhouse on Cape Cod can see Shirley Booth's Oscar displayed in the lobby. What the audience doesn't see are hundreds of posters of past productions hung on the backstage walls of the theatre. Occasionally, you'd see one poster hanging upside down. Why? When the star was particularly unpleasant or the production was a particular problem, the poster would be hung upside down. All the stars of the television show *M*A*S*H* who played the theatre in different productions have their posters upside down.

Angela Lansbury is one of the nicest people in the theatre. During the run of *Mame*, Anne Francine, who had rather large feet, wore a pair of blue satin shoes. One of the shoes got stuck in a track on the stage floor and Francine simply stepped out of it. Lansbury looked at it in wonderment and shot the cast a look of "What is it?" Finally, she went over, picked it up, and cradled the giant shoe in her arms like a baby.

Lansbury loved to play little tricks. One performance of *Sweeney Todd* had an unresponsive audience. During her "Worst Pies" number, she formed the dough into the shape of a large penis and balls. She put the penis on the cutting board with the head on the edge facing the audience. Slowly, gravity pulled the head of the penis down stretching it as it reached to the floor. Lansbury winked at the conductor, bringing him in on the joke.

During the run of a show, there are a lot of substitute musicians in the orchestra pit. One performance of *West Side Story* had a lot of subs. During the cha-cha at the dance in the gym, Tony and Maria and two other couples snap their fingers. At one performance, they noticed that the percussionist had gotten out of his chair and come to the edge of the stage. He put his hands on the stage and snapped his fingers in time with the dancers. The cast was mystified. During the intermission, they went down and found the percussionist to find out why he did that. He said, "It's written in my part: 'snaps on stage.'"

Here's an oft-told anecdote that has evolved over the years. This is the true story, told by Robert Schear, the stage manager of the show. Anna Maria Alberghetti was the star of *Carnival!* During one performance, Alberghetti was offstage in the ladies room unaware that her microphone had not been turned off. It was rumored that producer David Merrick was trying to punish her, but the soundman insisted that the mistake was completely his fault.

Jackie Gleason, the well-known star of television's *The Honeymooners* and "The Jackie Gleason Show," decided he wanted to return to Broadway and signed on to do the musical version of Eugene O'Neill's *Ah! Wilderness*. When it came to negotiate Gleason's fee for *Take Me Along*, he wanted to be paid the highest salary on Broadway. Since Alfred Drake had earned $10,000 a week for appearing in the musical *Kismet*, Gleason signed with producer David Merrick for $10,001 per week.

When he wasn't onstage, Gleason would go across the street to Sardi's for a couple of drinks and return to the theatre for his entrance.

Gleason started missing performances, saying he had a stomachache. Producer David Merrick quipped, "Gleason with a stomachache is like a giraffe with a sore throat."

John Gielgud, Peter O'Toole, and another actor were performing in London's West End. One of the actors forgot his line so the stage manager whispered it from stage left. No one reacted, so he ran around to stage right and whispered the line. Again, no one did anything. Then he ran around behind the set and yelled out the line. Peter O'Toole called back to the prompter and said, "Yes, we know the line, we just don't know who's supposed to say it."

When George S. Kaufman's daughter Anne was a child, she was told she was welcome to attend any of her parents' parties, which featured such illuminati as Harpo Marx, Moss Hart, Kitty Carlisle, and other prominent persons. Her parents told her the only caveat was that she had to be either witty or silent.

Charles Lowe always made sure that his wife Carol Channing was on the far left of any photo so the caption would always start with "Carol Channing. . . ." Lowe also arranged to get photos of Channing with practically every famous person she met. Channing was instructed to put her hand on the celebrity's shoulder. If that famous person died, Lowe would send in the photo to the local papers' obituary departments. And because her hand was on the person's shoulder, she couldn't be cut from the picture.

The Westbeth Theatre in the West Village had a one-stall ladies room that was shared by the cast and audience. The theatre was booked with a terrible play, *Don't Look Now*, written by Michael Wilding Jr. At one performance, Wilding's mother, Elizabeth Taylor, came to the see the show. During intermission, she used the restroom. After the show, Anita Gillette went to the ladies room only to find that someone had stolen the toilet seat previously sat on by Miss Taylor.

Frank Root, a wonderful actor, was in a production of *Funny Girl* and found himself unable to get a laugh on a line he knew should get one. So he asked fellow cast member Selma Diamond for advice. She told him, "You've got to say your line and then squat. You'll get your laugh." He was doubtful, but he followed her direction and, amazingly, got his laugh.

In *Where's Charley?* an actor asked Abbott, "What should I be thinking during this speech?" Abbott replied, "Just say it and get off."

During rehearsals of *Guys and Dolls*, some of the actors were actually acting. Many, like Stubby Kaye and B.S. Pully had no theatre experience. And their acting was better classified as overacting. George S. Kaufman told Cy Feuer, "I'll put a stop to this!"

He addressed the cast thusly: "Gentlemen, you've all been hired because of your odd shapes and the great way that you look and the terrible sounds that you're capable of making. We don't want you to change anything. We love you all exactly as you are. There's just one thing—a fundamental thing—which we will observe from this moment on. Just read the lines and get off. Above all, no acting!"

Abbott was directing *Norman Is That You?* and he'd direct the actors thusly. "Walk behind the couch, stop at the third pillow, look down, count two, look up, and say the line." He instructed them to say the first half of the line facing the audience, wait for the laugh, and then turn with their backs to the audience and say the end of the line and the audience would laugh again. Two laughs on one line!

Sometimes during a long run, some lines lose their punch, and the actor can't figure out what went wrong and how to get back the emotion or the laugh. Maureen Stapleton was in *Plaza Suite* and lost a laugh. She had no idea how to get it back. Director Mike Nichols told her, "Just say the second half of the line an octave lower." And it worked.

Julie Andrews had two sets of blocking while in *Victor/Victoria*. Normally she would do her blocking and dance as originally directed. But if she felt tired, her second set of blocking allowed her to sit down for much of the show.

Anita Gillette was cast as a replacement in the original production of *Gypsy*. She was one of the Hollywood Blondes. Though she didn't know it at the time, she was pregnant.

When they found out, the producers decided to fire her. But Ethel Merman took a liking to Gillette and said to her, "So you can't do your splits but you can still do a cartwheel." Merman went to the producers and told them, "The kid stays in the show." At every performance, Anita would watch "Rose's Turn." After the song ended, Merman would exit to the wings, pat Anita's stomach, and go back on stage.

At one point in the show, the girls appeared on a giant Christmas tree dressed skimpily with, as Gillette explained it, "Holly berries in all the appropriate places." But as the days went by, Gillette got bigger and bigger and asked the costumer to let out her costume. The reply was, "It's not my fault you got knocked up." That's when Gillette knew she'd have to leave. She stayed in the show still doing cartwheels into her eighth month.

Here's a list of people who sang to prerecorded tracks at some time during their performances: Julie Andrews in *Victor/Victoria*, Liza Minnelli in *The Act*, Sarah Brightman's high notes in *Phantom*, and the Phantom himself. The chorus in *Follies* was on tape.

The Broadway cast of *Me and My Girl* was a wonderful group of actors, and they all really enjoyed each other. Whenever someone was about to leave the show, the custom was that they would leave a present for everybody. When Jane Summerhays left the cast, she left a huge packing case with cartons of microwave popcorn. When Jimmy Brennan left the show, he put up what he called a "cruising board." It was a seating chart of the auditorium and a bunch of different colored pushpins. One color pushpin was for celebrities; another color was for relatives. There were pushpins for attractive men and pushpins for attractive women. At the end of the opening number, the cast members would run to the board and start putting pushpins by the seat locations.

On a lighter note, casts often recognize celebrities in the audience and spread the word through a simple code. The orchestra section is divided into four sections. Number one is the left section of the seating as seen from the stage. The center of the orchestra section is roughly divided in two and becomes numbers two and three. The right side of the audience is number four. Then simply count the number of rows back and the number of seats off the aisle.

So if Julia Roberts is sitting in row D, two seats from the aisle in the left side of the center section of the orchestra, the actor will whisper to the cast, "Two, four, two—Julia Roberts."

When a famous actress was cast in what would become a disastrous revival of *Bye, Bye, Birdie*, the cast could hardly stand to hear her off-pitch singing. They complained to the soundman, and he told them that he could easily autocorrect her singing through the soundboard and no one would be the wiser. At the next performance, the audience heard her singing perfectly on pitch. But on the stage, the actors still heard her singing off pitch live, and a second later, her corrected voice was coming from the house. That sound was even worse than hearing her off-pitch singing, and the autocorrect was turned off for the rest of the show.

That production also featured John Stamos in the lead, in the part originated by Dick Van Dyke. Stamos's acting was good and he had real charisma and a wonderful rapport with the audience. Having already had two successful appearances on Broadway in *Cabaret* and *Nine*, this should have been a triumph, except that he wasn't a great dancer. And the director of the show had him do a lot of dancing, and it was terrible. Now that wasn't his fault. It was the director's fault for having him do something at which he wasn't proficient.

The same thing happened to Greg Louganis when he was cast as the Prince in the Long Beach Civic Light Opera production of *Cinderella*. He looked fantastic in the costume, everyone's dream of a handsome prince. And his acting was fine. But he couldn't sing. Instead of having him speak his songs to musical accompaniment, the director had him sing. And so what could have been a charming performance became an embarrassment.

Sam Levene was up for the part of Nathan Detroit in *Guys and Dolls*. There was only one problem, he couldn't sing. Frank Loesser had written four songs that involved Detroit. Finally, Levene was left with only one duet, "Sue Me," which didn't require much hitting of the notes. And as for the group numbers, Levene was told to just mouth the words. If he tried singing, his bad notes would throw everyone else's harmonies off.

Levene couldn't believe that he couldn't learn to sing. So he corralled the rehearsal pianist and asked Loesser, producer Cy Feuer, and Abe Burrows to sit in the audience and listen to him match the notes played on the piano. One by one, the pianist hit a note and the assembled shook their heads. Finally, after about six tries, Levene matched a note! He was thrilled until Loesser asked him to do it again. Naturally, he couldn't and that made him angry. Finally, he looked out at the three men judging him and shouted, "I know what you three are doing! It's a lousy trick! You guys have agreed every single time. It ain't possible that you always agree on what's the right note. It was a trick!"

Before rehearsals of the original production of *Half a Sixpence*, John Cleese admitted to musical director Stanley Lebowsky that he couldn't sing. Lebowsky didn't believe him and, anyway, anyone could be taught to sing. "John, let me tell you something. I've been working on Broadway for forty years. *Everybody* can sing." After trying to match notes on the piano, even Lebowsky admitted that Cleese couldn't sing. But he could learn the songs and mouth them when called to sing in a group. He couldn't dance either.

Jack Carson was playing at a theatre in the round as Professor Harold Hill in the *The Music Man*. Because the stage was surrounded completely by the audience, entrances and exits had to be made up the aisle leading to the top of the seating area where there was a bar. At each of his exits, Carson would run up the same aisle that led to the bar and treat himself to a shot or two. As the show went on, Carson's performance became looser and looser.

Terry Saunders replaced Dorothy Sarnoff in the original production of *The King and I*. When the tour played in Los Angeles, she was seen by the executives at Fox and hired to repeat her role of Lady Thiang in the film version. When asked who played the best Anna, Saunders replied, "Deborah Kerr," followed by Gertrude Lawrence and Constance Carpenter. When she was asked who played the worst Anna, she stated firmly that the booby prize went to Celeste Holm. Holm filled in when Lawrence went on vacation and promptly announced that she wouldn't be using an English accent when playing the part. She said her audience expected her to be like Ado Annie, the role she portrayed in the original production of *Oklahoma!*, a very American role. *The King and I* company took an immediate dislike to her and dubbed the musical *Ma Kettle Goes to Siam*.

Holm starred in the Harold Arlen and E.Y. Harburg musical *Bloomer Girl*. Right after the opening, Holm became bored and wanted to leave the show. Her contract stated that she was forbidden to cut her hair for the time she was in the show. Holm had a nightclub appearance and cut her hair and got her wish; she was dismissed. So Nanette Fabray took over her part and played most of the run of the show.

When Ellis Rabb was directing *The Grass Harp* on Broadway, Barbara Cook and Celeste Holm were cast. Holm was making a lot of demands including her billing. Rabb said, "I suggest we put her name in a box toward the bottom in which it says, 'But Celeste Holm.'" Holm was subsequently fired from the production.

They're Playing Our Song had a recalcitrant turntable during the preview performances. At one performance, Robert Klein was going around and around while musical director Larry Blank kept the music going and going.

Robert Klein finally arrived in the right spot and said that it was a very long trip and the traffic was terrible. This was his actual next line, but it got a big laugh.

Jean Simmons was wonderful in the road company of *A Little Night Music*. Her costar Margaret Hamilton was not so good. In fact, Stephen Sondheim quipped, "No man would have a liaison with Margaret Hamilton."

Ethel Merman was touring the hinterlands in an updated summer stock tour of *Call Me Madam*. In every city, there was a different choreographer. Merman's contract stated that only she was allowed to be center stage. Even if she was offstage, no one could stand in that spot. She also hated cast members moving behind her while she sang. In one city, the choreographer knew this about her and had the chorus stand stock still when Merman was singing. After the show, she told him, "You're the best damn choreographer I ever worked with."

Sondra Lee and Joe Layton were appearing at the Oriental Theatre in Chicago. Both of them were constipated and took some Milk of Magnesia. They toasted each other in the dressing room and went onstage to dance. All of a sudden, the medicine worked. Lee whispered to Layton, "Joe, don't lift me!" Layton replied, "Sondra, don't worry. And don't touch me whatever you do!"

When Sondra Lee was playing in the original company of *Peter Pan*, she met a young dancer named Paul Taylor. You may recognize his name since he became a famous choreographer with his own troupe of dancers. Taylor was told he had to do a back flip as part of his role. He tried and tried again. Finally, he flipped over, fell, and broke his nose. He had to leave the show.

While we're on the subject of *Peter Pan*, at the final preview before opening, Jerome Robbins came up to one of the children and asked him why he wasn't saying his lines. The actor responded, "There have been so many changes, I'm saving them for opening night!"

During the Nathan Lane revival of *Guys and Dolls*, the chorus girls appearing in "Take Back Your Mink" carried long white acrylic cigarette holders in their gloved hands. When they would throw out their hands to gesture, the holders would slip out of their hands and fly across the stage.

The Hot Box Girls would play a little trick when one of them was in their final performance before leaving the show. At the end of "Take Back Your Mink," the girls were directed to have a lot of stage chatter—whooping, giggling, etc. When a girl was set to leave that evening, the other Hot Box Girls wouldn't speak when they exited, leaving the one girl to be caught giggling and whooping on her own.

When Nanette Fabray replaced Ethel Merman in *Annie Get Your Gun*, during duets with Ray Middleton, he'd grab her hard around the waist and squeeze when he had to hit high notes. She felt that he was breaking her ribs. "Look," she told him, "you can do that with Merman but not with me!"

Ralph Bellamy started his career in the theatre, stock theatres to be exact. Once he was in a show with a leading lady who knew her lines but not always those of the other actors. One time, she heard a cue but didn't recognize it. So she ad-libbed, "Well, what are you going to do about it?" The actor stared at her and replied, "I'll tell you what I'm going to do. I'm going offstage into the prop room and get a prop cigar and I'm going to sit down and smoke it until you think of your next line." He then walked off leaving her alone on stage bewildered as to what to do next. She stood there until the stage manager convinced the man to come back and finish the scene.

Dennis King, a hugely popular operetta star in the 1920s, was in a show that featured a fake fireplace toward the rear of the set. Just as the curtain rose to reveal the house, the theatre cat strolled from the frigid backstage onto the stage and settled itself in the warm lights of the fake fireplace.

King entered grandly attired in his Edwardian costume. He came on to the tittering of the audience members who were laughing at the cat. King was confused. He looked around uncomfortably trying to figure out why the audience was laughing. This only made the audience laugh louder. Nothing satisfies an audience more than feeling a sense of power over an actor. King checked his pants to see if his zipper was down. The audience laughed even harder.

Another actor came onto the scene, equally confused by the audience's laughter. They looked at each other unable to begin their lines, completely thrown off by the reaction of the audience. The laughter rose. They checked each other's zippers. Still-greater laughter ensued. Francis L. Sullivan entered, also impeccably dressed in Edwardian garb. Equally confused, he drew up a chair and just stared at his fellow performers. Now the audience went crazy with laughter. Finally, there was nothing to do but bring down the curtain.

Now that's entertainment! *Typical unamusing remark by the "Author" of this book*

Arlene Francis was cast in a revival of *Dinner at Eight* opposite Walter Pidgeon. At one point in the play, she comes through customs and says, "Mrs. Isadore Goldberg, that son-of-a-bitch."

Just before the opening night performance began, the author Edna Ferber came running up to Francis and told her, "Arlene, you know George and I wrote this play before Hitler, and in those days you could make jokes like 'Goldberg, that son-of-a-bitch,' but now, well Jews are very sensitive and I don't think it's such a good idea. Can you make it a nice neutral name like Tom Jones or Jack Smith?"

Francis agreed, telling her that there was a lot on her mind, it being opening night, but that she'd try her best.

The way the scene was written, she would come through customs, see Pidgeon, and he would hail her, "Carlotta!" She would exclaim, "Oliver!" and they would hug.

While she was waiting to make her entrance, all she could think of was "Don't say Isadore Goldberg, don't say Isadore Goldberg, "When the scene began, she entered, and Pidgeon said, "Carlotta!" and she replied, "Isadore!"

Francis was starring in the Harry Kurnitz play *Once More with Feeling* when she was instructed to run through a doorway wearing only a brief teddy. At one performance, the teddy got caught on the door and Arlene found herself onstage practically nude. Backstage afterward, her costar Joseph Cotten remarked, "Well Arlene, there's one audience that knows your true colors!"

Martin Gabel played the leading character in Orson Welles's production of *Danton's Death*. In one scene, Gabel rises up from the basement on an elevator in the grip of a prostitute played by Arlene Francis. As the days went on, the scene under the stage was getting steamier and steamier. There was little acting going on. What Gabel and Francis didn't know was that the chorus was also in the basement waiting to make crowd sounds, standing quietly in the dark watching the show taking place below the stage.

The Sammy Davis, Jr. vehicle *Mr. Wonderful* was basically a musical wrapped around a nightclub act. Even during the show itself, Jack Carter and Davis would ad-lib and try to make each other break up, much to the audience's delight. During the nightclub-act part of the show, stars would show up and take seats on the set. Carter remembered that the audience was sometimes confused about this. "People would say, 'Jesus, that looks like Rex Harrison and Julie Andrews onstage.'" Jerry Lewis once came on, and the audience erupted.

During the nightclub scenes, Davis would announce baseball scores, discuss politics, and generally have a good time. Though the show had gotten tepid reviews, Davis saved it with his energy and antics.

Chita Rivera was shocked by the show, "I was a little snot sitting there watching a nightclub performer in a Broadway show. I thought the theatre was being ruined. But I learned some things: genius is genius."

One day in the middle of the show, columnist Walter Winchell came on the stage followed by a troop of newsboys, and gave a lecture about patriotism. It was crazy, and audiences would come to the show multiple times to see just what might happen on any given night.

When *Where's Charley?* opened, Ray Bolger got terrible reviews, and the show was failing at the box office. Then a miracle occurred. During one matinee, Bolger was singing "Once in Love with Amy" when he forgot the words. He broke character and went down to the front of the stage. He addressed the audience, "Ladies and Gentlemen. I forgot the words. Does anybody here know the words to this song?"

From the audience came a small voice, "I do, Ray." It was Cy Feuer's son Bobby. Bolger was surprised but he went along with what was happening.

"Then why don't you sing along with me?" Little seven-year-old Bobby Feuer started singing, "Once in love with Amy, always in love with Amy."

The audience went crazy for the number, but Bolger hated what had occurred. "What the hell is going on here! Kids screwing up my number! Why the hell do they let kids in the theatre in the first place?" Later, he learned it was Bobby Feuer, of whom he was very fond. And then he calmed down and realized that the moment worked. The number, complete with the sing-along, went into the show. And the song that was four minutes long on opening night became a twenty-minute number. And the show was saved. The word-of-mouth was remarkable.

Joseph Buloff was one of the busiest and best actors on Broadway. He came from the Yiddish theatre and even after playing over 164 roles, he still had the spirit of the old days on Second Avenue. Stella Adler was asked if she wanted to play in a show with Buloff. She absolutely did not, under any circumstances, want to share the stage with him. The producers told her that their time together onstage would be her big scene, and he would only sit there and have no lines. Reluctantly, nervously, doubtfully, she agreed to take on the role.

To her surprise, everything went along great in rehearsals. But on opening night, she faced the audience in her big scene and noticed that they weren't looking at her. She stole a glance to find that Buloff was cracking nuts, spitting out the shells, and eating them.

Here's a story about the "crossover beard." When shows went on tour, they sometimes played not only theatres, but also halls and meeting rooms, lodges, and even barns. Sometimes, there wouldn't be enough room backstage for an actor to exit from one side of the stage and later enter on the other. So the actor would put on a false beard, a slouch hat, and an overcoat to cover his costume. Then he would simply walk across the stage while another scene was going on. If it was an outdoor scene, maybe the audience would just assume it was a passerby. But if the scene took place inside, one of the other performers would say something like "Who is that guy?" and the other actor would say, "I don't know." And that is the "crossover beard."

Whenever the Shuberts wanted to send out yet another company of *Blossom Time* to the hinterlands, they'd have a first performance before an audience on Broadway, usually in the Ambassador Theatre. Then it could be advertised as "direct from Broadway."

Touring shows, even those coming "direct from Broadway," could be pretty cheap. Harry Carey, later a western star mostly in John Wayne movies, started in the theatre. He once saw a Broadway touring company whose entire cast consisted of a leading man, a leading woman, an Irish comic, the heavy, and eight chorus girls, twelve people in all. The rest of the chorus girls were painted on the backdrop!

Damn Yankees got rave reviews from the papers and the next day, Richard Adler was excited to go to the theatre to see the lines in front of the theatre.

But there were only three people in line. What happened? The reviews were raves. Where were the people?

For a week, the producers and creative staff pondered the problem. Finally, it was decided that the logo, Gwen Verdon in a baseball Jersey against a green background, was just not alluring. So the shot of her in the baseball uniform was replaced by a photo of her in the "Whatever Lola Wants" costume, wearing a sort of black bustier. Business immediately picked up. Hooray for sex appeal!

Ken Bloom — go to hell

When Lillian Russell opened in the Shubert Brothers' production of *Lady Teazle* on Christmas Eve, 1904, there were eighty-six chorus girls in the cast. This was a shocking fact. For how could the Shuberts afford to pay eighty-six chorus girls in a show that they advertised as a limited engagement of fifty-seven performances? The producers, through their ace press agent Channing Pollock (also an author and lyricist), let it be known that the girls were not earning that much money for appearing in the show. So how did these poor beauties make ends meet? Suddenly, articles appeared in the papers where the chorus boasted of their jewelry and furs. In other words, men were making sure they were well cared for, very well cared for, wink, wink.

Little things can mean a lot when performing in a show. Part of the magic is making the scenes seem realistic, no matter if the backdrop is painted and the orchestra is playing in the pit.

Kay Medford gave a wonderfully funny performance in Woody Allen's *Don't Drink the Water* opposite Lou Jacobi. Throughout her rehearsal, she carried a pocketbook over her arm. The director Stanley Prager told her, "You can lose the pocketbook." Medford replied, "Never!" She knew it would help her characterization and get a surefire laugh. And it did.

Gertrude Berg appreciated small things that would subliminally get her character across to audiences. In *Dear Me the Sky Is Falling*, when she would lie down on the psychiatrist's couch, she would take her shoes off.

When Robert Alda was starring in *Guys and Dolls*, in the Havana scene at an outdoor café, when it was time to pay the check, he'd put his glass down on top of the money so it wouldn't blow away, a small piece of business but it made the scene, even subconsciously, become real for the audience.

George S. Kaufman was a famous wit. Once he was accompanying his wife to Bloomingdale's department store. They were in the furniture department when a salesperson asked, "Can I get you anything?" Kaufman replied, "Yes, have you got any good second-act curtains?"

Merry-Go-Round was a musical revue that lasted only 135 performances in 1927, but that was enough for it to go out on the road to such exotic locales as Ashtabula, Altoona, and Possum Trot, Tennessee. One of the featured dancers was Rosemary Farmer whose main skill was her high kicks. She could also bring her foot up and wrap it around her head, a talent only suitable for two occupations, one of them being a life on the stage.

Well, at one performance, her leg went straight up and around the head. Just then Farmer got a cramp. She couldn't get the leg off her head. She was wobbling on one foot, high-heeled at that, when Libby Holman, noted torch singer/narcissist ran onstage and dragged Farmer into the wings. It took Holman and two stagehands to disengage the leg from her head.

SLAPPING

During rehearsals of *Destry Rides Again*, director Michael Kidd was so frustrated with Dolores Gray, he slapped her across the face. The next day, Gray's mother strode into rehearsal and slapped him.

During a performance of *Lady in the Dark* at the MUNI Theatre, Dolores Gray was ranting to her dresser about a quick change that had jammed her up. So the stage manager walked up to Gray, slapped her in the face, and threw her out on the stage. When she came offstage, Gray went up to the stage manager and thanked him.

Frank Loesser slapped Isabel Bigley during a rehearsal of *Guys and Dolls*. Loesser was chagrined that he had done it. *Guys and Dolls* librettist Abe Burrows took that and put it into the play with music *Say, Darling*.

RAYMOND MASSEY AND HIS PROGENY

Raymond Massey was starring in the title role of Robert E. Sherwood's play *Abe Lincoln in Illinois* and quite proud of his performance as the future president. Perhaps he was taking it all too seriously. Playwright, director, and Broadway wag George S. Kaufman quipped, "Massey won't be happy 'til he's assassinated."

Years later, Massey's son Daniel was starring in the musical *She Loves Me* opposite Barbara Cook and Jack Cassidy. The show was rehearsing prior to Broadway when the director and producer Harold Prince came running down the aisle waving a record album. "Look!" he shouted,

"Lena Horne has made a recording of our title song." Barbara Cook replied, "That doesn't surprise me. After all, Daniel, your father freed her people."

TWO DIFFERENT SHOWS—ONE DAY

Dick Van Patten, whom you may know from the television show *Eight Is Enough*, was an extremely nice guy and started early on his career as a child actor. He was kind and talented and so he was in demand. He recalled, "I would have a cab waiting for me downstairs, a special cab. I'd get off the air in the TV program *Mama* at 8:25. I would run down to the cab and they would shoot me right over to the Alvin Theatre, I would put on the Navy uniform and I was [Ensign] Pulver with Henry Fonda, in *Mr. Roberts*, and I would go out and do the show. There were a couple of times they would hold the curtain 'til I got there; they had to hold the curtain five or ten minutes longer and the audience would start to applaud because they were anxious to get the show going. But it worked out. I was also in *The Male Animal*. I was in three plays while I was doing *Mama*, during the course of the [run] . . . but it was exciting."

Rita Gardner was performing in *Jacques Brel* off-Broadway while standing by for two Broadway shows. She understudied both Constance Towers in *Ari* and Linda Lavin in *The Last of the Red Hot Lovers* at the same time. Since they didn't have beepers or cell phones, she'd have to show up at both theatres to see if she was needed. Since that would take a lot of time, Larry Hagman would pick her up on his motorcycle and drive her around.

Sylvia Miles was commuting by motor scooter between two downtown shows every night. She would do the first act of *The Balcony* (the only part of the play in which she appeared) in the West Village, and then perform in a revival of Tennessee Williams's *Camino Real*, which was playing in the East Village and featured her only in the second act.

Elaine Stritch was Ethel Merman's understudy in *Call Me Madam*. Every evening, she'd go to the theatre, knock on Ethel Merman's door, and make sure she was going on. Then she'd jump on a train to New Haven where she was appearing in *Pal Joey*, singing the song "Zip." Her entrance was at 10 p.m., which left plenty of time to ride between New York and New Haven. But one day, there was a terrible snowstorm. Stritch made the train but it sat in the station before finally pulling out. She arrived in New Haven and grabbed a cab. After threatening the driver as only Stritch could, she made it to the theatre and heard her cue to enter, and she strode onto the stage and sang her song as if nothing had happened.

On September 17, 1947, Iva Withers played the female lead in *Carousel* in the afternoon and the female lead in *Oklahoma!* in the evening.

John Raitt told Ken Kantor that Howard Keel, who originated Curley in the London production of *Oklahoma!* was playing Billy Bigelow across the street in *Carousel* on Broadway. The Curley understudy was new and unprepared to do the show that night. They tried to contact John Raitt, but he was unavailable and since the understudy at *Carousel* was ready to go on, Howard Keel went across the street to *Oklahoma!* doing two principal roles on Broadway in the same day.

In London, Olive Gilbert (who Ivor Novello insisted be in all his shows) was in two shows at the same time, *The Dancing Years* and *Arc de Triomphe*. They'd have a taxi waiting for her to drive her to the other theatre. During a wartime blackout, she almost missed the second show. That's when she gave up trying to be in both shows in the same evening.

Critic Robert Benchley had a different problem some evenings. He was performing in the *Music Box Revue* with his monologue "The Treasurer's Report." The piece of dramatic art began at 8:50 and concluded at 8:58. Benchley was also a critic and after his piece in the revue, he'd take off his makeup, change his suit and run, literally run, to catch the opening of another show on Broadway. In those days, Broadway was a happening place, and most nights, there was an opening somewhere on The Great White Way.

THE PHANTOM OF THE OPERA

Phantom has run long enough to generate a bunch of anecdotes.

Phantom has a saying, "Shove with love." Meaning, if you're standing in the wrong place, someone will tell you the right place. During "Masquerade," Marilyn Caskey, a terrific Carlotta by the way, asked someone where she was supposed to stand. She got no answer. The actor wouldn't even deign to acknowledge her presence. She asked again. No response. It was only then that she realized she was talking to one of the onstage mannequins.

The elephant and the chandelier each have names. They're written on the inside of the elephant and the upstage side of the chandelier. The elephant's name is Yo Bimbo and the chandelier's name is Ruthie II, named after assistant director Ruth Mitchell. Ruthie I is in England.

The electric portcullis is the giant metal grate that drops down and defines the Phantom's lair. The final scene takes place in the Phantom's hidden room. Raoul has to be immobilized while the Phantom and Christine argue about their affection for each other. Then Raoul is paralyzed by the Punjab

Lasoo. The Phantom slips it around Raul's neck. It's on a rope that goes up into the rafters so that Raoul hangs there throughout the musical section. If he weren't immobilized, he'd become part of the scene. One night the Phantom didn't have time to put the Punjab Lasoo around Raoul's neck. The actor playing Raoul, Jim Weitzer, realized that without the rope, he would be free to enter the scene. So he improvised and took the first opportunity to throw himself against the portcullis and scream, "Electric portcullis!" and writhe in pain as if he were being electrocuted.

Actor Ken Kantor was new to the show and still a little unsteady. When it came time for him to introduce the opera stars to the new managers, instead of identifying the tenor as Ubaldo Piangi, Ken slipped up and said, "Adobo Pasquale." Of course, the actors then had to continue to refer to him by that name throughout the show. Before the scene was even over, word of Ken's goof had gotten out to the *Phantom* tour in Los Angeles.

Most of the people working on *Phantom* have been there between eight and ten years. For Christmas one year, the cast was given a two-CD set of the Royal Albert Hall recording of *Phantom*. They were not amused.

Phantom has run for so long, it's difficult to make repairs in the theatre since there's no opportunity to close it for an extended period; so most fixes are patches. One evening, there was a drenching rain in New York and a waterfall was coming down the backstage stairs, past the dressing rooms, and down to the basement. Sparks were coming out of the walls when the water hit the electrics. In the auditorium, it was raining on the audience. The whole right side of the auditorium was soaked. They had to move the audience out of those seats for the evening performance. There was a time at *Phantom* when the basement was always flooded, so two-by-fours were put down so the actors could crossover and towels were used to stop the water from seeping under the doors of the wig room.

DANNY KAYE'S BAD BEHAVIOR

Never has a previously unknown actor achieved stardom faster than Danny Kaye in *Lady in the Dark*. In thirty-nine seconds, the time it took him to sing "Tschaikowsky," he became a Broadway star. Naturally, this did not please the titular star of the show, Gertrude Lawrence. And so an onstage feud began. When Kaye was performing, Lawrence would strike a match, and hold it as it burned closer and closer to her fingers, and then she'd light a cigarette in an extra long holder. She'd wear shiny, jangly bracelets when she was in his scenes. Kaye, who previously sang his song with his hands at his sides, suddenly started to use extravagant gestures. Lawrence would then wave a long red scarf. When she sang "The Saga of Jenny," Kaye would be pulling faces behind her.

Kaye's pulling focus wasn't limited to his own show. When Kaye was starring in the Cole Porter musical *Let's Face It*, he suddenly showed up at the Hollywood Theatre where Eddie Cantor was starring in *Banjo Eyes*. He joined a group of chorus boys onstage doing a military dance. Cantor, in front of the battalion, heard some laughter that he had never heard in that place before. He turned around to see Kaye eating a banana. Cantor had the wherewithal to acknowledge Kaye to the audience as a "guest star" before continuing the show as staged.

Now we flash-forward to Kaye's return to Broadway in the Richard Rodgers musical *Two by Two*. Kaye was a horror beginning on the first day of rehearsal. At one point during the show, Kaye tore a ligament in his foot while dancing and was out of the show for two weeks. When he returned, sitting in a wheelchair or hobbling on crutches, his disdain for the show and his fellow performers was acted out onstage in front of the audiences. When Joan Copeland was singing a touching duet with Kaye, he'd be unzipping the back of her dress from top to bottom. He'd ad-lib about other shows playing on Broadway, acknowledge audience members, and do other unconscionable acts. The Tony Award committee took note and Kaye nine months.

CHITTY CHITTY BANG BANG

One night, the title character of the show, a flying car, stalled in the flying position. No matter what the stagehands tried, the car would not move and the show had to stop. Because of the precarious finances of the show, the management wasn't going to have the audience leave and refund the tickets. The cast came out to try to entertain the audience until the car was fixed. It got so bad, at one point the cast sang "Happy Birthday" to those in the audience celebrating birthdays. Even the stagehands came out and told jokes. Christmas carols were sung. This went on for about forty-five minutes until the car could be moved into proper position and the show could continue.

Here's a tragic story with a humorous element. Ken Kantor and Jan Maxwell were singing the immortal song "Cuchi Cuchi Face" when there was a commotion in the house right box. Apparently, a man had had a heart attack and died. But all the cast could think of was that the last words he heard were "Cuchi cuchi wuchi little cuchi face."

It's traditional for the producers to give the cast and crew Christmas presents if the show is doing well. At *Chitty*, all the principals got cases of fine wine. The children in the show got the newly released iPods. The dogs in the show, of which there were nine, were given a large wicker basket of gourmet dog treats and toys. And the singing and dancing ensemble got . . . nothing. The dogs got more presents than the chorus.

INHERIT THE WIND

Here's what happened at a performance of *Inherit the Wind*. Paul Muni, the star of the show, developed an eye tumor. Producer Herman Shumlin had Ed Begley read a speech that Shumlin had written announcing that Muni would be out of the show, but his understudy Simon Oakland was a wonderful actor. Upon finishing the speech, Begley went backstage and the audience went back home. No one was left in the theatre, so the play took a hiatus until Muni's replacement Melvyn Douglas could learn the part and the play could continue.

Later on, Douglas came down with laryngitis. By then, Simon Oakland had left the show but Shumlin found him rehearsing with the Lunts and had him take a leave to fill in for Douglas. This time, the announcement was about how lucky the audience was to see Oakland, "Isn't that great? He returned just for this evening's performance."

Later in the run, both the cast and audience were surprised and disappointed when the stage manager said, "Melvyn Douglas will not appear in today's performance." The stage manager went on: "Instead, a special guest star will play the role of Henry Drummond." And that special guest star was Paul Muni.

There was another switch of performers during the revival of *Inherit the Wind* produced by Tony Randall's National Actors Theatre. Randall had played in the original production of the show, so it was especially meaningful when he produced the revival. During one performance, George C. Scott took ill while onstage and said, "I'm going to faint." The stage manager announced that they would take a short intermission and then the play would resume. But from on high in the mezzanine, Tony Randall yelled, "No we won't!" He ran downstairs and onto the stage and took over the part then and there and the play continued.

BOREDOM

Alfred Lunt once said about boredom in a long-running show, "I don't understand it. I am never bored. There's always something new to learn about a part. The only time I am bored is when I'm shaving or washing my teeth before going to bed."

In the Zero Mostel Broadway revival of *Fiddler on the Roof*, during "To Life," Mostel kept a bottle filled with water behind the bar. While the dancers were on, he would go behind the bar, take a swig, and spritz somebody in the cast. They couldn't figure out where the water was coming from until one of the chorus members found the bottle, spritzed Mostel, and was promptly fired.

Mostel was playing the Kennedy Center in Washington, D.C., in his final go-round as Tevye in *Fiddler on the Roof*. He was really bored and so was acting out onstage. During the dream sequence, while lying with Golde in their bed, she went to get up and he grabbed her by her nightgown, ripping it up the back. During the song "Do You Love Me?" when he sang the line, "Do you love me?" to Golde. Instead of answering, "Do I what?" she got up, walked away, and answered, "I'm not sure."

THREE STORIES ABOUT *REUBEN, REUBEN*

On *Reuben, Reuben*, Kaye Ballard did the backers' auditions and was so convinced that the show was going to be a hit, she cashed in a life insurance policy and invested in the show. The show ran one week in Boston.

The day after the opening of *Reuben, Reuben* in Boston, director Robert Lewis found composer Marc Blitzstein sitting on the floor of his hotel room with all the reviews around him. Blitzstein looked up at Lewis and said, "They don't hate me because I'm Jewish, they don't hate me because I'm a Communist, they don't hate me because I'm a homosexual. They hate me because I'm a songwriter."

At the end of one of the performances, Blitzstein and Lewis were standing in the back of the theatre. There had been a steady stream of walkouts all evening long. Some man walked up to them and said, "Excuse me, do you have anything to do with the show?" Blitzstein said, "I wrote it." And the man punched him in the face.

TO SLEEP PERCHANCE TO MISS YOUR CUE

Sometimes, unbelievable as it may sound, actors fall asleep onstage during a show! When James Garner was in *The Caine Mutiny Court-Martial*, he and three other actors played members of the tribunal who would rule on the case. They got so bored, having few lines and just sitting and watching the same scene over and over, night after night, sometimes they would fall asleep. So they painted eyeballs on their eyelids to make it look like they were awake.

Actor David Schmittou was performing in a production of *Camelot* in St. Louis, and Pellinore liked to take his time. After the ensemble finished "The Lusty Month of May," Pellinore, Arthur, and Lancelot would come on and there are a few scenes while the ensemble's still onstage. At one performance, one of the guys in the ensemble was sitting against a rock and fell asleep. When the blackout came for a scene change, the actor was still asleep and the stage manager had to come out and wake him up before the lights went up again.

Likewise, Josh Ellis had a friend in *1776* who fell asleep during the show and at some point, one of the other actors nudged his feet to wake him up. "How long have I been asleep?" he asked groggily. He and the other actor looked at the onstage calendar that counted down the dates until the Declaration of Independence was signed. It turned out by that reckoning, he had been asleep for a month!

Stephen Porter had narcolepsy. He was the authority on directing the plays of George Bernard Shaw, but he would always fall asleep during rehearsals.

TWO EDIE ADAMS STORIES

Rosalind Russell was not a singer by trade, but she acquitted herself well in *Wonderful Town*, which Leonard Bernstein wrote especially for her. Still, she had trouble getting her opening note. Bernstein tried all the instruments in the orchestra to give her the cue but none worked. Finally, it was Edie Adams who whispered the note to Russell every night. Eventually, Russell could find the note on her own, but she still insisted that Adams help her.

Adams wore glasses when offstage, so she couldn't see too well onstage. When *Li'l Abner* opened, she got her first pair of contact lenses. Now she could see *too* well. She noticed things that she'd never seen before: comic books on the orchestra's music stands, people eating in the audience, and other distractions. So she gave up the lenses. There was only one problem: When exiting from the bright lights of the stage to the darkness of the wings, she couldn't see when to stop, so two stagehands waited in the wings to catch her as she ran off. Also waiting offstage was a pair of pink bunny slippers since she was barefoot and the St. James stage was kept very cold.

Since she was skimpily dressed, she said she spent more time putting makeup on her legs than her face. She had to have five-gallon pails of Elizabeth Arden's fake tan makeup in her dressing room. Running around in bare feet every night also had its problems. When the show closed, not only had she lost twelve pounds, she wore one shoe size larger than when the show opened. Her husband Ernie Kovacs quipped, "Many an actress has gotten a swelled head playing a starring role, but Edie's the first to get swelled feet."

MORE STORIES FROM PARAMUS

One of Harold J. Kennedy's noteworthy all-star revivals was 1969's *The Front Page*. Doro Merande, taking a leaf from the self-righteous book of Celeste Holm, decided to be the morals inspector backstage. Robert Ryan and Kennedy would have a quick smoke backstage. Every single time they did, Merande would call the fire department. And every time she did, somebody overheard her and warned the miscreants. When the fire marshal showed up, a page came over the intercom, "Paging Will Steven Armstrong (the show's set and lighting designer)." But by then, all signs of cigarette smoking were extinguished. This went on over and over again. Finally, the marshal, exhausted by the routine, told Ryan and Kennedy, "Will you get that woman off our backs? We don't really care if you smoke or not. And obviously we're never going to catch you. Also, I don't know what she's making such a fuss about. She's rolling her own in the basement!"

Merande played some other "tricks." One evening the stage manager called for "places," but the stage crew didn't show up. Where were they? Someone heard a distant sound. It turned out that they were in the basement locked in the wire cage that held lights and props. They had been playing cards, as stagehands are wont to do, when Merande locked them in the cage. When Kennedy asked the actress why she did it, she replied, "It's where they belong." Perhaps true, but still the show must go on.

During the same production of *The Front Page*, Molly Picon replaced Helen Hayes. During rehearsal, Picon asked if she could make a small change in the blocking. Instead of standing by the phone table, could she please sit on it? She explained that she thought she might get a laugh by doing so. And indeed, when she sat on the table, there was a huge laugh. Kennedy was puzzled and mentioned to Maureen O'Sullivan that he couldn't figure out what was so funny. O'Sullivan, who was coming into the show and had sat in the audience, said, "I know exactly why." O'Sullivan laughed: "She was wearing red bloomers."

Renee Taylor, whose name is usually associated with her husband Joseph Bologna, was rehearsing for the Broadway revival of the Sidney Kingsley play *Detective Story*. The show was trying out in Paramus. Taylor was rewriting her part, adding jokes, and generally not getting the point of having a playwright at all. So it was decided that Paramus would be the end of the line for Ms. Taylor.

On opening night, the stage manager reported that Taylor would not be going on. Why? There was no pickle with the sandwich she ate in the show. It seems that for the previous three previews, there had been a pickle spear accompanying the onstage sandwich. But on opening night, her sandwich was sans pickle. So she wouldn't go on. She announced, "No pickle, no performance."

The director Harold Kennedy told the stage manager to get the prop guy to go out and get a pickle, fast. The problem was that Paramus was a town that observed blue laws, which meant that nothing was open on Sundays and, of course, the opening was on a Sunday. Half hour—no pickle, fifteen minutes—no pickle, 8 p.m.—no pickle. The curtain was being held, but still no pickle. Finally, almost ten minutes after the curtain was meant to go up, a pickle arrived! The show went well and everyone was happy, especially the stage manager. Kennedy inquired why he was so gleeful. After all, he had had to make a needless, frustrating trip around New Jersey in search of a pickle. But he was still grinning ear to ear. The stage manager dryly replied, "You don't know what we did with that pickle!"

THREE STORIES ABOUT BAD ACCIDENTS ONSTAGE

During *Redhead*'s number "The Pickpocket Tango," the large steel bars indicating a jail came down hard on Gwen Verdon's feet. She cried out and fell down. The curtain was brought down and Bob Fosse jumped over the orchestra pit to her aid. She said she was OK. Someone cracked, "Thank god it didn't land on your head." Verdon replied, "I wish it had, I'm a dancer."

Milton Berle was in *The Ziegfeld Follies of 1943*. While backstage, he accidently put his hand through the window. The show was held up for forty minutes while his hand was bandaged by a doctor. Berle asked the doctor to make the bandage huge, and he used it as a comic prop throughout the performance.

During the out-of-town tryout of *Anyone Can Whistle*, Henry Lascoe fell into the orchestra pit, landing on the drummer, who suffered a heart attack and died. Later, while out of town, Lascoe himself died from a heart attack and was replaced by Gabriel Dell.

THREE MORE ANITA GILLETTE STORIES

During rehearsals of *All American*, Joshua Logan didn't know what to do with Anita Gillette's performance. He blamed everything on the nightgown she was wearing. So he sent his wife Nedda Harrigan (daughter of musical theatre giant Edward Harrigan) out to buy a bunch of baby doll nightgowns. Logan brought them onto the stage. Then he had Gillette try each of them on before the entire company. While she was trying them on, he'd criticize her by saying, "You have the most unfortunate thighs," and "Those shoulders of yours!"

Ray Bolger's wife was banned from rehearsals of *All American*. When the show was in previews prior to opening, Gillette's performance in the song "Animal Attraction" stopped the show. Bolger's wife sat in the orchestra seats and reported back to her husband. Bolger had the number cut from the show.

Nanette Fabray, making her return to Broadway in *Mr. President*, kept insisting that costume designer Theoni Aldredge change the costume Gillette wore while singing "Laugh It Up." Fabray felt that Anita was pulling focus, and it took Aldredge five designs before Fabray approved the final costume.

BRUSHES WITH DEATH AND ACTUAL DEATH

Alan Alda had two mishaps that could have actually killed him. At the opening night of *Fair Game for Lovers*, he had to light a cigarette. Not a smoker, he wasn't quite adept at actually lighting the cigarette, but after much trial and error, he mastered the technique. On opening night, he successfully lit the cigarette, blew out the match, and held it at his side. Unfortunately, he didn't realize the match was still glowing and when it came in contact with his cheap acetate robe, Alda heard a gigantic whoosh and looked down to see the front of his robe in flames. Thinking fast, he furiously patted out the fire and luckily wasn't burned or worse. In the next morning's *Herald-Tribune*, Walter Kerr wrote that Alda was the kind of actor who would do anything to get attention.

When Alda was onstage in the second act of the musical *The Apple Tree*, one of the heavy lights fell from the grid, brushed by his face, and crashed to the floor, pinning his cape. Alda tugged to release the cape, a movement that also released the tension in the theatre when the audience laughed to see that he wasn't hurt. Director Mike Nichols sprang from his seat and rushed backstage to lighting designer Jean Rosenthal and screamed at her,

"How could that *happen*?" Rosenthal calmly replied, "Mike, the theatre is a dangerous place."

Eva Le Gallienne's dog Nana (yes, named after the dog in *Peter Pan*) died. That afternoon, Ms. Le Gallienne had to go to New York to appear in her production of *Alice in Wonderland*. She felt bad leaving the dog's body at home, so she took it to the theatre and put it in the dog bed in her dressing room. After the show, producer Liz McCann came to the dressing room to speak to the actress. She saw the dog and said, "That is the most well-behaved dog. It doesn't move or bark. A great backstage dog."

Betty Buckley had a brush with death in *Cats*. The cherry-picker crane that lifted her to kitty heaven while she sang "Memory" while astride a tire broke through the trapdoor with a horrible sound. Buckley reported, "I was on the tire with Ken Page and I thought, 'Sunday night I win the Tony, Monday night I'm killed.'"

THREE STORIES ABOUT SAM LEVENE

Because Vivian Blaine liked Sam Levene so much when they were in *Guys and Dolls*, she agreed to join him on a tour of *Don't Drink the Water*. During the performances, Levene would mutter under his breath to other cast members, "Is that the way you're going to say that line? It's not funny. I thought you said you could act." Blaine said it was a nightmare.

Levene was once on a tour of *Light Up the Sky*. Every day he'd have breakfast with the stage manager Bruce Blaine. When Blaine left the show, Levene sat at the usual table. The waitress came over and inquired about Blaine. When told that he had left for another job, the waitress said, "Well, the wrong one left. Now will you please move to somebody else's station. I don't want you on mine." Levene was so pleased he told the story to everyone.

Levene might be curmudgeonly, but he had a great sense of humor. After playing over 600 performances of *Light Up the Sky* with Harold J. Kennedy, he asked Kennedy if he would be at Sardi's the next Monday as usual. When Kennedy answered in the affirmative, Levene told him that exactly at eleven o'clock he was going to come into the bar and give Kennedy a big kiss on the lips and then leave. Kennedy laughed but, as you might suspect, on the next Monday, Levene walked up to the bar, kissed Kennedy, and left. The bartender couldn't believe it was Levene: "Well, I never would have guessed it."

TWO ETHEL MERMAN STORIES

Benay Venuta, Ethel Merman's best friend, came to see Merman in *Happy Hunting*. They got into Merman's limo after the show and Merman asked Venuta, "What'd you think of the show." Benay answered, "I liked it fine but there's one thing. In the scene when you come out wearing a turban, your hair's supposed to be completely tucked in, but you have a lock of hair sticking out of the front." Merman answered, "Fuck off Benay, it gives me softness."

Venuta was cast in a summer stock production of *Gypsy* and she called Merman for advice. Venuta was having trouble with the "Small World" scene. Merman said, "Oh Benay, it's easy. You walk downstage, push the kids out of the way, and sing, "Funny. . . .'"

TWO BETTY HUTTON STORIES

Betty Hutton had a strange habit when she'd do shows. At some point, she'd forget that she was in a show and she'd suddenly break character to introduce the performer she was playing opposite. In the middle of the number, she'd say, "Isn't he wonderful?" and then ask the audience to applaud. She did this to Dick Patterson in *Fade Out, Fade In*, in *Gentlemen Prefer Blondes* in Chicago, when she was Miss Hanigan in *Annie* on Broadway, and when she was Madame Rose in the Kenley Circuit's production of *Gypsy*.

The actor playing Herbie hated her doing this, and he gave notice to quit the show. At his last performance, Hutton turned to the audience and said, "Can you believe he's leaving us? He doesn't like me, I guess. But I know what he *does* like. Woo-hoo!" And she made a limp-wristed gesture.

When Betty Hutton came in to rehearse *Fade Out, Fade In*, she had an assistant who stood in the rehearsal room with a tall glass of vodka and every so often during the rehearsal, Hutton would throw herself down on the floor, kicking and screaming, "I can't do this!" Then she'd pick herself up and get back to the rehearsal. That's when Lou Jacobi knew their days were numbered.

THREE STORIES ABOUT GWEN VERDON

Gwen Verdon really wanted to be an actress and worked especially hard on *New Girl in Town*, a musical version of O'Neill's *Anna Christie*. She wanted to be the best Anna Christie that the world had ever seen. She sat in back of the set before she made her first entrance and tears would stream down her face. Director George Abbott would tell her, "Just say the lines. Just say the lines." Dancers weren't thought of as actors before Verdon. When people would tell her, "You're a dancer," she'd answer, "Well, what do you think we do between numbers?"

One day, out of town with *New Girl in Town*, she was physically weak and had to miss a few performances. But she wasn't easily replaced. Ann Williams had to do the acting, Marie Lake had to do the dancing, and someone else did the singing.

Sadly, Gwen Verdon and Stephen Douglass didn't get along in *Damn Yankees*. He was too full of himself for Verdon, who, like Chita Rivera, was always part of the chorus at heart.

TWO STORIES ABOUT STOPPING THE SHOW

The Fig Leaves Are Falling was a disorganized mess (Composer Allan Sherman's girlfriend was giving notes). Dorothy Loudon didn't originally have the song "All of My Laughter"; it was Jenny O'Hara's song. But George Abbott realized how heavily Dorothy Loudon was landing with the audience, so he gave her the song only two days before opening night.

Throughout the show, Loudon was dressed in gray. When it came time to perform the song she stood behind a giant heart-shaped cutout. The heart would split in half like Loudon's character's broken heart, and behind it Loudon was standing in a deep pink dress and she sang the song. When she finished, the audience went insane.

An actor came out to start the dialogue for the next scene, but the audience wouldn't be silenced. He shrugged and left the stage. Loudon broke character and took a bow, and the audience just kept cheering. Finally, she physically silenced the audience and told them that there wasn't an encore. And the audience started yelling, "Sing it again. Do it again." Loudon looked at the conductor who shrugged.

The stage manager reset the scenery, putting the heart back together, she got in place behind it, the heart split and she sang the song again. After the applause finally stopped the second time, she said, "Thank you, you've made an aging chorus girl very happy."

This was at the matinee, and the show closed after that evening's performance. She got a Tony nomination even though the show ran for only four performances. By the way, Dolores Gray won the Tony even though *Carnival in Flanders* played less than a week. Maya Angelou got a Tony nomination for the play *Look Away*, which closed on opening night.

Patricia Routledge was in the Alan Jay Lerner and Leonard Bernstein musical *1600 Pennsylvania Avenue*. The show ran for only a week. At the Friday night performance, Routledge sang "Duet for One," in which she simultaneously played two presidential first ladies, Lucy Hayes and Julia Grant.

Tony Walton had designed a very clever wig that was a bouffant when it was flipped up and had a hair ribbon and bangs when it was flipped down. Routledge finished the number and the audience cheered. And the applause carried over into the next scene.

She left the stage, the scenery changed, and the actors for the next scene came onstage, but the audience would not stop applauding. Finally, she came back onstage because the stage manager realized it was fruitless to start the next scene. She took a bow twice. Once with the bouffant wig and then again with the bangs and hair ribbon, thereby taking one bow for each of the first ladies.

THREE STORIES ABOUT *MINNIE'S BOYS*

The late, great Julie Kurnitz told this story. She was playing the Margaret Dumont character in the Broadway musical about the Marx Brothers, *Minnie's Boys*. She had only one scene and one song that was a showstopper. During previews, the scene was being completely rewritten, so they decided to take it out of that evening's performance. So Kurnitz did not appear in the show. But the show's curtain call was arranged in such a way that the actors' bows were timed to music.

So there were sixteen bars intended for Kurnitz's bows. The producers told her she had to go out and take the curtain call. She begged not to go on but they insisted.

At the finale, she came out to take her bow and the applause petered out because the audience had no idea who she was and why she was bowing. Kurnitz said it was the most humiliating moment of her career.

Also during *Minnie's Boys*, Groucho came backstage to meet the actors. And they were thrilled to meet him. Danny Fortus, the actor playing Harpo, said to Groucho, "Tell me about Harpo." And Groucho said something like "He was really funny." Then Irwin Pearl, the actor playing Chico, inquired, "What was Chico like?" And Groucho answered, "Chico was a great guy." Alvin Kupperman, the actor playing Zeppo, asked the same question of Groucho. Groucho responded, "He was a great straight man." Then Gary Raucher, the actor playing Gummo, asked Groucho to tell him about Gummo. Groucho looked at him and said, "Fag."

Jim Coleman was the musical director on *Minnie's* Boys, which was playing in the Theatre on the Mall in Paramus, New Jersey, with Shelley Winters repeating her Broadway role. He was taking Winters out to dinner between shows and went down to her dressing room. Actually, dressing room was too fancy a term for what was just a bunch of canvas flats and a sink in the corner. It was a little sink, like the one in a dentist's office. Coleman knocked for Winters, who said, "I'll be out in a second." And the next thing he heard was a huge crash. He rushed in and there she was on the floor with her dress up around her head, surrounded by porcelain shards and water rushing out of the sink. She had been trying to pee in it.

CHILDREN AND ANIMALS

An old adage of the theatre goes "Never work with children or animals."

The *Anything Goes* revival at Lincoln Center needed a dog. The plot had the male ingénue Billy Crocker disguising himself with a beard made from dog fur. There were two dogs in the show, a Pomeranian from whom the fur was supposedly clipped and a Chihuahua offstage acting as the dog after it was shaved for Crocker's beard.

To make the joke land, they trained the Chihuahua to walk the apron of the thrust stage so everyone could see it. But they could only get the pooch to walk straight from stage left to stage right and not along the curve of the thrust. No matter what they did, the dog would only walk straight across the stage. Director Jerry Zaks shrugged and said, "I guess the dog only works proscenium."

Chitty Chitty Bang Bang had a pack of six dogs. All six had to appear according to the contract with trainer Bill Berloni. During the run of the show, the cocker spaniel developed cataracts. It was soon apparent that the dog was slowly going blind. For Berloni to maintain his contract, he couldn't get rid of the spaniel. So Berloni trained the beagle to be the cocker spaniel's seeing-eye dog. Everywhere the beagle went, the cocker spaniel would follow blindly. Berloni found a vet to remove the spaniel's cataracts. While the dog was recovering, the understudy dog went on. The spaniel recovered and was put back in the show, but the beagle kept trying to help him and was rewarded with the spaniel constantly snarling and biting at the beagle whose services were no longer needed. That's what thanks the beagle got. It's so typical of actors, no gratitude.

The Paper Mill Playhouse was presenting a production of *Candide*, which was being performed on a raked stage tilted toward the audience. The director's bright idea was to have the overture staged in such a way that every time a musical theme changed, a new character would come on and do something symbolic of his or her character. *Candide*, who was played by director Robert Johanson, came on leading a lamb. After making a circle during the music, they would exit. The lamb was rehearsed repeatedly, using the cast album of the show playing through the loudspeakers so that the lamb would be comfortable onstage.

At the first dress rehearsal, the orchestra was playing for the first time at full volume. As usual, Johanson came out with the lamb. Hearing the live orchestra for the first time scared the lamb, and it relieved its entire bladder onto the stage. The cast, watching the pee stream down the stage toward the orchestra pit, screamed in warning. Unfortunately, the orchestra was playing so loudly the musicians couldn't hear the screams onstage. The urine flowed inexorably down the rake of the stage toward the orchestra pit. The more the cast yelled, the more scared the lamb was, and the louder the orchestra played. Finally, the orchestra caught on and the players, with nowhere to go, fruitlessly held their instruments aloft to protect themselves from the torrent. For the next performance of *Candide*, a toy lamb on wheels was procured.

THREE MISSIVES FROM GEORGE S. KAUFMAN

During a performance of *Of Thee I Sing*, William Gaxton was overacting to a fault (something he was wont to do). Director and coauthor George S. Kaufman was standing in the back of the theatre fuming at Gaxton's performance. Kaufman walked into the lobby and sent Gaxton a telegram that reached the actor backstage when he came off from his scene. The telegram read: "I'm watching your performance from the back row of the theater. Wish you were here."

At another of the shows he directed, Kaufman sent the following telegram to the cast: "I was here tonight. Where were you?"

Kaufman hated when actors' performances changed during a show's run. He posted a note backstage at one of his shows: "11 a.m. rehearsal tomorrow to remove all improvements to the play put in since the last rehearsal."

SEVERAL STORIES ABOUT *APPLAUSE*

Lauren Bacall was making her musical theatre debut and the score was by Charles Strouse and Lee Adams with a libretto by Betty Comden and Adolph Green. How could it go wrong?

When Strouse, Comden, and Green decided to call their new show *Applause Applause*, director/choreographer Ron Field came in after getting hair transplants and announced that they show's title had to be changed.

Why? Because his hairstylist told him that the title looked like the word "applesauce."

Len Cariou auditioned four times for *Applause*, the musical version of *All about Eve*. Lauren Bacall was at the final audition to give her approval. When Cariou and director/choreographer Ron Field were walking out of the Alvin Theatre (now the Neil Simon), Field told Cariou, "I'd really like to cast you, but could you tell me what you've done." Cariou pointed across the street to the ANTA Theatre (now the August Wilson) where there were three six-foot pictures of him as Henry V and said, "That's what I'm doing."

Applause tried out in Baltimore's late, unlamented Morris Mechanic Theatre. The theatre was a concrete barn and Mechanic had bought the historic Ford's Theatre in Baltimore and promptly knocked it down when he built the Mechanic. So many people in Baltimore hated him.

Life Magazine sent a photographer down to the Mechanic Theatre in advance of a feature in the magazine. After a performance, the *Life* photographer came up to Bacall's dressing room to discuss the shoot. "What did you think of the show?" asked Bacall. The photographer paused and said, "Well. . . ." After a long pause, Bacall offered him the following advice: "Go fuck yourself!"

Diane McAfee was playing Eve in *Applause* while it was in Baltimore. Unfortunately, she wasn't working out, so the producers sent for Penny Fuller. Fuller flew in from Los Angeles and went to the theatre to see that evening's performance. She was given a seat in the third row, but she asked to be moved farther back because she thought if anyone in the cast saw her, they'd know why she was there. The "Applause" number began, Gene Foote came out and spotted Fuller and ran backstage to tell everyone.

Fuller continued the story: "I saw the show and I thought I knew what was wrong, they needed a strong person who wasn't a girl but a woman. She had to have some kind of strength to balance it with Bacall. They said I had to meet Betty (Bacall) and I thought, 'please God let her know that if I'm good it will only help her.' She approved me. On Monday, I had a music rehearsal. On Tuesday I had a rehearsal with the understudies. On Wednesday, my predecessor and I learned a new dance for the gay bar, which I hadn't noticed was a gay bar till Saturday. On Thursday I had a rehearsal with the cast for the first time. On Friday, I had a full dress rehearsal with the cast, orchestra and lights. They hadn't time to make me costumes so I'm wearing Diane's clothes for the most part.

I'm sitting on the steps that are leading up from the audience to the stage. And the producer brings me a tuna sandwich. And I'm thinking, 'This is as good as it gets, the producer brings you a tuna sandwich and there's a full dress rehearsal just for me!' Then Larry Kasha, god bless him, gives me a kiss on the head and I thought, 'Away we go.' I walk on stage and I look out at the audience and sitting next to our director, Ron Field, is Diane McAfee. And I turned to Larry Kasha and asked, 'What is she doing there?'

I, in my youthful ignorance, said to Betty Comden and Adolph Green that the speech Eve has in the dressing room about her past should be filled out a little more, it wasn't quite pithy enough. So, they rewrote it for me.

Anyway, I asked Larry Kasha what she was doing there watching this. And Larry says, 'She thinks if she had that speech she wouldn't have gotten fired.' And I looked out at her and said to myself, 'OK, baby. You wanna know why you're not doing this? Watch this!"

McAfee's life turned out okay. She had a run-of-the-play contract with *Applause*, meaning she was paid whether she was in the show or not. She later played a tour of the show and most importantly ended up marrying Brandon Maggart, whom she met in *Applause*, and became the mother of Maude Maggart and Fiona Apple.

Katharine Hepburn was playing up the street in *Coco* and decided to drop over to the Palace Theatre to see *Applause*. When she came back to the Mark Hellinger Theatre where *Coco* was playing, a stagehand asked Hepburn, "How was the show?" She replied, "Full."

When *Applause* went out on its first national tour, Virginia Sandifur was playing Eve. Though she's a good performer, she just wasn't working out in the part, and it was decided to replace her. Everyone liked her so much no one wanted to be the bad guy and give her the news, but Bacall stepped up and said, "I'll take the heat."

About three months into the run of *Applause*, on a Wednesday matinee, Len Cariou was standing in front of Lauren Bacall who was sitting at her dressing table. He was singing his first number to her. The song was going along fine except, out of the corner of his eye, he spied a woman nudging her husband and pointing to the stage. She kept pointing excitedly. Soon, Bacall also noticed the woman and looked over at Cariou standing right in front of her and started to smile. Cariou looked down and saw that his fly was open. Cariou deftly turned around, zipped it up, and continued singing, "So, smile that famous smile. The one that gets them all."

Penny Fuller wasn't interested in touring with *Applause*, so she stayed with it through subsequent Margo Channings. One of the replacements was Anne Baxter who had originally played Eve in the film *All about Eve*.

At one performance, Fuller was aware of a jingling sound coming from the wings. She didn't have a chance to look offstage and the sound of jingly metal continued as the show went on.

During intermission, she went to the restroom and heard the jangling coming from the stall next to hers. The door opened and out stepped Bette

Davis, wearing an armful of bracelets. It seems that she had wanted to see the show but there weren't any tickets available, so she was led backstage to watch from the wings. All through the second act, Fuller saw Davis moving around backstage watching her performance.

So for that one performance, the original Margo Channing was watching the original Eve Harrington play Margo Channing opposite the new Eve Harrington.

By the way, Lee Adams thought that Eleanor Parker was the best Margo Channing.

At the first night of Anne Baxter's taking on the role of Margo Channing in *Applause*, Penny Fuller gave her a small silver apple from Tiffany's. It was inscribed, "Goodbye Eve. Hello Margo."

During the run of *Applause*, Lee Roy Reams's mother was having heart problems, and he flew out to be by her side. He got a call from the producers who told him, "Betty (Bacall) is upset that you're not going to be here for the closing and Anne (Baxter) doesn't want to go on without you." Lee Roy's sister convinced him that his mother would want him to go back to the show. So he did and on the day of Anne Baxter's opening in the role, on his dressing table was an envelope with a round-trip ticket and $100 in cash from Baxter. By the way, the producers docked his pay for the time he took off to be with his mother.

CHAPTER 21

Spectacles

When Andrew Lloyd-Webber and Charles Hart's musical *The Phantom of the Opera* was to open in London, the stage effect of the falling chandelier was to be the coup de theatre of the evening. Originally, the chandelier was to fall straight down toward the audience below, but it was decided that the effect might actually cause panic in the seats. So it was determined that the chandelier would fall at an angle, eventually landing on the front of the stage. The effect was still impressive, but the chandelier was moving too fast. Then there was concern that the audience would still be traumatized by what was ostensibly the theatre's chandelier falling. Finally, it was decided that the opening of the play would show the chandelier already onstage from which it would float to its position over the audience, thus letting them know that it was all a stage effect.

But in the late 1800s, spectacular stage effects elevated the drama and some were definitely not as safe as the chandelier in *Phantom*.

Under the Gaslight, an 1867 melodrama, featured what now has become a cliché but at the time was a dramatic and shocking effect. When act three opened, the stage was set with a railroad track running from upstage down to the orchestra pit. To the left of the track was a switch house and, most dramatically, the hero was tied on the track with the villain gloating and exclaiming, "The Lake Shore Express is due on the hour."

Just then the whistle of a train is heard. Then again it comes but louder. From the back of the stage the beam of a headlight appears getting ever closer. As the train hurtles forward, the heroine runs in and throws the switch to send the train onto a different track.

For audiences of the time, it was an electrifying effect.

Having live horses onstage always brought out the crowds. In *The County Fair*, a down-on-his-luck jockey is helped by the Widow Bedott. He has a hunch that one of her horses has the potential to become a winning race-horse. He trains it and enters it in a race. The race is actually mounted on the stage with live horses running on treadmills. It's no surprise that the jockey and his mount win the race, the winnings, and pay off the mortgage on the widow's farm.

And most famously, 1899's *Ben-Hur* had its chariot race onstage with horses running on treadmills. It was a tremendous success, running 194 performances and touring throughout the United States.

CHAPTER 22
Original Cast Albums

A mystery was solved when people were searching for the identity of the singer who sang, "I feel like I'm not out of bed yet" on the studio recording of *On the Town*. He's not credited on the album. Noted Broadway critic and historian Kenneth Kantor recognized the voice as that of Michael Kermoyan. George Gaynes wasn't credited for the Miss Turnstyles dialogue and song. And it's Adolph Green acting as Rajah Bimmy under a fake name.

Adolph Green performs Speedy Valente on the Columbia recording of *On the Town*'s "Come on sister, gather a crowd around you."

Harold Arlen sang the last notes of "I Never Has Seen Snow" for Diahann Carroll on the recording of *House of Flowers*. Arlen is also the singer of "Man for Sale" on the cast album of *Bloomer Girl*, though this time he was credited.

On the Capitol stereo studio recording of *Kiss Me, Kate*, it's Alfred Drake playing both gangsters singing "Brush Up Your Shakespeare" under two fake names, Aloysius Donovan and Alexis Dubroff. You'll notice both their initials are A.D.

In "Gorgeous" on the cast recording of *The Apple Tree*, Carmen Alvarez sings the operatic section for Barbara Harris.

Stephen Sondheim says the line, "You ain't getting 88 cents from me, Rose" on the cast album of *Gypsy*. Because Erving Harmon, who played Pop Hovick, didn't sing in the show, he wasn't asked to come to the recording session.

Ezio Pinza's anguished cries, "Marius, Marius," in a musical montage in *Fanny* were sung by his understudy Henry Michel on the recording. They neglected to call Pinza in for that.

Jerry Bock played the siren at the beginning of the overture on the recording of *Fiorello!*

Martin Charnin played the thunder in the beginning of *Two By Two*.

Austin Collyer was in the cast of *Let It Ride* and told the following story. When they were finished recording the original cast album, the ensemble was dismissed. They went across the street to a bar and had a jolly celebration. Suddenly, one of the engineers came flying into the bar to announce that they all had to return to the studio. Somehow the finale to the show was never recorded. And that's why the singing on the Finale sounds so bad. The cast was drunk.

Speaking of drinking, Elaine Stritch had been drinking a lot of champagne at the recording session of *Company*, and by the time they got to her big number "The Ladies Who Lunch," she was plowed. They were forced to record the music only and she came in the next day to do her vocals.

CHAPTER 23

Tragedies

Not all anecdotes are funny. There's a fair share of tragedies too.

The play *My Sister Eileen* opened under a pall. Four days before the opening on Broadway, the real Eileen McKenney, whose sister Ruth wrote the original story for *The New Yorker* and the person on whom the title character was based, was killed in a car accident along with her husband, the novelist Nathaniel West. They were driving to Los Angeles to catch a plane for New York in order to be at the opening night. Her sister Ruth was so distraught, she did not come to the opening and, despite the play running over 800 performances, she never saw the show.

Misfortune also dogged the musical version of *My Sister Eileen*, *Wonderful Town*. Every night after the performance, a man showed up outside the stage door waiting to talk to Edie Adams. He was there every night, rain, shine, or snow. He was around so often even the stage doorman would let him wait inside if the weather was bad. One night Adams's understudy Florence Fosberg went out on a date with him. The next day Hal Prince called Adams to say that Fosberg was found stabbed to death in a hotel room.

Though showgirls are depicted as beauties wooed by rich stage-door Johnnies, who marry into wealth and live happily ever after, that wasn't always the case. True, many did have money and millionaire husbands, but that didn't ensure them happy lives. In fact, many of Florenz Ziegfeld's beauties met unhappy ends.

The most famous of these is Olive Thomas who, distraught over her marriage to Jack Pickford, took an overdose of a sleeping potion in Paris. (Jack,

Mary Pickford's brother, also had an unhappy end.) Although Thomas died in Paris, she is said to haunt the New Amsterdam Theatre to this day.

Dorothy Dell crashed her car in Pasadena; Myrna Thomas died of sun poisoning; Cynthia Cambridge, known as "Miss England," was thrown by a horse in Hyde Park and died instantly; Helen Walsh was burned to death in a fire aboard a yacht owned by Harry Richman; Jessie Reed died in the charity ward of a Chicago hospital; and Peggy Shannon was found dead with a half-burned cigarette in her hand.

Lillian Lorraine, perhaps Ziegfeld's greatest beauty, had an accident that damaged her spine and spent the rest of her life in bed and in poverty. Hilda Ferguson, one of the most iconic of Ziegfeld's beauties, lost half a million dollars and the love of many millionaires when she became an alcoholic, finally collapsing on the stairway of a rundown speakeasy.

And Will Rogers, one of Ziegfeld's greatest stars, took a plane trip with pilot Wiley Post against the wishes of his wife. She felt "something awful" was going to happen and begged him not to go. Rogers was a devil-may-care sort and said to his wife, "Tell you what. I'll toss a coin. Heads I go, tails you can keep me here." The coin landed heads up. Rogers said, "See—I win!"

Savoy and Brennan were a fantastic team in early musical theatre. Bert Savoy might have been bald, overweight, blind in one eye, and middle-aged, but he cleaned up great as one of the premier female impersonators on the stage. Jay Brennan was the straight man (no pun intended) in the act. One day, Savoy, three friends, and John Murray Anderson's dog Henry went for a swim in Long Island Sound. When they were in the water, a thunderstorm blew in and the four ran for the beach house. Lightning struck Savoy and Jack "Ohio" Vincent and they were killed instantly. A doctor at the inquest thought that the metal clasps on their swimsuits attracted the lightning.

Four days before Michael Bennett died of complications from AIDS, a revival of *Dreamgirls* opened on Broadway. Bennett knew he could not be there on opening night and so decided to hold a grand opening night party in his house in Tucson. He invited all the doctors, orderlies, nurses, and caregivers who had helped him so much during his illness.

August 25, 1980, may go down in theatre history as the saddest opening night on Broadway. It was the opening of David Merrick's *42nd Street*. The show was a smash hit with eleven curtain calls. Merrick walked out on the stage and tried to quiet the cheering throngs. "This is tragic," said Merrick. The audience laughed and applauded, knowing that the show was a triumphant hit. "No, you don't understand," intoned Merrick. "Gower Champion died this morning." Every television station and newspaper covered it.

Lee Roy Reams, a treasure trove of Broadway anecdotes, was there and recalled hearing the following on opening night. Bob Fosse quipped, "Gower once again did me one better. I filmed my death. Gower Champion had the nerve to do it on opening night."

Jeanne Eagels made a smash in the show *Rain*, the most successful drama of the 1920s. She stayed with the show for four years and became associated with the character of Sadie Thompson. When she finally got a new part in *Her Cardboard Lover*, she didn't have the technique required for a totally different kind of role. She was stuck in the melodramatic style of *Rain*. She died at age thirty-two, probably of a drug overdose, never repeating her success.

On the subject of death: Lillian Hellman was in the hospital with emphysema. She couldn't see or walk anymore though she did keep on smoking. Her friend, the writer Peter Feibleman, visited her shortly before she died and asked her, "How are you feeling?" Hellman looked toward him. "Terrible," she rasped. "Oh, Peter, I have the worst case of writer's block I've ever had in my life."

CHAPTER 24

They Died With Their Boots On

Bob Fosse suffered a heart attack on the second day of rehearsals of *Chicago*. Then the conductor had a heart attack and producer Martin Richards was hospitalized with colitis.

Fosse died in Washington, D.C., on his way to the National Theatre where a revival of *Sweet Charity* was about to open.

Howard Da Silva had a heart attack after the final preview of *1776* but insisted on playing on opening night.

Arnold Soboloff died after exiting the stage during a performance in the Sandy Duncan production of *Peter Pan*.

During a performance of *70, Girls, 70* out of town in Philadelphia, the cast was quite elderly. David Burns quipped, "At half hour some of the cast calls in dead."

A few days later, during a performance, Burns got up from a desk, shuffled a few feet, and got a big laugh. He repeated the action, but before he could deliver the joke, he fell to the floor and got another big laugh. But he didn't get up; he was dead.

At Burns's funeral, lyricist Fred Ebb said, "How perfect for him that the last sound he ever heard was laughter because he lived for that."

Dick Shawn was appearing in a one-man show in Los Angeles. During intermission, he usually stayed onstage and sat quietly in a chair until the start of the second act. At one performance, he didn't wake up for the second act. He had died during the intermission.

CHAPTER 25

You're Fired

Back in the 1970s, the Ford Motor Company was using the slogan "There's a Ford in My Future." Lyricist/director Martin Charnin was fired from *I Remember Mama*, a musical about a Swedish immigrant family. He took out a full-page ad in *Variety* that said, "There's No Fjord in My Future."

Julie Kurnitz told a story about Laurence Kornfeld, the original director of *Minnie's Boys*. He had in his contract that they couldn't fire him before the first preview. So they did the first preview and then they fired him. He ripped the payphone off the wall.

Actor Denny Martin Flinn found legendary set designer Jo Mielziner sitting all alone in the restaurant at the Watergate Hotel, which was next to the Kennedy Center in Washington, D.C., where the musical *Sugar* was trying out. Flinn knew then that Mielziner and his sets were being replaced.

The Ziegfeld Follies of 1936 was a success with Fanny Brice, Gertrude Niesen, Eve Arden, the Nicholas Brothers, Josephine Baker, and Bob Hope. When the show was out of town, there were two vaudeville-type acts, Stan Kavanaugh, a juggler who was a tremendous success with audiences and a ventriloquist act that just didn't go over. The ventriloquist and his dummy were fired. But that didn't seem to hurt the career of Edgar Bergen and Charlie McCarthy.

The Sidewalks of New York was a new musical in 1927. While the show got respectable reviews, the producers felt they had to cut down the cast to save money. Among the casualties was the dance team of Hope (Bob Hope whose Broadway debut lasted eight weeks) and Byrne.

CHAPTER 26

Quotes

"It's not enough to succeed. All others must fail."—David Merrick's philosophy of theatre.

"I wonder why nobody ever did?"—Russel Crouse's retort to Christopher Plummer when Plummer said that anyone could write about children and nuns and have a hit.

"You can't cut her out. She's got the best costume in the show!"—Lucinda Ballard, *The Gay Life*'s costume designer, after Anita Gillette's part was cut during tryouts.

"All I did was just what (George S.) Kaufman told me to do. And it worked."—Abe Burrows crediting Kaufman for the structure of *Guys and Dolls*.

"Mr. Burrows, would you consider giving Mr. Pedi credit as coauthor?"—George S. Kaufman when Tom Pedi as Harry the Horse changed his lines in *Guys and Dolls*.

"At least they are letting me shoot my own horse."—Jonathan Tunick on reducing his orchestration of *Promises, Promises* for the 2010 revival.

"I can handle 'em."—Ethel Merman upon hearing the two songs Jerry Herman had originally written for her when he wanted her to star in *Hello, Dolly!* They both went into the show when she took over the part at the end of the show's run.

"Oh, God!"—Richard Burton, head in hands, reacting to hearing Robert Goulet at the first read-through of *Camelot*'s script.

"I remember seeing *Les Miz* when I was seven. I cried when Fantine died, fell asleep for awhile, woke back up in time for Javert's suicide—that is actually a great way to experience that show."—Lin-Manuel Miranda in *The New Yorker*.

"I can pee a melody."—Richard Rodgers.

"Don't knock love, my boy. I'd be out of business without it."—Ira Gershwin to a friend.

"An audience never knows what they do not get. But they sure know when you give them something."—David Merrick.

"You get a good play and you get a good cast and what have you got to do?"—Elia Kazan.

"Who wrote that? That's really good!"—Stephen Sondheim after playing "Someone in a Tree" for the first time.

"If you want to know if the scene works, don't watch the stage, see the audience."—David Merrick.

"I'd as soon write a show for the Barbary apes"—George S. Kaufman when asked if he'd write a show for the Marx Brothers, which he did end up doing to great success.

"I wanted to be sure myself that I was willing to rent a room in the lunatic asylum."—Sam H. Harris explaining why he wanted to see the Marx Brothers perform before he would produce a show with them. The show turned out to be *The Cocoanuts*.

"In the throes of composition, he seems to crawl up the walls of the apartment in the manner of the late Count Dracula"—Alexander Woollcott on George S. Kaufman's writing style.

"This is not muscular philanthropy."—Fritz Loewe to Agnes de Mille upon giving her a royalty for her work in *Brigadoon*. Lerner and Loewe were the only songwriters who gave de Mille a royalty on their work.

"Excuse me. Are the actors speaking too loudly for you?"—Mike Nichols to two women talking during a play.

"Only telephone operettas."—playwright Russel Crouse when asked if he liked operettas.

"See, I'm acting, I'm acting."—Ethel Merman to director Jerome Robbins after her heartfelt performance of "Rose's Turn" in *Gypsy*.

"Fuck the music. Sing the words."—Jule Styne's advice to actors who over-sang. Styne always said that the lyrics were more important than the melody.

"Don't talk in hotel rooms. We all live next door to each other."—Hal Prince after Bob Fosse heard him criticize a dance through the walls of a hotel during the out-of-town tryout of *Damn Yankees*.

"I learned when I was very young that I cannot sleep unless I know I'm annoying somebody."—Paddy Chayefsky

"In show business it is said that the three most overrated things in the world are Japanese food, extramarital sex, and going out of town with a musical."—press agent Harvey Sabinson.

"Mary Tyler Moore is going to be the next Mary Martin. Mark my word. Who do we have in musical comedy now anyhow? Barbara Harris can't sing, and Streisand you can't get."—Harvey Sabinson as quoted by writer John Gruen.

"God, I wish I could write like that."—Neil Simon after watching a performance of *Lost in Yonkers*, a play that he himself wrote!

"If you close this play, I will personally stab you in your sleep with a fork."—Maureen Stapleton to Neil Simon when *The Gingerbread Lady* was in trouble out of town.

"If you don't take this part, I'll stab you in the balls. It's our first chance at security and you're blowing it."—Kate Mostel to husband Zero when he considered turning down *Forum*.

"Go out on the corner and give the tickets away—anybody who walks by. Get them into the theatre."—Wally Fried, general manager of Neil Simon's first play *Come Blow Your Horn*, trying to build up word-of-mouth.

"Because I hate having fourteen fucking neurotics between me and the audience."—George C. Scott on why he always came back to the theatre after doing a film.

"It's too much, Gower! You're driving this company into the grave!"—Lucia Victor to Gower Champion out of town with *Hello, Dolly!*

"Champion's a cold fish and I mean that as a compliment. He keeps his distance from the actors; they don't argue with him, they do what he says"—Albert Selden after bringing in Champion on *Irene* to replace John Gielgud.

"*I* have a contract, and she isn't going on and make a fool of herself. *I'll* go on and make a fool of myself!"—Debbie Reynolds suffering from laryngitis in Toronto during *Irene* and refusing to have her understudy Janie Sell look bad onstage when she hadn't had any rehearsal.

"I could kill the owner of this theatre."—producer Kermit Bloomgarden fuming about the state of the Majestic Theatre during *The Music Man*.

"I could kill the son of a bitch who owns this place."—Richard Burton fuming about the state of the Majestic Theatre during *Camelot*.

"I'm the son of a bitch who owns this place!"—John Shubert to Richard Burton.

"Go ahead and shoot me!"—John Shubert to Richard Burton after handing him a gun. Burton passed on the opportunity.

"I hope one day to have enough fuck-you money that I don't have to listen to Mike anymore."—producer Liz McCann on working with Mike Nichols on *The Gin Game*.

"No collaborators."—Jerome Robbins response when the Shubert Organization's Gerald Schoenfeld asked him why he quit working in the theatre after *Fiddler on the Roof*.

"I'm Jane Seymour and I'm presenting an Oscar."—Ian McKellen with a mop on his head in imitation of Jane Seymour after she missed two performances of *Amadeus* in order to present on the Oscars.

"Well, I hope we still have the same title."—Howard Lindsay after he and Russel Crouse walked in on director George Abbott giving new lines to the cast of *Call Me Madam*.

"All right, young lady, may we now go ahead with 'The Dance of the Sacred Cow?' Music please!"—Director J.C. Huffman after Fred Astaire stopped rehearsal and Adele explained to Huffman that the dance they were doing was sacred to them.

"The first taste-free musical."—Tharon Musser on *Teddy and Alice*.

"You know, I just feel like throwing up all the time the show is on."—producer Alex Aarons about opening night nerves.

"I seem to have dropped my Goddam program."—a society type to her escort after the first act of *What Price Glory*, a show that was known for its profanity.

"Any minute it may turn a little too far, and eighteen somewhat surprised stagehands will have to go into an impromptu ballet."—Frank Morgan warning the audience what might happen if the turntable in *The Band Wagon* breaks down.

"Where is that little son of a bitch Michael Bennett?—Katharine Hepburn during rehearsal of *Coco*. "You know, though, he is a genius."—Katharine Hepburn amending her remarks.

"No show lasts forever."—Michael Bennett to his lawyer and friend John Breglio when Breglio asked him what should be said about him after his death.

"I read this on the train, and I wanted to jump off and call you before I got home."—George Abbott to Comden and Green after reading the script of *On the Town*.

"A playwrote."—What George Axelrod, author of the play *The Seven Year Itch*, dubbed someone who wrote only one play.

QUOTES BY AND ABOUT DAVID MERRICK

David Merrick was a giant of the American theatre and the most successful producer in Broadway history. There are so many quotes about and by Merrick, he deserves his own section.

"He had to be controversial and confrontational all the time. With David, people were to be *used* and used at what they did best."—associate producer Biff Liff.

"Actors never forgive me for having employed them."—David Merrick.

"The pursuit of a smash at any cost."—director Tyrone Guthrie describing Merrick's producing style.

"I wouldn't give that schmuck a glass of water if he were on fire."—Richard Rodgers on Merrick.

"The most valuable force in the theatre today, the most vital figure as producer and showman to come along in years."—Richard Watts Jr.

"I was in an insane asylum, trying hard to hold a rational conversation with one of the inmates but losing ground. Merrick's hypnotic talents were going to work on me. *'Don't look at his eyes!'* I thought to myself, 'DON'T LOOK AT HIS EYES!'"—Stan Freberg, who had a successful record album, *The United States of America*, that Merrick optioned.

"He is the embodiment of pure disinterested commercialism. As a producer he has about as much identification with his products as the manufacturer of trusses."—Robert Brustein.

"I would like to throw his fat Limey posterior out on the street."—David Merrick on *The New York Times* critic Clive Barnes.

"I came to see that he was a 24 ct. gold prick."—producer Alexander Cohen.

"Mr. Merrick is best known as the distinguished producer of the musical *Breakfast at Tiffany's*"—David Merrick's bio in the program of *How Now, Dow Jones*. The previous season, *Breakfast at Tiffany's* had closed in previews.

"Every element in the New York theatre—from playwright-and-his agent to actor-and-his agent—is brutalized by the permanent harsh conditions on Broadway. Before a season starts, everyone knows how many fortunes will be lost, how many people will be fired, how many plays will close in three days. As a result, there's a lack of simplicity, confidence and frankness in everyday dealings. There is no point of repose in the Broadway theatre. In such a situation, the man in the key position—the producer—can pretend that this isn't the case. Or he can come in like the sheriff who recognizes that to operate efficiently he must shed his illusions and learn the law of the Underworld. Merrick has done this and now *is* Broadway. In a theatre that is glued together by sentiment and emotion, Merrick's great strength is that he has this dark sense of humor which enables him to find detachment and irony in the most outrageous occurrence. In his detachment, he is the purest man in the American theatre. When the Day of Judgment comes for Broadway—to the fury of his enemies and rivals—the first citizen who will be seen going through the Gates of Heaven will be David Merrick. The man who knows how to fix the harm done by a critic will have used his energies more potently than those who pay far more lip service to the cause of High Art."—Peter Hall.

FURTHER READING

[handwritten annotation: which is mostly NOT amusing and also severely handicapped by lack of footnotes and precise bibliography]

In researching this book I spoke to a lot of theatre professionals who gave me stories from their experiences going back to the 1950s and '60s. And, of course, there's those legendary and perhaps apocryphal stories about the great personalities of the theatre like Mary Martin, Ethel Merman, David Merrick and their ilk. Friends who are aficionados of the musical also know a hell of a lot about shows in the 1920s and beyond. But for the earliest stories of the last century and even the one before that, memoires and biographies are invaluable.

If you don't live in a big city, where do you actually find a good used bookstore? And that's where the Internet comes in. Sites like abebooks.com, amazon.com and others make searching for specific titles a breeze. What's missing is the thrill of the hunt and the serendipity of coming across a great theatre book that you never knew existed. But now you can find almost any book you want to read. *[handwritten annotation: meaning you didn't keep track]*

Having said all that, here's a highly subjective list of some of the books that I consulted in putting together this book. It's not a complete list but rather a compendium of biographies and autobiographies that are very much worthwhile for your reading pleasure and Broadway education. Mostly, they're really funny.

As I mentioned in my foreword, some people are just born raconteurs and books by those people are loaded with stories told in a most amusing way. The best of these books include the following:

No Pickle No Performance (Doubleday 1977) is the name of one of the best books on the American Theatre. Producer/director Harold J. Kennedy tells stories about the greats and near greats of the American theatre who appeared in his many productions. The stories spare no one and are equally hilarious and jaw-dropping. Trust me, this is not a dull recitation of Kennedy's career. It's the juiciest of all theatre memoirs and is highly recommended.

The wives of Zero Mostel and Jack Gilford, Kate Mostel and Madeline Gilford tell it like it was with nobody spared, including their husbands in their double biography—*170 Years of Broadway* (Random House, 1978). It's a fun read that gives a lot of insight into the lives of performers and the mishegas that goes into a career in the theatre.

Tony Randall is best known as the star of the TV version of *The Odd Couple*. But he had a distinguished career in the theatre and, in fact, was considered one of the best actors of his generation. Randall's biography, *Which Reminds Me* (Delacorte Press, 1989) is, like Randall himself, smart, funny, and amused by it all.

Similarly, Alan Alda is renowned for his work on television but his two memoirs *Never Have Your Dog Stuffed* (Random House, 2005) and *Things I Overheard While Talking to Myself* (Random House, 2007) also cover his significant Broadway career and in addition give an insight into his father Robert Alda's life upon the stage in shows like *Guys and Dolls*.

Kaye Ballard's career is hard to grasp today. She was big on Broadway in the 1950s and early '60s. She had a cult television show along with Eve Arden, *The Mothers-in-Law*, and then mostly unsuccessful attempts to return to Broadway. She tells it all in *How I Lost 10 Pounds in 53 Years* (Back Stage Books, 2006). Surprisingly, she didn't include some of the stories she's told others (who told them to me for this book—including a few that can't be repeated) but there's plenty Ballard's personality in the book and that makes it a fun read.

Now here's as unlikely a recommendation for an honest, interesting, and enjoyable book as you could think of. When I picked up Jerry Schoenfeld's recounting of his years at the top of the Shubert Organization, *Mr. Broadway* (Applause, 2012), I expected a dry, recitation of the many financial and artistic triumphs of the Shubert Organization when he and Bernard Jacobs ruled Broadway. But what I found was a perfectly frank story written with the enthusiasm of a true theatre lover. It was a unexpected pleasure to read this behind-the-scenes-on-Broadway autobiography. He spares neither himself nor the artists with whom he worked. There's a bit of defensiveness in his writing as if this book would set the record straight once and for all.

Richard Maney was Broadway's most successful, most audacious, smartest press agent and his book, *Fanfare* (Harper & Brothers, 1957), is a celebration of all that theatre and its denizens can be: crazy, inspired, insecure, audacious, brilliant. But mostly crazy. It's a terrific book. Maney was the press agent of Tallulah Bankhead and that should say it all. And speaking of Tallulah Bankhead. . . .

Tallulah Bankhead was one of the theatre's most outrageous personalities and her autobiography (Harper & Bros., 1952) as well as Brendon Gill's oversized biography (Holt, Rinehart & Winston, 1972)—both of which are titled *Tallulah*—are hilarious romps through her career. She exhibited a talent and personality that were uninhibited and often out of control. And "exhibited" is exactly the right word, there was none of the shrinking violet in her character. The Gill book repeats some of Tallulah's stories from her book but it has a much needed arms' length viewpoint that is very appreciated.

Speaking of withholding nothing from an oversized personality, Maureen Stapleton spares herself nothing in her autobiography, *A Hell of a Life* (Simon & Schuster, 1995). Wow, what a gal! One of our best actors, Stapleton has a lot of fun revealing to the reader what a career in the theatre is all about—the egos, the fears, the insecurities, and the triumphs. And boy, was she a talented mess! This is a book that any aspiring performer should learn from and enjoy.

In her later years, Ruth Gordon had a reputation of being no-nonsense and somewhat nuts. But that was a role she played equally as well as her brilliant performances on Broadway. Her autobiography, *Myself Among Others* (Atheneum, 1971) is a perfect reflection of her unique personality; insightful, honest about herself, and quite wry. And mostly, her love of the theatre and those with whom she worked shines through.

John Cleese had a short theatrical career in London and on Broadway but his recollections in *So, Anyway* (Crown, 2014), are as sharply observant and as funny as you'd expect. Oh, and intelligent, too. This book is as enjoyable a read as you'd expect from this master comedian. You can tell there was no ghostwriter on this book. Every word you read sounds like Cleese himself is telling you the story while sitting next to you.

Another legendary comedian, Fred Allen, isn't as well known today but in his time he was considered one of the smartest and wittiest men in show business. He conquered vaudeville, Broadway, radio and television and his book, *Much Ado About*

Me (Little, Brown and Company, 1956), spends most of its time in his early career in vaudeville and on Broadway. His is a wry sense of humor and that's the way he approached his life. He has a healthy skeptical view of people and that makes this book all the richer. When you finish it you'll want to move right ahead to his second book, *Treadmill to Oblivion*, about his years in radio and television.

George Abbott was the greatest man of the theatre in the Twentieth Century. He wrote, directed, produced, and gave first-time opportunities to a host of great writers and performers. No one knew more about the theatre than Mr. Abbott and, most importantly, knew enough to know what he didn't know (see *A Funny Thing Happened on the Way to the Forum*). His career lasted from his first Broadway appearance in 1913 to the last show he directed on Broadway in 1987, the aptly named *Broadway* (of which I had my one and only experience as a Broadway press agent). That show opened on his 100th birthday! And his career continued after that almost up to his death in 1995. He was a good man and a no-nonsense professional and that's reflected in his fascinating autobiography, aptly titled *Mr. Abbott* (Random House, 1963).

Perhaps Mr. Abbott's greatest achievement was mentoring, supporting and teaching the young Harold Prince beginning with Prince's third Broadway assignment with 1953's *Wonderful Town*. Their collaboration continued through 1965's *Flora, the Red Menace*. In 1974, Prince himself wrote an autobiography of the first part of his long, distinguished career, *Contradictions: Notes on Twenty-six Years in the Theatre* (Dodd, Mead & Company, 1974). It's a fascinating look at a Broadway that will never again exist. Throughout the book is a spirit of respect for and love of the theatre that is somehow gone from today's theatre where finances seem to have more to do with what is produced than real passion. Now, forty years later, he's finally working on the sequel.

Finally, this is my choice for the greatest theatrical autobiography of all time. You probably won't believe me but Joseph Jefferson, who acted from the time he was in swaddling in 1833 when he was but four-years-old until his retirement over 40 years later. Jefferson travelled throughout America and the world and was the most beloved of all 19th Century performers. Like many 19th Century performers he travelled for years in one definitive role, Rip Van Winkle. His autobiography is thrilling and inspiring and the last chapter, which talks about what being an actor is all about, should be read by every actor, director, and producer. Unsurprisingly, Jefferson's autobiography is titled, *"Rip Van Winkle": The Autobiography of Joseph Jefferson* (Appleton-Century-Crofts).

Here's some more very worthwhile biographies and autobiographies.

Maxwell Anderson is unfairly forgotten to a large extent. Two books are worthy of your time. *The Life of Maxwell Anderson* (Stein and Day, 1983) by Alfred S. Shivers, Ph.D. is a well-researched biography that's happily not an academic slog. Anderson's daughter, Hesper, has written a beautiful memoir of her life with her famous father, *South Mountain Road* (Simon & Schuster, 2000). It's always nice to read a book that's more about emotion and personality rather than professional achievement.

John Murray Anderson was one of the most beloved producers. And his autobiography, *Out without My Rubbers* (Library Publishers, 1954), is full of his warm personality. It's a highly recommended read.

As is producer Leonard Sillman's irrepressible autobiography, *Here Lies Leonard Sillman* (Citadel Press, 1959). And how many memoirists admit in their title that all they offer may not be one-hundred-percent true? Sillman's career may not have been the greatest but it's astounding and hilarious, too. It's a great book.

Desi Arnaz only appeared in one Broadway show, *Too Many Girls*, but he humorously captures his innocence and insecurities about appearing in a musical for the first time in his book, honestly titled *A Book* (William Morrow, 1976). And I think he went on to a successful career on television but I didn't get that far in the book. Desi's wife, Lucille Ball, had her own one-off on Broadway with *Wildcat*. She recounts the experience in her autobiography, *Love, Lucy* (G.P. Putnam's Sons, 1996). It's an interesting take on the proceedings. She doesn't tell that Desi advised her not to undertake the part. Nor does she report that she basically financed the production. But she has interesting things to say. She also went on to television but I didn't get that far in the book.

Peter J. Levinson's *Puttin' on the Ritz* (St. Martin's Press, 2009) replays some of the stories from Fred Astaire's autobiography, *Steps in Time* (Harper & Row, 1959). But it ably fills out Astaire's triumphant Broadway career and that of his sister, Adele. Astaire himself is as charming and self-effacing in his writing as in real life. This is a mostly sunny autobiography written in the days when if you couldn't say anything nice, don't say anything at all was the mantra of autobiographies. And Kathleen Wiley's beautifully researched and well-written biography, *The Astaires* (Oxford University Press, 2012), deepens their story and holds the theatre in warm regard.

Milton Ager is an undeservedly forgotten songwriter but his daughter, Shana Alexander has written, *Happy Days: My Mother, My Father, My Sister and Me* (Doubleday, 1995). It's always nice to read about someone who's life has not been retold ad infinitum. Ager was a giant of Tin Pan Alley but had limited success on Broadway. Still, Alexander's wonderful book has nuggets like the story of Ager's song, "A Young Man's Fancy" from the show, *What's in a Name?*, that had the subtitle, "The Music Box Song" and that subtitle gave Irving Berlin a name for his new theatre.

David Roper's, *The Unauthorized Life and Times Ins and Outs Ups and Downs of Lionel Bart* (Pavilion, 1994), is certainly frank and is a fascinating read that covers Bart's career in London. His only Broadway show, *Oliver!*, was a smash hit but it did Bart no favors.

Howard Dietz's *Dancing in the Dark* (Quadrangle, 1974) is a true reflection of the theatrical genius. Yes, that's right, genius. He had, perhaps, the most agile mind in the theatre. A wit as well as a huge talent, Dietz's story is a must-read.

Producer Max Gordon wrote his autobiography *Max Gordon Presents* (Bernard Geis Associates, 1963) with theatre reporter Lewis Funke and the result is a perfectly charming, bemused, and excellent mirror of Broadway from the 1930s to the 1960s. Gordon was a gentleman of the theatre with exquisite taste and the good sense to largely leave the artists to what they did best.

Phil Silvers' writes about his life in burlesque, Broadway, Hollywood, and television in *This Laugh Is on Me* (Prentice Hall, 1973). Silvers seems to have laughed through life and you'll have a great time in his company. He was one of those comics whose inspiration knew no bounds. A true star who could make the worst material into gold.

Neil Simon was the most successful playwright of his time and his book, *Rewrites: A Memoir* (Simon & Schuster, 1996), is just as funny, ironic, charming, and sometimes sad as his great plays. His follow-up, *The Play Goes On* (Simon & Schuster, 1999) is good too but not a touch on *Rewrites*.

Louis Sobol was a leading columnist in the vein of Dorothy Kilgallen. Only she was despised by everyone and Sobol was loved by everyone. His book, *The Longest Street* (Crown, 1968), practically covers every famous person from Broadway, Tin Pan Alley, and Hollywood. It's a great read even if you don't recognize all the names.

Eddie Cantor wrote a bunch of books (actually David Freedman wrote most of them). His life from the Lower East Side to international fame is more interesting as many at least told by Cantor whose career spanned show business from the beginning of the 20th Century. In Cantor and Jane Kesner Ardmore's *Take My Life* (Doubleday &

Company, 1957) he write personal reminiscences of such greats as Florenz Ziegfeld and that's particularly fascinating.

Producer Cy Feuer wrote *I Got the Show Right Here* (Simon & Schuster, 2003) with the help of Ken Gross. Like all autobiographies, Feuer tells his story as he saw it without a lot of self examination. But he and his partner Ernie Martin produced some of Broadway's biggest hits and the stories of getting those shows on is fascinating.

John Kander, Fred Ebb, and Greg Lawrence's *Colored Lights; Forty Years of Words and Music, Show Biz, Collaboration, and All That Jazz* (Faber and Faber, 2003) is straight out of the proverbial horses' mouths. Kander and Ebb's personalities jump from the page. Lawrence asks just the questions you'd ask the songwriting team only better.

Sondra Lee's *I've Slept with Everybody* (BearManor Media, 2009) is a small but fun bunch of anecdotes of her fascinating theatrical life. Irreverent, just like the characters she danced in a series of great Broadway musicals.

Wakefield Poole recounts his career on Broadway and pornography. The book is *Dirty Poole* (Alyson Books, 2000) and he discusses his contributions to *Do I Hear a Waltz?* And *Follies*. In fact, he filmed the entire production of *Follies*!! Where is that film!!! And the porno part of his career is interesting, too.

INDEX

Collyer, Austin, 290
Colonial Theatre (Boston), 151, 158
Color Purple, The, 68
Colored Lights: Forty Years of Words and Music, Show Biz, Collaboration, and All That Jazz, 309
Columbia Records, 81
Comden, Betty, 22, 60, 67, 71, 83, 107, 157, 244, 245, 283, 285, 302
"Come and Be My Butterfly," 154
Come Back, Little Sheba, 218
Come Blow Your Horn, 301
"Come On, Play Ball with Me, Dearie," 198
"Come On-a My House," 43
Come Summer, 133
"Comedy Tonight," 60
Company, 146, 251, 290
Complete Lyrics of Irving Berlin, 12
Connell, Gordon, 250
Connolly, Marc, 77, 101, 123
Conoli's Opera and Theater Ticket Agency, 86
Conquering Hero, The, 50, 146
Conreid, Hans, 173
Constant Wife, The, 174
"Contradictions: Notes on Twenty-six Years in the Theatre," 307
Conway, Blade Stanhope, 108
Cook, Barbara, 194, 261, 267
Cook, Carole, 39
Cook, Joe, 20
Cooper, Gladys, 21
Cooper, Marilyn 251
Cope, John, 117
Copeland, Joan, 271
Copperfield, 123, 193
Corbett, James J., 208
Corned Beef and Roses, 77, 78
Cornell, Katherine, 103, 104, 236
Corsaro, Frank, 147
Cort, Harry, 127
Cort Theatre, 5, 75
Cotten, Joseph, 263
Cotton Club, 12, 166
Countess Maritza, 239
County Fair, The, 288
"Couple of Swells, A," 73
Cowan, Jerome, 50

Coward, Noel, 8, 16, 21, 35, 36, 63, 65, 66, 117, 141, 158, 238
Cradle Snatchers, The, 13
Crawford, Cheryl, 104
Crawford, Michael, 95
Crazy October, 6
Crosby, John, 242
Cross, Beverly, 69
Crouse, Russel, 54, 76, 144, 203, 299, 300, 302
Cryer, David, 97
"Cuchi Cuchi Face," 271
Cukor, George, 174
Cullman, Howard, 83
Cummings, Robert, 108
Curtis, Tony, 93

Da Silva, Howard, 96, 295
Dahm, Marie, 102
Daily Mirror, 216
Daily News, 216
Dale, Alan, 182, 187
Dale, Jim, 125
Damaged Goods, 211
Dames at Sea, 148
Damn Yankees, 56, 110, 112, 116, 226, 253, 265, 280, 300
Dance a Little Closer, 55, 68
"Dance at the Gym," 120
"Dance of the Sacred Cow," 302
Dancers, The, 8
"Dancing in the Dark," 308
Dancing Years, The, 269
Daniels, William, 97, 111, 234
Danton's Death, 105, 263
Darien Dinner Theatre, 227, 229
Dassin, Jules, 56
David, Hal, 21
Davis, Betty, 121, 223, 285
Davis, Buster, 15, 90
Davis, Owen, 59
Davis, Jr., Sammy, 90, 96, 130, 264
Daw, May, 208
Day in Hollywood, a Night in the Ukraine, A, 62
De Cormier, Robert, 69
De Lys and Clarke, 64
De Mille, Agnes, 95, 158, 300
De Roy, Jamie, 23
DeSylva, B.G., 83

137

143

150

155

J89